D1757263

GERMANS ON WELFARE

GERMANS ON WELFARE

From Weimar to Hitler

DAVID F. CREW

OXFORD
UNIVERSITY PRESS

OXFORD
UNIVERSITY PRESS

Oxford   New York
Athens   Auckland   Bangkok   Bogotá   Buenos Aires   Cape Town
Chennai   Dar es Salaam   Delhi   Florence   Hong Kong   Istanbul   Karachi
Kolkata   Kuala Lumpur   Madrid   Melbourne   Mexico City   Mumbai   Nairobi
Paris   São Palo   Shanghai   Singapore   Taipei   Tokyo   Toronto   Warsaw

and associated companies in
Berlin   Ibadan

Copyright © 1998 by Oxford University Press, Inc.

First published in 1998 by Oxford University Press, Inc.
198 Madison Avenue, New York, New York 10016

First issued as an Oxford University Press paperback, 2002

Oxford is a registered trademark of Oxford University Press

All rights reserved. No part of this publication may be reproduced,
stored in a retrieval system, or transmitted, in any form or by any means,
electronic, mechanical, photocopying, recording, or otherwise,
without the prior permission of Oxford University Press.

Library of Congress Cataloging-in-Publication Data
Crew, David F., 1946–
Germans on welfare : from Weimar to Hitler /
David F. Crew.
    p.   cm.
Includes bibliographical references and index.
ISBN 0-19-505311-7; 0-19-511878-2 (pbk.)
1. Public welfare—Germany—History—20th century.   2. Poor—
Germany—History—20th century.   3. Germany—Social policy.
4. Germany—Social conditions—1918–1935.   I. Title.
HV275.C74   1998
362.5'8'094309041—dc21   97-8445

9 8 7 6 5 4 3 2 1

Printed in the United States of America
on acid-free paper

For Sara and Kate

Acknowledgments

In the process of writing this book, I have accumulated debts to a large number of institutions and individuals. It is a pleasure to be able, finally, to express my thanks in print. The generous financial assistance provided by the German Marshall Fund of the United States made it possible for me to spend the academic year 1987–1988 doing research in Germany. Grants from the University Research Institute of the University of Texas, the German Academic Exchange Service (DAAD), and the Max Planck Institut für Geschichte (MPI), Göttingen, allowed me to finish my research in Germany during subsequent summer visits.

Without the patient and professional assistance of the staffs of the following archives and libraries, I would not have been able to undertake the extensive digging in local sources that this book required: the municipal archives in Dortmund, Bochum Essen, Cologne, and Frankfurt, the Hauptstaatsarchiv Düsseldorf (Kalkum), Staatsarchiv Hamburg, the Staats- und Universitätsbibliothek Hamburg, the Staatsarchiv Ludwigsburg, the Hauptstaatsarchiv Stuttgart, and the Friedrich Ebert Stiftung library and archive in Bonn–Bad Godesberg. I am particularly indebted to the remarkably pleasant and helpful staff of the Caritas-Bibliothek in Freiburg who opened their doors early, closed late, and allowed me to monopolize a copying machine so that I could make optimum use of my limited time there. The interlibrary loan service of the Perry-Castaneda Library at the University of Texas at Austin also deserves thanks for relentlessly tracking down obscure German publications.

The organizers and sponsors of a number of seminars, lectures, and conferences gave me the opportunity to present installments of my research and to benefit from thoughtful responses and criticisms. My thanks, in particular, to Richard Evans and the School of European Studies, University of East Anglia, Norwich, England; Professor Dr. Karl Otmar, Freiherr von Aretin, Director of the Institut für europäische Geschichte, Mainz; Professor Dr. Dieter Langewiesche, Dr. Friedrich Lenger, and the History Seminar at the University of Tübingen; the Max-Planck-Institut für Geschichte, Göttingen; Professor Dr. Adelheid von Saldern and the History Seminar at the University of Hanover; Michael Geyer and Konrad Jarausch, who organized the conference on German Histories: Challenges in Theory, Practice, Technique at the University of Chicago (October 1989); Geoff Eley and Thomas Childers, co-organizers of the conferences on The Kaiserreich in the 1990s: New Research, New Directions, New Agendas (February 1990) and on Germany and Russia in the Twentieth Century in Comparative Perspective (September 1991), both held at the University of Pennsylvania in Philadelphia; the Arbeitskreis-Geschichte von "Sicherheit" und "Wohlfahrt" at a meeting in Basel, Switzerland (July 1991); Professor Dr. Ulrich Herbert, former Director of the Forschungsstelle für die Geschichte des National-sozialismus in Hamburg; Professor Dr. Detlef Junker, Director of the German His-torical Institute, Washington, D.C.; and, finally, Professor Dr. Bernd Weisbrod's seminar at the University of Göttingen.

Many friends and colleagues on both sides of the Atlantic supplied very neces-sary encouragement, support, and constructive criticism at every stage in the writ-ing of this book. In Bochum, at the Ruhr University, Ian Kershaw, Hans Mommsen, and Bernd Weisbrod (who has since moved to the University of Göttingen) helped me to think through some of my early ideas about this project during a preliminary exploration of archives in the autumn of 1983. In Hamburg, Liz Harvey, Christa Hempel-Küter, Klaus Saul, and Klaus Weinhauer introduced me to the archives and to the life of a city that I continue to find fascinating. John Breuilly, who was visiting from the University of Manchester, shared working hours in the archives during the autumn of 1987 as well as evening meals and lively conversation in the university guest house. Uwe Lohalm became a special friend and colleague during the months in 1987 and 1988 when I was working in the Hamburg archives; he and his wife, Sigrid, have continued to welcome me into their home on all my sub-sequent visits to Hamburg. During long walks on the neighboring Ginsterheide, Uwe and I have talked for hours about Hamburg's welfare system, German his-tory, contemporary German politics, and our mutual family concerns and pleasures. When the research for this book took me from Hamburg to Stuttgart in the spring of 1988, Andreas Gestrich went out of his way to be helpful, arranging for a place for me to stay, introducing me to the local archives, and inviting me to spend time with his family.

Over the past eight years, Göttingen has become my home away from home in Germany, thanks to the generosity of the Max-Planck-Institut für Geschichte and to the warm welcome extended by the Göttingen team of researchers. Indeed, much of this book was written during the periods I spent as a visiting fellow at the MPI. My thanks, especially, to the former director of the modern-history side of the institute, Rudolf Vierhaus, the current director, Hartmut Lehmann, Hans Medick, Jürgen Schlumbohm, and Peter Becker (now at the European University, Italy) for helping to make my frequent stays in Göttingen so productive.

My debt to Alf Lüdtke is immense. From the first time that he asked me whether I was interested in coming to Göttingen as a visiting fellow at the MPI in the summer of 1989, right up to the most recent transatlantic E-mail exchange, Alf has played a major role in the way I think about my work. Alf, his wife, Helga, and their daughter,

Insa, have also helped to make my frequent visits to Göttingen personally pleasant as well as intellectually rewarding.

On my first trip to Göttingen in 1989, when there was a temporary problem with my original accommodations, Adelheid and Manfred von Saldern took me into their wonderful home on short notice and ended up asking me to stay for the rest of the summer. I have enjoyed their marvelous hospitality on every subsequent visit and feel myself privileged to be considered a part-time member of their household. Heidy von Saldern is a remarkable colleague and friend. Over the past eight years, whether in Göttingen, in Hanover, or in cyberspace, she has been exceptionally generous with her time, her knowledge, and her insights. In the spring of 1996, she gave the manuscript of this book a close and careful reading, from which the final version has profited enormously.

As this book was taking shape, it was very helpful to talk with Young-Sun Hong about our shared interest in the history of the German welfare state. In locations as diverse as Berlin, Freiburg, Ann Arbor, and Los Angeles, she and Larry Frohman offered me not only food for thought but also unstinting hospitality and excellent Korean meals. Conversations and correspondence with a long list of other scholars, colleagues, and friends have also contributed to this book's development and to my own intellectual growth: in Germany, Christoph Sachsse (Kassel), Michael Grüttner and Ursula Nienhaus (Berlin), Dieter Dowe, Friedhelm Boll, Beatrix Bouvier, Dieter Rebentisch, Patrick von zur Mühlen (Bonn), Istvan Hont (Göttingen), and Gregory Claeys and Christine Lattek (Hanover); in England, Richard Bessel and Richard Evans; in the United States, Jack and Jane Censer, Belinda Davis, Elizabeth Domansky, Kathleen Canning, Jane Caplan, Greg Egighian, Geoff Eley, Atina Grossmann, Rudy Koshar, Robert Moeller, and George Steinmetz.

At the University of Texas, I am lucky to have exceptionally supportive and stimulating colleagues. The charter members of the interdisciplinary reading group on modern culture and theory—Kit Belgum, Martha Newman, Joan Neuberger, Irene Kacandes, and Lynn Wilkinson—deserve special mention as does a somewhat newer but already cherished colleague, Judith Coffin. Whether they know it or not, my undergraduate and graduate students have also made important contributions to this book by constantly challenging me to formulate and communicate my ideas as clearly and precisely as possible. My skilled, efficient, and understanding editors at Oxford University Press, Thomas LeBien and Paula Wald, have made it a pleasure to move this book from typescript to print.

Above all, I want to express my deepest thanks to my wife, Sara, for her intelligence, vivacity, love, and warmth, and to my lovely and talented daughter, Kate, who grew up with this book and who repeatedly helped me to remember that the theater, Borges, and going to college are equally as important as the history of the German welfare state. I dedicate this book to them.

Material in Chapters 5, 7, and 8 has been previously published in part or in different versions in the following articles:

"'Wohlfahrtsbrot ist bitteres Brot': The Elderly, the Disabled, and the Local Welfare Authorities in the Weimar Republic, 1924–1933." In *Archiv für Sozialgeschichte*,

30 Bd. (Bonn: Verlag J. H. W. Dietz Nachf, 1990). Copyright 1990 by Verlag J. H. W. Dietz Nachfolger. Used by permission of Verlag J. H. W. Dietz Nachfolger.

"'Eine Elternschaft zu Dritt'—staatliche Eltern?: Jugendwohlfahrt und Kontrolle der Familie in der Weimarer Republik, 1919–1933." In Alf Lüdtke, ed., *"Sicherheit" und "Wohlfahrt": Polizei, Gesellschaft und Herrschaft im 19. und 20. Jahrhundert* (Frankfurt: Suhrkamp Verlag, 1992). Copyright Suhrkamp Verlag 1992. Used by permission of Suhrkamp Verlag.

"Gewalt 'auf dem Amt': Beispiele aus der Wohlfahrtsverwaltung der Weimarer Republik." In *WerkstattGeschichte* 4 (1993). Copyright 1993 Ergebnisse Verlag GmbH. Used by permission of Ergebnisse Verlag GmbH.

"Gewalt 'auf dem Amt': Wohlfahrtsbehörden und ihre Klienten in der Weimarer Republik." In Thomas Lindenberger and Alf Lüdtke, eds., *Physische Gewalt: Studien zur Geschichte der Neuzeit* (Frankfurt: Suhrkamp Verlag, 1995). Copyright 1995 Suhrkamp Verlag. Used by permission of Suhrkamp Verlag.

"The Ambiguities of Modernity: Welfare and the German State from Wilhelm to Hitler." In Geoff Eley, ed., *Society, Culture, and the State in Germany, 1870–1930* (Ann Arbor: University of Michigan Press, 1996). Copyright 1996 by the University of Michigan. Used by permission of the University of Michigan.

Austin, Texas   D. F. C.
February 1997

Contents

Abbreviations

The following abbreviations are used throughout this book.

ADGB Allgemeiner Deutscher Gewerkschaftsbund (General German Trade Union Federation)

ARSO Arbeitsgemeinschaft sozialpolitischer Organisationen (Working Group of Social Policy Organizations)

AVAVG Gesetz über Arbeitsvermittlung und Arbeitslosenversicherung (Law on Labor Exchanges and Unemployment Insurance)

DDP Deutsche Demokratische Partei (German Democratic Party)

DIZ *Deutsche Invaliden Zeitung*

DNVP Deutschnationale Volkspartei (German National People's Party)

DVP Deutsche Volkspartei (German People's Party)

FAD Freiwilliger Arbeitsdienst (Voluntary Labor Service)

FE *Fürsorgeerziehung* (correctional education)

IB Internationaler Bund der Opfer des Krieges und der Arbeit (International League of the Victims of War and Labor)

KPD Kommunistische Partei Deutschlands (Communist Party of Germany)

NSDAP Nationalsozialistische Deutsche Arbeiterpartei (National Socialist German Workers' Party)

RAM Reichsarbeitsministerium (Reich Labor Ministry)

SPD Sozialdemokratische Partei Deutschlands (Social Democratic Party of Germany)

USPD Unabhängige Sozialdemokratische Partei Deutschlands (Independent Social Democratic Party of Germany)

GERMANS ON WELFARE

Introduction

The Meaning of the German Welfare State

The Narratives of Modern German History

If narrative theorists are right and meaning is constructed by the way in which a story is told, then it is difficult to attribute a single meaning to the history of the German welfare state since Bismarck.[1] If there ever was an authoritative "master narrative," it has certainly dissolved in recent years into a variety of new, often competing narrative possibilities. This narrative pluralism has been produced by the broader debates about modern German history in which scholars have engaged since the late 1960s. The search for the origins of Nazism has dominated discussions of both the Wilhelmine Empire (1890–1918) and the Weimar Republic (1919–1933). In the late 1960s and early 1970s, Hans-Ulrich Wehler, Jürgen Kocka, and other members of the Bielefeld school proposed a view of recent German history that rapidly attained the status of a "new orthodoxy."[2] This interpretation saw Nazism as the inevitable end product of Germany's political and social "misdevelopment" in the Wilhelmine and Weimar periods. Unlike other western European nations (especially Britain), Germany failed to establish a stable, liberal parliamentary system of government, a democratic political culture, or an egalitarian civil society. Instead of following the "British road" to democracy, the new German industrial nation traveled a quite different path of "Prussianism." The old, "preindustrial" elite, the aristocratic Prussian *Junker* class, refused to give way to the rising German middle classes. The middle classes, in turn, increasingly frightened by the emergence of a socialist working class, forsook their "historic mission." Renouncing their earlier liberal goals, they allied, albeit as junior partners, with the reactionary Prussian aristocracy and the authoritarian German state to resist the forces of democracy in Germany. By 1933, this conspiracy of preindustrial *Junker* and "feudalized" bourgeoisie could turn only to

3

Hitler in a last desperate and ultimately disastrous gamble to overturn Weimar democracy and resist the threat of Bolshevism in Germany.

In *The Peculiarities of German History*, which appeared in 1984, David Blackbourn and Geoff Eley challenged the Bielefeld school's arguments about Germany's "failed development" and its "special path" (*Sonderweg*) to fascism. Blackbourn and Eley attempted to "normalize" recent German history by shifting the focus of their discussion from "pre-industrial continuities" to the "silent bourgeois revolution in economy and society," which by the end of the nineteenth century had transformed Germany into one of the most "modern" of the European industrial nations.[3] But if Germany was a "normal" western European country before 1914, as Blackbourn and Eley claimed, why then did it plunge into genocidal barbarism after 1933? Detlev Peukert sought the answers to this problem in the "pathologies of modernity." In major works on Weimar and Nazi Germany, Peukert called for a "sceptical de-coupling of modernity and progress," arguing that historians must "raise questions about the pathologies and seismic fractures within modernity itself, and about the implicit destructive tendencies of industrial class society, which National Socialism made explicit and which it elevated into mass destruction."[4]

The Bielefeld school had located the origins of Nazism in the persistence of fatal "preindustrial traditions." Peukert detected a different set of continuities between Nazism and Germany's pre-1933 past. He argued that the Kaiserreich (1871–1918) introduced a period of "classical modernity" that experienced its crisis years during the Weimar Republic.[5] The Third Reich was the result of Weimar's failure to resolve the multiple crises of "classical modernity" within the political framework of bourgeois democracy: "The NSDAP was at once a symptom, and a solution, of the crisis." Peukert insisted that the Third Reich was a pathological variant of Germany's pre-1933 modernity, an exaggerated development of modernity's "dark side."[6]

Peukert's "classical modernity" is characterized by advanced capitalist forms of production and economic organization, by bureaucratization, by the growing "rationalization" of society and culture, and by the "social disciplining" and "normalization" of the everyday lives of the masses. In the epoch of "classical modernity," instrumental reason and the spirit of science assumed hegemonic roles in the ordering of German society. Peukert's discussion of Germany's classical modernity owes much to Max Weber. Yet this is a very different Weber than the social theorist to whom the Bielefeld historians laid claim in the 1960s and 1970s. That Weber was seen as the German prophet of a teleological American-style "modernization theory," which could serve as a liberal/Social Democratic West German antidote to the dogmas of East German Marxism. By contrast, Peukert's Weber is a symptomatic thinker of the German and European *Jahrhundertwende* ("turn of the century") who confronts not Marx but Nietzsche and who refuses to embrace the Enlightenment master narrative of "progress." Peukert's Weber is sensitive to and troubled by the "antinomies of modernity," which can be summarized as the progressive "rationalization" of everyday life through the processes of secularization and bureaucratization that threatens to produce the complete "disenchantment of the world" and the growth of a misplaced faith in the capacity of rational science to solve all human problems. Indeed, Peukert's almost postmodernist Weber presents an ambiguous and contradictory "modernity" with a "Janus" face.[7]

Telling the Story of the Welfare State

The Pathologies of Modernity?

The welfare state became a central fixture of Germany's twentieth-century modernity, yet the history of German welfare has, until recently, been poorly developed by comparison with Great Britain.[8] Early research was selective; historians focused on Bismarck's social insurance policies (sickness insurance in 1883, accident insurance in 1884, and old age and disability insurance in 1889) but neglected the history of poor relief and the poor law. This was no accident. Concentrating on Bismarck's social insurance policies allowed supporters of the *Sonderweg* thesis to argue that it was the political interests of the preindustrial ruling elites and not those of the bourgeoisie that both produced and profited from the precocious development of the modern welfare state. As George Steinmetz puts it in an excellent discussion of these issues, this "scholarship . . . often coded Bismarck's social policies as a result of neo-feudal paternalism and the weakness of liberalism, or as disqualified by the manipulative motives that inspired it." But Steinmetz argues that the German social insurance system was unmistakably "modern" and "bourgeois": It had much stronger support from industrial interests than from agrarian ones, and the practical ideologies according to which it functioned were quintessentially bourgeois.

By comparison with social insurance, poor relief might appear to have been a "traditional" form of social provision. But it, too, was emphatically "bourgeois." Before World War I, systems of poor relief were largely constructed and implemented at the level of the local state by the liberal middle classes who still dominated local government and administration. The major nineteenth-century model of poor relief—the Elberfeld System—"stressed individual responsibility, self-monitoring, and quick reintegration of the poor into labor markets."[9] Regular visiting to achieve the intense "individualized" treatment and surveillance of the poor anticipated the central practices of twentieth-century social work.

By the late nineteenth century, however, bourgeois social reformers were beginning to insist that the German state would have to do more to promote the health and welfare of the German people as a whole than the existing framework of the poor law allowed if Germany was to become a world power and if its political order was not to be undermined by the spread of socialism among the poor. Alongside the poor-relief system there now emerged maternal and infant welfare centers, youth welfare officers, housing inspectors, and public health agencies that campaigned against tuberculosis. Advice and information would be dispensed even to "healthy" families and individuals in order to educate them in rational and scientific methods of reproducing and raising children, caring for the body and the home, and managing family economies. "Welfare was . . . increasingly understood as education in the methodical, rational conduct of life, as conformity of the everyday existence of the lower orders to the demands of scientific rationality."[10]

World War I produced a rapid expansion of the welfare system. The national military emergency and the domestic crisis caused by mass deprivation and hunger on the home front forced the German state to assume responsibility for a much wider range of "clients" (war widows, war wounded, and others) and to expand social rights in return for the population's "sacrifices to the nation."[11] After 1918, the success or failure of the Weimar Republic depended to no small degree upon the welfare state's ability to give millions of Germans at least a fundamental level of material and mental security in the face of the new risks to which they had been exposed by the effects of the lost war, the Revolution, and inflation.[12] Yet the economic problems of the postwar period meant that, even in its best years, the Weimar Republic was an "over-burdened welfare state."[13] The onset of the Depression and the growth of mass unemployment after 1929 destroyed republican democracy and the welfare state upon which it was based.[14]

The Nazis insisted that social policy must serve the priorities of "racial hygiene." Instead of supporting the "weak" and the "unproductive," as the Weimar system was alleged to have done, social policy in the Third Reich devoted its resources to the "biologically" valuable, who could contribute to the economic and racial health of the nation. The "biologically inferior" were denied economic assistance and subjected to "negative" eugenic measures, including forced sterilization, even euthanasia. In any relatively "benign narrative of [the] modernizing welfare state," the Nazi "racial state" can only appear as a radical break from the previous history of the German welfare system and from "a central, secular developmental trend of modernity."[15] After 1945 (so this argument continues), the German welfare state resumed a "normal" trajectory that eventually produced the social justice and "security" that, until recently, and with some exceptions, has characterized the Federal Republic since the 1950s.[16]

Detlev Peukert's examination of the "pathologies of modernity" forces us to confront a much darker history. Peukert argues that the growth of Germany's modern welfare state was inspired by and in turn nourished a "utopian" view of social policy. Welfare reformers maintained that just as medical science had learned to cure diseases previously thought to be hopelessly fatal, so, too, modern social welfare would be able to heal the body social. This *Fortschrittsoptimismus* seduced social policy experts into believing that they could soon achieve a "final solution" of the social problem. Weimar represented the high point of this enterprise when social policy became firmly anchored in the state. Yet Weimar was also the crisis period of classical modernity in social policy, as in other areas of social, political, and economic life. Especially after 1929, when the Great Depression, mass unemployment, and state welfare cutbacks created previously unimaginable material deprivation and social dislocation, "the limits of what social-technology could achieve were reached in every direction."[17] Rather than accepting that German history had frustrated their ambitions, welfare experts began to redefine their Utopia. If German society as a whole could not be cured of its social problems, then healthy individuals must be protected from the influence of the "incurables." The "scientization" of the social and the "medicalization" of social problems had, Peukert argues, opened the door to a new and distinctly modern "pathology" that found its ultimate expression in the Nazi program of separating the "healthy" Germany *Völk* from its "degenerate" racial and biological enemies, followed by their sterilization or extermination.[18]

However, Peukert's discussion of the pathologies of modernity in its German context does oversimplify a complex, conflict-ridden history. I would offer at least four major criticisms. First, Peukert stresses continuity at the expense of seriously underestimating the significance of the ruptures produced by World War I and by the Nazi accession to power. Second, for Peukert, the vital continuity is a consistent "uto-pianism" that eventually led social policy experts to embrace "social racism." Many of the participants in postwar social policy debates certainly believed that the Weimar welfare system would promote the "rationalization" of social behavior and every-day life.[19] Yet this commitment to social rationalization often drew its inspiration less from the confident faith in social progress described by Peukert than from Germany's desperate need for social reconstruction following war, defeat, revolu-tion, and inflation. Contemporaries often saw the Weimar welfare state more as a form of damage control than as the culmination of a utopian project initiated in the 1890s. Nor was the Weimar welfare state run by a monolithic regime of experts sin-gularly intent upon the pursuit of "the final solution to the social problem" but rather by a somewhat improvised chaos of competing authorities, underfunded agencies, and a mixture of private and public bodies. The ideological vantage points of most of the major welfare interests (whether Catholic, Protestant, or socialist) immunized them against exaggerated expectations. The Weimar welfare "establishment" also included local government officials and tens of thousands of volunteer workers (*ehrenamtliche Organe*), who were often more concerned with reducing the costs of welfare administration than with any utopian goals. Moreover, attempts to impose the dictates of instrumental reason on the organization of everyday life "from above" could by no means count on a warm reception from below, among the welfare clients who were the targets of social rationalization. The friction generated by the welfare system's invasion of the "life-worlds" of millions of Germans and the resulting "con-frontation of the concept of rationalization with other norms, or . . . behavioral ori-entations" made it difficult for the Weimar state to secure the popular legitimacy it so urgently required.[20] Third, most recent discussions of the Weimar welfare state recognize the influence of what Peukert calls "social racism" but emphasize that it was only able to become the dominant welfare discourse and practice (and hence a murderous reality) after its critics had been silenced by the Nazi destruction of the Weimar public sphere and of the legal rights of welfare clients after 1933. Fourth, Peukert expands the concept of the "final solution" to include the persecution and extermination of large numbers of non-Jews who were regarded by the Nazis as racially or biologically "inferior," as "lives unworthy of life." Wolfgang Ayass has recently cautioned against blurring vital distinctions between the Nazis' victims. Ayass reminds us, for example, that "unlike Jews and Gypsies, the 'asocial' had certain ways out. The main criterion of selection was always active participation in the labor pro-cess or the war machinery. Whoever demonstrated that they could be 'reeducated' also gave evidence that their deviant behavior was [perhaps] not hereditary."[21]

Feminist Historiography: Women/Gender and the Welfare State

Historians of women and gender have also begun to rewrite the history of Germany's welfare state. Seth Koven and Sonya Michel argue that largely middle-class women philanthropists and social reformers played a previously neglected but extremely important role in the early development of welfare states in America, Britain, France, and Germany. Under the banner of "maternalism," these women advanced new claims to participate in a previously masculine public sphere and attempted to expand the boundaries and transform the definition of "politics" itself by insisting that social policy take account of the interests of women and children, which male politicians had largely ignored.[22] However, Kathleen Canning suggests that Koven and Michel's claims for the importance of "female agency" are weakened by their own observations about Germany, where a strong state constructed "comprehensive social welfare programs for women," even though German women exerted less political influence than their American or British counterparts. Canning argues that "even where women lacked 'bureaucratic and political power' . . . ideologies of gender shaped the definitions and practices of welfare and were in turn recast by state interventions and anchored by state authority." Social policy "sought to fix gender roles, to align sexual divisions of labor with the social order, to regulate the social body through policing female bodies, even where bourgeois feminist-maternalists were unsuccessful or inactive."[23] In this book, I will argue that gender certainly played an important role in the shaping of the Weimar welfare state. But the gender lines drawn by the Weimar welfare state were complex, contradictory, and unstable. Bourgeois women struggled with bourgeois men but also with working-class men and women for power and influence within the administrative structures of the welfare state. The voices of bourgeois women competed with each other, as well as with those of bourgeois men, working-class men, and women in the new public spheres that formed to discuss welfare issues.

Gender must, however, be understood, as Eve Rosenhaft has recently suggested, as not just "the qualities attributed to empirical individuals but as a system of organizing social perception in which sexual difference is pivotal."[24] Adopting this perspective will allow us to see that the Weimar welfare state was traversed by divisions and tensions between (but also within) a series of gendered "spaces," practices, and identities. The rational principles of "administration," culturally coded as masculine, repeatedly collided with a more emotional, even spiritual ideal of "feminine caring." Both male and female welfare officials frequently felt themselves pulled in the opposing directions that "bureaucratism" and "social work" signified. "Social work" repeatedly attempted to differentiate its (gendered) practices from those of a "policing" conceived of as masculine—yet policing remained an integral component of social work. Consequently, the Weimar welfare state cannot be characterized as either simply patriarchical or maternal.[25]

History of Everyday Life

Peukert's analysis of the pathologies of modernity and Koven and Michel's attempts to gender the narrative of the welfare state concentrate largely upon the discussions of feminists, social reformers, and welfare experts and the laws and institutions that their debates produced. Yet the Weimar welfare state was not simply the product of discourse and discursive struggle; it was also constructed and reproduced by the daily interactions of hard-pressed officials and impatient, frequently desperate clients. To see how welfare discourses were translated into welfare practices by local welfare officials and appropriated, contested, or renegotiated by millions of welfare clients, we need the perspective that *Alltagsgeschichte* (history of everyday life) can provide. The history of everyday life insists on the importance of getting "inside" the "structures, processes and patterns" of social analysis.[26] Through the careful construction of historical "miniatures" that allow "thick description" of the social production and construction of meaning,[27] *Alltagsgeschichte* tries to understand how "big structures, large processes" were experienced and appropriated by ordinary people.[28] But it is important not to think of "structure" and "agency" as antagonistic categories. "Structures" should rather be seen as "at once the medium and the outcome of human interactions. They are transformed by agents, but they are also reproduced by agents. . . . Agents could not exist without the structures that provide their constraints and possibilities, and structures could not exist without the agents who enact and/or transform them."[29]

With very few exceptions, discussions of the German welfare state have simply ignored the voices of the millions of Germans who came in contact with the welfare system as its clients. Welfare clients appear as statistics, seldom as individuals. This is a peculiar silence, given the importance welfare authorities themselves assigned to the client's role in the welfare system. Weimar welfare offices distributed material support, but they also tried to educate their clients.[30] This pedagogical project could not succeed without the clients' cooperation.[31] Clients' responses to this project cannot be reduced simply to "compliance" or "resistance." Alf Lüdtke's concept of *Eigensinn* can help us to understand the "ambiguities and contradictions of ordinary people's perceptions and behavior as they actually live their lives."[32] *Eigensinn* describes the inconsistent, even contradictory, practices through which ordinary people tried to assert their identities and interests. These small physical or verbal acts of daily self-assertion might be directed against those "above" (the authorities and their rules) but also against those "around" one (other welfare clients). And *Eigensinn* has no simple, unilinear consequences or significance: "*Eigensinn* makes it possible, makes it easier for the individual just to keep going and thus also opens up space for further participation and hanging on. In other words, questions about *Eigensinn* by no means lead us only or even primarily to resistance or complete emancipation."[33]

The meanings and the consequences of *Eigensinn* did not remain constant from one historical period to another. War, revolution, and the promises of the Weimar constitution nurtured a historically specific "moral economy" that allowed Weimar clients to advance claims seldom voiced by Germans who turned to the poor law or private charity before 1914. Some Weimar welfare clients appealed explicitly to the social and political rights proclaimed by the constitution. Others cited the provisions of the new welfare laws. Even welfare clients who made no specific reference to constitutional or legal arguments may certainly have been encouraged to assert their interests by new conceptions of justice, right, and dignity. But self-assertion was an end in itself as well as a means to an end.[34] The very act of challenging the authority of welfare officials, of calling into question their definitional powers over one's case, could be just as important to many welfare clients as any concrete material benefit that such a challenge might produce. Yet enjoying the immediate symbolic pleasures of self-assertion could jeopardize longer-term material interests. Welfare authorities often disciplined or excluded clients they regarded as "difficult." Avoiding these painful sanctions called for more subtle and opaque forms of self-assertion, or what Michel de Certeau terms "surreptitious creativities" that "far from being regulated or eliminated by panoptic administration, have . . . insinuated themselves into the networks of surveillance, and . . . are merely concealed by the frantic mechanisms and discourses of the observational organization."[35]

Why Weimar?

Some of the best recent work on Germany's welfare state has refused to be confined by the periodization that Germany's political history supplies. Peukert's search for the pathologies of modernity transgresses the chronological boundaries between Wilhelmine, Weimar, and Nazi Germany. Andreas Wollasch, Ewald Frie, Young-Sun Hong, and Greg Egighian all see the "crisis" decade from 1914 to 1924 as a single, formative phase in the history of Germany's modern welfare state. And Peukert, Liz Harvey, and Marcus Gräser have identified important continuities in social policy that connect the last phase of the Weimar Republic to Nazi Germany.

Without denying the importance of these wider historical perspectives, I want to argue that the search for the meaning of the Weimar welfare state must bring us back to the specific circumstances of the Weimar Republic itself. The history of the Weimar welfare state was determined more by what distinguished it from its Wilhelmine predecessor and its Nazi successor than by what they all had in common. Revolution and defeat transformed the political, ideological, and economic contexts within which welfare institutions and practices were situated. The German Revolution of 1918/19 and the creation of the Weimar Republic destroyed the two foundations of the "imperialist motif" that had sustained and justified "bourgeois social reform" since the 1890s, namely, "a strong state and an expanding economy."[36] Bourgeois social reform and social work had not been able to strengthen the imperial state and prevent revolution. The labor movement now challenged the bourgeois monopoly of social work, demanding a democratization of welfare. The religious charities were able to resist the Social Democrats' demand for a complete state monopoly of welfare functions and to secure for themselves a special legal position in the Weimar welfare state.[37] However, their experience in the Weimar Republic taught the religious welfare interests that state welfare threatened to secularize and bureaucratize all welfare practices, leaving no room for the traditionally important spiritual dimensions.

Germany was also poorer after 1918. Armed with new legal rights, welfare clients battled with the state and each other for the scarce and shrinking material resources of the welfare system.[38] Welfare thus became a highly contested public sphere in the Weimar Republic, torn by incompatible visions of society and competing identities and interests. Between 1919 and 1933, the always fragile compromise that had allowed the Weimar welfare state to come into being began to unravel beyond repair. Those who had never been comfortable with Weimar's welfare state eventually turned their backs on it altogether and began to search for a completely different alternative. The Nazi accession to power allowed them to pursue that search untrammeled by the constraints—legal, political, and moral—that Weimar's public sphere had still managed to impose.

From a late-twentieth-century perspective, Weimar cannot be regarded as the period of Germany's decisive breakthrough to the modern welfare state; that transition is located in the years after Germany's defeat in World War II.[39] Yet the political commitment to the idea of the "social state" was a cornerstone of the Weimar social contract.[40] This promise of the welfare state created popular expectations that turned quickly into grievances when the economic and political context of the Weimar Republic prevented this *Sozialstaatspostulat* from being translated into a meaningful social reality.[41] Yet at the same time that clients were experiencing the manifest inadequacies of the Weimar welfare system, its opponents charged that the welfare state had grown too big, was too costly, and had made far too many Germans dependent upon handouts. It is important to remember that "the picture, so familiar to us, of the Weimar Republic as the first welfare state in German history was, for many contemporaries, only a pejorative designation."[42] In the Weimar Republic, we can observe the emergence of a political rhetoric about an overextended welfare system that continues up to the very present to nourish assaults upon the welfare state not only in Germany but in other western European countries and in the United States.[43]

Which Welfare State?

Until quite recently, discussions of Weimar's welfare state have focused primarily on labor legislation, public housing, and the introduction of unemployment insurance in 1927.[44] But the 1920s witnessed a massive expansion of public responsibilities (under the umbrella of the 1922 Youth Welfare Law and the 1924 National Welfare Decree) for a heterogeneous collection of often newly constituted welfare clients—ranging from single mothers, illegitimate children, and delinquent youths to all those whose lives had been damaged by the war and the inflation. Contemporaries described this complex of means-tested support and educational therapies that supplanted both the Wilhelmine poor law and private welfare activities as *Wohlfahrtspflege* or *Fürsorge*. These terms had not been widely used in the nineteenth century, when "*Wohltätigkeit*" denoted private charity and emphasized its voluntary nature and "*Armenpflege*" described the limited, disciplinary and demeaning state poor law. By the twentieth century, both *Wohltätigkeit* and *Armenpflege* were seen as backward and discriminatory and were thus increasingly replaced by the terms "*Wohlfahrtspflege*" and "*Fürsorge*." Both concepts intoned the importance of systematic, comprehensive treatment of social problems by the state in cooperation with private welfare organizations.[45] It is this sphere of public welfare activities that is the subject of this book.

The public welfare system touched the lives of millions of Weimar Germans. During two major periods of crisis in Weimar's history—the inflation of 1918 to 1923 and the Depression of 1929 to 1933—public welfare became the only means of assistance for the great majority of those in need (see Table 1). At the beginning of December 1923, for example, 22 percent of the Munich population was on welfare; in Frankfurt am Main this figure was 39 percent, in Nuremberg 49 percent, in Stettin 56 percent, and in Dortmund, as a consequence of the Ruhr occupation, 80 percent.[46] In the mid-1920s, the numbers of Germans who had to turn to public welfare decreased considerably, but after the onset of the Depression welfare dependency once again became widespread. In 1927, some 1,571,700 Weimar Germans were on welfare; this figure rose to 1,983,900 in 1930 and to 4,608,200 by the end of 1932 (an

TABLE 1. Permanent Welfare Clients, per 1,000 Population

Place	1926	1927	1928	1929
Hamburg	41.09	43.75	42.80	50
Cologne	95.46	75.44	71.77	69
Düsseldorf	64.96	42.98	57.39	42
Stuttgart	63.64	61.93	37.24	49
Germany		27.07		

Sources: *SJDR*, 46 Jg., 1927, p. 443; *SJdS*, 22 Jg., 1927, p. 441, 23 Jg., 1928, p. 126, 25 Jg., 1930, p. 431, 26 Jg., 1931, p. 333, 27 Jg., 1932, p. 324.

increase of 193 percent between 1927 and 1932).[47] The four cities whose records provide much of the information about local conditions and welfare practices analyzed in this book all had per capita rates of welfare clients that were considerably higher than the national average in 1927. Between 1927 and 1930, the growth of caseloads in these four cities was consistently higher than the national average (with the exception of Cologne in 1930).[48] By 1932, Hamburg's welfare clientele was eight times larger than it had been in 1925, and almost 23 percent of the city-state's inhabitants were on welfare.[49]

Toward (a) Possible Narrative(s)

How then should the story of the Weimar welfare state be told? Obviously, I do not think we should attempt to search for a new master narrative. What we need, as both gender history and *Alltagsgeschichte* have shown, is a way to tell the story that does not rely upon "a concept of reality which is monolithic, linear and does not allow for plural realities."[50] An adequate narrative will have to be skeptical about any "optimistic teleology of modernization,"[51] but it must also resist the temptation, as Atina Grossmann has recently put it, "to impute to social welfare in general, from the imperial era on, a kind of slippery slope trajectory of inexorability that led in a perhaps bumpy, but nevertheless logical line to forced sterilization, euthanasia, and then genocide."[52] An adequate narrative must, finally, be able to recognize continuities without effacing breaks, ruptures, and discontinuities. With regard to Weimar's welfare state, this injunction means being able to locate Weimar in a wider historical context but not at the expense of understating the importance of the ruptures produced by the German Revolution in 1918/19 and the Nazi seizure of power in 1933. I hope this book will show how these requirements can be met.

Scope and Sources

This book examines the history of the Weimar welfare system from a number of perspectives: national, regional, local, and individual. The types of sources examined are, correspondingly, quite varied. Three national welfare publications proved to be of greatest use for reconstructing the national debates and conflicts on welfare issues and policies in the Weimar period: the Social Democratic *Arbeiterwohlfahrt*, the Catholic *Caritas*, and the Protestant *Innere Mission*. Complete runs of each of these three national publications are housed in the Caritas-Bibliothek in Freiburg, where I was able systematically to work my way through every Weimar-era issue of each of these three journals. In Freiburg, too, I was able to explore what is undoubtedly one of the richest single collections of published contemporary materials dealing with both public and private welfare activities in the Weimar years. Here I also discovered and was able to begin to retrieve another type of extremely valuable source (although this search continued in a number of regional/municipal archives and libraries): the local welfare journals that a great number of Weimar welfare offices and agencies published, frequently in limited numbers and primarily for the use of local professional and volunteer welfare workers. These publications proved to be indispensable sources of information on local welfare practices and problems. In the library and archive of the Institute for Social History at the Friedrich Ebert Stiftung in Bonn, I found a rich collection of published material concerning the participation of Social Democratic organizations in the Weimar welfare system. The institute's extensive microfilm collection also gave me access to a wide range of regional and local Social Democratic Party (SPD) newspapers from the 1920s.

Primary responsibility for the implementation of national welfare laws and policies and for the day-to-day administration of public welfare lay in the hands of local authorities. Consequently, intensive research for this book was done in a series of local archives. I decided that it was important to pay attention to a range of different local social, economic, cultural, and political milieus. In northern and western Germany, I decided to focus upon Hamburg, Düsseldorf, and Cologne, three centers of industrial production with quite different political, cultural, and religious complexions. Hamburg, Germany's second-largest city (population 1,152,523 in 1925) and at the same time a federal state, was a largely Protestant stronghold of both the Social Democratic labor movement and the Communist party.[53] Hamburg was one of the most important ports in northern Europe, and its economic and social life was shaped by the postwar fortunes of international commerce and the shipbuilding industry. In 1925, 26.8 percent of Hamburg's workforce was employed in commerce and trade, 13.5 percent in transport, and 5.5 percent in machine construction (2.9% in shipbuilding); 5.2 percent worked in the building industry and another 5.2 percent in the clothing trades.[54] In the Rhineland, Düsseldorf (population 432,633 in 1925) and Cologne (population 700,222 in 1925) were heavily Catholic cities and Center party strongholds, where the political presence of the Social Democrats was considerably weaker than in Hamburg (although the Communists were just as strong).[55] Düsseldorf's most important sources of employment were commerce and trade (18.1% of the workforce in 1925), machine building and metal engineering (12.8%), basic metals production (8.6%), and transport (5.4%). In Cologne, the commerce of the Rhine River was a major source of employment; 20.0 percent of the local workforce was engaged in commerce and trade and 9.6 percent in transport in 1925. But 7.8 percent was also employed in machine building, 7.1 percent in the building trades, 7.0 percent in clothing manufacture, and 5.7 percent in the food trades. In south Germany, I focused primarily on Stuttgart (population 341,967 in 1925), a predominantly Protestant city where the Social Democrats were stronger than in Düsseldorf or Cologne but weaker than in Hamburg. In Stuttgart, the important sources of employment were commerce and trade (17.2% of the workforce), followed by the clothing trades (7.7%), machine construction (7.5%), electrical, optical, and fine mechanical engineering (7.0%), and transport (6.6%).[56] I also used archival materials relating to the entire region of northern Württemberg, which included several quite rural and agrarian districts as well as urban ones. In the Oberamtsbezirk Künzelsau, for example, where 56.7 percent of the population was Protestant, and the population density (excluding towns over 10,000) was less than 60 inhabitants per square kilometer in 1930 (compared with over 200 inhabitants per square kilometer in Stuttgart), 63.7 percent of the population was engaged in agriculture.[57] Small farms of less than 5 hectares constituted between 50 and 60 percent of all agricultural enterprises; the remainder were between 5 and 100 hectares in size. The average size of a Künzelsau farm was between 6 and 8 hectares.[58] It was not possible to engage in detailed research in East German local archives, but I have drawn wherever possible upon contemporary published sources from the eastern parts of Germany, especially the local welfare journals mentioned above. Indeed, local welfare journals have provided a great deal of information on a considerable number of localities in a number of different regions of Germany, beyond those for which it was possible to undertake detailed archival research.

The main aim of this book is to go beyond the type of discussion of welfare state policies and institutions that has largely occupied historians until now. I have examined the policies and the institutions of the emerging welfare system in considerable detail, but I have tried to show that these structures of the welfare state were the always provisional outcomes of complicated and contradictory interactions and relationships between welfare officials and welfare clients; in this book, "social practice moves to the center of the stage."[59] David Sabean points out that "once we center our attention on [social] relationships, we are forced into research strategies which favor the local and the particular."[60] Initial investigations of a number of local archives in northern, western, and southern Germany revealed that the administrative records of local welfare agencies have been quite unevenly preserved. My richest discoveries were made in Hamburg, Düsseldorf, Cologne, and Ludwigsburg. Among the very considerable treasures of the Hamburg Staatsarchiv are, for example, the detailed minutes of the regular roundtable meetings that brought the directors of each of the city's district welfare offices together to discuss current issues and problems of everyday welfare practice. In Ludwigsburg, I had the good fortune to discover detailed individual case records and petitions in a number of different administrative districts of northern Württemberg. However, the sheer abundance of administrative records in these particular archives does not solve the problem of gaining access to the voices of the people being administered. Welfare records reveal a close and reciprocal relationship between official claims to power and modes of representation. Although the construction of case files and other welfare documents often required taking direct testimony from welfare clients, welfare officials insisted on their exclusive right to interpret these statements and to define their authors' interests and identities. Officials tried to assert absolute control of the narrative constructed by their case files. Even the apparently most objective statistical lists were always, at least in some measure, "strategic representations of social reality."[61] We must, therefore, read welfare records against the grain, paying close attention not only to the strategies deployed by welfare officials to defend their monopoly of definitional powers but also to the tactics with which clients attempted to contest, subvert, or evade these official claims.[62]

At different points in this book, I have engaged in the thick description of certain individual cases that produced exceptionally rich paper trails. The individual voices that emerge from these particular case files are not representative in any strictly quantifiable sense. In many instances, these files are so rich precisely because the clients in question had assumed the anomalous role, at least in official eyes, of "professional complainer" (*Querulant*). In their thoughtful examination of one such case, Adelheid von Saldern, Karen Heinze, and Sybille Küster suggest, however, that the *Querulant/Querulantin* may be exceptional only insofar as he or she functions as an "extremely delicate sensor . . . who, in exaggerated . . . manner draws attention to structures of the social order that are open to criticism and thus concern more than just this individual case."[63] In my readings of the individual cases that are presented in some detail in this book, I have tried to listen to these suggestions and to pay attention to what the individual case may be able to tell us about the range, if not necessarily the quantifiable distribution, of possible experiences, perceptions, and responses among the welfare officials and clients who did not leave behind such extensive documentation of their individual stories.

Chapter 1 of this book shows that the Weimar welfare system was made possible only by a fragile compromise between religious welfare interests and the Social Democrats. The conflicts of worldview that marked the origins of the Weimar welfare system continued to traverse its subsequent history in the 1920s and eventually contributed, during the Depression, to the dissolution of Weimar's version of the welfare state. Chapters 2, 3, and 4 take us inside Weimar welfare offices by exploring the identities and interests of the major actors at the local level: welfare officials, volunteer workers, female social workers, and welfare clients. A major aim of this book is to examine the broadest possible range of encounters Weimar Germans might have had with the welfare system; consequently, Chapters 5, 6, and 7 examine the experiences and reactions of different major categories of Weimar welfare clients, beginning with "social pensioners" and "small capital pensioners" in Chapter 5, then moving on to women (Chapter 6), and children, young people, and families (Chapter 7). Chapters 8, 9, and 10 are concerned more with experiences (hunger, homelessness, and unemployment) that were shared by a variety of different types of welfare clients. The conclusion offers a summary of the range of identities and interests that emerged from these encounters with the welfare system and then moves on to a consideration of the transformation of the Weimar welfare state into the Nazi racial state.

CHAPTER ONE

Religion, Socialism, and State Welfare in the Weimar Republic

Detlev Peukert has argued that in the 1920s, Germany broke with its nineteenth-century past more abruptly, more distinctly than any other western industrial nation. But the "dream of reason" (*Traum der Vernunft*) that inspired the "project of modernity" was experimental, plagued with contradictions, and, consequently, crisis ridden. By demystifying the world, modernity produced a desire for a revitalization of everyday life by a charismatic leader and by irrational appeals to "new religions," such as race. Racism offered a way out of the normative crisis produced by the triumph of science and reason over religion. Although nineteenth-century medical science had been able to prolong life, it could not overcome death; and, unlike religion, it offered no spiritual consolation for this failure. Peukert argues that racism solved these problems by shifting attention from the individual body to the *Volkskörper* (the "eternal," eugenic "body" of the *Volk*). Although each individual must eventually die, the healthy race could survive. But while racism promised immortality for each individual's "healthy" genes, it also made the "elimination" of the "unfit" carriers of "deficient genes" a duty owed by the current generation to posterity. This prescription had murderous results during the Third Reich. But Peukert insists that social racism was not a uniquely Nazi deformation; it had in fact already been produced by the human sciences themselves: "National Socialism provides a special case, a particularly fatal form of the tense relationship that runs through the entire history of social policy between . . . the 'normality' that is to be fostered and required and . . . the 'non-conformity' that is to be segregated or eliminated."[1]

This is an intriguing and, in many respects, compelling argument. Yet it ignores the central role of the religious welfare interests and of religious and ideological conflict in the Weimar welfare state. Far from having been completely defeated by the new religion of science and reason, German Catholicism and Protestantism waged a bitter, protracted, and in many ways successful struggle in the 1920s to retain their influence over the practice of welfare. Although eugenic formulations of social policy became increasingly attractive in the early 1930s, it was this *Weltanschauungskampf* (conflict of world views) between the religious welfare organizations and the secular state, not the seductions of racism, that produced the ideological crisis of the Weimar welfare state. The discourse on welfare at the end of Weimar was dominated by a mounting ideological backlash against the utopian ambitions of the welfare state and not, as Peukert suggests, by eugenic reformulations of this Utopia.[2]

The 1871 constitution had given the new imperial government few significant powers over private charities, and the private welfare organizations remained intent upon maintaining their independence from state authority. To do this, they pursued two basic strategies. The first was to pioneer welfare activities in which the state had not previously been engaged. If these new institutions and practices were later taken over by the state, private welfare organizations could move into new, uncharted territory. Second, private welfare organizations began to form associations at the national level (i.e., Caritasverband in 1897) that played an active political role in attempting to influence state activity. The war significantly altered the relationships between the state and private welfare organizations. During the war, more than 600 new charities were formed, most financed by donations. Some were fraudulent, and some used all the money for administrative costs; prospective clients seldom benefited, and the imperial state felt moved to issue decrees in 1915 and 1917, taking this *Kriegswohlfahrtspflege* (war welfare) partially under state oversight. This made the major established religious welfare organizations, the Catholic Caritas and the Protestant Innere Mission, uneasy about possible further state expansion, especially as the nonconfessional German Association for Private and Public Welfare was beginning to urge that the private sector be more willing to cooperate with the municipalities and the federal and national states after the war, not least because it was clear that private charities would need access to public funds.[3] The new categories of welfare clients produced by the war—the war wounded and war widows—would have to be dealt with differently than the Germans who had previously come in contact with either the poor law or private charity. But the financial resources of private welfare organizations were not sufficient to meet the needs of these additional new welfare clients. The state would not provide financial support or the increasingly necessary legal restructuring of German welfare practices without subjecting the private welfare organizations to increased controls. In Kassel, for example, "the associations and private facilities were given municipal funds only on the condition that . . . a certain right of supervision be allowed to the municipalities."[4] It seemed likely, indeed, that the state and municipalities would simply take over large areas of the welfare sector.

The postwar inflation further undermined the financial independence of the private charities. In Hamburg, for example, the almost 1,000 private charitable foundations had invested their funds in "gilt-edged securities, ground rents, mortgages, savings bank deposits, state loans. . . . All of these investments were hit hard by the inflation."[5] A whole series of welfare institutions, previously in private hands, had to be taken over by the Hamburg state authorities to prevent them from going under completely. Many individuals who had previously been active in private welfare withdrew, in part angered by the political changes, in part lacking the financial means to continue their voluntary efforts.[6] In Munich, "the private institutions became more and more dependent during the inflation on the fees paid for patients and inmates by the public authorities."[7] This new dependence on public funds created a tense relationship between the private welfare interests and the state. After 1918, the private and public sector worked together "in systematic cooperation, which, however, in view of the importance of public funding, could also turn into the subordination [of the private institutions]."

Left-wing demands for the complete "socialization" of welfare in Germany during the Revolution of 1918/19 convinced "the functionaries of the Innere Mission and the Caritas who had been socialized under the empire . . . that now everything they had lived and worked for was threatened." The private welfare organizations certainly had material reasons for wanting to resist an extension of state control; they were afraid that their considerable infrastructure, including not only institutions but the jobs of the people working in the private welfare sector, would be swallowed up by the state. But fundamental issues of worldview were equally if not more important. Both the Caritas and the Innere Mission saw themselves as religious organizations, charged with the task of resisting secularization and attempting to promote the re-Christianization of German society. They were less concerned with the rationality and efficiency of welfare work than with its religious and moral effects. The fact that the most vocal supporters of "statification" or the "municipalization" of welfare were generally socialists and secular, left liberals sharpened the ideological dimension of the conflict. During the Revolution, and despite their own considerable differences, the German Association for Private and Public Welfare, Innere Mission, and Caritas formed a "defensive cartel." While admitting the mistakes of the past (in particular their refusal to recognize their clients' legal claims to support) and declaring their readiness to engage in a new cooperation with the state at all levels, the private welfare organizations nonetheless insisted upon the largest possible degree of continued independence from state oversight and regulation.

The Social Democrats did not have precise plans for the reorganization of the welfare sector, and their ability to act was in any case severely limited by their loss of support in the 1920 Reichstag elections. Nevertheless, the private welfare organizations continued to distrust the SPD throughout the Weimar Republic. If, before 1918, it was the Wilhelmine state that the private welfare organizations saw as their main enemy, after the Revolution, they "now turned . . . completely against Social Democracy as if every socialist city council executive, federal state government, and national minister was attempting to deal a death blow to 'free' welfare in one general attack."[8] "Social Democracy" and "state welfare" became virtually synonymous terms of abuse in the vocabulary of the religious welfare interests. Writing in 1923, Reinhold Seeberg lamented that the Weimar state had far too little understanding of the religious, spiritual, and moral goals of the Innere Mission. But Seeberg believed that "it will not be much longer before broad sections of our people decide to reject the dark compulsion to dogma, in which Social Democracy, with its materialistic 'enlightenment,' has imprisoned them. Then the hour of the Innere Mission will come, then it will bring the German people near to the heart of what they seek . . . a repositioning of the will is required . . . which protects . . . Christianity as a *Weltanschauung* [worldview] against [the triumph] of reason."[9]

In their attempts to resist what they regarded as the threat of Social Democratic statism, the private welfare organizations could rely upon the sympathies of highly placed Catholic officials within the Weimar state bureaucracy: Dr. Heinrich Brauns, a director of the Volksverein für das katholische Deutschland, who served as the head of the Reichsarbeitsministerium (Reich Labor Ministry; RAM) from 1920 to 1928,[10] and his department heads responsible for matters involving "free welfare activities," Oberregierungsrätin Julia Dünner and Ministerialdirektor Erwin Ritter, both Catholics who consistently supported the *Subsidiaritätsprinzip* (derived from Catholic social teaching), which gave precedence to private over public welfare activities. The religious welfare organizations, with their nationwide structures, were useful allies when the RAM encountered resistance from local governments to its attempts to construct a national welfare system. And the private welfare organizations worked more cheaply in the welfare sector than public agencies, which were bound by Weimar labor law to pay their employees according to a schedule of standard wages (*Tarifvertrag*).[11]

Until the national government issued new guidelines for the organization of public welfare in the 1922 Youth Welfare Law and the 1924 National Welfare Decree, the welfare departments that many German cities were beginning to create posed the greatest challenge to the independence of the private charities. In 1920, for example, a south German welfare journal carried a vehement diatribe against the "communalization" of private welfare organizations, claiming that this would only "demolish the works created by the warm-hearted love of humanity and . . . sacrifice without in the least being able to replace them with public services. . . . In short, altruism, welfare's soul, would be killed by 'bureaucratism.'"[12] But that same year, in a discussion of "the spirit of the welfare department," Adam Stegerwald, head of the Catholic Trade Union organization and director of the newly created Prussian Ministry of Welfare, conceded that it was time to reconsider the relationship between the private and the public welfare sectors.[13] Stegerwald acknowledged that a "people's welfare," conscious of its goals and focused on the special needs of the present time, "was a necessary precondition for an orderly, planned rebuilding and recovery of the life of the German people." Much had been done during the war; now it was time to combine all of the state, municipal, and private welfare activities so as to avoid the fragmentation of their efforts. The institutional sites where this vital work would be performed were the welfare departments, which were to be created in every administrative district; they would become the focus for "every social and charitable effort in the individual administrative area. . . . These welfare offices would become the central points of the internal reconstruction of the German people."

Stegerwald warned, however, that "nothing will be achieved and much will be damaged if we content ourselves with believing that the basic questions concerning welfare offices have been . . . solved because a large network of new administrative agencies has been spread across the country." More important than the administrative regulations that governed the new institutions were the capacities, the dispositions, and the desire to help of the leading officials of these new offices. And what applied to the leading officials was even more important when it came to the female social workers: "They . . . come most often, most intimately in contact with the people. In their house visits and their office hours, the female social workers should demonstrate a living empathy for the fate of the individual. . . . Here, emotional tact, basic experience of life are indispensable."

The new welfare offices would act as central clearinghouses that made sure that "every single case was referred directly to the responsible welfare association and everyone who sought advice was helped to find the most direct path to the relevant agency." The welfare departments must coordinate all public and private efforts to improve the physical and the moral condition of children and youth. Working closely with the "popular associations and local welfare corporations," the public welfare departments should attempt to reach those groups of the population who were in need of a doctor's advice and preventive health measures, making them aware of the available means of assistance through posters and flyers, the daily press and film, lectures and courses for mothers. Yet while the new welfare departments would be responsible for this essential work of centralization, or, as Stegerwald preferred to put it, "federalism," the real social work would continue to be performed by the private welfare associations. For this reason, "the spirit that informs the work of the welfare offices must . . . be compatible with the methods of private charity. The social and charitable organizations are well known and well loved by the people. By contrast, public authorities enjoy no particularly laudable popularity. Private welfare must thus be valued as a bridge between state welfare and the people."[14]

At a meeting in January 1920 in Berlin, representatives of all the private welfare interests warned that the new republican state could not afford to do without the human capital invested in private charitable activity. The love of one human for another would always be superior to bureaucratic practices in its ability to discover need "with open eyes and a warm heart" and in its healing powers. The private welfare organizations were prepared to learn from the criticisms that had been leveled against them, even where these were not fully justified. They would make every effort to adjust to and take account of the changed economic and political circumstances as well as the "new scientific knowledge" in the field of welfare. More than they had in the past, they would attempt to encourage members of all social strata, but especially of the organized working class, to join in the work of private welfare.[15]

A Catholic writer, Dr. Alexander Göbel, insisted in 1923 that municipalization must mean a reciprocal relationship between the local state and the private charities. Acting as the focal point for all welfare activities in a locality, the new welfare office should be able to achieve greater rationality and efficiency. But it was important to retain a division of labor between the public and private agencies because each functioned in different ways. Public agencies were bureaucratic, hence more suited to the types of welfare and the kinds of cases that did not require "education" (*Erziehung*). The private charities, by contrast, were more "mobile," dynamic, and better suited for types of welfare work where personal contact and educational influence played a much larger role.[16] Another Catholic commentator asked his readers not to forget the vital spiritual and religious aspects of welfare that the state would never be able to address: "The personal element, which is missing from the impersonal effect of the bureaucrat, [often] stands in the foreground . . . above all because it is regularly a matter of providing spiritual and religious-moral forms of help."[17]

The 1924 National Welfare Decree laid out the general framework (*Rahmengesetz*) of the new national welfare system. The individual federal states were to fill in the specific details, although the national government would specify certain general guidelines (*Reichsgrundsätze*). Conflict erupted over section 5, which stipulated that "welfare unions" (*Fürsorgeverbände*) be formed to act as links between state welfare and private organizations. The private welfare organizations—led by Caritas—claimed the dominant voice in these new welfare unions. No consensus could be achieved, and regional authorities were left to put together working arrangements between the private and the public sector as best they could.[18] The differences between federal states could be considerable; Saxony was, for example, the first German federal state to assume unified responsibility for youth and general welfare, and it obliged the local welfare unions to provide services that were not included in the 1922 Youth Welfare Law. In Prussia, on the other hand, youth welfare and general welfare were not united, and the local welfare unions were not obliged to provide more than the nationally prescribed minimum of services.[19]

The private welfare organizations had successfully resisted the Social Democrats' demands for a state monopoly of welfare functions. Public welfare departments were prevented from engaging in welfare programs or constructing facilities where private ones already existed. Yet these private activities and institutions were heavily supported by taxpayers' money. Private welfare organizations continued to play an extensive role in the administration of youth welfare. The great majority of social workers were trained in schools run by private welfare organizations (which also received public funds), and the private welfare organizations supplied many of the volunteer workers who conducted the daily business of municipal welfare systems in the neighborhoods.

Despite the differences in their worldviews and politics, the private welfare organizations were able to form a single umbrella organization in 1924—the Deutsche Liga der freien Wohlfahrtspflege—to represent their interests in future negotiations with the state. The newly founded Social Democratic organization, the Arbeiterwohlfahrt (Workers' Welfare), was excluded from membership, as was the German Association for Private and Public Welfare, on the grounds that it was concerned more with theoretical problem solving than with practical welfare work and that its worldview was too secular. The national welfare associations that were members of the new Deutsche Liga were able to establish a monopoly position in the representation of welfare interests and the formulation of policy. Unorganized welfare interests had no voice. The *Subsidiaritätssystem* meant in practice the formalistic allocation of responsibilities within the context of a neocorporatization of the political system after the war. In the years between 1924 and 1930, the private welfare organizations experienced "an unusual upswing. . . . These were years of high new investment and the consolidation of existing fields of work and institutions," with the help of public funds, their own bank, and also foreign loans. But the "free" welfare organizations also underwent a continuing process of "trustification" (*Vertrustung*) and "bureaucratization" that seemed to make them less flexible in responding to new problems and in developing new areas of social work, thus reducing the advantages they could claim over the supposedly less innovative state welfare bureaucracy.[20]

Social Democrats and Welfare

In the Wilhelmine Empire, most Social Democrats viewed the German state as an instrument for domination by the ruling classes and for the maintenance of capitalism. But even before the end of the nineteenth century, some socialists were prepared to concede that the state need not serve the ruling class alone. As political life in Europe became more democratized, as workers were enfranchised and as their numbers and organized strength grew, it seemed possible that the state might be transformed through the electoral process into a means of popular emancipation. This did not mean that the laws of capitalist social and economic development could be suspended altogether by the political power of working-class voters, even in a republic based on universal suffrage. But the working class or, more broadly, the "people" (in Edward Bernstein's revisionist formulation of the problem) could use the state to begin constructing elements of socialism within the existing capitalist economy. Democratization of the German state therefore constituted an important step in the transition to socialism because it enabled the working class to influence economic and social developments directly.[21]

It was with these understandings of the possibilities, as well as the limits, of parliamentary democracy that Social Democrats participated in the construction of the Weimar Republic. Historians have tended to focus on either the inability of the SPD to carry through a "true" socialist revolution in 1918/19 or their failure to nurture the popular democratic impulses exhibited in the revolutionary Rätebewegung (council movement).[22] However, these assessments of failure ignore the real sense of progress and possibility that pervaded Social Democratic political rhetoric in the early years of Weimar. To the Independent Socialists and the Communists, the Weimar Republic may have been a betrayal of the revolutionary German working class by its opportunist majority Social Democratic party leaders. But to Social Democrats themselves, Weimar represented a new political opportunity.[23] The republic provided the political space in which the organized working class might begin to lay the foundations of a future socialist political economy. Weimar Social Democrats regarded the expanded responsibility and activity of the state in such areas as industrial relations, welfare, and housing as among the most important achievements of the Weimar period. In 1921, a German Social Democrat proclaimed that "we are witnessing the gradual coming into being of the welfare state, of the 'social state.'"[24]

The poor-law system and the practice of bourgeois philanthropy under the Wilhelmine Empire had filled Social Democrats with anger and disdain. Wilhelmine charity and the poor law stigmatized the recipients and deprived them not only of their dignity but of some of their political and civil rights as well.[25] The SPD did not develop a coherent alternative welfare program, but Social Democrats did insist that state welfare must replace private charity because only a public welfare system "could gain an overview of the entire population and register everyone who is in need of care."[26] Private welfare activities were, by contrast, far too fragmented. Moreover, Social Democrats wanted the provision of public welfare to be made more democratic and less discriminatory; benefits should be received by all German citizens as a right, not tainted by the stigma associated with the poor law.[27]

Hedwig Wachenheim, a leading Social Democratic welfare expert, was willing to concede that under the political conditions prevailing before World War I, especially in municipal government where the franchise was normally quite restrictive, the private welfare organizations had rendered a pioneering service. Yet even before the war, in the larger cities, where the organized working class had begun to exert influence, the initiative had passed to the public sector. This trend could only continue in postwar republican Germany where the political disabilities hindering working-class political participation had been removed. Wachenheim felt that the methods employed by the private welfare organizations were not equal to the challenges presented by Germany's postwar social problems: "Free welfare lacks the uniformity that guarantees a comprehensive campaign against need, working systematically with the most modern methods to achieve the best possible effects with the most modest of means."[28] But even more important for Wachenheim was the fact that the Christian welfare organizations simply did not conform to the democratic spirit of the Weimar Republic. The religious organizations had yet to recognize or to accept that, as another commentator put it, "a democratic people's state has emerged from war and revolution."[29] The Christian welfare organizations continued to act as if they, the givers of assistance, were the only subjects and those who received help were mere objects. And all Christian welfare activities were motivated by the desire to "missionize" among the poor and the needy, to win converts to the faith, to exert religious influence. For socialists, on the other hand, the welfare client was "the [active] subject as well as the object of welfare."[30]

Marxism had taught German Social Democrats that poverty and other social problems were merely symptoms of much deeper contradictions in capitalist society that would disappear only when capitalism was overthrown. Even the most reformist Social Democrats did not believe that welfare alone could solve the "social problem." Indeed, they insisted that it was far more a "bourgeois" than a Social Democratic illusion

> to exhibit ideals, for whose . . . achievement every single precondition is lacking in a capitalistically organized society. . . . [We] must continually encourage recognition and understanding of the fact that every effort [of the welfare system], even if it has some success in individual cases, will be completely wasted . . . if everything simply remains the same in the overall condition of the proletariat. . . . The significance of welfare as such is much more modest in our eyes than in the opinions of our fellow bourgeois social workers, who want to heal the wounds of this society with welfare alone.[31]

But Social Democrats saw that in a Germany whose population had suffered long years of war, mass hunger, and hyperinflation, welfare would necessarily assume a much larger economic and social function and hence play a more significant political role than it had before 1914. Social Democrats could not sit on the welfare sidelines until socialism arrived, especially when the religious welfare organizations continued to exert such an important influence over welfare clients. In 1919, the socialist labor movement formed its own voluntary association, the Arbeiterwohlfahrt. This new socialist organization was not to imitate or to compete with the existing private welfare organizations but rather to lobby persistently for the expansion of state welfare and to recruit working-class men and women to serve in this important branch of public administration.[32]

The SPD's immediate goal was actively to contest the hegemony of bourgeois welfare interests and ideology by constructing a visible socialist presence in local welfare systems. Even where local political circumstances made it impossible for Social Democrats to play a prominent role, the party still attempted to act as the "tribune of the people," a critical voice speaking for welfare clients. Social Democrats could attempt to influence the administration of local welfare systems through voluntary work in the committees of the welfare office, by supplying social-work volunteers, and by providing professional social administrators and social workers. By 1930, some 60 percent of all local Arbeiterwohlfahrt committees were, indeed, represented in local welfare systems. But, the Caritasverband and the Innere Mission continued to exercise considerably greater influence. It was particularly difficult to introduce Social Democrats into the ranks of the paid, professional social-work staff. In Prussia, for example, only about 600 of the 3,606 female and 204 male social-workers in the field were connected to the SPD by 1929.[33] Women were restricted primarily to social work in families and the neighborhoods. Very few socialist men and even fewer socialist women managed to gain higher-level administrative positions. The Arbeiterwohlfahrt's practical ability to influence the development of local welfare systems had thus fallen well short of original expectations.[34]

The Communist Critique

Social Democrats expected their contribution to the welfare state to be rewarded with working-class votes. But the Weimar welfare system soon become a bitterly contested terrain where Social Democrats and Communists battled one another for the support of the German working class. In Communist eyes, the Social Democrats had betrayed the German working class during the Revolution by settling for a merely bourgeois republic whose trappings of formal democracy did not hide the capitalist interests it served. The Social Democrats' loyal support of this capitalist state drew unrelenting criticism from German Communists. During the Depression, this critique was distilled into a single epithet: "social fascism." Nowhere were the Social Democrats more vulnerable to this political assault than on the terrain of the welfare state, for as Eve Rosenhaft observes, "Social Democracy was the pillar of the Weimar system, its representatives in important regions like Prussia most visible to the working class as administrators and dispensers of state services (or, as they all too often appeared, withholders of services and dispensers of police justice)."[35] The communists offered an alternative public sphere for the circulation of discourses critical of Social Democratic welfare policies and practices. Communist city council members intervened in debates on the local welfare budget, criticizing what they deemed to be abuses (often, they described in detail the treatment received by individual welfare clients). Communists regularly proposed increases in welfare benefits that both their socialist and nonsocialist counterparts found totally unrealistic.[36] Communists used city council debates to present unfavorable comparisons between the Weimar welfare system and the achievements of Soviet Russia.[37] The Communist Party took politics from the city council chamber to the streets in the form of hunger marches and demonstrations of the unemployed. But it also tried to bring voices from the street into parliamentary debates. In 1926, for example, in the middle of a discussion of Düsseldorf's welfare budget, a Communist city council member pointed to the presence in the visitors' gallery of delegates from the local committee of the unemployed and suggested that they be allowed to give a report of their grievances and demands.[38]

Communists ridiculed "the Social Democratic leaders [who] use every key in the scale to praise the social institutions created after the Revolution." The Hamburg Communist paper *Volkszeitung* insisted that

> today, it is just the same as it was before the Revolution, even though Social Democrats sit in "all the important government bodies"; when it comes to the poorest of the poor, no money is to be made available. . . . The coalition senate, which unites with the middle classes against the workers, must carry through the interests of the *Bürgertum* (its employer [*Auftraggeber*]), against the interests of the working class. But it can continue to do this only so long as the Hamburg workers continue silently to accept this "coalition mess" [*Koalitionsschweinerei*] and do not mobilize all their forces to fight for a Workers' Senate.[39]

Irritated by these charges, the Social Democrats insisted that "in Russia, despite the Communist monopoly of power, social institutions are utterly inadequate. In Germany, social institutions are constantly being expanded, improved, and refined by the permanent, responsible cooperation of the representatives of the working class."[40]

The Communists insisted, however, that German workers had little to show for the constitutional promises to "maintain, protect, and promote the purity, health, and social position of the family as a task of the state and the municipalities." The "state lets proletarian families live in holes-in-the-wall, condemns proletarian children to a life of hunger, sends proletarian women to jail if they try to ward off starvation with an abortion."[41] The Communist Party also mocked Social Democratic pronouncements about the "protection of motherhood." Communists insisted that a massive housing crisis, widespread unemployment, and the legal restriction of birth control and abortion made it impossible for the majority of working-class women to achieve the modernization and rationalization of family life that Social Democrats desired. At a conference of Communist women in 1928, a speaker urged that municipal elections be used to "expose the hypocrisy of the bourgeois parties, especially the Catholic Center and the SPD, who certainly know how to talk about their compassion for women but who do absolutely nothing to combat housing problems and hunger wages, the shameful paragraph 218 [against abortion], and legal discrimination against women. We have to focus women's attention very specifically upon the social policies of the cities and the towns."[42]

Welfare and the Local State

Although the national state created the legal framework for the public welfare system in the Weimar Republic, local governments assumed the major responsibility for welfare activities. In many parts of Germany, urban governments in the Wilhelmine period had been elected on the basis of restrictive, often quite discriminatory suffrage systems that usually prevented Social Democrats from becoming a significant presence in town councils. The democratization of local government after 1918 allowed Social Democrats, Communists, and German women to penetrate this once exclusively middle-class, male, liberal preserve. In all German cities and regions where the Social Democrats had a significant political presence after 1919, they pressured for the expansion of municipal welfare and housing responsibilities. The construction of public welfare offices was a vital first step in the postwar transformation of municipal welfare practices. Contributing to a debate on welfare reform in the Württemberg Landtag in 1923, the Social Democratic deputy Heymann observed "no one wants to restrict the activities of the private welfare agencies; but . . . welfare must be undertaken by 'public-legal' institutions, and those are the state and the municipality."[43] Social Democrats also insisted on the right of the labor movement to participate fully in the administration of the new welfare agencies. Hedwig Wachenheim declared, for example, that

> it is not enough to have a socialist running a youth office; this person must also have under him people who are in close, daily contact with working-class youths and their parents, in other words, people who are "class comrades." . . . All of [the welfare system's] work serves the welfare of the working masses, its material well-being, but also its spiritual march forward, the raising up of its consciousness and self-confidence and its will to social action.[44]

Social Democratic welfare experts argued that the achievements gained by the painstaking and persistent daily "detail work" (*Kleinarbeit*) of Social Democratic city council members, welfare officers, social workers, and volunteers in local welfare systems would pay off at the polls. But the fundamental political and economic contradictions of the local state in the Weimar Republic put the SPD in an unenviable political position.[45] Weimar local governments were squeezed between their extensive responsibilities for the implementation of nationally decreed welfare policies and their dwindling capacity to finance these social programs. The SPD became the target of simultaneous attacks from both the left and the right. While the Communists viciously ridiculed Social Democratic claims that "the social institutions of the Republic are already a step toward socialism," the bourgeois parties savaged the Social Democrats for reckless welfare spending.[46]

The strength of the Social Democrats in local government and their ability, consequently, to influence the development of local welfare systems varied considerably. In 1929, the SPD newspaper in Stuttgart reported that "welfare activities are still exercised to a very considerable extent by . . . the charitable-religious associations, which receive large amounts of financial support from the city."[47] In Berlin, "the private welfare organizations, supported by all the bourgeois parties . . . are waging an energetic battle . . . for . . . the leadership of welfare activities, and they have managed to gain a very strong influence in the youth and other welfare offices."[48] In Düsseldorf, municipal authorities made public their intention to centralize the city's welfare activities in a single welfare office in July 1919. Yet it took two years until this project was completed. In 1923, Social Democrats were still waiting for the city to achieve "a tighter coordination in a single bureau of all existing branches of welfare."[49] As late as 1925, a local Social Democratic leader had to warn against delegating public welfare tasks to private welfare agencies.[50]

In the SPD "fortress" of Hamburg, however, Social Democrats were able to play a major role in the development and administration of local welfare services. The Hamburg parliament passed a law for the creation of a welfare office (Gesetz über das Wohlfahrtsamt) in May 1920 that went into effect in November 1921.[51] From 1919 to 1933, a Social Democratic senator was responsible for the Welfare Department (Paul Hoffmann until 1925, Paul Neumann from 1925 to 1933), and for some or all of the Weimar years Social Democrats also headed the Labor Office, the Youth Office, and the Public Health Office.[52] Social Democrats were active at all levels of the welfare bureaucracy. There were socialists among the professional social workers, women such as Hanna Stolten, founder of a group for SPD welfare professionals.[53] And the great majority of the volunteers who actually administered the welfare system at its lowest levels in the neighborhoods were drawn heavily from the Social Democratic working class. By 1928, no fewer than 1,463 of the 2,221 volunteer welfare workers (*ehrenamtliche Pfleger*) in Hamburg were members of the Arbeiterwohlfahrt.[54]

In the early 1920s, the private charities were reluctant to cooperate with the new Hamburg welfare office. A meeting of the advisory board to district welfare office IV learned in May 1922 that "the private welfare associations fear that the public welfare office wants to exercise some sort of supervision of their activities, even though this is not true."[55] In May 1923, a meeting of district welfare office directors discussed the creation of a central card file of welfare recipients to avoid duplication of support, but they acknowledged that such an arrangement might not work because "private welfare associations anxiously refuse to allow any outsider to look at their files."[56] In June 1923, the deputy director of welfare district office I reported that "the private welfare agencies are certainly not inclined to tell the welfare office who they are helping, especially as they lack adequate means and thus regard the help they give as merely supplemental."[57] After the promulgation of the National Welfare Decree in 1924, the Red Cross, the Inner Mission (Innere Mission), the Patriotic Women's Aid Association (Vaterländische Frauen Hilfsverein), Caritas, and the German-Jewish Community (Deutsch-Israelitische Gemeinde) jointly requested that the Hamburg Welfare Department set up a committee to discuss cooperation between private and public welfare agencies.[58] This led to the formation in 1925 of a free union of private and public welfare agencies in Hamburg with the goals of "promoting profitable cooperation . . . and agreement on the division of labor and delimitation of areas of competence." The Welfare Department was now able to report that "the public agencies work together, to the greatest possible extent, with the free welfare organizations to tackle welfare tasks."[59] Advisory boards had proved indispensable "as a connection between the public and the private welfare agencies in each welfare district."[60]

Yet cooperation between private and public welfare agencies was frequently accompanied by conflict between socialist and religious welfare organizations. Within the institutions of the new public welfare system, the Caritas and the Innere Mission struggled with the Social Democratic Arbeiterwohlfahrt for ideological influence over welfare clients. Catholics complained that "the socialist Workers' Welfare has strongly increased its activities and its claims, especially in the area of youth welfare, and it seeks ever more intently to push back religious youth work." Although the Youth Welfare Law prescribed cooperation between public and private youth welfare activities, "this is often not achieved . . . especially at the local level." The priorities to be served in the selection of the members of the directing committee of the Youth Office remained unclear; often, this committee was not allowed the practical influence that the law itself prescribed, and sometimes private youth welfare organizations were given little real responsibility, being degraded instead to the status of "messenger boys." Sometimes, too, the public youth welfare system simply appropriated for itself activities that the *freie Jugendhilfe* (private assistance to youth) had engaged in quite successfully up until that time.[61]

In heavily Catholic areas, however, Social Democrats found that they were the ones denied any real influence over the new welfare institutions. In 1924, for example, Social Democrats presented a motion in the Düsseldorf city council "that would check the influence of the Center party, and thus of the religious organizations, in the Youth Office."[62] Conflicts between Social Democrats and Catholics were especially intense in the Rhineland, where, according to Hedwig Wachenheim, active use was made of paragraph 11 of the Youth Welfare Law, which allowed youth welfare departments to delegate the tasks legally prescribed for them to private associations. In addition, the provision that the voluntary youth-welfare worker assigned to a case should have the same religion as the young client was being very narrowly interpreted. Even if both parents were committed Social Democrats, the child might still be entrusted not to the Arbeiterwohlfahrt but to a Catholic or Protestant welfare organization, simply because the family had never taken the difficult but necessary legal steps required to leave the church. Wachenheim interpreted what was happening in the Rhineland as an attempt not only to exclude the Arbeiterwohlfahrt but also to "tear the unity of the youth welfare system apart . . . along religious and ideological lines."[63]

Catholics placed a different interpretation upon paragraph 5 of the National Welfare Decree and paragraphs 6, 9, and 11 of the Youth Welfare Law, claiming that these provisions guaranteed them the right to be involved in "educational measures" prescribed for Catholic children. Attempts by the Arbeiterwohlfahrt to gain greater influence in local youth welfare departments appeared to Catholics as an "unjustified intrusion . . . into a religious, specifically, a Catholic, area of work." Catholics and Protestants rejected the Arbeiterwohlfahrt's claim to be "an organization with a worldview" when it demanded parity with the other forms of "free welfare" in all those areas "where the law takes note of religion or worldview." The socialist worldview seemed to consist largely of negative attributes, such as anticlericalism and materialism. And religious critics claimed that within the Social Democratic camp there were many, especially among the SPD voters and trade union members, who continued to attend church and pay their church taxes. Caritas argued that "only the clear and distinct renunciation of church membership or declaration of membership in a socialist *Weltaunschauungsgemeinschaft* [community of worldview] . . . gives the Arbeiterwohlfahrt any claim to responsibility for a case." Indeed, the Caritasverband maintained that "on the basis of the present law, the Arbeiterwohlfahrt can raise no claim to clients beyond those who have left the church and have openly declared themselves ideological socialists." The Caritas conference in Dortmund insisted that "attending a secular school, having parents who are party members, etc. are not grounds for making children clients of [voluntary workers from] the Arbeiterwohl-fahrt. . . . We demand that the responsible ministries instruct the courts and the youth offices that neither judges . . . nor social workers may ask the child or their parents which organization they wish to be responsible for the case." The Werl conference urged local Caritas organizations to stick to this position, even if that meant being deprived of funds that they would normally have received from the municipality.[64]

"Bureaucracy" versus "Welfare"

In the course of the 1920s, the religious welfare organizations began to realize that the strategy they had adopted after the Revolution was too costly. Working with and within the new state welfare system appeared to have trapped the private welfare organizations in a mechanistic and bureaucratic straitjacket that made it more and more difficult for them to fulfill their religious and ethical missions. In 1922, a Caritas spokesman had warned that "to be watched over, led, and patronized by public agencies completely contradicts the essence of free welfare. If the Caritas should become merely the instrument of a public agency set above it . . . then it would lose all initiative . . . and the best people would turn away from it; this would, in a word, be the death of Caritas."[65] After ten years of trying to work with the new public welfare system, religious welfare organizations feared that this dire prophecy had come true. In 1932, a commentator complained:

> Our Caritas work has been virtually forced to adopt the methods of the public sector in our joint work with the public welfare system, and even in the organization of our chari-table activity we have been compelled to imitate the model of a bureaucratic agency. . . . [The result has been] that we have to a certain extent neglected our most essential tasks and have lost much of our real connection with the *Volk*. We are now seen only as an extension of public welfare, and the person in need of help sees us as an alienated institution rather than as a part of the "community" in which we are all members, help-ers as much as those in need of help.[66]

Within Innere Mission circles, too, there was great concern that working closely to-gether with the public welfare system endangered the religious character of the Innere Mission's work, hence its deepest motives and highest goals.

The religious welfare interests repeatedly warned against the dangers of "overex-tending the idea of the state . . . which sees the state as responsible for all welfare."[67] In 1926, for example, the Caritastag in Trier complained that "the relatively inten-sive expansion of public youth care signifies a retreat of religious goals in this im-portant area."[68] A meeting of the Caritas in Württemberg held between 18 and 20 October 1926 gave recognition to the achievements of the public welfare offices "that are indispensable in the present time of mass need" but took a solid stand against "all attempts to create [state] monopolies in the area of welfare."[69] Another Württemberg commentator complained in 1927 that there was simply "too much" public welfare in Germany; there was a tendency "to organize too much, to regulate things legally too much, to force everything into articles of law, paragraphs, and basic rules, even when it comes to spiritual matters and even when developments are not yet ripe for a legal solution."[70] Dr. Kurt Erichson agreed that "today the state is on the road to an overorganization . . . in the face of which the client stands helpless, crushed by advice, house visits, investigation, etc."[71] A Catholic critic complained that "from the . . . ethical standpoint of the social worker, one can speak of a lamentable mechanization whose consequences completely contradict the intentions of those who wish to serve human beings. . . . Over and over again, we must . . . shield ourselves from the mechanization of our work."[72] In 1929, the director of the Hamburg Welfare Department admitted that the private welfare organizations had "to a large extent come to approximate the shape of public welfare in their organization and administration and in their use of professional social workers."[73]

It was impossible simply to reverse the growth of the state welfare system that had taken place since the war because "the contemporary crisis and the tasks confronting social welfare require as seamless as possible a network of welfare offices and activities. Only the state can create this network on the basis of legal regulation and with the support of public funds. . . . Welfare has become a public task and will remain so."[74] Yet the religious welfare organizations wanted more respect to be paid to the actual spirit of the National Welfare Decree, "which had no intention of making free welfare a subdepartment of the public welfare system but rather saw both as coordinate sources of strength."[75] The tasks delegated to the private organizations should not be too narrowly circumscribed by officially imposed restrictions and regulations; the individual organizations should be allowed to use their own initiative in doing their welfare work. The practice of welfare and, indeed, the good of the entire population could be served only by allowing private organizations to retain as much as possible of their own distinctive character (*Eigenart*). This did not mean that piety or the care of souls could simply replace the scientific and technical knowledge that had come to define modern welfare practices. Welfare work required professional training. But as the public welfare agencies came to realize that the problems they dealt with were not only material but also spiritual, they would begin to value the unique work of the private/confessional organizations: "There are a whole series of cases of need in which, in addition to material support, spiritual help is also required. . . . With the whole human being, care of the soul is as important as welfare."[76] In 1929, D. Erfurth observed that whereas Protestants saw that it was necessary to combine scientific knowledge and methods with "religious and moral" measures, "until recently, the state, science, and socialism had been completely blind to this perspective." Erfurth concluded that "the proper orientation of the needy person to God is, in the eyes of Protestant welfare, the beginning of self-sufficiency. . . . This way of thinking is naturally higher and more comprehensive than the [more limited material] goals of state welfare."[77]

In 1929, Oskar Martini, president of the Hamburg Welfare Department, admitted that it was not unreasonable to ask "whether it is today at all still possible for everything . . . that is symbolized by the concept of the 'heart' . . . to achieve recognition . . . as a force that contributes to the structure and the effects of welfare work in public agencies." But Martini refused to believe that "what one calls the 'value of the heart' . . . is to be found, exclusively or primarily, in the activities of private welfare." Certainly, the war and the inflation had hastened the pace of professionalization:

"Voluntary welfare work was neither strong nor capable enough to deal with the enormous new mass indigence." The demand for trained personnel increased from year to year, and the "social schools," originally intended solely for women, had begun to develop an extensive curriculum for all branches of social work. Yet Martini felt that the schools provided more than merely technical training; they had, in fact, become "lively nurseries of social conscience and understanding," imbuing their graduates with a strong idealism that they then carried into their practical work. In other words, the social schools "not only sharpened the minds and the knowledge of young people but also guided their hearts. . . . Thus, in the proper professional official we find the 'heart' and 'reason' combined."

Even the personnel trained in a more strictly administrative tradition were beginning to gain greater insight into the necessity of a "fundamental social training." At the same time, social workers were beginning to recognize the significance of clear and orderly administrative work: "We cannot properly understand social work if we allot the function of the heart only to the female social worker while claiming reason only for the [male] administrative official. Both must do their difficult job with the same spirit." Finally, Martini drew attention to the continuing, vital significance in the public welfare system of the volunteers, who "bring . . . their living contacts with the life of the people, their understanding for the views of different social strata, a variety of life experiences and perspectives . . . that the professional finds harder to achieve." The human warmth provided by the volunteer workers, "whose work is not a function of their public office but of the impetus provided by their worldview and their purely human sense of responsibility," was needed especially during periods of "mass need, which today make . . . a deep, individualized practice of welfare so difficult."[78]

CHAPTER TWO

The Welfare System in the Neighborhoods

Professionals and Volunteers

An Example: Hamburg's Welfare System

Martini had attempted to demonstrate that the social spirit, which the private welfare interests claimed as their ethical and religious mission could be reconciled with bureaucratic state welfare practices. But could the record of his own welfare administration in Hamburg justify this claim? The legal framework for Weimar Hamburg's welfare system was the law passed in May 1920 by the Bürgerschaft that united in a single welfare department the former "poor-law system, the agency supervising charitable foundations, workhouses, and homes for the aged, the welfare section of the Labor Office, and the welfare agency for war wounded and the survivors of men killed in the war."[1] The National Welfare Decree of 13 February 1924 created a single German system of welfare law, and the law that applied this decree to Hamburg, the Ausführungsverordnung of 28 March 1924, created four district welfare unions within the boundaries of the city-state.[2] In 1930, a Geschäftsordnung took account of the new structures of Hamburg's welfare system that had developed since 1924 "as well as the new national legal regulations and the reforms of Hamburg's local administration." Because Hamburg was a federal state as well as a city, the Hamburg welfare system "consisted of a state welfare union as well as several district welfare unions."[3]

By 1928, the Hamburg Welfare Department employed some 180 welfare officials with civil service status and 750 nontenured employees (*Angestellte*). Some 2,221 people served as volunteers, of whom 1,786 were men and 435 women.[4] Each of the eleven welfare districts was divided up into roughly twenty subdistricts, each with the "necessary number" of professional and volunteer welfare officers (usually between twenty and twenty-five per subdistrict). By 1926, there were some 214 subdistricts.[5] Subdistrict meetings (*Bezirksversammlungen*) "that decided on the support to be given to the needy" were held every fourteen days.[6] Attached to every welfare district office was "an advisory board, among whose tasks were . . . helping to promote a fruitful cooperation between local welfare agencies and the private welfare associations."

People seeking help applied to the welfare district office responsible for the area in which they lived. Their application would then either be investigated by the professional welfare officer (Pfleger) or would be handed over to a volunteer welfare worker. To qualify for public relief, an applicant had, in general terms, to be unable "to provide the necessary means of support for himself and his dependents." What was referred to as "expanded care" (*erweiterte Fürsorge*) could only be granted "when the character of the client and the nature of his circumstances appeared to make it possible to retain or restore his economic independence or to prevent permanent indigence or a significant decline in social position." Support could be granted on a one-time or long-term basis: "The table of standard rates [*Richtsätze*] issued by the Welfare Department is the basis for granting ongoing assistance. These are neither minimums nor maximums but should serve as general guidelines for the determination of the necessary amount of support."[7] In 1928, the standard rates in Hamburg were set at "38.60 marks per month for a single person, 60 marks for a married couple, 12.90 marks for each child in a family."[8] That same year, a Hamburg dockworker might expect to earn between 197.42 marks (February) and 243.08 marks (November) per month.[9] The Hamburg welfare system was supporting in "open relief" some 31,490 clients and their dependents in 1928: 19,900 "general" welfare clients; 7,520 "social pensioners" (*Sozialrentner*); and 3,680 "small capital pensioners" (*Kleinrentner*). There were, in addition, some 7,295 household heads and their dependents "who had such small incomes that the welfare office had occasionally to step in and award a one-time grant of support." Whereas fewer than 2 in every 100 inhabitants of Hamburg had received either long-term or one-time relief in 1912, this number had risen to 3 by 1928. In addition to their basic cash relief, most welfare clients also received some kind of supplement for rent, clothing, gas bills, as well as support in kind, such as subsidized foodstuffs (two-thirds of the price on the open market) and health care. The Hamburg Welfare Department had its own company to supply clothes to welfare clients, and shoe repairs were done by a work-creation project of the Hamburg Labor Office, organized as a limited liability company in April 1924. In the winter months, welfare clients also received "a supplementary fuel benefit in the form of coupons for two or more hundred weight of coal briquettes each month."[10] Certain privileged categories of welfare clients—those legally recognized as small capital pensioners, social pensioners, and war victims—were given the benefit of the so-called elevated welfare, which prescribed not only higher levels of support (usually at least 25% more than the normal, so-called general welfare) but also different standards of treatment.[11] Those eligible for the elevated welfare were, for example, not subjected to the same sorts of means test as the general welfare clients.

Because of the damage done by the war and the postwar years, public health became one of the Hamburg Welfare Department's most important fields of activity. There were special health programs for children and young people, but the Welfare Department also supplied medical assistance for the needy and paid for medicine, hospital stays, and rest cures. The Welfare Department set up a day camp near the city in Moorwärder, and the Arbeiterwohlfahrt ran another one in Kohlbrand, to which some 16,063 children had been sent the previous year. The Welfare Department also had health-cure camps in Wyck auf Fohr and in Lüneberg; several others were in private hands. Maternity allowances were granted to the needy "as a health care measure," and the Welfare Department distributed over 117,000 liters of milk to children, pregnant women, nursing mothers, and sick people in 1928. Some 70,000 lunches and 300,000 breakfasts were given to schoolchildren as well as 76,000 other meals to other persons in need. The Hamburg Welfare Department kept about 3,500 clients in so-called closed care; about 500 were in private institutions and 3,000 in the main public facility (Versorgungsheim) and its various branches. Some young homeless people were kept in closed care, as were young "psychopaths," girls considered to be in danger of becoming prostitutes, and adult chronic alcoholics. But the majority of the inmates were old people who were no longer able to look after themselves.[12]

The Hamburg Welfare Department prided itself on being one of the more advanced in Germany, providing social services that went beyond the minimum prescribed by national welfare regulations.[13] The Hansestadt developed some specialized areas of welfare, such as the treatment of chronic alcoholism, which was provided in cooperation with the Hamburg Association for the Promotion of Abstinence. Hamburg had "the first and only publicly supported treatment facility for alcoholics in Germany" and in 1925, the Welfare Department was also developing plans for the treatment of "persons addicted to morphine, cocaine, and other dangerous drugs."[14]

The neighborhoods that the eleven district welfare offices served displayed quite different economic, social, and political characteristics (see Map 1). In general, the central welfare districts were the most densely populated, although there were certainly considerable variations within some districts. Welfare districts I (Altstadt-Neustadt), II (St. Pauli), and III (Eimsbüttel) had the highest population densities in the city; in excess of 700 inhabitants per hectare (2.471 acres) of built-up land area. But within both districts I and II, there were large areas with considerably lower population densities (under 100 inhabitants per hectare) because both of these districts, along with district XI (Billwärderausschlag, etc.) included most of the Hamburg waterfront and dock areas. Although the high population densities in some parts of the centrally located welfare districts put welfare officials and social workers in close daily contact with welfare clients, the topography of the waterfront area made their jobs more difficult; in 1927, for example, welfare district office XI complained that "it requires a lot of time to make house visits in the harbor and dock district because the canals and inlets, as well as the railway facilities make it necessary to take considerable detours to get where one is going."[15]

The percentages of the general population on welfare varied considerably from one welfare district to the next (see Table 2). Welfare district II (St. Pauli, Steinwärder, Waltershof, Finkenwärder) had the highest ratio of welfare clients to inhabitants in 1926, 1927, and 1928 (in 1929, another inner city district, district I, Altstadt-Neustadt, took the lead) whereas district V (Winterhude, Geestvororte) consistently had the lowest ratio. The political contexts within which district welfare offices had to work varied considerably. In the 1924 elections for the national parliament, the Social Democrats received their three highest vote totals in Billbrook and Moorfleth-Stadt,

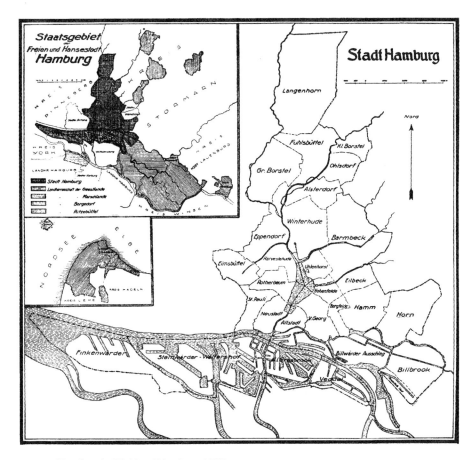

MAP 1. Hamburg's Welfare Districts, 1927

Welfare District   Neighborhood

I	Altstadt, Neustadt
II	St. Pauli with Finkenwärder, Steinwärder, and Waltershof
III	Eimsbüttel
IV	Eppendorf, Rotherbaum, and Harvestehude
V	Winterhude with Gr. Borstel, Fuhlsbüttel, Kl. Borstel, Langenhorn, Ohlsdorf, and Alsterdorf
VI	Barmbeck-Nord
VII	Barmbeck-Süd and Eilbeck
VIII	Hohenfelde and Uhlenhorst
IX	St. Georg (Hammerbrook)
X	Borgfelde, Hamm, and Horn with Billbrook
XI	Billwärderausschlag (Rothenburgsort) with Veddel, Moorfleth-Stadt and Kl. Grasbrook

From *Aus Hamburgs Verwaltung und Wirtschaft* 1 (September 1927), 4 Jg., Nr. 7.

TABLE 2. Hamburg's Welfare Clients by Welfare District, 1926–1929, per 1,000 Population

District	1926	1927	1928	1929
I. Altstadt, Neustadt	60.9	41.7	30.0	42.5
II. St. Pauli, Steinw.-Waltershof, Finkenwärder	64.4	56.1	38.9	40.0
III. Eimsbüttel	44.3	38.9	28.5	30.8
IV. Rotherbaum, Harvestehude, Eppendorf	40.4	37.7	27.5	30.5
V. Winterhude, Geestvororte	36.6	31.2	20.8	23.6
VI. Barmbeck-Nord	42.8	36.4	22.7	24.9
VII. Barmbeck-Süd, Eilbeck	43.7	40.9	28.3	31.5
VIII. Uhlenhorst, Hohenfelde	52.5	43.5	33.5	36.3
IX. St. Georg	48.8	38.4	31.7	37.7
X. Hamm, Horn, Borgfelde, Billbrook	41.3	36.8	26.3	27.8
XI. Billwärder Ausschlag, Veddel, Moorfleth-Stadt, Kleiner Grasbrook	43.2	38.4	24.6	27.6
All Districts		25.8	28.1	31.4

Source: SJFHH, 1926/27, p. 302, 1927/28, p. 312, 1928/29, p. 295, 1929/30, p. 302.

situated in welfare district I (45.5%), Veddel, also in welfare district I (43.84%), and Langenhorn, in welfare district V (43.4%). The Communists received their highest vote in St. Pauli, which belonged to welfare district II (28.9%), although the Social Democrats got 26.8 percent of the vote there. Communists also polled 28.9 percent of the vote in Neustadt (welfare district I) and 36.5 percent in Horn (welfare district X). The vote for the other end of the political spectrum, the conservative-nationalist DNVP (Deutschnationale Volkspartei, or German National People's Party), was highest in Hohenfelde, welfare district VIII (35.12%), Harvestehude, welfare district IV (31.56%), and Gross Borstel, welfare district V (30.52%).[16] The SPD's coalition partner in Hamburg, the DDP (Deutsche Demokratische Partei, or German People's Party), was strongest in the 1924 elections in Rotherbaum, welfare district IV (21.92%), Harvestehude, welfare district IV (21.71%), and Fuhlsbüttel, welfare district V (20.69%).[17] By 1931, the political complexion of the welfare districts located in the poorest, inner city neighborhoods had become even more contentious, with Nazis as well as Communists and Social Democrats receiving significant votes in local elections in Altstadt (26.3% for the Nazis), Neustadt (16.1%), St. Georg (20.3%), and St. Pauli (22.1%).[18]

The Officials in the Welfare Office

The new Hamburg welfare system was headed by Social Democratic political appointees—Paul Hoffmann from 1921 to 1925, Paul Neumann from 1925 to 1933—but administrative direction lay in the hands of the jurist, Oskar Martini, who retained his office from 1920 to 1945.[19] Most of the original personnel came from existing public and private welfare agencies or other sections of the Hamburg administration and had only administrative training; as Martini put it in 1922, "It was necessary to retain, from the past, some of the valuable elements."[20] Some war veterans and war invalids were also given positions in the Hamburg Welfare Department.[21]

A "Social Spirit" or "Bureaucratism"?

In 1926, an English-language newspaper presented the Hamburg welfare bureaucracy as it undoubtedly most liked to see itself: "President Martini is a broad-minded and generous hearted citizen who does everything in his power to make his officials realize that they are not dispensing charity but serving public welfare by ministering to those in distress who, largely through no fault of their own, have become poor and dependent on outside help."[22] When Paul Neumann came to sum up the transformation of Hamburg's welfare system after the war, he maintained that "not only the name has changed . . . but something more essential, the spirit."[23] Yet some observers doubted that this social spirit had actually penetrated the consciousnesses of the officials who worked in the new welfare offices across Germany. In 1920, E. G. Dresel warned that "the legal specialists . . . easily appear to become indispensable because they are the only ones who understand the enormous mass of legal regulations."[24] But Carl Mennicke acknowledged that it was often difficult for the official sitting in the welfare office to "imaginatively visualize the case, which exists only on paper."[25] For this reason, Dresel proposed that no man or woman should be allowed to rise to a leading position "who has not spent a certain amount of time in the field, in actual contact with real families."[26] Even as university students, the men, in particular, must be exposed to "real practice" by volunteering in one of the many branches of welfare activity, perhaps with the Innere Mission.[27] Mennicke agreed: "It would surely also be ideal . . . if only personnel who had practical training as social workers were employed in the administrative activities of the welfare and youth welfare offices. The danger of 'overbureaucratization' [*Verbürokratisierung*] is perhaps an even greater danger for men than for women, so that the spiritual . . . antidote that comes from rich, practical experience of welfare work is even more desperately necessary."

These recommendations were rarely (if ever) put into practice. Mennicke himself recognized that "fiscal considerations require the best possible utilization of local administrations, so that, for decades to come, the majority of officials working in welfare and youth welfare offices are unlikely to have practical experience."[28] Another welfare expert complained that "nowadays, we have mainly officials trained only in administration, who move from office to office, working today with this, tomorrow with that quite different set of tasks. Yet the welfare official has to deal not with functions but with people."[29] Marie Baum observed in 1927 that "it is a very basic consideration for state and municipal bureaucracies that individual officials . . . should be able to apply themselves to as many different areas of work as possible, to thus always be interchangeable, when conditions require."[30]

Hamburg welfare authorities had to concede that "shortly after the creation of the Welfare Department, complaints were made about 'formalism' and 'bureaucratism.'"[31] In 1923, for example, the Hamburg Communist newspaper charged that

> when the old poor-law system [Allgemeine Armenanstalt] was replaced by the Welfare Department on 1 Sept. 1921, some of those forced to ask for public assistance probably breathed a sigh of relief, hoping that now things would be better for them. Unfortunately, this has remained only a pious wish. Although at first the change in names appeared to be accompanied by a new spirit, this has long since been overwhelmed by the "bureaucratism" that rules in the Welfare Department. . . . The old spirit of the Allgemeine

Armensanstalt has very quickly broken through again, and "Saint Bureaucracy" is also at work.[32]

These complaints were in part symptoms of exploding client numbers and of budget cuts during the period of inflation, which made it difficult to engage in "orderly, individualized case work";[33] in 1922, district welfare office directors reported that "it is no longer possible to speak of proper social work; the cases are dealt with in a purely mechanical fashion." The tone adopted by certain welfare officials only compounded some clients' sense of injury. That same year, *Angestellten* (clerical staff) in the welfare district offices had to be admonished "to make a few more concessions to the pensioners and to show a bit more understanding for their mental condition."[34] The image of the insensitive and imperious welfare official continued to circulate, even after inflation was brought under control. In 1926, for example, Martini cited an article in the Communist *Volkszeitung* "that complained that a welfare applicant who had been unemployed for months was rudely interrogated about his finances." Martini urged that the first interview be conducted in an especially tactful and careful manner: "It was not acceptable simply to pose the formal questions listed on the printed questionnaire in the manner of a police interrogation."[35] Conceding that recent increases in distress had placed an additional strain upon officials in the local welfare offices, an article in the *Volkszeitung* in 1926 nonetheless condemned welfare officials who displayed a lack of "social feeling" and took out their frustrations upon the clients, not to mention "those elements who consciously regard welfare clients as low and inferior human beings."[36] A city council member in Düsseldorf likewise complained in the mid-1920s that at one of the city's welfare offices "the way many officials treat the clients leaves much to be desired. Several officials seem to believe that they are the only ones who should have anything to say and that everyone who has to wait in line for hours on end just to get a few measly pennies should keep their mouths shut. . . . I managed to determine that in the Bändelstrasse [welfare office] old men, aged sixty to seventy, have to stand in line from the early morning hours until noon if they want to have the 'pleasure' of receiving their money."[37]

Male Social Workers: *Berufspfleger* and *Ermittler*

The administrative and functional division in Weimar welfare systems between the external and internal services (*Aussen- und Innendienst*) generally marked a gendered boundary line between female social work in the field and male administration inside the welfare offices. This divide reflected different conceptions of male and female "nature," aptitude for administrative versus social work, and the relative value of each of these different welfare practices. It also signaled real differences in the organizational strength of female social workers and male administrative officials, who were able to bargain with municipal administrations for better wages, job security, and status. Yet the *Aussendienst* was not exclusively female; in Hamburg, two types of male welfare professionals worked in the field as well: the *Berufspfleger* and the *Ermittler*. In 1926, there were thirty-five *Berufspfleger* and forty-eight *Ermittler* in Hamburg. The *Berufspfleger* was to act as a sort of troubleshooter, assuming responsibility for all particularly difficult cases deemed too demanding for either the volunteer workers in the neighborhoods or the female social workers. The *Berufsp-fleger* also investigated all applicants for one-time support, insofar as these were not the responsibility of the female social worker "or involved the simple establishment of certain facts."[38]

The *Berufspfleger*'s reports and recommendations for action on individual cases were supposed to be based on the intimate knowledge of the client and his or her family that could be gained only from house visits. But in May 1926, a report concluded that "the *Berufspfleger* are overloaded with work, and, with the passage of time, this has affected the thoroughness of their investigations. Especially in the cases of long-term assistance, follow-up visits are not being made with the necessary frequency."[39] In May 1927, a meeting of welfare district office directors was told that "the reports of the *Berufspfleger* often do not show whether they are based on house visits or simply upon the documents. It has become more and more common for the *Berufspfleger* to summon the client to the district office and interview them there [rather than making a house visit]." Martini emphasized, however, that "it is absolutely one of the main tasks of the *Berufspfleger* to visit the client at home, because the environment in which the client lives is of the greatest importance for the determination of assistance." The welfare district offices were admonished to remind the *Berufspfleger* "that the main emphasis of their work is fieldwork."[40]

The duties of the *Ermittler* were more menial than those of the *Berufspfleger*. The *Ermittler* physically transported information between the welfare district offices, the volunteer workers, and the clients themselves—"especially . . . written and oral decisions and reports, as well as documents and letters"—and carried the relief money from the district welfare office to the volunteers each week.[41] In the spring of 1927, the *Ermittler* in district office VI were engaged in the transport, among other items, of "gas, light, and rent payments."[42] The *Ermittler* were also responsible for presenting demands for the repayment of support directly and orally to those clients who were not meeting their legally prescribed responsibilities.[43] The *Ermittler* were expected to be persistent in these attempts, "even when the documents in the casefile seemed to indicate that the prospects were hopeless."[44] In 1927, welfare district office V reported that the *Ermittler* were often able to bring in money that would otherwise never be repaid to the welfare office.[45] Welfare officials recognized, however, that the results achieved were sometimes not worth the effort expended and that persistent pressure for repayment created unnecessary tensions between the client and the welfare system.[46] There were cases in which the *Ermittler* threatened to use legal compulsion, even though it was clear that clients could not repay the support they had received without being forced back into poverty. Welfare district office directors were reminded that "only the legal department should use the threat of compulsory measures, [but] this regulation was often ignored."[47]

The Volunteer Welfare Workers in the Neighborhoods

Most experts agreed that the more comprehensive and more difficult tasks assumed by the welfare system after the war required a greater number of professional social workers and welfare officials. But no one thought it would be possible or desirable to dispense altogether with the help of unpaid volunteers (*ehrenamtliche Pfleger*). As one commentator in Berlin put it, "I would think it absurd for public welfare to be administered solely by the professionals."[48] Dorothea Hirschfeld explained that "if the official cannot rely on the assistance of volunteers, then he cannot devote the necessary amount of attention to the difficult cases."[49] Siddy Wronsky insisted that "if the volunteers were excluded, there would be a severe reduction in both the quantity and the quality of work that could be done." Many commentators believed that the unpaid volunteers provided a vital link to the welfare clients because the volunteers had a more direct and personal knowledge of "everyday needs and of the unbearable living conditions under which a large part of the population suffers."[50] And, of course, the financially hard-pressed municipalities could save money by delegating some welfare tasks to unpaid volunteers.

Recruitment: "Democracy" at the Base of the Welfare System?

Social Democrats insisted that ordinary working-class men and women must participate in the welfare system as volunteer workers if public relief was to become more responsive to popular needs than it had been under the empire: "Through the participation of workers, the people's trust in the poor-law system, which is today even more diminished than it was before the war, would certainly increase." Although the Hamburg regulations governing the Wilhelmine-era poor law "exclude no occupational group from participation in the public poor-law system, in Hamburg, as in most other German cities, the artisans, the tradesmen, and the state officials are most strongly represented." At the end of the war, the director of the Hamburg poor-law system estimated that approximately 34 percent of the poor-law guardians in Mühl-hausen were workers, with about 20 percent in Nuremberg and about 9.4 percent in Mannheim; but in the entire Hamburg poor-law system, there were only ten workers.[51] In 1919, the welfare division of the Hamburg Labor Office reported that the volunteers "let no new elements join their ranks . . . from Hohenfelde, complaints were made that the poor-law guardians here form an exclusive circle."[52] A USPD (Unabhängige Sozialdemokratische Partei Deutschlands, or Independent Social Democratic Party) city council member in Düsseldorf also pointed out in 1919 that at present "among all of the volunteers, there are only one clerk, one turner, one foreman; all the rest are teachers, tradesmen, master butchers, bakers, locksmiths, smiths, tailors, and plumbers, and every other sort of master craftsman. But workers and women are altogether absent. . . . Working-class women, who have felt the sting of poverty on their own bodies, would be especially useful here."[53]

The Weimar Republic gave Social Democrats the opportunity to democratize the welfare system by implanting a working-class presence in welfare administration. By 1925, 226 of Hamburg's welfare volunteers were workers, another 289 artisans, and 203 master craftsmen. By 1927, some 40 percent of the city's 2,485 volunteer welfare workers were drawn from the working classes, and in 1928 no fewer than 1,463 of the 2,221 volunteer welfare workers in Hamburg were members of the Arbeiterwohlfahrt.[54] As the SPD senator for welfare in Hamburg put it, "All social agencies in Hamburg depend on a large volunteer staff . . . among whom the working class dominate. So far as voluntary work is concerned, our welfare agencies are democratized in the truest sense of the word."[55]

By 1926, Stadtrat G. Binder, a Social Democratic welfare expert, was able to observe with some satisfaction that, "I know cities where 30 to 50 percent of the poor-law guardians are workers." Binder thought that a strong working-class presence among the volunteers was certainly to be welcomed because, "belonging themselves to the property-less class, dependent solely on . . . their labor power, the working-class volunteer is intimately familiar with the conditions confronted by people who apply for relief."[56] But Binder's contemporaries were well aware of the hindrances to working-class participation in the welfare system. In some localities, political prejudice still continued to restrict the working-class presence among the volunteers. In 1924, for example, the Social Democratic newspaper in Hamburg complained that in neighboring Bergedorf "they have lost no time in pushing our comrades out of public offices, thus opening the door wide to the return of the spirit of the prewar poor law. . . . The city council of Bergedorf, which has a bourgeois majority, has delegated [responsibility for welfare matters] to only one representative of the working class. . . . [The middle classes] are not always comfortable cooperating with our comrades in welfare matters."[57]

Only workers whose "own circumstances are well ordered" could be considered for positions as *ehrenamtliche Pfleger*.[58] Hamburg authorities suggested that people who had criminal records or occupations that required them frequently to be away from home, such as train drivers, could not properly fulfill the responsibilities of an *ehrenamtliche Pfleger*.[59] Some working-class candidates could not meet even these rudimentary requirements. In 1925, for example, a man who had served since 1923 as an *ehrenamtliche Pfleger* in Hamburg was found to have a long police record, stretching back to 1893.[60] Even workers with clean police records and whose present economic circumstances were relatively orderly might still find it difficult to afford the time (and the loss of income) that voluntary welfare work required. A commentator warned that "people who already have other functions and offices [in the labor movement] usually do not have sufficient time to act as a volunteer welfare worker."[61] Binder acknowledged that "many intelligent workers prefer a position as functionary in the trade unions, the cooperatives, or the party" rather than working as a volunteer in the welfare system. Moreover, "the often very cramped living conditions of many workers . . . make it impossible, or at least very difficult, to receive visitors [clients] and to discuss, undisturbed, the subtleties of their situation."[62] In September 1926, a meeting of Hamburg welfare district directors learned that there was a pressing need for more *ehrenamtliche*, but suitable people were hard to find. In welfare districts I, II, III, and VII, "the volunteers all have at least fifteen to twenty cases and are thus overburdened. Some chairmen of the district committees of volunteers already have the intention of resigning their office. . . . Some volunteers are themselves unemployed and not able to manage the expenses that go with the office." Yet in a meeting later that same month, it was suggested that the volunteers be given even more cases so as to relieve the greatly overburdened professional social workers.[63]

Given the hindrances to greater working-class participation in the Weimar welfare system, it is not surprising that the middle and especially the lower-middle classes

(*Mittelstand*) continued to exert an important influence on the unpaid administration of welfare. In the county of Calau in eastern Germany, the limited range of occupations exercised by the heads of district committees in 1925 included "cabinetmaker, teacher, pastor, municipal civil servant, railway man, master baker, tradesman, glass maker, wife of a local administrative official."[64] In Hamburg, no fewer than 380 of the volunteer staff in 1925 were merchants and small businessmen, while 307 were civil servants and white-collar employees.[65] Among the 497 *ehrenamtliche Pfleger* who were selected for office in Cologne in 1929, only 9 were unskilled workers; 88 were skilled workers and artisans, but 18 were master artisans and 35 were male teachers.[66]

Women could serve as nonprofessional volunteer welfare workers, but they appear to have remained a minority unless local regulations specifically mandated a certain quota. In Calau in 1925, women constituted half of "the welfare volunteers [*Wohlfahrtsordner*] who come from all occupations, layers of society, religions, and political orientations."[67] In Hanover, where it was stipulated that at least half of the volunteers must be female, women were actually in the majority.[68] Of the 497 volunteers in Cologne in 1929, 97 were married women (including housewives), 162 were women without occupational or marital description, 13 were women teachers, and 1 was a nurse.[69] But a report from Berlin in 1929 complained that "it is especially the women who are taken too little account of, even though they are well suited for this work."[70] And in Hamburg in 1927, only 407 or 16.3 percent of the 2,485 *ehrenamtliche Pfleger* were women, of whom 345 were listed as housewives (*Hausfrauen*).[71]

Volunteer workers could be appointed individually, or they might be nominated by one of the private charitable organizations.[72] Marie Baum observed in 1927 that in a number of cities the private welfare organizations put forward their own candidates for positions as volunteer workers. Baum found that in Lübeck half of the volunteers were proposed by the Arbeiterwohlfahrt and the other half by the Protestant Welfare Office (Evangelisches Wohlfahrtsamt).[73] A report for 1932–1933 showed that in the heavily Catholic Rhineland metropolis of Düsseldorf, the Caritasverband supplied 49.5 percent of the volunteer workers, the Protestant Welfare Office some 28.5 percent, and the socialist Arbeiterwohlfahrt only 15.2 percent. However, the distribution of members of these three welfare organizations varied considerably from one welfare district of the city to another. So, for example, in one of the two welfare districts in working-class Gerresheim, 17 of the 49 volunteers were Arbeiterwohlfahrt members, compared to 16 from the Caritasverband and 13 from the Protestant Youth and Welfare Office. In the second welfare district in Gerresheim, the Arbeiterwohlfahrt supplied 12 of the 42 volunteers, the Caritas 13, and the Protestant Welfare Office 13 as well. By contrast, in welfare district Ib\1, located in the Altstadt, 29 of the 44 volunteers came from the Caritasverband, 9 from the Protestant Welfare Office, and only 4 from the Arbeiterwohlfahrt. In six of the city's fifty-one welfare districts, the Arbeiterwohlfahrt had no representatives at all among the volunteers. On the other hand, the distribution of volunteers in each of the city's welfare districts was not always a direct reflection of the relative influence of each of the private welfare organizations; in welfare district IIib\1, for example, where the Caritas had 9 volunteers and the Arbeiterwohlfahrt only 2, a member of the Arbeiterwohlfahrt nonetheless acted as a deputy to the Catholic district chairman. And in welfare district Iid\1, where the Caritas had 15 volunteers and the Arbeiterwohlfahrt only 10, there was nonetheless an Arbeiterwohlfahrt district chairperson with a Catholic deputy. In welfare district IVc, where the *Caritas* had 11 volunteers, the Protestant Welfare Office had 9, and the Arbeiterwohlfahrt had 5, the district chairperson came from the Arbeiterwohlfahrt and the deputy from the Protestant organization.[74]

Training

The expansion of state welfare activity created a growing demand for "expert knowledge" of social problems. One observer claimed in 1933 that "welfare has become a science [*Wissenschaft*]."[75] In the Weimar Republic, there were a great many more new laws and regulations governing the administration of welfare than there had been under the monarchy.[76] In a speech given to a meeting of the German Association for Private and Public Welfare in Hildesheim, the general secretary of the German League of Free Welfare Organizations (Deutsche Liga der freien Wohlfahrtspflege), G. Vöhringer, complained about the difficulties that private welfare organizations had recently experienced in recruiting volunteers and in soliciting donations. He thought that a good deal of the problem could be explained by the economic difficulties faced after the war by the social groups who had played such a vital role in charitable activities before 1914. But other factors exercised an equally powerful influence. The practice of welfare had, for one thing, become more demanding, more complicated, requiring specialized knowledge to which fewer and fewer volunteers had ready access. Indeed, Vöhringer estimated that out of any twenty people who volunteered for welfare work, scarcely five would now be competent, even though previously all twenty could have done the work.[77]

Welfare offices did attempt to train their voluntary workers in the new knowledge. In 1926, for example, the Cologne Welfare Department invited the voluntary workers from six of the city's welfare districts "to five evenings of lectures . . . which offer an overview of the welfare system's different areas of responsibility and which will arm the volunteers for their tasks. . . . This is the first time in the history of volunteer welfare work in Cologne that such a comprehensive course has been offered."[78] In 1928 in Hamburg, welfare authorities suggested that each year not only the professional welfare staff but also the *ehrenamtliche* should be taken on tours of all the major institutions in the Hamburg welfare system.[79] In the county of Calau,

> if the large circle of volunteer workers in the county welfare office . . . are to do their jobs successfully, then they need systematic and permanent (re)training. . . . This goal is served in the first instance by the official journal, *Die Nachbarschaft*, which deals . . . with the implementation of welfare responsibilities within the county. . . . This journal is given to all volunteer workers . . . free of charge. In addition . . . the professional staff of the county welfare office and other experts give lectures and hold discussions. . . . There are also regular slide and film presentations, which are combined with informative lectures. . . . Some female volunteers who would profit from the opportunity are sent to inspect particular facilities . . . or to take special courses (i.e., in infant care). Volunteers may also consult an extensive collection of specialist literature (periodicals and books) housed in the main county welfare office.[80]

Symbolic attempts were also made to improve the status and the public image of volunteer welfare workers. In 1926, for example, Elena Luksch-Makowsy was commissioned by the Hamburg Senate to design "an artistic medallion . . . that would be awarded to volunteers as a sign of their long years of service. . . . The inscription 'For faithful work in the service of the people' expresses . . . the spirit in which this medallion will be awarded. . . . The thirteen-centimeter-high, nine-centimeter-wide bronze medal portrays, in a beautiful unity of form, a train of people, meant to symbolize the laboring population." This medallion was to be awarded once a year "on constitution day."[81]

Practices

The *ehrenamtliche Pfleger* had responsibility for the majority of the cases requiring long-term public support. They held monthly or bimonthly meetings in each welfare ward (*Bezirk*) to discuss applications for support and to review old cases. In 1926, an observer described the course of a district meeting in Cologne:

> All of the male and female volunteers, the responsible female social worker and an official from the district welfare office are present. . . . One volunteer recommends changes in the level of support for his clients. . . . Every volunteer has his or her "special case" to submit for discussion . . . then come the new cases. The welfare official . . . discusses the individual details. . . . Every volunteer defends the cases that his [or her] house visits have revealed are genuinely in need of help. . . . Every single case is voted on. . . . Then, however, from the document file, two "bad" cases are taken out. One failed to declare income from a pension, which he had been drawing for some time; another had kept the details of a significant amount [of assets affected by the inflation] secret. . . . The volunteers' displeasure can be read on their faces. That one cares so loyally for one's clients, that one expends so much time and energy . . . only to find that one has been deceived, is always disappointing. . . . From now on, be ever more alert, so that something like this cannot happen again. Everyday practice shows that there are cases in which the laws and the rules and even the knowledge of the individual are not enough to find the right decision. In these cases, volunteers, female social workers, and welfare officials all have to work together, trying to do the best for everyone. . . . Finally, the case files are distributed and the welfare journals passed out.[82]

Volunteer workers were expected to provide the same kinds of detailed reports that the professional social workers used as the basis of their "social diagnosis":

> The personal details of the client are obviously the most essential elements of a case file: name, birth date, marital status. Yet not in the form of a simple questionnaire . . . but rather as a picture of personalities that can give deeper insight into the causes [of the client's] condition of need and so as to determine . . . how the family itself can be won over to cooperation in the healing of their own circumstances. . . . In this respect it is important not only to establish the husband's occupation but to give facts that . . . cast light on his relationship to his work; that means looking at his "workbook," which shows whether he has a stable pattern of employment or has changed jobs often. . . . It is important to provide details of the way in which [the wife] runs the household, her influence on the family; special attention should be paid to the children's health, how well they are cared for, including spiritually.

In other words, "the essence of the case report is at odds with any inflexible, pre-scribed set of questions. . . . It must avoid all schematic forms. . . . In the report, it is not a matter of dead facts but of human experience and human fates in all their plu-rality and complexity." Instead of simply recording how many rooms a family has and how much rent they pay, volunteer workers should construct a "vivid depiction of the family's domesticity [*Häuslichkeit*] . . . which, proceeding from the descrip-tion of external, especially hygienic, characteristics, the furniture, the sleeping ar-rangements, can provide very valuable keys to the family's living habits, relation-ship with the landlord, and with the neighbors." The volunteers must also periodically update their reports on individual cases because "even the best report . . . needs to be constantly corrected and expanded . . . so that better ways to help can be found."[83]

Yet despite these efforts to induct unpaid volunteers into the mysteries of "scien-tific social work," the volunteers were by no means always committed to the meth-ods championed by the paid professional staff. In 1927, a complaint was made against one *Pfleger* in Hamburg whose report on a client "essentially consisted of the asser-tion that the client's economic situation had not changed. But the police soon reported that the client was completely uncared for, so that he had to be taken into an institu-tion."[84] This example demonstrated how important it was that the welfare district offices examine each case carefully to decide whether or not the *Pfleger*'s reports were satisfactory, "even if they must request that the *Berufspfleger* clarify the case himself."[85] The volunteer workers were also encouraged to pay closer attention to health problems: "In this respect, much is still neglected. . . . So, for example, a fam-ily was in the care of a volunteer for three whole years, but . . . one of the children who was crippled was never taken to a doctor. Similar conditions exist with regard to psychopathic children."[86]

Nor did the volunteer workers always agree with or understand the decisions made by the professional staff. In April 1925, President Martini pointed out that although the volunteers might want to withdraw supplemental benefits paid to women when it appeared that they were living with a man, the Welfare Department was restricted by clear regulations in such cases. In July 1926, it was reported that "some of the volunteers are upset because they think the rent support some clients receive is too generous."[87] And in 1928, a Hamburg welfare official observed that "the volunteers find it hard to understand why a 'child-rich' family, whose breadwinner has a per-manent but poorly paid job should be granted ongoing rent support, or why clients with severe lung diseases should be given special benefits. . . . [District welfare of-fice director] Valentin has often felt that the volunteers see the district office as no more than a countinghouse."[88]

Unpaid Volunteers and Welfare Clients

The relationship between the voluntary welfare workers and their clients was direct and personal. The transaction of everyday welfare business, including payment of support money, normally took place in the *Pfleger*'s own home. General guidelines for the appropriate levels of support were laid down by the central welfare office and, increasingly, by the national state. But the volunteer workers were allowed to award relief that was as much as 33.3 percent higher than the official guidelines, and they did, at times, respond to pressure from below. In 1921, there were complaints that some volunteers in Hamburg were too liberal with grants of relief.[89] In 1923, at a meeting of district welfare office directors, an official observed that "the attitudes of the volunteers play a significant role" in the awarding of relief and that "volunteers in Barmbeck-Nord have always displayed a certain generosity . . . and usually agree unanimously to award the highest level of support."[90] In 1927, a welfare official complained that "it is easier to get ongoing assistance from the volunteers than from the professionals."[91] Two years later, volunteer workers in welfare district XI actually paid some applicants 50 percent more than the official standard rates "because the rents are so high in the new housing [*Neubauten*] that tenants have to take in subtenants to meet their rent. The subtenants often move out, and for a period of time the room remains vacant and the district must step in with a one-time rent support payment."[92] In some districts there appeared not to be "enough movement" from one year to the next; clients were allowed to draw long-term support for far too long. District directors urged that individual cases be checked more regularly and more carefully. The differences in the numbers of cases that each subdistrict had been able to remove from the welfare rolls (between 3.5% and 33.13%) were so dramatic that they could not be explained in terms of differences in the populations of each area "but only by the different orientations and intentions of the volunteers."[93]

However, the *ehrenamtliche* system could also generate intense and extremely personal antagonisms. Social and economic relationships in the neighborhood sometimes intruded into the connection between the client and the *Pfleger*. One person on welfare complained that he had been given food on credit from his *Pfleger*'s shop instead of cash.[94] A second Hamburg client was told to apply for money to pay his *Pflegerin* the rent he owed her.[95] Some clients' dealings with the volunteer workers in their district convinced them that the nonprofessional staff was neither fair nor impartial nor, for that matter, honest; several volunteer welfare workers, including an "SPD secretary, Iron Front man, and shopkeeper," were reported to have embezzled money they were supposed to have given to their clients.[96] Because they lived in the same neighborhoods as their clients, the volunteer workers' surveillance of everyday life might also be more intrusive than the professional social worker's home visit. One welfare recipient complained that he had been given a *Pfleger* who actually lived in his own apartment building.[97] In 1932, one welfare district introduced the procedure of summoning all welfare clients to the district meetings, "to question them on the spot. . . . By these methods it was, for example, possible to confront one client with the fact that he had some extra income from street trading."[98]

CHAPTER THREE

The Gender of Welfare

Women and Social Work

Representations of Social Work

Wilhelmine social reform and social work were supposed to strengthen the imperial state and prevent revolution. According to Alice Salomon, prewar bourgeois social reformers "undertook their work in the belief that it was possible to bring about reform of social conditions peacefully, through the insight and the efforts of the privileged classes."[1] After 1918, these ideological foundations of prewar social reform lay in ruins. German defeat in World War I plunged the country into revolution and deprived Germany of its empire. Socialists then challenged the bourgeois monopoly of social work, demanding a "democratization of welfare."[2] These dramatic changes put bourgeois reformers and welfare experts on the defensive; Salomon argued, for example, that social work must help to construct a new *Volksgemeinschaft* (people's community), "so that the class conflicts of 1918/19 would not assume even more threatening dimensions."[3] Else Wex thought that social welfare could act "as a means of reconstructing the . . . lost collectivity, as a new means of connecting the state with the social estates."[4] Salomon insisted that social welfare "is, at its innermost core, the work of reconciliation."

Wex and Salomon also believed that social welfare would play a vital role in Germany's postwar recovery. If a weakened Germany was to survive the postwar competition among nations, it would have to produce not only quality goods and machines but also "the healthiest, most productive, best-trained human beings." Yet the challenge posed to social welfare in the 1920s was immense; Salomon observed that "with the increasing impoverishment . . . in the last years . . . ever wider strata of the people . . . need assistance. . . . Today, many millions of Germans . . . are being supported by public funds."[5] The war had weakened the social attachments and relationships that helped people to cope with their troubles before 1914: "The family is

... atomized. ... Youth is uprooted, alienated from *Heimat* and family."[6] Local welfare authorities agreed. In 1927, the director of the Hamburg Youth Office warned that "the intense endangerment of youth caused by the influence of the big city, by poor housing, and by unemployment ... requires constant protective work."[7] Even in rural areas, the war had produced "deep transformations. ... The men coming back from the war are changed, and they also find a different village-*Heimat* [when they return]. 'Mammonism' has entered the countryside and has altered its spiritual complexion."[8]

For nonsocialists, then, social welfare was to contribute to class reconciliation and to moral and cultural as well as economic reconstruction after the war. To achieve these goals, social welfare must certainly offer material assistance to those in need, but Salomon insisted that "every purposeful type of welfare cannot ... simply ... support the poor but must, when possible, bring about the reconstruction of economic independence. It must strive to restore the client's strength within the existing economic system."[9] The aim of the newly constructed Kassel Welfare Department was described as "the promotion of the individual's thrift and economy ... and the prevention of dissipation that leads the individual to require social assistance. ... By providing help now, welfare protects against greater costs in the future."[10] This project required "instruction, enlightenment, and advice aimed at changing ... the way the client lives."[11] Social work was thus intensely personal. Unlike social insurance, social welfare was addressed not to entire categories of collective juridical subjects but to the individual welfare client and his or her family, to whom it offered an "education in independence, education in self-help."[12] Elizabeth Neumann described the activities of the rural district social worker as "serving and helping, because [social work] deals directly with the individual, with the entire person; [social work] must understand the person's world. ... It must attempt to win and likewise offer trust."[13]

Salomon articulated a secular vision of social work that proposed "a new understanding of the client. ... The new social welfare was no longer to be responsible to God, the state, the community, but rather to the worth of the individual person in need."[14] Throughout the 1920s, this secular social-work ideal, "temporal and aimed at the material betterment of welfare recipients and the political position of the women welfare workers themselves" had to compete with a religious perspective that saw social work "as an essentially spiritual act of charity."[15] In 1922, a Catholic commentator, Christine Thomas, complained that there was a noticeable lack of "social spirit" in the everyday life of "our dear Fatherland." Neither social policy nor social welfare could awaken and cultivate this social spirit by themselves; it must flow from the heart, "from person to person ... and who has a better calling for this than the female social worker?" In Thomas's mind, it was the combination of the Catholic social worker's religious faith with her feminine nature that allowed her "to transport the charitable into the social and in this way to cultivate the social spirit." The word of God that made it clear that "the poor would always be with us" challenged Catholic social workers to help their needy "brothers and sisters" to develop those "strengths and forces that help and heal and love and console, whose unfolding warms our hearts and allows us to engage our complete humanity, our feminine being, and our Christian nature."[16]

Social Democrats warned, however, that "the bourgeois and the socialist camps bestow such a different significance upon welfare that mutual understanding" was virtually impossible. Working within the Weimar welfare system, Social Democrats were not able to pursue independent socialist welfare policies. They did, however, hope to import a class-conscious perspective into the welfare state and to give its everyday practices a democratic inflection.[17] But Social Democratic welfare experts warned that participation in Weimar's welfare system might also cause socialists to lose sight of the class perspective that distinguished them from their bourgeois counterparts. In the case files of the bourgeois social worker, the prescription of various measures for the individual client counted as a successful treatment of a case.[18] Bourgeois social workers might sincerely believe that they were helping to build a *Volksgemeinschaft*, but socialists should not succumb to these illusions. Although welfare might help certain individuals, it could not contribute to the transformation of society so long as the condition of the working class as a whole remained unchanged. A socialist social worker warned that "we are not permitted . . . ever to fail to see welfare for what it really is: a partial labor, extracted from the more general framework of social relations. We must always understand and be aware of the interrelationships between social work and all the other tasks of the state and society."[19] Socialists must also seek to connect their efforts to the larger movement of proletarian "self-help" embodied in the trade unions, the youth organizations, the workers' educational associations, and the sports clubs.[20]

Even so, socialists engaged in welfare work might be forced into the unwelcome role of defenders of the existing social order against "its dissatisfied, grumbling victims." If welfare clients did not understand "the deeper social and economic causes of their suffering but rather directed their anger against the individual welfare official with whom they had to deal," even socialist welfare officers might feel compelled to justify their decisions by citing laws and regulations with which, in their hearts, they did not agree. These were the moments when the socialist welfare worker must display class solidarity with the unhappy welfare client:

> When, for example, an unemployed man, embittered by his exclusion from the process of production and by the inadequate public assistance [he receives] . . . slams his fist down on the table and threatens "to make short work of the welfare office," then a socialist welfare officer must not dismiss him with harsh words as an "insolent disturber of the peace." Instead, with friendly objectivity, the socialist official must make clear to the client that the way he is acting will get him nowhere, that the official can only implement the existing regulations, and that these laws are made by the elected representatives of the whole people. If the welfare client wants to change things . . . then he should exercise his right to vote and participate actively in political life.[21]

The socialist welfare worker must act neither as a police officer nor as a "patronizing schoolmaster." A Social Democratic social worker in Hamburg urged her colleagues to "make yourself superfluous. Take care [of your clients] only as long as is absolutely necessary. . . . Where I cannot do positive social work, I may not rob the criminal police of their job."[22]

The socialist social worker must recognize that welfare clients' problems are not simply the result of their own "unwillingness to work, inability to manage money, dissipation, weakness of character, or a general lack of will," as many bourgeois social workers appeared to believe.[23] But cultivating a more class-conscious attitude did not solve the dilemma of the socialist who participated in the disciplinary power that was inseparable from modern welfare practices. Even the class-conscious social worker had to follow the officially prescribed rules for the construction of a case file.[24] The knowledge presented in a case file was produced by a "disciplinary microtactic," a form of "the gaze" identified by Michel Foucault as an indispensable technique of "power/knowledge" that allowed welfare administrators to know and to control the clients with whom they had to deal.[25] This kind of "individualizing visibility . . . aimed at exhaustive, detailed observation of individuals, their habits and histories. Foucault claims that this visibility succeeded in constituting the individual for the first time as a 'case,' simultaneously a new object of inquiry and a new target of power."[26]

The Gender of Welfare?

Nineteenth-century female social reformers constructed public identities as the "other" of male reason. "Maternalists" appropriated and redefined arguments about women's difference that had been used by men to legitimate women's exclusion from the public sphere.[27] They argued that women must play an important role in the developing welfare state, which was bringing private relationships into the public sphere, precisely because women were more emotional, caring, and nurturing than men. By the 1920s, however, female social workers found themselves trapped in an impossible dilemma. In the context of an "increasingly legalistic and bureaucratic structure of the welfare system," the claim that social work was a uniquely feminine calling, advanced originally by feminists to lay claim to a public role for women, became a justification for placing men "in positions of administrative authority by virtue of their presumed rationality and capacity for 'universalistic' bureaucratic thought."[28] The attempts to represent social work as a new profession, requiring specialized training and expertise, that became increasingly common in the 1920s also tended to undermine women's claims that their gender gave them a natural monopoly on social work.[29]

   Accreditation as a professional social worker increasingly required training at one of the state-approved "social women's schools" (*soziale Frauenschulen*).[30] Marie Baum thought that the specific focus of social-work training would, to some considerable extent, be determined by the needs of the local welfare offices. If a welfare office placed great emphasis upon preventive care, then the social worker must be well trained in "hygienic, pedagogic, and economic " dimensions of social work. But these skills would not be required by a welfare office that limited its activity to dealing with problems only after they had become apparent. Baum insisted that every social worker required "a certain measure of domestic knowledge." But, in addition, the social workers should have training and experience "in the hygienic as well as the pedagogic area ." Female social workers needed also to deepen their knowledge of "administrative law and practice ." Finally, Baum urged that "every social worker . . . be . . . as well versed in the larger context of the economic life of the people, the social and political struggles that flowed from it, and their consequences in social and labor legislation as she was in the laws of consumption, the regulation of the private household, workers' budgets, etc."[31]

As early as 1920, however, E. G. Dresel warned against putting too much weight upon specialized knowledge and official certifications. Though certainly these were necessary, it was important not to lose sight of the general ethical and moral motivations that should always guide and inform welfare work.[32] Social workers must have certain inclinations toward "idealism and belief in humanity [and] the ability to empathize with others."[33] Like many of his contemporaries, Dresel thought that "the female sex possesses a disposition that men usually lack" that suited them for welfare work: "the mothering instinct . . . the ability to make sacrifices for the weak . . . and those needing care." The women who applied to the *soziale Frauenschule* should not be too young and should, preferably, already have had some practical experience, especially with housekeeping: "Care of the household, which was already badly neglected before the war, suffered a severe blow from the mobilization of young women during the war. Here, the female social worker . . . must solve an enormous challenge in the ceaseless work of detail. The social-work schools . . . must require that their students possess the requisite household knowledge and are capable of giving guidance in this area." Dresel concluding by insisting that the formal training could only provide a first step toward what would actually be learned in daily practice. Social workers could not really become experts in the various areas they studied at school; at best, they could gain an understanding of the way in which different specialisms looked at the world and which problems concerned them. All political positions "that are particularly eager to interfere in economic issues" must be excluded from social-work training, and a perspective on these "human questions" that stands above political parties had to be found. In short, the "social women's schools" had to attempt to become "nurseries for a social conscience . . . from which great strength could emerge to overcome the contradictions within and between individual strata of the people."[34]

Numbers of middle-class women did became professional social workers, but they were seldom admitted to the predominantly male, permanent, tenured welfare bureaucracy. Fewer working-class women could afford the expense or time needed to receive accreditation as a professional social worker by taking courses at one of the state-approved schools.[35] Many trained social workers had to content themselves with poorly paid, insecure positions.[36] In 1925, almost all social workers in Württemberg were hired with civil service status, but in Prussia only 23 percent were given such positions.[37] Until 1928, very few of the Hanover social workers had permanent positions (which meant they could be fired with one to three months' notice and had no pensions), and, as a rule, women were paid 10 percent less than men, "with the justification that because their female abilities allowed them to cook, sew, and wash their clothes, they had fewer clothing and household expenses." In December 1928, all social workers previously hired as nontenured, salaried employees in Hanover were made *Beamtenanwärterinnen*, which meant that after ten years on the job they could lay claim to a tenured civil service status (*Beamtenverhältnis*).[38] In Hamburg, however,

the social workers in every welfare district employed by the health service, who, at the same time, act as so-called family care social workers . . . are not salaried employees of the state in a proper sense but are, rather, employees of two private associations . . . the

Central Federal State Organization for the Protection of Nursing Infants and Small Children and the Central Federal State Association for People's Health Care, which, however, receive some of the money for the social workers' salaries from the state treasury, some from the Health Office, and some from the Welfare Department.[39]

Female social workers found it difficult to move from fieldwork to office work because they generally lacked the administrative training required for these positions, especially at higher levels. When Margarete Cordemann, who had been a social worker during the war, was appointed the first director of the Düsseldorf Family Care Agency, she was not awarded the status of a municipal civil servant. Her original contract provided for termination of her employment on three months' notice. She was to receive a monthly salary of 300 marks, but in August 1919 it was recommended that she be paid 550 marks per month.[40] In February 1920, the average monthly salary for female office workers in their twenties was 417 marks, so Cordemann was not being paid particularly well.[41]

Social workers were subjected to considerable physical and nervous strain by their daily work. Gertrud Bäumer claimed that "working with people is incomparably more demanding—both physically and spiritually—than working with documents. Fieldwork is ten times as strenuous as office work."[42] One commentator in Württemberg warned in 1925 that "one most not forget that the female social worker can only begin her actual work after a physically demanding trip on foot, in all sorts of weather. Every day, year-round, the social worker must deal with every sort of misery. . . . She requires all her spiritual strength. She is repeatedly exposed to contagious diseases, especially when caring for tubercular clients." Another report observed that "colds and flu, symptoms of exhaustion, nervous complaints are all the social worker's occupational diseases."[43] Social workers could seldom expect adequate or, indeed, any vacations during which they might recuperate from their exhausting work.[44] A Hamburg social worker recommended that "every female social worker should do gymnastics to keep both mind and body supple."[45] Working conditions were especially demanding and difficult in rural areas: "The geographical extent of the social workers' territory is usually too large in Württemberg, as it is elsewhere."[46] Citing a recent study, Marie Baum found the size of rural welfare districts to be "almost a curiosity—although not a humorous one. Although a rural postman was not required to travel more than 28 kilometers each day, some rural social workers had territories as large as 400 square kilometers." In rural areas, too, the social worker often did not have access to adequate office space to write her reports or to hold consultations with clients.[47] Margarete Cordemann complained that "there is not only a struggle for work space but also a small daily war over writing paper, pen nibs, and file folders."[48]

Weimar welfare systems created divisions and tensions between a series of gendered "spaces," practices, and identities.[49] Emilie Zadow, a social worker charged with the care of families of Sinti and Roma [Gypsies] living on the outskirts of an unnamed large city, described the contrast and the tension between the two gendered spaces of the welfare system as she moved from the welfare office to the field in the course of one day:

She has a small consultation room in the welfare office of this suburban district. Here documents wait for her, every type of document; their external appearance already speaks volumes: thick, black ones, dirty with greasy spots . . . brand new ones, still in the full sparkle of their youth. Green ones from the Youth Office that one gladly picks up because they still seem so hopeful—especially so long as they are still clean; red, yellow, and blue ones. An entire rainbow. When the "sister" finds a really thick, old packet from the poor law, she sighs and does not really want to open it; here is a "hopeless case." What delights her the most, however, are the rose-colored sheets that announce the birth of a new little Gypsy. Then she would really love just to head off and find out how the child looks and to look right at the mother's face, which exhibits such lovely changes in the days after the birth.

But as much as she wanted to, Zadow could not simply run off to talk with the human being whose "official story" she held at that moment in her hand. She still had meetings to attend and telephone calls to make. She had to hold office hours, then write "endless reports." Sometimes, "when all she has done is spend the whole day in conferences and with documents, she has the feeling that 'family care' was made of nothing but paper, and she as well."

> Once she was back in the *Aussendienst*, both she and her clients came alive again. Ten minutes later, she was in the middle of the Gypsy village. In front of the barracks, there was colorful life. Old and young, on four feet and in feathers; everything that could be out in the open was. . . . Yes, this is certainly different than what is in the files. Greetings fly here and there; the people know their "sister" well. She has been looking out for their children for years, ever since they came as infants to the mothers' advice center.[50]

A clearly gendered distinction was drawn between masculine administration and feminine social work. Female social workers tried to represent what they did as a type of skilled and gendered "quality" work that was intrinsically superior to the routinized, rationalized, assembly-line *Massenarbeit* (mass production) of the male welfare official. In 1922, a female welfare officer in Düsseldorf complained that

> unfortunately, our male welfare officials, who are today concerned with youth welfare, are too focused upon the technical details of administration. Many know only the youth's name, enter his offenses schematically in the documents . . . summon him to the office . . . when it appears necessary, give him a good talking to, and then possibly move him to another apprenticeship. . . . It is nonsense for the female social workers to undergo years of specialist training when the male office personnel only have the same training as any other administrative official.[51]

Hedwig Stieve, a social worker in Nuremberg, described her anger and dismay when she first observed how a male welfare official "disposed" of "her" cases at a meeting of the city's central welfare commission:

> Quite breathlessly, the official sprinted through the documents, describing the situation of a whole family in just two sentences and frequently influencing the decision with a slight intonation or a random word. . . . Those listening to him were really not familiar with these cases and could only see things as the official painted them. . . . Then the meeting was adjourned, the exhausted official packed up his documents, muttering to himself that "nonetheless, it had been possible to get through no fewer than fifty-seven cases." How much . . . misery was condensed into just two sentences here and formed into a "decision." I took my document case and went back to my district. I had to work out my consternation.[52]

Female social workers' frustration at the *Bürokratismus* of male welfare officials was only compounded by "the structural contradiction . . . between their considerable responsibilities for observation and their minimal decision-making powers."[53] Female social workers were seldom permitted to exercise more than a modicum of bureaucratic authority: "The social worker can instruct, advise, even warn . . . but only the bureaucrats in the welfare office can grant real assistance."[54] At the end of the 1920s, one female social-work director bitterly complained that "women are needed only to visit the poor districts in all kinds of weather. . . . Receiving . . . a client's application is a female activity. Making decisions . . . that is male. . . . So, when people say that women are particularly suited for welfare work, this means . . . that they are just [to be] used [to] . . . provide a kind of messenger service."[55]

The gendered division of labor within Weimar welfare systems produced "repeated points of conflict."[56] In 1924, a south German social worker complained about "the lack of understanding among the men for the physical and spiritual costs of this work. . . . Because it does not produce concrete, material items of value, [social work] is looked down upon; in some places, it is declared to be unnecessary."[57] At the Kiel Workers' Welfare conference in 1927, a female social worker from Berlin grumbled that "it is not the work . . . but rather the daily guerilla war with the [male] administrative officials over areas of responsibility . . . that wears us out."[58]

Yet gender was not the only division that structured social workers' perceptions. Female social workers were also committed to worldviews—Protestantism, Catholicism, socialism—that they shared with men. While not suppressing gender conflicts, each worldview had the power to unite some women with some men in their orientation to state welfare practices, while dividing them from other men and women who adhered to opposing worldviews:[59]

> As a result of the conflict of worldviews over welfare, there are many contradictions between the law and morality that are larger than the ethos of the profession itself. . . . Here, we are thinking, for example, of the conflicts that a Catholic social worker must have who is employed in a "sexual advice center" run according to socialist views. . . . Similar, more or less severe conflicts emerge in other branches of our work—the guardianship of young children . . . or family care. . . . Here, our moral standpoint requires us to register a clear, strong "no!" This refusal may cost the individual his or her job; it can cost a private organization the public funds it needs; and yet, this "no" must still be unequivocally expressed.[60]

"Family Care"?

A formulation of the social question that placed deficiencies in working-class family life at the epicenter of most social problems made "the job of the female visitor or social worker . . . pivotal to the achievement of social change."[61] Weimar social workers felt that they were charged with the responsibility of "ferreting out the weak spots, plugging the holes, and holding back the decline of individual families."[62] Female social workers "had the task of going into homes and restoring the will of family members to become independent and self-supporting."[63] Marie Baum insisted that "because caring for the household . . . as well as the regulation of . . . consumption is the job of the housewife and mother, then a woman must also be the one to advise and influence the housewife within the framework provided by the public welfare system."[64]

World War I immediately presented public and private welfare agencies with the tasks of caring for and holding together the families of men sent to the front. By 1916, the attempts to mobilize women for war production posed another threat to the German family. In order not to pay "for the production of war materiel with the lives of young children and the destruction of the families," it was necessary to supplement "the family's now reduced ability to nurture and educate with social-hygienic and social-pedagogical institutions."[65] The wartime and postwar "crisis of the family" appeared to require a transformation of the goals of state welfare from "those of the poor law, which only gave relief, to those of a preventive and constructive form of welfare" and, consequently, the integration of previously separate and diverse welfare organizations and practices within a comprehensive framework of "family care" (*Familienfürsorge*).[66] Marie Baum, the foremost exponent of family care, suggested that the concept had several meanings. It could, first of all, represent a "social-political goal," meaning that all welfare measures should respond to paragraph 119 of the new Weimar constitution, which promised to strengthen the family. *Familienfürsorge* could also be defined as a method that took as its starting point "not individual need, not the individual's fate or responsibility, but saw the entire family as the necessary starting point for a therapeutic plan." Finally, *Familienfürsorge* might also be a form of welfare activity that fused together "the various, specialized branches of economic, health, and educational welfare so as to prevent overlapping and inefficiency but, above all, to better serve the interests of the family itself . . . which would only need to deal with a single agency and which would be helped according to a unified plan." Baum believed it was necessary to combine these three perspectives in a comprehensive definition and set of practices.

Even before the war ended, Hamburg had begun to consider the "combination of all branches of welfare in both field and office work." The federal state of Saxony issued its first welfare law in May 1918, laying the foundations for "a unified health care, including housing care, organized on a district basis, which can only be effectively implemented as family care." And in 1919, Düsseldorf introduced "district housing care with a clear inclination toward family care." A conference of the German Association for Private and Public Welfare in Nuremberg in 1921 called for the "unification of . . . fieldwork in district family care." But the postwar crisis presented serious hindrances to the further development and expansion of *Familienfürsorge*, whose real function was the "preventive social-hygienic and social-pedagogical work" that would allow it "to heal damaged and endangered lives" and not the distribution of material assistance, which, of necessity, became its primary activity in the immediate postwar years. By the time her book was published in 1927, Baum could find only a few German cities that had actually achieved the kind of integrated, unified social work that was the basis of a genuine family care approach; Düsseldorf, Nuremberg, Halle, Hamburg, Chemnitz, Pforzheim, and Freital. Many others "are still stuck in transitional stages, some of which are quite unsatisfactory (e.g., Frankfurt am Main, Dresden); elsewhere the problem hardly appears to have been even addressed (Stuttgart)." The system in Berlin "does not conform to the concept of family care presented in this book." In many rural districts, however, "the incorporation of a system of family care into the welfare apparatus has proceeded with less friction than in the cities, at least in the initial stages."[67]

In Düsseldorf, "housing welfare" was the point of departure for comprehensive intervention into everyday family life. The Family Care Office owed its existence, in legal and administrative terms, to the Prussian Housing Law of 1918.[68] The inspiration for a comprehensive system of family care, however, was derived from the welfare and charitable activities of women's organizations in Germany before the war and, in Düsseldorf, from the war work of the Zentralstelle für freiwillige Liebestätigkeit, an umbrella organization set up to coordinate the relief work of private welfare associations and to create a link between them and municipal government.[69] *Familienfürsorge* was meant to act as a preventive form of care, not merely as a palliative. To do this, it had to "grasp the whole family." As the agency put it in 1923:

> Family care, as such, is translated into reality in the sense that it is not the individual whose social misery has become manifest, who is grasped [by the system] but that person's family as a unit. The preventive character of the welfare care is emphasized [for example] insofar as . . . the protection of mothers before and after births, and infant and child care are being undertaken. This means that the activity of the social worker is extended to include families who are, in essence, socially "healthy."

It was obvious that this kind of social work required fairly detailed, ongoing, and quite personal knowledge of the circumstances of individual families in the city. To procure that knowledge, *Familienfürsorge* was organized on a district basis. Offices were set up in designated districts of the city. Each office was to be staffed by a professional social worker, hired and paid directly by the city. In 1925, there were twenty-five separate districts in which each local office had responsibility for about 17,000 "souls."[70] By 1930, the number of districts had been increased to thirty-six.[71] The local district office was meant to be the focal point of all welfare work, public and private, in the neighborhood: "The district offices are thought of as 'social settlements,' as central points around which all the social life [of the neighborhood] crystallizes. Everyone who is in any way concerned with social work should participate in the internal and external development of the district welfare office. . . . *Familienfürsorge* should provide the foundation upon which the whole public welfare system can be built up."[72] Great emphasis was laid upon the need frequently to visit families in their homes all over the district. Consultations during office hours were mainly intended as follow-ups to the original house visit. As the agency put it in 1923, "the focal point of [family] care activity lies in the house visit."[73] Indeed, an early set of guidelines for the organization insisted that "office work is to be kept to the necessary minimum, [so that] the contact of one human being with another may be expanded."[74] In the administrative year 1924/25, the social workers conducted 44,593 house visits; by 1931, the annual number of visits had risen to 90,121.[75]

Hamburg welfare authorities insisted that even though they had not been using the name, they had, in effect, also been employing a family welfare approach for years. Although as late as 1927 the Hansestadt had not yet formally unified the implementation of all fieldwork, considerable efforts were made to ensure that within each welfare district "overlapping and duplication of the various social workers' efforts are avoided." Regardless of the agency for which she worked, the social worker who made the first visit to a family was thereafter entrusted with their "entire economic, health, and educational care." The *Aussenfürsorge* of the Youth Office remained separate from that of the Welfare Department, especially with regard to endangered children and youths, but the twenty children's social workers responsible for preschool-age children did work closely with the Welfare Department.[76]

Could female social workers actually expect to gain greater power and authority in those cities that reorganized their welfare systems on the principle of *Familienfürsorge*? A report from Charlottenburg claimed that "the district social worker has a very independent and respected position that raises her from the level of merely supplying facts to that of a . . . social diagnostician. The difference between field- and office work has vanished."[77] The new approach clearly increased the responsibilities of the female social worker. Hanna Hellinger, a Social Democratic welfare expert, felt that "family care deserves its name only where it has health, educational, and economic responsibilities."[78] In the Frankfurt system, the female social worker was charged with a broad range of tasks, including the supervision of foster children, submitting petitions for "correctional education," the investigation of applications for economic assistance from families with children, and surveillance of the health of all children in the families for which she was responsible. House visits were the core of the social worker's activities, but she was also expected to hold at least one to two office hours, four days per week.[79] In Hanover, social workers "had to pay attention to . . . all areas of welfare."[80] In Württemberg, where, with the exception of Stuttgart, social workers were "almost always family care social workers," they were likewise responsible for a wide range of welfare tasks.[81]

Some social workers feared, however, that in practice this increased workload only amounted to "a devaluation of . . . professional standards. . . . This opinion was strengthened by the fact that the propagandists for family care harked back to the historical traditions of the preprofessional era of welfare, to the volunteer work that was the basis of the Elberfeld system."[82] Baum insisted that a family care approach had no chance of working properly if it was forced to embrace too many clients. *Familienfürsorge* would clearly have to concentrate on certain categories. Social workers must be allowed to concentrate their efforts on the more difficult cases, leaving simple problems to either the volunteer workers or trainees.[83] To avoid overloading the *Familienfürsorge*, Hamburg authorities thought social workers should not have to bother with care of the elderly, "except in cases where children were also involved." And it was absolutely clear that "care for single people and certain unemployed people" did not belong to the province of family care.[84] Dortmund's family care system explicitly recognized the need to relieve the female social worker of the purely economic cases that did not require educational measures: "In these times of mass need, there is a danger that economic relief will take up too much space. Thus, a number of male *Ermittlungsbeamten* have been assigned all those cases that do not require and are not responsive to therapeutic care and surveillance."[85] But what Hamburg and Dortmund excluded from the *Familienfürsorge* many other welfare offices included.[86]

Knowledge and Power?: The Female Social Worker's "Gaze"

Reading the Signs: "Social Diagnosis" and "Social Therapy"

The most advanced social work in the 1920s attempted to pattern itself upon medical diagnosis and treatment: "The social worker is the doctor to whom the clients turn in their distress."[87] Like a physician diagnosing an illness, the social worker had to be able to understand what the symptoms of each case might tell her about the underlying causes of the welfare client's problems.[88] Weimar welfare experts were guided by the assumption that clients were incapable of correctly assessing their own problems and needs: "The person seeking help comes to the welfare agency without any real knowledge of his condition of need but rather as a result of certain symptoms, which are signs of a social illness but which do not permit him to recognize the essence of this disorder. The person in need . . . turns to the welfare agency for money, not for treatment."[89] In *Methoden der Fürsorge*, a handbook for the instruction of social workers in the principles and practices of "scientific" social work, Siddy Wronsky argued that what clients had to say about their own lives was distinctly less important than the way that the welfare officials read this evidence and created a case history from it. And it was not only the client's spoken words that were expropriated by the social worker to construct a "social diagnosis" and to prescribe the necessary treatment.[90] Wronsky suggested that even the client's body language should be read for the clues it could provide about his or her problems:

> Examination of the influence of the personality of the client can extend to . . . gestures, speech, and handwriting. . . . This can aid in the recognition of depressive and chaotic personalities. . . . A repressed self-presentation, muted gestures, heavy, monotone speech, and drawn-out . . . handwriting often allow us to recognize a depressive personality who tensely carries their fate around with them . . . and who requires extra effort and attention if they are to be moved to act.[91]

Social workers were not content merely to respond to the symptoms of distress but sought to treat its deeper causes: "How can the condition of need be removed on a permanent basis? How can a temporary condition of need be prevented from turning into a permanent condition? What preventive measures are necessary? How can the person in need be made capable of once again earning their livelihood?"[92] After constructing the appropriate social diagnosis, the social worker would prescribe the necessary treatment.[93] But the welfare client must follow this prescription. That meant, as a female Hamburg welfare official put it in 1928, that

> all welfare work is a matter of trust. The welfare system has the task of making itself superfluous in the individual's life by securing the proper assistance but at the same time by exercising an educational influence that makes the individual once again economically independent, which strengthens his will by influencing his desire to help himself. Welfare must therefore always work with the individual or his family.[94]

Social therapy was meant to exclude politics from the administration of the welfare system. Although the Revolution of 1918/19 had transformed the welfare client from a passive object into an active subject, it was more important that the client cooperate with the social worker in the treatment of his or her case than that clients exercise any political influence, individually or collectively, over the administration of the welfare system. As Wronsky put it,

> The precondition for an effective treatment is to bring the individual to the recognition of his own situation, his own lack of energy, as well as the causes of what is lacking. Real healing is only possible . . . when the client applies all his strength to the achievement of the . . . goal. In this new method we see a parallel with the new status of the client in the welfare system . . . [but] his personal involvement in the therapeutic measures . . . required for the removal of his own condition of need is of much greater importance than his participation in the advisory boards of the welfare unions.[95]

Ordinary social workers in the field certainly expressed many of the same ambitions that Wronsky formulated and theorized in her various writings on social therapy. In 1922, for example, a social worker in a rural area of eastern Germany observed that "it is certainly not enough simply to get rid of the immediate condition of need, which must be recognized and grappled with, at its roots."[96] A meeting of Hamburg welfare district directors in 1927 also gave recognition to the need for detailed modern casework: "It should repeatedly be emphasized how absolutely necessary a proper social diagnosis is for any sensible form of welfare."[97] But the everyday realities of the Weimar welfare system made the consistent and widespread implementation of scientific social work, the intensive casework approach, social diagnosis, and social therapy virtually impossible. To begin with, few social workers had the time or energy to inform themselves about the latest developments in the scientific knowledge of social work. Women social workers often complained that it was difficult enough just to keep up with all the new welfare regulations while attempting to deal with the everyday problems of social work. Most social workers were simply too exhausted by the demands of their job to be able to digest anything at the end of the day unless it "did not make too many demands upon them and, above all, focused on everyday practice."[98] In recognition of these problems, Hamburg welfare authorities decided that social diagnosis and recommendations for "the measures suited to the case" should be made not by the social workers themselves but by those "male and female welfare officials" who were more familiar with the theoretical literature.[99]

Reading the Signs: Everyday Practices

In everyday practice, social workers' readings of the signs that each case presented were informed less by scientific knowledge than by often quite rigid middle-class values and sensitivities with respect to cleanliness, orderliness, sexuality, and "proper" family life. Social workers paid a good deal of attention to the cleanliness of their clients' homes and to the state of their clothes. Social workers also routinely questioned relatives, neighbors, employers, and other social authorities, such as clergy, about the behavior and the reputation of applicants for relief. In 1932, one Hanover social worker was pleased to report that "questioning neighbors in the house . . . revealed no signs of unreported income or anything else negative concerning the applicants, who are judged to be solid, orderly, and thrifty, and whose will to work is not to be doubted." The reports of other Hanover social workers contained such observations as "according to the neighbors, the daughter gladly goes dancing on

Saturdays . . . but nothing unfavorable about her was reported" and "the family does not have a bad reputation in the house, but people have apparently heard that the family buys things on credit, which has created offense in this otherwise orderly building." The wife in one family "has the worst possible reputation all over the neighborhood" and was thought to be a casual prostitute. The social worker refused, however, to believe that the husband gained any economic advantage, "as some people maintain," from the wife's "immoral earnings" because "by contrast with his wife, he . . . is described as solid by credible neighbors." Another social worker's report was larded with innuendo and rumor:

> S. was not previously known to us, but her mother was. There have always been rather strange circumstances in this family, which is impossible to get to the bottom of; even now, precise details about the mother and the son are hard to come by. Certainly, the son does not seem to have a regular job, and one supposes that he has some illicit income. It is rumored that he has connections to gangs of thieves. He dresses very well and, according to neighbors, gives nice presents to all his frequently changing girlfriends, although no one thinks he is being kept by a woman. This information was given to me quite confidentially, because it is only a suspicion, but also because people are afraid of the family, who are quite unpleasant and easily angered.[100]

Social workers were forced to admit, however, that some of their information amounted to no more than neighborhood gossip. A manual published by the Arbeiterwohlfahrt to instruct volunteer social workers in proper casework cautioned that "one should by no means rely upon information from the neighbors, in which gossip often plays a major role, but one should rather trust one's own observations and personal impressions."[101] Yet if a client was really intent upon dissimulation, the social worker's gaze might not be powerful enough to uncover the most important details: "It is not easy to clarify the situation of the 'antisocial' elements, because the person in need and their dependents make every effort to deceive the welfare agency. Seldom do you get a clear picture of their real characters and the way they live their lives."[102]

Even if female social workers did manage to compile a lengthy, detailed case file that looked like the model reports and analyses presented in their training handbooks, the male officials in the welfare office who made the final decisions about how to treat each case might simply reduce the client's file to a string of keywords that distilled (and probably also distorted) the female social worker's more complicated reports and analyses into a much shorter, more easily readable list of signs. So, for example, the welfare records of one Hamburg woman, clearly thought to be a difficult case, covering a period of nine years and filling several hundred pages, was reduced to a one-page abstract that presented a string of lapidary remarks, confirming the official judgment that she was an "uneconomic woman" (*unwirtschaftliche Frau*) responsible for her own economic difficulties.[103] The guidelines laid down by the Hanover Welfare Department in 1923 put a greater premium on case files that were concise and easy to read than on the kind of elaborate analysis presented in the more progressive textbooks: "The female social worker should be friendly and patient during her house visits and office hours but should not spend more time than is necessary and should not bother with matters that do not concern her. Her reports must also strive for pointedness and brevity (names, numbers, facts!)."[104]

"Massification"

The kind of intensive casework required for a detailed social diagnosis was realistic only, if at all, when the absolute number of cases assigned to each female social worker was relatively small.[105] It was generally agreed, for example, that two large categories of postwar welfare clients—the social pensioners and small capital pensioners—did not normally require the attentions of a social worker.[106] Nor were female social workers given responsibility for all of the remaining welfare clients. In 1925 in Hamburg, 59,242 new applications were received by the welfare offices, but only 9,019 of these, or 15.2 percent were given to the female social workers for investigation.[107] Even so, women social workers complained that their caseloads were much too large. In a review of Baum's book, a female Hamburg welfare official drew attention to Baum's assertion that the district served by a *Familienfürsorgerin* could not include more than 7,000 inhabitants "if fundamental and successful work is to be performed." But in most German cities this precondition could simply not be achieved; in Hamburg in 1927, for example, each *Bezirksfürsorgerin* was responsible for a district with almost 8,000 people.[108] Hamburg welfare authorities reported in January 1927 that female social workers had average caseloads of 160 families and made an average of 197 house visits per month. In Chemnitz, the average number of house visits was 210. Marie Baum discovered in 1927 that the average number of inhabitants in each district served by a social worker ranged from 21,000 in Frankfurt to 16,000 in Düsseldorf and 10,000 in Cologne. Baum thought it remarkable "that the city of Düsseldorf can conduct orderly welfare work with only 0.7 female social workers for every 10,000 inhabitants, but this has been achieved . . . only at the expense of uncommon strain upon the social workers and also with the considerable involvement of the private charities."[109]

Among those welfare clients for whom female social workers did have some form of direct responsibility, by no means all received the amount of attention that the ideal of intensive casework prescribed. In 1923, for example, the Düsseldorf Family Care Agency reported 6,995 families on its books: 249 of these were visited twelve times or more in the course of that year; 1,359 families received between six and twelve visits; but the great majority, 5,387, had social workers in their homes only once a year. In most instances, the social worker went to the family simply to make observations and gather information for some other state or municipal agency. Such activity "could only be seen as an 'external' determination." It was quite clear to the director of the agency that "families that are visited only once a year are not being properly 'grasped' by the system of care." That is to say, such visits did not serve the central purpose of the *Familienfürsorge* to create a "relationship of trust" between social worker and family that could then be used not only to channel the "correct material relief to the correct people" but also to allow the social workers to educate the whole family in ways of preventing future problems.

The ethos of the *Familienfürsorge* prescribed that home visits should be given the highest priority; office hours were meant to be used as a follow-up to the original home visit. But from the middle of the 1920 onward, office hours came to take up more and more of the social workers' time. One of the main reasons for this was that during periods of extreme distress and unemployment the welfare offices were invaded by hundreds of people trying to get some form of support. In 1923, for example, the Düsseldorf agency reported that "at the beginning of the exceptional period of distress, the district centers . . . have been visited by hundreds of people seeking help. . . . The social workers could only attempt to pacify these people and encourage them to go home."[110] Conditions such as these, which became increasingly common after the onset of the Depression, frustrated the central goal of the agency and put an end to any pretension of being able to engage in serious, individual casework.

The Realities of "Social Therapy"

Ordinary social workers' responses to clients' problems seldom resembled an elegantly conceived, carefully thought-out social therapy. The knowledge required for the everyday practice of social work was scarcely esoteric, and social workers were often forced to engage in an improvised strategy of makeshifts: "Such activities were tiring and demanding but required nonspecific and quite general capabilities, not specialized professional qualifications: alertness, endurance, sensitivity, the ability to come to grips with things."[111] In the early 1920s, for example, a Düsseldorf social worker described what she had done to help the family N., consisting of a husband who had lost an eye in the war and who suffered from rheumatism, a wife who had a lung disease, and six children, aged one to fourteen. The family had no sheets on their beds and very little furniture, and they were nine months behind on their rent. The landlord had already gone to court to have the husband's irregular income garnisheed. The social worker began by promising the landlord that the rent would all be paid if he would withdraw the case and begin to make necessary repairs in the flat. After obtaining some initial financial help for the family from private charities, the social worker busied herself with educating the wife in proper household management: "Although at first she did not trust me at all, eventually the wife began to accept my efforts and . . . came to confide in me about her daily woes." Every two weeks, the social worker visited the family and discussed with Frau N. the ways in which economies could be made in the family budget so as to pay back the rent that was in arrears. By Christmas, the family was on a much better footing: "Frau N. asserted that she now had the courage to go on living; she was once again strong enough to manage without outside help."

In 1927, a social worker in Cologne had to devise a therapeutic plan for a family of six consisting of a father who was a skilled mechanic/fitter (*Schlosser*), a mother, and four children, aged four, eight, fourteen, and fifteen. The family had come to the Welfare Department's attention through the health services six months earlier, when the mother, who was not in good health, had a difficult birth and the infant subsequently died. The social worker's house visit revealed that the family had only two rooms and a kitchen in an outbuilding with "little sun and a great deal of dampness." The entire family slept in two full-sized beds, a child's cot, and the sofa. Their only set of bed linens was completely worn out. Although the father was healthy, an examination of the mother revealed signs of a developing lung illness. The children were delicate but, according to the mother, quite healthy. A year earlier, the father had been fired from his last full-time position because he had been caught in a petty theft. Since then, he earned an "irregular and unverifiable" income as a casual

laborer. He seemed no longer interested in his wife or children, and his sense of responsibility for the family had greatly diminished. Of necessity, and despite her poor
health, the wife was now working as a cleaning lady early each morning, before she
had to get the children ready for school. She made a very good impression on the
social worker, not least because she had assumed the entire responsibility for raising
the children. The children's dispositions (*Veranlagung*) seemed on the whole good;
only the eight-year-old—so the mother complained—had inherited the father's "irresponsible and superficial attitude." The fifteen-year-old girl had already been training as a sales apprentice for a year.

The social worker's family care plan included health, economic, and educational
measures. First of all, the social worker insisted that the mother and the children be
examined by the tuberculosis clinic and that the children continue to be kept under
medical surveillance by the school doctor. The social worker also procured a single
bed (*Isolierbett*) to prevent the mother from infecting other family members. The
family received new bed linens. The mother was given "strengthening foods" in the
form of milk and butter. To improve the family's economic situation, "the attempt
must be made to find the man a steady job as a fitter." But above all, it was important
to exercise a "personal influence" upon the husband so as "to awaken in him a feeling of responsibility for his family, so that he no longer leaves the entire job of caring for the family to his physically so weakened wife." The educational component
of the social worker's prescription consisted of speaking with the eight-year-old boy's
schoolteacher about putting him in a day-care facility (*Hort*), a measure that appeared
to the social worker to be "urgently necessary." The social worker also intended to
ask the *Berufsamt* to find the fourteen-year-old boy a suitable apprenticeship when
he left school at Easter: "It was in the interest of the young boy and of the family that
he learn something orderly so that he did not take a dead-end job just for the money.
. . . The school doctor prescribed a rest cure so that the boy could become physically
stronger before going out to work." Above all, the social worker thought that "for
this family it is exceptionably valuable to have someone they trust . . . to whom they
can talk about all their problems. The family care social worker has won this trust,
knows all the family's strengths and weaknesses and how to strengthen their ability
to reach the desired goal."[112]

Frustration and Despair

It was not surprising that social workers registered disappointment and frustration
with their own position in the welfare administration. In 1927, Marie Baum complained that "it would be quite easy to cite numerous cases that display a naive over-
estimation of administrative work and an equally naive underestimation of social
work." Baum was particularly critical of welfare departments that "use trained and
talented female social workers just to gather information, which is no different than
if one were to give unskilled work to a trained technician or make the doctor a nurse."
Baum cited the example of a "welfare district with 40,000 inhabitants . . . that had
only one social worker, who was told by the district director to make about 250 visits each month, solely for the purpose of checking out applications for clothing, beds,

stoves, and the like," as well as other routine tasks. Under these conditions, any real social diagnosis or plan of social therapy was impossible. Baum insisted that female social workers must be accorded a vote in the meetings held to discuss cases. In this respect, Düsseldorf was exemplary: "The entire work of the district committee depends very much upon the efforts of the social worker, who presents and explains each case before it is passed on to the volunteers."[113] But in both Cologne and Stuttgart, female social workers were simply expected to provide the district committees with the facts they needed for their deliberations.[114]

It was not easy for social workers to console themselves with the belief that they had at least managed to win the trust of their clients. Official representations of social workers liked to present them as welcome visitors in poor neighborhoods.[115] But a Hamburg social worker urged her colleagues to remember that "when we social workers go into a family, we are generally not eagerly awaited guests that people are happy to see. We show up, unannounced, in the middle of situations that cannot really support the presence of a stranger."[116] Social workers were well aware that "social work is largely a matter of house visits. . . . It is the insight into family conditions that permits a precise determination of need, but getting this information is often made very difficult by the distrust with which the client responds."[117] Marie Baum warned that the social worker must proceed slowly and carefully; she cautioned against "asking too many questions, intruding too deeply into the life of the other. . . . It is better to avoid taking care of someone against their will, even though much can be said in its favor." It was clearly much easier to win the trust of (normally female) clients who had themselves approached the social worker for help; greater difficulties were created when "the welfare system intervenes on its own, to protect young people, or to prevent the spread of disease, for example." Yet the same social worker who offered advice on the health of the children might also come to remove an "endangered" child to a reform school. Baum concluded that "it was always necessary to achieve a tactful balance between the extent of welfare measures and the maintenance of the family's own sphere of power."[118]

In 1922, Elizabeth Neumann portrayed the social worker as a "bridge between the public welfare system and the people in need. . . . The female social worker must attempt to remove the mistrust that is nowadays directed at the municipal welfare system."[119] In 1930, a welfare expert still insisted that "the female social worker provides the indispensable living connection between the office and the outside world, which the most diligent office staff cannot replace. If this connection is lost, then the welfare office's work inevitably sinks into being a more or less mechanical disposal of cases."[120] But Gertrud Bäumer had to admit that social workers often found it very difficult to overcome "the obstructions that people naturally set in the path of everything connected with the authorities [*alles Obrigkeitliche*]" and the "suspicion of those in need aimed at the members of another social class."[121] The "sheer number of cases" also made it hard to establish the kind of more personal relationship with individual welfare clients that could allay their distrust. In 1924, Schwester Martha Mehl, a social worker in Backnang, northern Württemberg, complained to a south German welfare journal that recent cuts in local government personnel meant that social work is even further devalued and would eventually become no more than "mass production," a superficial activity that completely failed to get at the real essentials because of insufficient time. It is this that constantly makes it almost impossible for the female social worker to stick at her job, for she must be blind if she does not notice that the gaps of three, four, even five months between house visits [to the same client] exclude the possibility of any fruitful work. . . . The individual social worker must therefore decide whether she should renounce a profession that takes no real account of her own physical and spiritual strength [and] . . . compels her, in her dealings with individuals, to turn away from female nature and treat the people only as a mass.[122]

In 1927, Marie Baum complained that "for an occupation built upon so much idealism and, for the most part, on such good expert knowledge, it is a misfortune that during and after the war the main focus of the work has shifted to . . . the provision of [simple] economic relief to masses of the needy." The results were disastrous: "In numerous cities . . . and to some extent in the rural areas, individualized, preventive . . . welfare has sunk under the weight of material assistance, [and] the social adviser has been denigrated to the status of a simple provider of information."[123]

In Nuremberg, Hedwig Stieve confided to her diary that "we never manage to drive down to the roots. Our entire system of welfare seems to me no more than a wretched attempt to heal appearances without ever getting down to the causes ." Confronted with the "sensual concreteness" of her clients' poverty ("Today, I saw living conditions that defy description") on a daily basis, Stieve's feelings swung from guilt to disgust to despair ("This one case can speak for many, and it allows me once again to feel the powerlessness of welfare") and the desire to escape.[124] In 1927, a *Familienfürsorgerin* in Nuremberg summarized her working week as follows: "The week is at an end. What has happened that is positive? The pile of cases there on Monday has been somewhat reduced, but now there are new ones." One of her colleagues working in another district concluded, "All in all, one has the feeling at the end of the week that, despite being constantly active, one has really not done what should be done. Personally, I would like also to remark that living in the district itself has two sides: You become a good neighbor and can take care of some matters quite informally, but you never have a moment's peace, either before or after the working day, on Saturday afternoon or on Sunday."[125] Emilie Zadow insisted that "the system itself is neither good nor bad; it is what we, as human beings . . . make of it." But she, too, had to admit that "it is, after all, only a scratching around at the periphery!"[126]

From the vantage point of the Depression, even the war years could be viewed with a certain nostalgia. Bäumer claimed that the women who served in the War Welfare Agency of the National Women's Service in Berlin had enjoyed a more personal relationship with the soldiers' wives (*Kriegerfrauen*) and were not viewed as "authority" but as "service." Yet unfortunately, "the public's attitudes have gotten sharper, as the number of those in need . . . grows and the female social worker's job has more and more come to consist of checking and controlling and saying no; in other words, the functions of authority." The "connection of social service with its functions of authority" created a fundamental contradiction that constantly threatened to damage the social worker's relationships with her clients: "Both elements disrupt and diminish each other. As an instance of the structure of power, [social work] does not, in a certain sense, have enough authority; nonetheless, the authority it does have hinders its effect as a form of social help."[127]

Some commentators worried that social workers might become so troubled by "feelings of immense helplessness when confronted with mass need" that they would simply "capitulate before the masses." Helene Weber warned, for example, that

> even in the circles of social workers there has slowly slipped in a . . . tired pessimism. People suggest that welfare has "run dry." . . . The sheer flood of mass poverty in working-class circles and in the broken *Mittelstand* grows unceasingly in many urban neighborhoods and in the countryside. . . . One goes up and down many staircases and always finds the same story. . . . Broken family lives . . . endangered youth. Male and female social workers who draw up their accounts at the end of the year arrive at a sad result. Some write the word "futile" at the bottom. Others take consolation in their growing card files and document indexes. But those who look more deeply know that numbers and cards mean nothing. Today we stand before a definite bankruptcy of our human powers.[128]

Religious commentators suggested that only a "professional ethos, rooted in deepest modesty, in religious humility" could provide an effective antidote to the kind of pessimism produced by daily confrontations with "mass need." The individual social worker was admonished "to overcome pessimism through the force of their inner will." In addition to their "sense of duty," social workers needed a " true calling" that demanded for its fulfillment "that the human being is prepared to sacrifice . . . their own sense of self."[129]

CHAPTER FOUR

Becoming a Welfare Client

W̲ho became a welfare client? A description of an ordinary morning's business at a district welfare office in Cologne in 1926 introduces us to some of the types of people who tried to get help from local welfare systems;

> It is eight o'clock in the morning. The clients of the district assemble in the main waiting room of the welfare office, people of every type, every class, each gender—joined together by no other fate than that of being a welfare recipient. Here sits the former domestic servant, twenty years with the same employer, who has lost her small savings; next to her, a young worker who still has not found a job. . . . There, a formerly independent tradesman who . . . neglected his business and now, when there is so much competition, cannot keep it on its feet. Next to him, an old worker. . . . An industrial accident has made him unable to do his former work. Now, he draws a small pension, but, despite his every effort, he has not been able to find another job. . . . His pension, along with the casual labor his wife does, are not enough . . . for the family to afford more than the most meager existence.[1]

The ability to stay clear of welfare dependency was by no means a direct reflection of occupational status or social position. The inflation produced a "generalization of poverty . . . that gripped social strata that had previously not had to turn in such numbers to the welfare system."[2] After the war, being a member of the middle or lower-middle classes was no longer, as it had been before 1914, a guarantee of economic security. Welfare clients classified as small capital pensioners came from the "previously well-off layers of the *Mittelstand*" whose savings or investments had been wiped out by the inflation. Social pensioners (the chronically ill, disabled, and elderly drawing social insurance pensions that had to be supplemented by welfare) came primarily from the ranks of "artisans, workers, rural circles, and the lower-level civil servants."[3]

As late as 1927, one observer thought that "the *Mittelstand* and the working class are about to exchange their relative positions in the social structure." Yet despite the changes in the relative socioeconomic status of the middle, lower-middle, and working classes caused by the war and inflation, dependence on wage labor remained an important source of economic insecurity. In Esslingen, the largest single group of welfare clients were unskilled workers (41.7%), although there was almost an equal number of skilled factory workers.[4] In Nuremberg,

> from February 1925 onward . . . there were clear signs of increasing unemployment. The number of people out of work receiving supplemental benefits from the welfare office rose . . . from the middle of 1926; the curves for the unemployed and for the total number of welfare recipients were almost congruent. . . . In the past few years, the total number of welfare clients is almost exclusively the result of the changes in the unemployment relief and insurance systems that force people onto welfare."[5]

Between 1927 and 1932, the distribution of welfare clients changed in Germany as a whole as shown in Table 3. Individual cities and regions displayed significant differences from the national averages (see Table 4). In 1927, for example, Stuttgart had almost four times the national percentage of war victims. Düsseldorf, Cologne, and Stuttgart all had smaller contingents of social pensioners and small capital pensioners than the nation as a whole but larger proportions of general welfare clients. Nor were the distributions of welfare clients the same from one city to the next; for example, Cologne and Düsseldorf had considerably larger proportions of clients on general welfare and commensurately smaller percentages of social and small capital pensioners than Stuttgart.

In 1925, looking back over the preceding four and a half years, the Hamburg Welfare Department reported "that the people who are most closely tied to the state . . . namely, the war victims, are today far less frequently found among welfare clients than they were during the inflation. In those days, the welfare office had to give them considerable assistance because their pensions were becoming quite worthless. . . . The revaluation of their pensions . . . has now made it unnecessary for the great majority of war victims to draw regular support from the welfare system."[6] By the mid-1920s, "the increases and decreases in the numbers of welfare clients strongly reflects the ups and downs of the economy."[7] Hamburg's position as a center of international trade made its economy extremely vulnerable to the changes produced by the war. The growth in the size of other nations' merchant shipping fleets during

TABLE 3. Categories of Welfare Clients for Germany as a Whole, 1927–1932

Category	31 July 1927	31 July 1928	31 July 1929	30 June 1930	30 Sept. 1931	31 Mar. 1932
War victims	4.7%	3.8%	3.0%	2.0%	1.2%	1.0%
Small capital pensioners	21.1	20.9	19.8	16.0	10.0	7.3
Social pensioners	36.7	37.3	36.6	31.5	20.9	14.8
General		28.2	27.8	24.0	17.4	15.3
Unemployed	37.5	0.9	1.9	2.6	5.2	5.7
Welfare unemployed		8.9	10.9	24.0	45.2	55.9

Source: SJDR, 51 Jg., 1932, p. 411.

TABLE 4. Categories of Welfare Clients in 1927

Category	Düsseldorf	Cologne	Stuttgart	Germany
War victims	5.5%	1.5%	19.6%	5.1%
Small capital pensioners	2.7	7.2	10.3	19.8
Social pensioners	28.4	21.1	14.8	35.7
General	63.4	70.1	55.3	39.3

Sources: SJdS, 22 Jg., 1928, p. 126; *SJDR*, 58 Jg., 1929, p. 394.

and after the war intensified competition. Only in 1926, 1928, and 1929 did exports from the port of Hamburg exceed the amount of pre-1914 exports. The volume of imports also declined in response to the reduced postwar purchasing power of German consumers. Hamburg shipbuilding concerns were largely dependent on the big shipping companies for new contracts, with the result that even though Hamburg companies such as Blohm and Voss and the Deutsche Werft were able to procure a lot of repair and maintenance work, shipbuilders were underemployed. In 1927, for example, the Hamburg docks were using only 50 percent of their shipbuilding capacity.[8] The "permanent crisis" of Hamburg's shipbuilding industry and the continuing weakness in foreign trade made employment in these branches insecure and irregular, with the result that "both in the middle and the later years of Weimar, building and metalworkers joined with dockers and sailors in forming a large proportion of those standing in the dole queues. White-collar workers from the tertiary sector associated with the harbor and export trades also had a precarious hold on their jobs in these circumstances."[9] (See Table 5.)

Age, health, gender, and the presence or absence of family and relatives willing and able to provide support all worked to amplify or to mitigate economic vulnerability. Those between the ages of fifteen and twenty-five in 1925 were "the product of a particular peak in the birth rate." When this "superfluous" younger generation left school, they "entered a labor market that was already stagnant and oversubscribed." But after 1910, the birth rate had already begun to drop noticeably.[10] This meant that between 1925 and the end of the Republic, "a heavy decrease in the younger generations in the population pyramid" was, as Hamburg officials complained in 1932, combined with an "exceptionally strong increase of old people who were no longer able to work" and who would have to turn to the welfare system for assistance in times of need.[11]

TABLE 5. Hamburg's Welfare Clientele, 1925–1928, Absolute Numbers and Percentages

Category	1925	1926	1927	1928
War victims	220 (0.9%)	399 (1.3%)	536 (1.9%)	614 (1.9%)
Small capital pensioners	3,709 (15.5%)	3,621 (11.7%)	3,517 (12.3%)	3,158 (9.9%)
Social pensioners	6,885 (28.8%)	7,787 (25.2%)	8,609 (30.2%)	9,373 (29.7%)
General	13,054 (54.7%)	19,086 (61.8%)	15,888 (55.6%)	18,447 (58.4%)
Total	23,868	30,893	28,550	31,592

Source: SJFHH, 1928/29, p. 293.

Gender was vitally important. A study of Frankfurt drew attention to "the strong increase in the female portion of the clients, especially widows and divorced women."[12] In Hamburg, female welfare clients (62.4%) outnumbered men (37.6%) by a ratio of 1.7:1 in 1927. Women constituted 60.6 percent of general welfare clients, 59.4 percent of social pensioners, 77.5 percent of small capital pensioners, and 58.1 percent of the small group of war victims (*Kriegsopfer*). Females outnumbered men in all age groups of all categories except for the tiny numbers of *Kriegsopfer* younger than thirty. Single people made up 26.7 percent of all of Hamburg's welfare clients in 1927, while 21.5 percent were married, 7.4 percent were separated, 6.1 percent were divorced, and 38.4 percent were widowed. Widows and widowers constituted 28.9 percent of the clients receiving general support but some 51.8 percent of social pensioners and 50.8 percent of small capital pensioners.[13] In Altona, Hamburg's next-door neighbor in Prussian territory, the largest single group among the women on welfare in 1927 (45%) had no occupation at all: "Not a few were separated from their husbands, divorced, or abandoned." But female casual laborers accounted for 22 percent of the total and domestic servants for 10.9 percent.[14] Hamburg's economy, based on shipping and shipbuilding, did not offer large numbers of employment opportunities for women. Although the postwar ratio of women to men in Hamburg was even higher than in Germany as a whole, "the proportions of women working . . . were lower than the national average."[15] Although the numbers of women working had clearly increased since 1907, in 1925 women still constituted only 22.9 percent of the workforce in industry and 25.8 percent of those employed in trade and commerce.[16] The growth of the clerical/service sector did offer new opportunities but primarily for young, single women, which meant that "older women had greater difficulties finding a full-time job than elsewhere."[17]

In-migrants were also at greater risk than the native-born population. A male worker, native to the city in which he lived, who had a wife and children who also earned an income and whose relatives could provide assistance in times of need, was less likely to have to turn to the welfare authorities for support than a recently arrived, young migrant with no family or friends. A study of Esslingen found that only about 20 percent of the city's welfare clients came from the city, compared to 80 percent who were born outside.[18] In Altona, the in-migrants represented "by far the largest number of welfare clients."[19] In Frankfurt, an investigation of one particular welfare district found that "the settled population provides a much smaller contingent of the welfare recipients than the migrants."[20]

The single most important development between 1927 and 1932 was the explosion in the numbers, both absolute and relative, of the "welfare unemployed": jobless Germans who no longer had any claim to the benefits paid by the unemployment insurance system established in 1927 (*Alu*) or to "crisis relief" (*Kru*). In 1928, the welfare unemployed accounted for only 8.9 percent of all welfare clients in Germany. But by 1932, the welfare unemployed had become the largest single group (55.9%) on municipal welfare rolls. The new importance assumed by the welfare unemployed in the cities listed in Table 6 was already evident in 1930, with the exception of Stuttgart, where the proportion of war victims had actually increased since 1927.

By 1930, average daily employment on the Hamburg docks had dropped to 75 percent of what it had been in 1928, by 1931 to 64 percent, and by 1932 to only

TABLE 6. Categories of Welfare Clients, 31 December 1930

Category	Hamburg	Düsseldorf	Cologne	Stuttgart	Germany
War victims	1.8%	0.7%	2.5%	27.3%	1.8%
Small capital pensioners	5.0	4.3	6.1	9.8	12.6
Social pensioners	21.4	21.6	18.3	20.0	26.0
General	29.4	28.4	21.5	9.2	22.1
Unemployed	6.1	13.5	—	18.4	33.5
Welfare unemployed	36.4	31.6	51.7	15.2	3.9

Sources: SJdS, 27 Jg., 1932, p. 324; *SJDR*, 1932, p. 411.

49 percent. This decline in activity had an immediate effect on shipbuilding. Between 60 and 70 percent of the workforce in the Hamburg shipbuilding concerns were out of work by 1930. The biggest Hamburg shipbuilding company, Blohm and Voss, reduced its workforce from 10,700 on average in 1929 to 4,879 by the end of 1930, 2,639 by the end of 1931, and 2,449 by the end of 1932.[21] But the massive increase of the welfare unemployed in Hamburg and other German cities had been produced not only by the Depression but also by a series of emergency decrees that shifted the burden of assisting the unemployed from the national to the local governments by reducing the length of time that the jobless could draw insurance benefits and by excluding some categories, such as women and young workers, altogether. When the insurance system was established in 1927, the unemployed who qualified could expect to be supported for up to thirty-nine weeks. After Chancellor Franz von Papen's emergency decree of 14 June 1932, those out of work who were still eligible could draw insurance benefits for only six weeks. Increasingly, municipal welfare offices became the only sources of support for millions of unemployed Germans. In September 1930, 49.7 percent of the registered unemployed received insurance benefits, 15.7 percent received crisis relief, and 18.0 percent were on local welfare rolls. By September 1932, 40.1 percent were on municipal welfare, 24.1 percent on crisis relief, but only 12.1 percent were still able to draw insurance benefits.[22]

Constructing Welfare Clients

Although a variety of "objective" factors and circumstances caused some Germans to turn to the welfare system for support more commonly than others, the actual welfare clientele was produced less by these people's needs than by the decisions of welfare officials to grant the status of welfare clients to some of these applicants while denying it to many others. Certain categories of potential welfare clients were excluded a priori from consideration for normal welfare benefits: young, single people "on the tramp" around Germany in search of work, for example, or "beggars and vagabonds," who were only allowed "a night's shelter and morning coffee" in exchange for several hours of chopping wood or equivalent work. The length of stay in municipal shelters was usually limited to just a few nights. Longer stays were possible only in the *Arbeiterkolonien*, usually run by private charitable organizations, where applicants were required to do agricultural or other labor in exchange for a place to sleep, food, and a small amount of "pocket money."[23] In general, workers who were on strike or were locked out by their employers could not expect any support from the welfare office, though their wives and children might be given some help.[24]

Applicants who did not fall into any of the excluded categories could by no means be sure that they would be granted support. A study of two welfare districts in Cologne during several months in 1928 and 1929 revealed that between 45 and 65 percent of all new applications were rejected. Applications were most commonly turned down because the individual had too much income to qualify. People with earnings, often from casual labor, that exceeded the guidelines for public relief accounted for between roughly 19 percent and 35 percent of all cases rejected. Support was also refused if the applicant had relatives (including wives, parents, and children) who were legally obligated to provide support or had a claim to unemployment insurance or crisis relief, or if the petitioner could be directed immediately toward a job.[25] Welfare clients were guaranteed the right to contest welfare office decisions, but the chances of having an unfavorable ruling overturned appear not to have been very substantial; in the administrative year 1928/29, some 1,554 complaints were received by all of Berlin's welfare districts. Of these, 59 percent were rejected.[26]

"Individualisierung"

Provision 33a of the 1925 national guidelines (*Reichsgrundsätze*) guaranteed that clients admitted to "elevated welfare" (*gehobene Fürsorge*) would receive at least 25 percent more than those on the general welfare. These divisions among the welfare clientele were reinforced by differences in clients' rights to participate in welfare administration. The recognized organizational representatives of those on elevated welfare were granted advisory rights (*Mitbestimmungsrecht*) that were denied to all other welfare clients.[27] Yet even though welfare administrations were required to make distinctions between collective categories of welfare clients (such as pensioners or the unemployed), the authorities nevertheless insisted on their right to judge each individual application on its own merits and according to social workers' and welfare officials' determinations of the clients' needs. As a Düsseldorf deputy mayor put it, "a schematically determined level of support does not really help. Individualized welfare is always the right thing."[28]

This approach to popular needs assumed that although there were clearly general social and economic conditions that brought welfare clients to the welfare system, the factors with which welfare officials should be primarily concerned were personal and familial rather than social, economic, or political. Although the general, structural economic causes of poverty and distress could not be ignored, the welfare system was not designed to provide a basic safety net for all the victims of inflation, unemployment, and so on but for those who could prove that they had real "need." Its central task was to "rehabilitate" individuals and families who by their very application for public relief had proved themselves in some way deficient in the economic struggle for existence. But if the welfare office was to "remove the causes of the person's condition of need," then individualized social work, not restricted by any schematic table of benefits, was essential.[29] As an advice book prepared by the Social Democratic Arbeiterwohlfahrt to train its voluntary workers put it in the mid-1920s, "In welfare, which is concerned with the individual person, each case has to be treated with regard to its own unique character. . . . One can only provide the correct forms of help when the specific causes of the problems are known."[30]

The crisis years of the postwar inflation severely tested this fundamental principle of "individualization" (*Individualisierung*). Far too few welfare officials had to process exploding numbers of applications for assistance. In 1921, the administrative head of the Hamburg Welfare Department insisted that the standard rates must not be applied schematically "but that every applicant must be treated individually, according to his [or her] own specific needs."[31] Yet one year later, in July 1922, district welfare office directors complained that lack of personnel meant that they could not consistently engage in "orderly, individualized casework."[32] Martini agreed that "we can no longer really call this social work."[33] Looking back on the inflation years from the perspective of 1926, the Hamburg Welfare Department observed that

> the galloping inflation, which made it necessary to alter the standard rates over and over again so that they could keep pace with the devaluation of the currency, made it difficult for welfare workers to understand the importance of the standard rates. By 1923, when the currency completely collapsed, it was no longer possible to do any real social work. In the last months of 1923, the levels of support payments, which had to be changed on an almost daily basis, were decided on a completely schematic basis with no reference to individual need; clients got their money two or three times a week. . . . Welfare work was transformed into mere accounting. But the stabilization of the currency gave real social work a new and firmer foundation.[34]

The end of the inflation and the reductions in the number of clients crowding into welfare offices across Germany did make it possible to insist upon a return to *Individualisierung*. Yet a south German welfare expert complained in 1925 that although "the principle of individualized welfare is often intoned," in reality the welfare system continued to be far too schematic and bureaucratic in its practices: "The disadvantage of this schematic procedure is not only that assistance is not tailored to the needs of the individual case but that many applicants are given support without adequate investigation of their situation, and these people then burden the welfare system permanently or for long periods of time."[35] In November 1925, Hamburg welfare district directors criticized the district committees of volunteers who were granting advance payments in the amount of the standard rate to an increasing number of applicants without thoroughly investigating the client's circumstances. This was a dangerous practice because "it gave the impression that . . . support would be granted without adequate verification of need."[36] In April 1926, Hamburg welfare officials also found disturbing the "requests that were frequently made not to take certain portions of the client's income into account when determining the level of support . . . [which] would mean departing from the basic principle of individual welfare."[37]

Welfare authorities and clients gave quite different, often opposed meanings to key terms in the administrative vocabulary of the welfare system. To welfare authorities, *Individualisierung* meant their right to determine clients' needs, whereas clients and their advocates argued that individual needs were not being taken account of and that officials were acting in an arbitrary fashion or were sticking strictly to the letter, rather than the spirit, of the welfare rules and regulations. To welfare authorities, "schematization," or the construction of differentiated classes of welfare entitlements, was an evil to be avoided at all costs, because it failed to draw the all-important distinctions between individual welfare clients. But for clients, a schematic approach promised greater equity and entitlement. In 1931, an SPD critic asked whether the scales of standard rates in the individual welfare regions in Germany could not, perhaps, "be more differentiated. This is not 'schematization' but only protection against . . . arbitrary decisions, which is much worse than 'schematization.' . . . The welfare system could certainly do with more objectivity and differentiation." While some observers agreed with welfare authorities that each case required individual treatment, they warned against an excessive *Individualisierung* that completely ignored or attempted to destroy any notion of parity or "equal benefits for the same types of cases." It was simply inequitable when welfare authorities awarded "very different amounts of support for very similar cases of economic need." This made welfare practices appear arbitrary, almost "accidental" in clients' eyes.[38]

Normalization and Labeling

Local welfare agencies constructed representations of the "normal" and the "abnormal" that legitimated the satisfaction of some popular needs while ignoring or suppressing others. Welfare officials approached their clients with preconceptions and prejudices concerning normal family life and gender roles, images of certain neighborhoods within the city, and "acceptable" and "difficult" forms of individual behavior, which very much affected what they saw in their clients' homes.

"Normal" Families

Social-work practices were informed by a vision of the "normal" family that often collided with the more complex and variegated family forms and household structures in which many Germans lived after World War I. In 1932, for example, the Düsseldorf Family Care Agency attempted to remove and rehouse two families who were living in a condemned building. One of the families went without a quarrel into the emergency housing that the agency provided. But the widow H. rejected the room she was offered because, she said, it was too small for her family. Investigation revealed that the "family" included a certain Frau K., still legally married to another man but living with the widow H.'s son as the mother of his child. The outcome of this investigation cannot have been anticipated or appreciated by the widow H.'s son, by his common-law wife, or even by the widow herself: In the eyes of welfare authorities, Frau K.'s relationship did not constitute a proper marriage, and Frau K. was deemed not a member of the family. She therefore had no right to move with them into the emergency housing that had been provided, and the agency required that she be separated from her common-law husband and put into a shelter for the homeless.[39]

"Tough" Neighborhoods

Welfare authorities agreed that the Gängeviertel in central Hamburg was without doubt one of the most "difficult" and dangerous urban neighborhoods in Germany.

> The Gängeviertel in the old part of Hamburg, with its dark, crooked houses and canals . . . is well known and ill reputed. It is inhabited by a population consisting, in part, of antisocial elements and of families whose lives are completely disordered, whose household heads and members are unemployed, a population that vegetates like a dull, seething mass. Political disturbances announce themselves early here; these people, who live in a world apart, are closely tied to each other. Just a whistle and the whole alleyway is alive, another whistle and . . . the same narrow street lies empty and desolate.[40]

When a worker who had recently arrived in Hamburg applied to the welfare office for help in paying the rent of a room in the Gängeviertel, he claimed to have been told, "Yeah, that's a fine neighborhood, you won't get any money from us to live there."[41] He was advised instead to apply for a place in a homeless shelter.

The Gängeviertel was in some ways unique, but welfare authorities in most other German cities could easily name districts that they considered to be particularly "rough," "difficult," and dangerous. In 1929, for example, the head of the Düsseldorf Family Care Agency described the Oberbilk neighborhood as one of the city's more "difficult districts, although one cannot say that it is unconditionally the worst; other districts, such as the harbor area or Gerresheim, have very similar problems."[42] That same year, the Hanover welfare journal *Wohlfahrts-Woche* warned its readers that "the dark recesses of the big city too easily become hiding places for criminals and all other elements who dislike daylight. The lowest circles of prostitution move into such nooks; narrow courtyards, dark houses, stranded human beings!"[43]

"Difficult" Welfare Clients

Labels were also attached to people, collectively and individually. In 1930, one welfare client in Württemberg was described as "a malicious, treacherous, and unfair person who can no longer pull himself together and integrate himself into the social order like other people. . . . Humanity should be protected from such individuals, who constitute a serious danger. . . . [The client] sees every public agency and its personnel as his enemies."[44] Another south German welfare client was categorized as one of "those persons who avoids real work and knows all too well how to squeeze money out of the public treasury."[45] A third client in Esslingen was described as "an intriguer who does not quite bother with honor and honesty and is well known for this."[46] The complaints of a fourth client were dismissed because "he lives with the permanent delusion that he is somehow being dealt with unfairly . . . that an exception should be made for him. . . . He is known in almost every public agency."[47] Welfare officials may have sincerely believed these characterizations of their more troublesome clients, but these epithets also served a rhetorical strategy aimed at silencing the voices of welfare recipients and rejecting the validity or legitimacy of their claims and complaints. As one welfare official in Esslingen put it in 1927, "The worst thing is that we have to listen to every imaginable harsh word from the mouths of such riffraff. Instead of doing social work, we get bogged down in endless feuding."[48]

"Cash" or "Things"

Even if their applications were successful, welfare clients found that they might each be assisted in quite different ways. Welfare authorities wanted to maintain clients' ties to the market economy and to cultivate in their clients habits of self-reliance and attitudes of responsibility for their own and their family's fate. These priorities meant that welfare authorities tended to favor cash support over support in-kind. But during the postwar inflation, support in-kind became more and more widespread as it rapidly became more difficult to keep pace with the violent devaluation of money: "The quicker the worth of money sank, the more important support in-kind became for the client." In Munich, this meant that "the relief system was, to a considerable, extent 'renaturalized' [i.e., converted to payment in-kind]."[49] In 1927, the Social Democratic welfare expert Herta Kraus insisted that the return to cash payments represented a definite "step forward . . . compared to the prevalence of payment in-kind . . . which, quite understandably, expanded greatly during the inflation. This was the more practical [form of relief], but it had unpleasant effects upon the maintenance of the client's responsibility for himself [or herself]." Cash payments had a useful educational effect because the individual welfare client had to decide how "to apportion the money for household expenses."[50] But at the same time, welfare authorities feared that some welfare clients would use the money that was given them for illegitimate purposes, such as drink.

Applicants whom the welfare authorities deemed to be completely "unreliable" might well be offered *only* support in-kind; in 1931, for example, one south German welfare authority reported that "the practice maintained until now of giving unreliable clients support in-kind (flour, fats, coal) has proven quite satisfactory, and we will continue to employ it. . . . In cases in which either the husband would misuse cash support or the wife does not know how to manage household expenditures, we have preferred to give relief in-kind."[51] Another local authority reported that "if it is to be feared that the client will make improper use of cash support, the money has been paid out to the wife or to other [responsible] family members."[52] But most welfare clients lived in a "mixed welfare economy," consisting of some support in cash combined with other assistance in the form of things or services, including subsidized foodstuffs or meals at soup kitchens, milk for infants and small children, fuel for heating and cooking, clothing, eyeglasses, artificial limbs, shoe repair, health cures, as well as medical and dental treatment.[53]

Clients' Voices: Procedures for Complaints

During the German Revolution, radical demands were raised for welfare clients' councils (*Räte*), on the model of the workers' and soldiers' councils. But after 1919, the advisory boards (*Beiräte*) and complaints committees attached to the new welfare offices were the only officially recognized institutional sites at which clients were allowed to contest welfare authorities' decisions. One of the primary aims of the advisory boards was to promote "systematic cooperation between the public and private welfare agencies."[54] But delegates of various welfare clients' organizations—primarily those representing pensioners and war victims—could also claim a voice, along with the representatives of private charitable organizations, as well as the professional and the volunteer welfare staff of each district.

The representatives of clients' organizations who sat on advisory boards or other committees within the welfare system were expected to transmit their members' grievances to the authorities. In November 1927, for example, the Reichsbund der Kriegsbeschädigten, Kriegsteilnehmer, und Kriegshinterbliebenen, Bezirk Esslingen (a veterans' and "war victims'" organization) complained to local welfare authorities that "increases in the cost of living have hit war widows and the parents of war orphans especially hard because these people generally have no income from a job." The organization did not challenge the basic welfare principle of *individuelle Fürsorge* but nonetheless asked for a "special winter allowance" for several categories of war victims.[55] This advocacy of welfare clients' interests and grievances occasionally made the welfare authorities quite uncomfortable. In 1924, for example, the Hamburg Welfare Department complained that "the spokesmen for the organization of small capital pensioners are much too eager to encourage the pensioners to lodge complaints with the central welfare office."[56]

Yet the representatives of clients' organizations did not always champion the clients' causes in conflicts with welfare authorities. In March 1927, for example, the representative of the war wounded on the district welfare committee in Esslingen voted to reject an appeal against a welfare office decision submitted by Karl L., a mechanic, judged to be 50 percent incapacitated.[57] In November 1928, the same representatives supported an action taken by the district welfare office against another war invalid, Emil N. In 1926, Emil N. had charged that he had been treated in a "partisan manner" by an Esslingen welfare officer, S., who was also an official of the Reichsbund der Kriegsbeschädigten, Kriegsteilnehmer, und Kriegshinterbliebenen, Bezirk Esslingen. However, S. claimed that Emil N. was a particularly difficult client who had recently threatened S. with "all manner of unclear intimations. . . . Three times I had to ask him to leave the room, but he simply kept on insulting me, so that I had to warn him that he would be escorted out."[58] In June 1927, S. was the target of another complaint, this time from another war veterans' organization, the Landesverband des Deutschen Reichskriegerbunds Kyffhäuser. It alleged that, for "purely agitational purposes," S. had quoted from official internal welfare files dealing with one of their members at a public meeting of the war wounded held in Winnenden on 15 May.[59]

If welfare clients could not gain satisfaction from the advisory board, they could turn to the complaints committees. But critics charged that in Prussia, at least, the procedures governing oversight of the welfare bureaucracy's practices and the provisions that allowed clients to lodge complaints were unsatisfactory. Düsseldorf Social Democrats thought it particularly unfair that welfare authorities sat in judgment on their own decisions. In 1925, the Düsseldorf SPD newspaper suggested that a system of advisory committees composed of welfare clients, like those already at work in the agency responsible for assisting the war wounded, should be developed in all the branches of the welfare system.[60] From a more politically conservative point of view, Marie Elisabeth Lüders, a Reichstag deputy, voiced similar criticisms in 1929: "The welfare authorities . . . more or less act as the judges in their own cases . . . because they are the ones who provide the appeals board with the documents that serve as the basis for a decision, even though [the welfare authorities] are, so to speak, the 'accused.'" Lüders charged that reviewing and responding to a complaint could take several months, sometimes even years, involving "repeated requests for information that is already known, combined with the constant refusal to acknowledge . . . well-known facts and the reckoning of support that is blatantly at odds with the national guidelines."[61]

In September 1921, the president of the Hamburg Welfare Department recommended that a "provisional complaints committee" be formed that would include one district head of volunteers and one volunteer welfare worker from each welfare district in the city.[62] In February 1922, the welfare district offices were reminded that they were obligated to accept complaints from people who had applied for public assistance and that it was important "to avoid sending people from one office to the next unnecessarily."[63] However, a female official insisted in March 1925 that the current procedures for processing complaints were too slow. It often took several months for a complaint to be submitted first to the advisory board, then passed on to the complaints committee. Some petitions filed in October of the previous year had only just arrived at the welfare district office at the beginning of March 1925.[64] The fact that "investigations . . . often take many weeks" only to end in a refusal of the application "without one word of explanation" was beginning to damage the "good reputation of the welfare office and the atmosphere of trust among the population."[65] From the complaints of petitioners "one can hear just how embittered they are that the welfare office does not think it necessary to give them any sort of explanation, after having laid out every detail of their troubles." President Martini requested that "in suitable cases, when the applicant is not a well-known troublemaker," the welfare district offices should "carefully and tactfully explain the reasons for the refusal."[66] People who intervened to get help from the welfare office on behalf of someone else hardly every received news of the outcome; they, too, should be given an answer, but only if they "were not trying to make trouble and were not motivated by some desire for revenge."[67] By August 1926, the number of complaints had increased considerably. A male welfare official suggested that the welfare district offices should try harder to resolve these cases before they were sent to the central office. The welfare district directors claimed, however, that welfare clients believed it was easier to get their applications approved at the central office and threatened to go directly there.[68] Earlier that year, some welfare clients, impatient with the long delays, had even sent letters to Martini's private address.[69] Berlin welfare authorities reported that complaints filed by welfare clients had risen from 986 in 1926/27 to 1,666 in 1927/28. But they claimed that the great majority of these complaints were unfounded and were simply "a considerable extra burden for the administrations concerned."[70] The percentage of cases decided in the plaintiff's favor remained low, not exceeding 2.7 percent.

The Language of Complaint

Counternarratives I: Clients' Appeals to Welfare Authorities

The normal administration of welfare made it extremely difficult for the client's own story to be heard. Case files were, in effect, miniature biographies, written with the aim of explaining why a particular welfare client had come to the attention of the welfare authorities and offering an assessment of their character and a representation of the causes of their neediness. Clients might provide the raw material for the story of their own lives in combination with the testimony provided by neighbors, friends, relatives or employers, but it was the social worker and the welfare official who constructed an officially acceptable narrative from these details. Although there was certainly an attempt to present case files as the products of scientific analysis, welfare authorities were necessarily interested in controlling the narrative, the specific details it included and deemed significant, along with the interpretation of these details and their causal interrelationships. They were certainly not prepared to allow the subjects of these stories to construct their own storylines. Welfare authorities' desire to control the case-file narrative extended even to the official record of welfare clients' complaints. Instead of presenting the original letters and statements filed by welfare clients in their appeals against official decisions, welfare offices were frequently content to paraphrase or to present merely a summary or abstract that retained few traces of welfare clients' own voices.[71]

The language used by the clients in the letters that have been preserved was often constrained by the need to present arguments that would appear legitimate in the eyes of welfare authorities (usually not the officials whose decisions were being contested but those higher up who had the power to review decisions made at a lower level of the welfare administration). It was all too easy to be simply dismissed as a "chronic complainer" (*Querulant*). But within certain rather narrow limits there was still room for welfare clients to contest the official representations of their characters and the official narratives of their lives and problems. If the story that the welfare client tried to tell proved to be more accurate, more compelling than the case file, then decisions made at a lower level of the welfare administration might be overturned or revised by a higher authority.

Clients' attempts to assert their identities and interests were often directed against each other as well as against welfare officials. Greg Egighian observes that in the early years of the Weimar Republic,

> as suffering became universalized, it simultaneously became, like currency, a medium of social relations within the social state. Individuals judged themselves and were judged by each other with reference to the kinds and degrees of distress that marked their lives. . . . The Germany of the early 1920s was overrun with victims, wave upon wave of individuals who represented themselves as having sacrificed their health or their husbands or their limbs or their income for a state, which, they now believed, wanted to abandon them. The fact that the social state had only limited resources at its disposal added another element to this environment—competition. . . . Once inflation set in . . . it was necessary to prove that one's needs were more pressing, one's predicament was more dire, one's sacrifice was far greater than anyone else's.[72]

The claim to be the innocent victims of the war and inflation allowed both social pensioners and small capital pensioners to amass "a kind of cultural capital in the Weimar social state" that they were able to "invest" in the construction of national organizations that campaigned against abuses and lobbied for special treatment.[73] Pensioners "approached the state, which they held morally responsible for their fate . . . with a basic sense of being entitled to some form of restitution."[74] Although armed with new legal rights and even the promises, however vague, set out in the Weimar constitution, other welfare clients—the mother of an illegitimate child, the abandoned wife, the family evicted for not paying their rent, the unemployed male worker whose insurance benefits had run out—could not draw upon a fund of cultural capital like that available to the pensioner. Unable to exert the same organized, collective influence upon the welfare system, these other welfare clients devised more informal and individualized tactics to assert their identities and pursue their interests.

Pensioners frequently saw themselves as victims of the welfare bureaucracy, as well as of recent German history. Welfare officials were not always willing to grant pensioners easy access to the benefits of elevated welfare that they felt they deserved. With varying degrees of success, pensioners tried to contest negative decisions. In 1929, for example, the small capital pensioner Pauline H. of Oberteuringen sent a letter to the Württemberg Interior Ministry complaining about a recent decision by the district welfare authority in Tettnang. Her appeal was based largely on her claim that the "facts" used by the welfare authorities to determine what assistance she would receive were actually "gross misunderstandings and mistakes." First, the decision took no account of a doctors' judgment that she was "completely incapable of working" as a result of having lost one eye. The ruling had also maintained that Pauline H. could be supported by her relatives, but she insisted that "exactly the opposite is true: My sister and brother-in-law and the heirs to their property have vehemently contested this obligation and refused to recognize a legal responsibility in any form whatsoever." Indeed, the idea that her relatives would or could take care of her was "at best a pious wish and an absolutely groundless assumption . . . [made] with the obvious purpose of trying to save the public treasury . . . some [money]. The position taken by the local authorities has not sprung from any sense of justice, social feeling, or Christian belief, and it grossly violates any decent morality." Pauline H. also displayed some familiarity with welfare regulations by claiming that the decision of the Tettnang authorities contravened the Interior Ministry's guidelines, "issued on 27 July 1928" for the implementation of the National and Federal State Welfare Decree. Placing her "absolute trust in the highest authorities in the state" of Württemberg, she demanded that "the facts . . . laid before you be assessed and evaluated as corresponding to the harsh reality." Only the higher level of support that she had originally requested from the Tettnang welfare union on 8 September 1928 would, she argued, conform to "the intentions of the socially conscious lawmakers."[75] The authorities in Tettnang responded by charging that Pauline H. was receiving "free board and lodging and perhaps even a little money" from her relatives, even though "attached to her complaint is a declaration from her relatives that they have refused [this assistance]." While agreeing to review the case, the authorities also decided to cut off Pauline H.'s support from the next month onward on the grounds that "she did not meet the requirements for the administrative status of a small capital pensioner" because the "stipulations of paragraph 14 of the National Welfare Decree of 4 December 1924 had not been met." Pauline H. was, the authorities insisted, "still able, despite her physical infirmities, to earn an essential portion of her livelihood, as many others in her condition must do. Moreover, there is, in her case, no real condition of need, according to the provisions of the Kleinrentnergesetz, because she does receive free food and lodging and also has revaluation assets of about 1,600 marks."[76] But in August 1929, the Interior Ministry ruled in favor of Pauline H., instructing the Tettnang authorities to give her 30 marks (instead of the 60 marks she had originally requested) per month on the grounds that she was, indeed, "unable to work" and also that "any voluntary contributions to support made by a third party in the form of food should not be taken into account in the present case."[77]

The case of Friedrich K., a social pensioner in Esslingen, born on 30 December 1867, followed a very different trajectory. In April 1926, Friedrich K. filed a complaint with the Württemberg Ministry of State (Staatsministerium) against the welfare office in Esslingen, stating that

> because of severe stomach problems, I am unable to work for the foreseeable future. . . . I need to eat heartily. Eggs, butter. But can't afford this. Have filed request for supplemental assistance of 40 marks per month. Up to now, no success. Sent a bill from Herr S., master baker in Esslingen for bread, flour, 11 marks, which I can't pay. My son, Albert, has also been out of work for three months. . . . I should be granted the 40 marks per month. Now I can't pay my rent. Will the high state government decide on my case? I stand here, without means, no property, no assets. I want to hear news. That my petition has been taken account of? Hurry.[78]

However, the Ministry of State returned this letter to the Esslingen welfare office, which then informed Friedrich K. that "any further attempt would be totally useless, and we ask you to stop making requests because they will simply find their way into the wastepaper basket."[79] Despite this warning, Friedrich K. did not relent, and his perseverance paid off, at least temporarily. In March 1927, Friedrich K. was granted a back payment of 289 marks to cover the period from February to May 1926.[80] Yet despite repeated requests from the welfare authorities, Friedrich K. did not submit evidence of the way he had spent this back payment. When it became clear that Friedrich K. had used some of this money to settle debts incurred after he had received the back payment, the Esslingen welfare authorities decided to cut him off for a period of three months. This time, Friederich K. carried his appeals all the way up to the RAM in Berlin, which, however, told him that it could not intervene and that the Württemberg Economics Ministry was "alone competent. It made the final decision."[81] Even this response did not stop Friedrich K. In June 1930, reporting on the latest of Friedrich K.'s apparently endless appeals, the welfare office in Esslingen complained that "Friedrich K. is really a harmless person but certainly a well-known grumbler who always wants something other than what the welfare authorities give him."[82] In November 1933, the Esslingen district welfare authority complained that although they now routinely threw his letters away, "it appears to give K. particular pleasure to burden as many agencies as possible with his petitions." In October, he even sent an appeal to the president of the Weimar Republic.[83] As late as May 1941, K. was still firing off letters of complaint. On 10 May 1941, a government official described K. as a "pathological complainer, well known to the authorities." His records showed that he had been filing complaints since 1923. Seventy-four years old in 1941, Friedrich K. was " described by the Esslingen county authority . . . as the biggest troublemaker of all the local welfare recipients and as . . . the terror of the Post Office sickness fund." The official concluded his report with the remark that "if K. was not an old social pensioner, moved by his abnormal disposition to make complaints, considerably sharper measures would, in my opinion, have to be taken."[84]

Counternarratives II: Letters to the Hamburger Volkszeitung

If welfare clients could not get what they considered to be an adequate hearing within the official channels provided by the welfare system, they might take their stories to city council members or to the local press, especially the Communist newspapers. In September 1930, for example, Frau Alexandra Maria H. wrote to the Oberbürgermeister of Cologne, Konrad Adenauer, warning that "before I accept the help in my sad situation already offered to me by the local press, I turn, once again with a report, and a complaint, to you, with the request that you take on my case so as to hasten a resolution, as my complaint has already sat for four weeks at the [welfare] office without being answered."[85]

In Hamburg, an active "worker correspondents" movement, which used a network of ordinary workers (non-Communist as well as Communist) to report on everyday life in the factories and the neighborhoods, generated a stream of letters to the Communist newspaper that detailed ordinary workers' experiences with the welfare system.[86] The *Volkszeitung* tried to show how the individual stories sent to it by readers should be read from a class perspective. But readers' letters could not simply be subordinated to the Communists' political agenda. Indeed, the editor's comments often stood awkwardly at odds with the texts themselves in which the readers usually presented melodramatic accounts of their experiences of daily life in the Weimar welfare system.[87] Patrice Petro has observed that "melodrama was an important representational mode in Weimar"[88] and that the popularity of melodrama can be explained by its ability to address

> the real, the ordinary, and the private life. . . . Yet, in contrast to realism, melodrama seeks excessively to expose and draw out the implications of everyday existence. . . . It is a melodramatic convention to use characters as types so as to stage a drama of ethical conflict and violent contrast. . . . The very unambiguous social and psychic function assigned to characters in melodrama . . . allows them to be instantly recognizable to spectators and deployed in such a way as "to reveal the essential conflicts at work-moments of symbolic conflict which fully articulate the terms of the drama."[89]

As a genre, melodrama appears to have been particularly appealing to women.[90] Many readers' letters were, indeed, sent by women or described their dilemmas and grievances. Yet even when men were the authors of these letters, they often assumed what might be described as the female voice and the female subject position in a melodramatic narrative.

Despite differences in the concrete details of the individual stories, the letters published in the communist newspaper were preoccupied with at least one of two major themes: time and dignity.

Time

Official time ran much slower than clients' time. Readers expressed enormous frustration and anger at the amount of time that they were forced to wait in endless lines in welfare offices, or that they spent while being sent, often with no apparent purpose, from one welfare agency to another or while having to wait for weeks, months, and sometimes even years before hearing the outcome of an appeal against an unfavorable decision. However, welfare officials insisted that proper casework took time and that the welfare system was overburdened and understaffed. For the most desperate clients, time was vital. Without immediate assistance from the welfare office, they would go hungry or homeless right away. But even for those who still had some resources, the time spent waiting for help was important. It became a symbol of the indignities to which clients felt they were routinely subjected by welfare authorities. Being made to wait was a humiliation; it showed that welfare officials felt their clients' time was simply worthless. In 1923, for example, an unemployed worker complained that when he had gone to his local welfare office to file a request for milk, he had been forced to wait in line for hours: "The unemployed have time. But it is time that things be put in order here. The entire welfare office is . . . badly built. . . . Downstairs, only thirty people can sit, hundreds must stand. Upstairs, five men can sit, everyone else, about fifty people, have to stand waiting for hours. If you come at 9:00 A.M. or even later, you have to wait two to three hours. Conditions are frightful. It can't go on like this."[91] In 1927, another reader told the story of his workmate who had no new linen for his newly born ninth child, even though he had made an application seven weeks before the infant's birth. The friend had waited for several hours in line in order to submit the application, then had returned to the district office on several different occasions, trying, vainly, to speak with the female director of social work. Now the welfare district office claimed to have no idea where his application was: "This is a big waste of time. It is already a shameful feeling when you are forced by economic need to go and beg at the welfare office. For what reason do you have then to wait for several hours until it's your turn?" Were the officials really so overloaded with work or "does this torture serve the purpose of rubbing the client's nose in his own misery?"[92]

Dignity/Humiliation

Readers' letters also claimed that the ways in which welfare officers spoke to and treated clients assaulted their dignity and their rights. So, for example, a story published in 1923 described what had allegedly happened to the wife of a "comrade" who had been "disciplined" (i.e., fired) by the Blohm and Voss shipyards when she went to the volunteer worker, Claus, who lived in the Geibelstrasse, to ask for welfare: "He asked me . . . whether I wasn't ashamed to turn to the welfare system. Didn't I have any idea why my husband had been let go? He was probably ashamed to tell me that he was one of the rowdies that the shipyards could be happy they were now rid of. Now things could return to being more peaceful." After being subjected to a "long sermon," the woman received 1 million (inflated) marks for ten days for herself and her two children; the volunteer worker claimed that he was being generous because, in fact, the guidelines called for only 60,000 marks.[93]

In 1928, a man filed a complaint with the welfare office, against the *Bezirkspfleger* (district volunteer worker), Kruger. On the fifteenth of the month, the plaintiff had visited Kruger on behalf of his "bride Frl. H. Kl., who was confined to bed . . . but who needed a countersignature on a chit for money." The woman had already revealed to the man that she had been treated like a common prostitute by Kruger. When the man arrived, "he was treated completely like a beggar." Even though he knew that she was sick, Kruger demanded that Frl. Kl. appear in person. Kruger then exclaimed, " That's just dandy! . . . She claims to be sick. Now we are going to get her!" The man drew Kruger's attention to the doctor's note stating that Frl. Kl. must remain in bed, but Kruger then began to interrogate the man about his relationship to Frl. Kl. "I told him that she was my bride. Herr Kruger began to equivocate and re-sisted signing the promissory note. . . . I did finally get a signature, but it was made clear that I should disappear and never come back to his shop; I want to say that my bride is not the only one to have been treated this way by Herr Kruger. Complaints about him can be heard everywhere in Borgfelde."[94]

From these individual examples, readers were meant to conclude that such harsh and unfeeling *Pfleger* had no real understanding of the new social rights granted Germans by the Weimar constitution, nor of the real causes of poverty and unem-ployment. But rather than using these examples to drive home the political point that the system should be overthrown, the *Volkszeitung* was often content to conclude that volunteers such as these should either reform their ways or resign their posi-tions. As the *Volkszeitung* put it in 1923, "Someone has to put an end to this disgust-ing behavior and to tell [the volunteer worker in question] that he should either change his attitude or bid good-bye to the welfare system."[95]

Readers' letters were equally unsparing in their criticism of some of the profes-sional female social workers and male officials in the district welfare offices. In 1926, a reader's letter, which the *Volkszeitung* introduced with the title "A Wooden Crate as a Child's Bed," offered a harsh portrait of a female Hamburg social worker. The man who sent in the letter was unemployed and could not afford to buy a baby's basket for the child his wife was soon to deliver. He applied to the welfare office for help, and after a couple of days a "sister" came to visit the family. But the man claimed that instead of providing the help he needed, the social worker "offered her opinion that I had known for nine long months that a baby was on the way and I should have bought everything it would need when I still had work." The man insisted that he had, indeed, procured all that the child would require, except for a basket. But the social worker then allegedly suggested that he buy a small, wooden crate in which the baby could sleep; she claimed "that this works very well. My wife was also dealt with in the rudest manner when she filed the application."[96]

Other readers' letters drew attention to the treatment clients received at the hands of certain male officials in the district welfare offices. In 1927, a reader described the case of an "old man, aged fifty-five," tailor by profession, who had suffered from epilepsy for the past twenty-eight years. For the previous sixteen weeks, the old man had been receiving welfare assistance. But when he went on 22 March to the district welfare office to pick up his money, the official told him "without beating around the bush, 'You are getting no more [relief].'" When the old man asked for the rea-son, the official told him only, "You heard me, you are getting no more. Get out of here, fast!" The old man pleaded with the official to give him the money and finally began to cry. When the official threatened to summon the police, the old man sat down in a chair and declared, "Call a cop if you want, I am staying. What am I supposed to live on? I need some money, or at least give me a coupon for foodstuffs, so that I can still my hunger." This only made the welfare official more furious. When the policeman finally arrived, the old man asked to be allowed to finish weeping before he was taken out, so that he would not have to appear on the street in tears. The policeman was willing, but the official insisted that the old man leave immediately.[97]

Melodrama "was a remarkably malleable cultural form, containing a variety of potential meanings and scenarios," but it definitely "set limitations on what could be said."[98] With the publication of their letters, welfare clients were able to satisfy some important needs, foremost of which was the chance to tell their own stories. Melodramatic representation also allowed welfare clients to inflict rhetorical revenge upon welfare officials, who were often cited openly by name.[99] By being held up to public ridicule, specific welfare officials could perhaps be made to feel personally exposed and vulnerable to popular outrage, which might even take the form of physical violence.[100] The personal might become political when the welfare officers who had allegedly engaged in abuses of their office could be identified as members or supporters of the SPD. The *Volkszeitung* claimed in 1929, for instance, that "the Social Democrats, who are to be found everywhere in the district welfare offices, torment the poor women who are welfare clients."[101] Yet the fixation of these little melodramas upon specific villains and victims could very easily lead to the conclusion that the problems of the Weimar welfare state were located in the personalities of the people who administered it rather than in the system itself—clearly not the message that the Communists intended to convey.

"Self-Help"

In 1928, a high-ranking female official emphasized that the Hamburg welfare office and, indeed, the Weimar welfare system in general "had the task of making themselves superfluous for the individual client by providing the necessary help but at the same time exerting an educational influence that helps the individual to become once again economically independent and that strengthens his will to help himself."[102] However, it is clear that at least some clients had discovered rather different ways to engage in self-help.

Fraud and Falsifying Documents

At least some welfare clients were able, knowingly or unknowingly, to exploit the gaps in welfare regulations and the welfare office's inability to double-check the details of all applications. In March 1924, for example, a meeting of Hamburg district welfare officers considered the case of Erna H., against whom charges had been brought for drawing both unemployment benefits and welfare support at the same time over a period of several months. However, this case fell apart because the welfare authorities could not show that the woman had been warned beforehand that she was not allowed to receive both forms of support.[103] The district welfare office directors insisted that this was not an isolated case and suggested that the appropriate regulations be printed in a form that could be handed to clients when they applied for assistance. In February 1926, a Hamburg welfare official reported that the state prosecutor was having difficulty proving intent to defraud in several cases and suggested that the questionnaire that each applicant was required to complete should be amended to make it absolutely clear that "all forms of income must be declared [and] that . . . the applicant is obliged to report any change in his economic situation, even without being asked to do so."[104] In July 1928, another Hamburg official reported that charges had been brought against a married woman who received support and had failed to declare income; the woman was acquitted because it was not clear that she had completely understood all the forms she had been required to sign.[105]

Other welfare clients actively subverted the welfare bureaucracy's "monopoly of administration" by altering or counterfeiting official records. In November 1926, a Hamburg official reported the case of a swindler who managed within a short period of time to get a total of 100 marks from several different district offices by presenting falsified documents. The district offices were encouraged to give out only small amounts of money upon the first application because it was not always possible to phone the central archive to see if the applicant already had a file.[106] In January 1928, the Labor Office asked that the district welfare offices put their own stamps on the cards of the unemployed as soon as they received support so as to prevent swindling.[107] In November 1928, it was reported that "a very disorderly couple with a bad reputation" had been given rent support money but were told they would get more only when they could submit proof that they had in fact paid their landlord. The couple then submitted a fake rent receipt. Charges were brought against them for fraud and falsification of documents.[108] In the summer of 1929, welfare district office directors discussed the falsification of the books used to record earnings and social insurance contributions with the intent of swindling the unemployment insurance office or the welfare office: "In one case, the unemployed person used two different . . . books at the same time; he bought the second one somewhere for a mark." Again, this appears not to have been an isolated instance. In fact, a district welfare office director claimed that

> counterfeiting has already assumed startling dimensions. But in any case, it is possible to buy [such] a book at the revenue office [*Finanzamt*] as a replacement for one that is [supposedly] lost for a mere 50 pfennig. The official stamps of the Labor Office and the Welfare Department have also been copied. The owner of the counterfeit stamps makes a good little income out of it. [The] book is not infrequently tucked inside a special cover, upon which is noted the name of the person seeking support, although the . . . book actually belongs to someone else from whom it has been borrowed just to draw the money.

To hinder the falsification of these books, the Labor Office began to punch them with a variety of different holes.[109]

Denunciations

Welfare authorities encouraged clients to inform on one another about undeclared income, mistreatment of children, and other abuses. In 1926, for example, a municipal officer in Düsseldorf told a city council meeting that it is obvious that the apparatus of the welfare system has become so monstrously huge . . . that, here and there, it is possible for some people who do not really deserve support to pass unnoticed. . . . Let me take this opportunity . . . to ask . . . that cases be reported to the welfare office . . . in which it is known that support is being drawn illegitimately and that the recipient could really manage to support themselves.[110]

In 1929, the Communist newspaper in Cologne claimed that welfare officials in the Rhineland metropolis could rely upon "an enormous number of spies, all over the city, drawn from the ranks of the welfare recipients themselves . . . who did not shrink back from the basest and most mendacious denunciations. Anonymous letters provide additional material to hang the poor from the gallows of hunger and to save money at the expense of the poorest of the poor."[111] In 1929, Karl B., for example, learned that the support he had been receiving from a Cologne welfare office was to be reduced because one of his neighbors had informed the welfare office that he had concealed income:

Karl B. was summoned here yesterday. He is twenty-six years old, has been unemployed for some time, and his crisis relief benefits have just recently come to an end. He presently receives 34 marks welfare relief each month, from which he must also support his sixty-year-old mother. A little while ago, a rent supplement was added to his support payments, which increased the amount to 58 marks. However, we have now reduced his benefits because someone in the neighborhood reported that his mother brings in money with her sewing.[112]

Some denunciations were motivated by sincere moral outrage and the desire to bring abuses to the attention of the welfare authorities. In 1927, a south German welfare official reported that the neighbors of a war invalid who owned a small piece of land that he had totally neglected "complain that such people are . . . supported from public funds. . . . It would have been easy for him to have grown the potatoes and vegetables he needed for the winter. His own friends came to the district welfare authority to make this statement."[113] But denunciations were also colored by the conflicts, passions, hatreds, and feuds generated by the frictions of everyday life in families, neighborhoods, tenement blocks, and courtyards. In 1931, for example, a client, Frau S., appeared in a Düsseldorf welfare office to give evidence supporting her petition that her children be taken away from their father. Frau S.'s husband had left her and was now with a Frau W., whom Frau S. described in her testimony as a woman "who drinks and smokes a lot, so that the youngest child is endangered by living there." It was not clear whether Frau W.'s drinking and smoking were as bad as the fact that the child was made to work selling Communist newspapers until as late as 9.30 P.M. Undoubtedly, all these charges weighed heavily. Even though she herself had earlier given up her children to her husband when he left her because she claimed she could not support them, Frau S. clearly knew how to present her case in a way that would sound the appropriate alarms in the minds of the authorities.[114] Welfare authorities sometimes found, however, that the information they received from relatives, friends, and neighbors could be completely useless: "A considerable number of . . . denunciations . . . are unfounded and can be traced back to neighbors' and relatives' desires for revenge."[115]

"Mis-"Appropriation

Some welfare clients appear to have found ways to (mis)appropriate material objects that circulated in the welfare system economy, although it is difficult, perhaps even impossible, to disentangle the reality of these self-help practices from the ideological image of the "welfare cheat," held up as a symbol of the welfare state's failures by its political opponents. In 1926, for example, a Hamburg welfare official recommended that the men working on public job sites not be given tools by the welfare office because they sometimes quit work after a few days and then sold the tools.[116] Other clients found ways to convert relief in-kind into cash. In 1927, a DNVP member of the Hamburg parliament claimed that in neighboring Geesthacht,

> on 12 February 1927, a welfare recipient purchased fifteen *Pfund* [pounds of foodstuffs] at the welfare office for his household. Ten minutes later, he returned and bought . . . ten pounds of lentils for a third party, who was not a welfare client. These cost 28 pfennig per pound on the open market, but only 20 pfennig at the welfare office. On 13 February, an inhabitant of Geesthacht got an unemployed single man . . . [to] buy ten pounds of sugar at 27 pfennig per pound (about 38 pfennig on the open market). . . . Indeed, sugar has allegedly been purchased in large quantities, often two or three times the amount normally used by a single family in a week. The same appears to be true of coal. . . . Welfare recipients are alleged to be drawing, on average, 140 to 150 *Zentner* [hundred weight] of coal yearly, much of which is sold to people not entitled to welfare.[117]

Street Trading

Some welfare clients also turned to street trading, or other semilegal and illegal market or nonmarket economic activities to supplement the support they received from the welfare office.[118] In some instances, the welfare office knew about the welfare clients' street trading and even encouraged it. In 1925, for example, Hamburg district welfare offices actually asked the police to issue permits for street trading to some of the people who had applied for relief; but by June, the police were refusing to issue more permits.[119] In July 1929, the police warned once again that they could grant no more permits for street trading and that the district welfare offices should not support or encourage attempts by clients to get permits.[120] Yet it was clear that welfare clients continued to engage in unlicensed and illegal street trading. In 1929, for example, the Association of German Flower Shop Owners complained to the Hamburg police and welfare authorities about "the ever-widening trade in flowers on street corners. It was especially to be lamented that the Welfare Department gave the money to these traders to pay for their licenses and their stock of goods (this was unfair competition). . . . In certain cases, the turnover of flower businesses has declined so much that the proprietors themselves must apply for welfare." The Welfare Department insisted, however, that as a rule it did not give welfare clients money to pay for the license and that it certainly did not regard "street trading in flowers . . . as an adequate source of income; the department had no 'welfare interest' in the sale of flowers on the street without a fixed location." Indeed, the welfare authorities claimed that the clients who engaged in street trading frequently appeared to be "completely physically capable of work" but were attempting to make some money without reporting it to either the Labor Office or the Welfare Department.[121]

CHAPTER FIVE

Pensioners in the Welfare System

A primary goal of the new social insurance system introduced before World War I was to relieve the overburdened poor law of the large numbers of elderly and disabled who constituted the great majority of its dependents.[1] Disability and old-age pensions would enable workers who could no longer earn their own living to stay off the poor law. By offering manual workers greater security in old age, the framers of this new benefit also intended to undercut the political appeals of Social Democracy. But not all manual workers were covered by the new pensions; industrial workers received the greatest attention from the Bismarckian and Wilhelmine states because they were thought to be the most vulnerable to socialist appeals. Agricultural workers, employees in small workshops, and, in particular, women were either neglected altogether or received only second-class benefits. And even those who received pensions could not always survive without additional help from the poor law. Thus, social insurance had failed even before 1914 to achieve its two primary aims. The burden of the elderly and infirm upon the poor law was somewhat reduced, but thousands of aged or disabled workers were not spared the indignity of being forced to apply for poor relief. And, of course, the growth of Social Democracy was not halted. Between 1914 and 1924, the depreciation of the German mark severely weakened the social insurance system's ability to provide benefits. Costs outran previous contributions, and the numbers of claimants increased as the war took its toll on the health of the nation. By 1923, it was clear that neither contributions nor benefits could keep pace with inflation: "The pensions . . . earned through years—or decades—of paying contributions were so worthless that many did not even bother to collect them at the post office."[2] For more and more social pensioners ("the chronically ill, the disabled, and elderly pensioners from German social insurance, along with their surviving dependents"), "[municipal] welfare took the place of their pensions, which eventually were significant only insofar as they formed the basis for the legal claim to public assistance."[3]

The other major category of pensioners who found themselves in receipt of welfare support was quite different from the mainly working-class social pensioner. Although a "heterogeneous group" in terms of their "levels of education, previous lives, and activities," the *Kleinrentner* "or, as contemporaries . . . put it, 'small capital pensioners' [Kleinkapitalrentner]" were very conscious of having previously belonged to the middle or lower-middle classes.[4] As *Der Rentner*, the publication of the small capital pensioners' major organization, put it: "Before the war . . . there was no so-called pensioner question—many were actually in the position to make donations that helped other people in hard times. Others supported the arts and the sciences, still others worked as unpaid volunteers for the common good. . . . Those who are today pensioners were once pillars of public life and prominent upholders of civilization." The small capital pensioners felt that through no fault of their own they had been reduced to poverty by the lost war and by the ravages of the German inflation. They expected some form of reparation from the state for their losses: "It is . . . a debt of honor that the state should compensate [pensioners] for the losses they have suffered. . . . Pensioners are not seeking alms. They advance only justified demands. The Reich is . . . morally and legally obligated adequately to care for its creditors, who gave it their last pfennig."[5]

Pensioners rapidly formed organizations to represent their interests. Social pensioners became an organized political force toward the end of World War I, forming a number of local associations to press their claims with government authorities. In July 1920, these groups came together to form the Central Association of German Invalids and Widows (Zentralverband der Invaliden und Witwen Deutschlands), which became the largest organization of disabled pensioners in the Weimar Republic.[6] The Zentralverband campaigned for the improvement of pension benefits so as to make it less necessary for indigent, aged workers to go to the welfare authorities for supplementary support (*Sozialrentnerfürsorge*). But years of experience with the political economy of aging in imperial Germany, along with their more immediate observation of the political and financial hindrances to a significant expansion of state pension benefits, convinced the leaders of the Zentralverband that they must campaign energetically for improvements in the welfare system at the same time as they continued to push for better social insurance provisions. Although the Zentralverband declared its political neutrality, it had strong connections to both the majority and the independent Social Democrats. The major national organization of small capital pensioners was, by contrast, politically conservative, as were smaller local groups such as the Bund Bayerischer Kleinrentner, formed in July 1920 in Munich.[7] The small capital pensioners pinned their hopes on a "revalorization law" that would allow them a measure of restitution of their savings and investments. When it became apparent that no such law was likely to emerge from the labyrinth of Weimar party politics, the small capital pensioners demanded that the Weimar Republic provide them with state pensions, similar to those granted the other war victims.[8] The political struggles over the fate of the small capital pensioners dragged on until the very end of the Weimar Republic. In the meantime, many of these dispossessed members of the *Mittelstand* were forced, against their wills and with considerable injury to their self-esteem, to petition local welfare agencies for public assistance.

Local welfare authorities, however, appeared to be less interested in the problems of Germany's 4 million social pensioners and 280,000 small capital pensioners than in those of children and young people.[9] The "problem of youth" had already begun to attract attention before World War I.[10] But the social disruptions caused by the war and the Revolution, pronatalist concerns fueled by wartime population losses, and the apparent affinity of youth for political radicalism all combined to make children and young people major targets of welfare professionals and social policy experts in the Weimar Republic.[11] In 1925, Senator Neumann in Hamburg explained, for example, that "the shock dealt to the health of the nation by the war and the postwar years [required] the Welfare Department to view health care and special measures for children and young people as one of its most significant fields of work."[12] This focus on youth intensified during the Depression. In December 1931, for example, the director of a Hamburg welfare office observed that "at the present time, when there are endless numbers of young unemployed to take care of, it is no longer possible to give special consideration to old people, especially as, with advancing age, needs become diminished in every respect."[13] A meeting of north-west German welfare offices decided that so far as the institutional care of the elderly and infirm was concerned, "the present economic crisis requires that expenditures be reduced to an absolutely necessary minimum. The extent of provision in homes for the aged must be made consonant with the reduced living standards of wide circles of the working population, especially as the inmates of institutions do not have to worry about their economic survival."[14] Indeed, by 1931 the care of the elderly had become such a low priority for Hamburg welfare authorities that they now gave out "a 'meat-wolf' [a meat grinder], which costs only about 3.95 marks" to pensioners who really needed false teeth.[15] There were good reasons, then, why both social pensioners and small capital pensioners should feel that in the Weimar welfare system they were viewed as "more or less worthless persons."[16]

Pensioners and the Local State

In the early 1920s, invalids' organizations, as well as federal, state, and insurance officials, pressured municipal administrations to set up special relief programs for social pensioners.[17] In 1920, an emergency law created the basis for a separate *Sozial-rentnerfürsorge* to which the Reich contributed 80 percent of the necessary funds. The *Deutsche Invaliden Zeitung* (DIZ), mouthpiece of the Zentralverband, took this step as a "most striking indication that the poor law was a totally inadequate institution, to which the social pensioners could not be handed over."[18] But the director of the Hamburg Welfare Department insisted that creating special categories for each group of people receiving welfare support was impossible and would contravene the fundamental principles upon which the department was built.[19] Like most other German cities, Hamburg preferred "not to create special institutions for each new group of clients . . . but rather, to expand the poor law as a whole and to raise it to a higher level." But in December 1921, a new national law (Gesetz über Notstandsmassnahmen für Rentner der Invaliden- und Angestelltenversicherung) made "special welfare"

(*Sonderfürsorge*) for social pensioners binding. The municipalities were now required to give social pensioners assistance that would bring their annual income up to a specified level, initially 3,000 marks. The Reich would continue to provide 80 percent of the necessary funds, the municipalities the remaining 20 percent.

German cities felt that the Reich should be primarily responsible for the "small capital pensioners because . . . the national government, not . . . the federal states or the local governments . . . had to assume responsibility for the lost war and the inflation." But the municipalities were forced to wait until February 1923, when a national law laid the foundations for *Kleinrentnerfürsorge*. In the meantime, local authorities experimented with a variety of special arrangements for small capital pensioners.[20] These measures included subsidized foodstuffs, loans and other financial aid, tax concessions, life annuities, and the construction of municipal homes for the aged. In Düsseldorf, the Welfare Department set up a special office that

> is primarily an agency for information and mediation and works closely with the local League of Small Capital Pensioners. . . . From case to case, the municipal welfare office may provide support . . . [but] special emphasis is placed upon letting the League give the money to the pensioners . . . because they generally want to have as little as possible to do with the poor law. The city welfare agency has repeatedly learned that pensioners much prefer being provided with a suitable form of employment to being given monetary relief. . . . In cooperation with the Rentnerbund, a workshop for fine-quality handwork has been set up, which is to be commissioned by the larger private companies.

A 1923 Reich law expanded the circle of potentially eligible applicants to include "needy, old persons, incapable of work, who had made, or for whom a third party had made, provision for the future and would not have been forced to turn to the welfare system had it not been for the inflation." In Munich, the numbers of applicants increased from 2,000 in February 1923 to 6,000 by the year's end.[21] In October 1923, the Hamburg Welfare Department assisted some 3,500 small capital pensioners; by January 1924, that number had risen to 5,108.[22] As inflation spiraled out of control, grants of food, clothing, shoes and boots for the winter, medical treatment, and prosthetic and orthopedic aids became more important than the increasingly worthless money payments.[23] In January 1923, for example, the Hamburg Welfare Department wrote Josephine Kreplin at the Eilbeck local branch of the German Rentnerbund, recommending that some of its members who had asked about getting help with their gas bills should apply to their district welfare office, "where they will receive tactful treatment." The Eilbeck Rentnerbund local wrote back in August 1923, complaining that in the period from 18/19 July to 15/16 August, "just two loaves of bread per week for a married couple [cost] 135,000 marks." But a single pensioner got only 90,000 marks and a married couple 170,000 marks. The price of the gas used for cooking, lighting, and washing had also risen to the point where it constituted "a mountain that . . . crushes not only the small capital pensioner but also all of the people of little means."[24]

Local welfare authorities found it difficult to deal with these new clients because "the small capital pensioner did not fit any of the images of the needy client in the heads of welfare officials."[25] The *Kleinrentner* resented the conditions under which they received support, especially the means test and the intrusion of social workers into their "bourgeois privacy."[26] In 1922, a local official in Wasseralfingen, northern Württemberg, claimed that "the people want nothing from the poor law; they would rather freeze and starve."[27] Düsseldorf poor-law authorities reported that "the 'new poor' from the *Mittelstand* . . . shun the path to the poor-law guardians (*Quartierpflegern*), who seem . . . to show no understanding for their circumstances."[28] In a letter sent to Oberbürgermeister Konrad Adenauer in 1923, the former "manufacturer, now unemployed," Fritz K. in Cologne expressed his outrage at the way he had recently been treated by local welfare authorities:

> I . . . have been totally ruined by the Reich . . . because I worked honorably and did not speculate with foreign currency! My aunt . . . now in her seventy-third year of life, who is well known to your blessed wife, was once well-off but has been made poor by the Reich. When the condition of the national economy forced me to close down my chocolate and confectionery factory, my aunt registered as a small capital pensioner and began to draw support. But how badly people are treated there, much worse than a beggar, and once these people were the backbone of the nation! At the office on Breitenstrasse 78 . . . there sits a personnel who have no idea of real misery!!!!! They snap at the clients, saying such things as "What! Are you still here? Wait outside until you are called," etc. It is really a scandal. . . . Many women who have to draw support leave the office in tears, asking, "Do we deserve such bad treatment?" . . . A Frau D., Deutz, Arnoldstrasse 10, after being subjected to just such an experience, declared that she intended to give all the money back.[29]

Hamburg welfare office directors were warned in 1922 that "the complaints about bad treatment of the pensioners in the district offices just will not subside. The personnel must be more obliging toward the pensioners and must attempt to adjust to their mentalities." The welfare districts were encouraged to schedule special office hours just for the "small capital pensioners."[30] But in March 1924, a Hamburg welfare official reported that "many of the ladies active in caring for the small capital pensioners have asked that [they] not have to wait for unnecessarily long periods of time. . . . Some . . . especially the women, would rather do without welfare and slowly perish than have to wait so long at the welfare office."[31] The welfare volunteers were sometimes reluctant to raise levels of support because they "let themselves be deceived by the external appearance of prosperity." One Hamburg welfare official insisted that cases could not be decided on the basis of the clothes or furniture that the small capital pensioner still owned, but another cautioned against giving the impression that the *Kleinrentner* were receiving special treatment.[32]

Private welfare organizations tried to spare needy small capital pensioners the indignity of turning to poor relief. In January 1921, "women in Düsseldorf came together to form a Welfare Committee for the Support of Small Capital, Social, and [other] Pensioners." This committee became the Düsseldorf local of the German Rentnerbund, chaired by Oberbürgermeister Marx, with an office in the Rhineland Women's Club, where every member of the Rentnerbund could go for advice and help.[33] In Munich in 1921, the Catholic Women's Association founded an organization that distributed foodstuffs donated by the rural population, gave advice on selling off "articles of value," and tried to obtain socially appropriate employment for the mainly female small capital pensioners. In the winter of 1922/23, the Caritasverband opened four shelters where needy persons from the *Mittelstand* could get food, stay warm, and perform some work for wages.[34] The umbrella organization for private charities in Württemberg set up workshops in both Stuttgart and the countryside for the "many older women of the *Mittelstand* who used to live on the return on their assets but are now forced to work, yet find no employment in the normal economy. . . . With typical feminine, Swabian industriousness, they make some goods on order and sell the rest at markets and bazaars."[35] To protect needy members of the *Mittelstand* who had to sell some of their possessions from being cheated by "dealers and profiteers with no conscience. . . . [Women's organizations] in Stuttgart and other Württemberg localities began to arrange such sales [with prospective buyers]" in 1922.[36] In Hamburg, two private organizations delivered cooked meals directly to the homes of small capital pensioners, provided several hundred places at the lunch tables of volunteers, and sold foodstuffs at reduced prices.[37]

With the National Welfare Decree of April 1924, needy social pensioners and small capital pensioners became the permanent responsibilities of the municipal welfare offices.[38] Pensioners were predictably outraged. The decree eliminated separate, special welfare programs for social and small capital pensioners, although it did require local welfare offices to treat these pensioners as privileged categories of welfare clients enjoying the benefits of elevated welfare. Yet pensioners feared that the planned consolidation of "social welfare . . . with the poor law in federal state welfare unions" would be used "to imprint the stamp of the poor law on social welfare so as to scare people away from laying claim to their rights and thereby to reduce expenditure." To a speaker at a protest meeting in Esslingen in April 1924, the decree seemed merely a maneuver at pensioners' expense "to shift the responsibility, which, in the first instance, the Reich should assume, onto the federal states and local government authorities. . . . This measure is theft of the rights of those sections of the population that the Reich itself . . . has made dependent upon welfare."[39]

After 1924, the Reich continued to funnel considerable amounts of tax revenue into local welfare measures for social and small capital pensioners and often attempted to use its financial leverage to pressure for better treatment of pensioners by local authorities. Local authorities, however, found themselves under great fiscal pressure to be less than generous with the pensioners who applied for relief.[40] But more than money was at issue. Welfare administrations stubbornly resisted all pressures coming from the elderly themselves or from the national government to establish pensioners as a collective category of welfare clients possessing general rights to a certain level of support and definite standards of treatment. Instead of the collective principles embodied in the idea of the elevated welfare that had been promised to the social and small capital pensioners by the 1924 decree, local welfare authorities insisted on their right to judge each individual application on its own merits (*Individualisierung*). In the mid-1920s, pensioners complained repeatedly that some local authorities refused to provide any basic guidelines on levels of support. This was particularly important to those on elevated welfare because, according to Reich specifications, they were to receive at least 25 percent more than ordinary welfare recipients.[41] But even where definite guidelines for levels of support had in fact been issued, these often provided no more than a broad and general framework within which each case was still to be decided individually on its own merits and according to welfare officials' determinations of the needs of their clients. The pensioners' orga-nizations were well aware of the consequences for those social and small capital pensioners who were forced into the arms of local welfare authorities. In 1925, for example, the *DIZ* remarked that "poverty thus becomes a pure hell and going to the poor law is as degrading as going to jail. . . . The signs on the offices . . . have been painted over. . . . It is no longer called the poor-law office but rather the welfare office. [Yet] this name change is often the most important, sometimes the only, transformation."[42]

Until the Depression, the central state seemed to offer the main hope to pension-ers for an improvement of their situation. The small capital pensioners insisted that the Reich must take over the administration of support for the elderly, whereas the social pensioners concentrated more on attempting to reform local practices with the help of pressure from the central state. The National Labor Ministry (RAM) repeat-edly insisted on adherence to its interpretations of the various provisions for elevated welfare laid out in the 1924 decree and its subsequent revisions. But local authorities ignored, evaded, or outright refused to comply with the directives sent from Berlin.

Throughout the 1920s, the *DIZ* published a stream of horror stories detailing the abuses engaged in by local welfare authorities. In 1929, for example, readers learned that the city council of Kamenz had warned elderly women on welfare that they would have to work if they wanted to continue to draw public assistance.

> A few weeks ago, it sent the following letter to some welfare recipients, among them two old women, aged sixty-eight and seventy-two. . . . "In accordance with paragraph 19 of the National Welfare Decree, continuation of your support . . . [will] be contin-gent upon the performance of work that 'contributes to the common good.' In other words, you must work for the assistance you receive. . . . You are required to report tomorrow morning . . . to the municipal director of gardens . . . in Kamenz. . . . There you will be given light work. If you do not show up for work, you will no longer re-ceive support."[43]

But the authorities in Kamenz might easily have taken lessons from their counter-parts in Follmersdorf (Bavaria)[44] where "a large contingent of those seeking help are now made . . . to depend upon alms; instead of being given adequate public assis-tance they get licenses to beg in the streets or are sent from one house to the next for their meals."[45]

Social pensioners found it particularly unfair that each time the Reich made an improvement in the level of pension benefits they received, the local authorities attempted to deduct this amount from the welfare assistance they had already granted, even though this practice clearly contravened the welfare guidelines issued in De-cember 1924.[46]

The Responsibilities of Relatives

Local welfare authorities commonly attempted to retrieve or reduce their expendi-tures by insisting on the responsibilities of relatives to contribute to the support of elderly or disabled kin. This was a legally prescribed obligation, set out in both the

1924 National Welfare Decree and in the earlier civil code (1900). But the application of these provisions varied from time to time and from one locality to another. In
1921, for example, welfare authorities in Hamburg conceded "that relatives are seldom in a position to contribute to support, so that we should probably stop trying to
press such claims."[47] In 1929, a regional welfare office in south Germany made it
clear that it would be unacceptable to make relatives help if it could not be shown
that they could actually afford to support needy kin.[48] But in 1925, another south
German welfare authority insisted that it was increasingly necessary to take strong
action against the relatives of those drawing public relief: "Recently, the number of
cases has increased, in which children do not support their aged parents, even when
they are able. . . . In addition to forcing relatives to pay, the [district administration]
regularly also puts them in jail; often the base mentality of these miscreants makes a
mere fine useless."[49] Local welfare authorities assumed that women had a natural
obligation to care for elderly relatives, regardless of any other burdens on their time
and energies. Women who dared contest these responsibilities risked severe reper-
cussions. In 1931, for example, a woman teacher in Hamburg was actually fired
because she had resisted local welfare authorities' attempts to make her assume responsibility for her aged parents.[50]

Welfare professionals argued that a decline in familial feeling was a major cause
of poverty in old age: "The reason why [the welfare system] has to assume far greater
responsibility than in the years before the war is to be found not only in the old people
themselves but lies to no small degree . . . in the egoistic and materialistic attitudes
of our time and, not least, in the absence within the family of a sense of responsibility, a spirit of sacrifice, and a readiness to take care of . . . old people."[51] Consequently,
welfare officers felt they must use every opportunity to remind relatives of their moral
responsibilities. In 1922, just a year after the Hamburg Welfare Department had
admitted that the chances of retrieving money from relatives were remote, it nevertheless decided not to abandon attempts to recover support from relatives "because
it was important to remind relatives of their duties, a reminder which might help to
deter people from seeking public assistance."[52]

Welfare authorities' shrill insistence on the responsibilities of relatives caused
unwelcome intrusions into family relationships and family economies. In 1923,
Hamburg welfare offices were told to monitor all changes in the financial fortunes
of relatives, especially those living with their parents; had a son or a daughter who
was earlier unemployed found work or, if already working, begun to bring more
money into the household? Had the family perhaps recently taken in a boarder? If
so, then the children could be made to bear more of the burden of supporting elderly
or disabled parents.[53] Although admitting that each case was different, Hamburg
welfare authorities concluded in 1924 that "as a general rule, an unmarried son, earning at least 20 marks per week, should be able to give something to his old mother,
and, for ethical reasons, attempts should be made to hold him to this obligation."
The director of the welfare office, Martini, wanted to be even more specific, suggesting that relatives not living together in the same household must contribute four
hours' wages per week, while those living together with elderly parents would be
asked for six hours' wages.[54] That same year, the Hamburg welfare offices started
holding special office hours to which they summoned relatives for a discussion of

their family obligations. The hours were held at the unusual time of 5:00–7:00 P.M. on Fridays

> to save the people summoned a loss of wages but at the same time because Friday is payday. As soon as possible after the welfare office becomes involved, attempts are made to get the relatives to pay up. . . . Discussions are held with them during office hours, and when possible a contribution is taken from them on the spot. The receipt of further contributions is closely monitored, and relatives are warned by letter if they get behind.[55]

After the onset of the Depression, welfare offices took an extremely hard line with regard to the responsibilities of relatives. Under intense fiscal pressure after 1929, local authorities began to insist that a broader circle of relatives should provide aid. Sometimes, even relatives who were not required by law to maintain their elderly or disabled kin were made liable for support because they were thought to be "morally responsible." In 1929, for example, a welfare office in Altona cut off a seventy-two-year-old worker who had been drawing public relief for many years because "he lives with a widowed sister. A detailed inspection . . . revealed that the sister and her daughter who has a child and lives in the same household, have a joint income of 637 marks per month. Support for the old man was stopped immediately on the grounds that, although the relatives he lived with had no legal obligation to assist him, there was, nonetheless, a moral responsibility."[56]

Even if children had no income and were themselves drawing unemployment benefits or welfare relief, the mere fact of cohabitation could be regarded as a benefit that disqualified an elderly parent from relief. In 1930, the regional welfare authorities in Besigheim, north Württemberg, refused a request for support made by social pensioner Christian A., a former night watchman, because "he lives with his married son, Alfons, and only has to pay 10 marks toward the total monthly rent of 21 marks; in addition, he is able to live much more cheaply in the shared household with his son than he would if he and his wife had to maintain their own household. To be sure, the son is unemployed at the moment and draws *Alu* in the amount of 18 marks from the Labor Office in Ludwigsburg."[57] In April 1931, a female social pensioner, Sophie H., complained to the Economics Ministry in Stuttgart because she had been refused assistance by the local welfare authorities in Esslingen. The woman stated:

> I live with my daughter and I require nursing care. As a recompense for my food and lodging, I can offer only my disability pension of 31 marks 95 pfennig. But my married daughter's own income is small, her husband has been unemployed for some time, they have many expenses . . . and cannot cover the costs of my upkeep from the sum of my disability pension alone. . . . From time to time, I am bedridden and could not maintain my own household nor can I help in my daughter's home. I politely request that the exalted Ministry of Economics in Stuttgart help me to obtain a social pension.

The regional welfare committee claimed, however, that Sophie H. was still able to do a lot of housework by herself and that her married daughter should have been able to find paid employment. Consequently, the family did not need public assistance. The Economics Ministry supported the local welfare authorities' rejection of Sophie H.'s petition for support.[58] The complaint of another social pensioner, Wilhelm B., was refused on the grounds that there is no serious condition of need when the daughter's income is taken into account. The daughter's claim that she gives up no part of her earnings at home does not appear credible. If the daughter had really not contributed money to the household, the father, who has a violent disposition, would long since have thrown his daughter out. . . . Account has been taken . . . of the fact that the daughter eats her midday meal in the factory canteen, but this still means that the income that can be assessed is 104 marks, which exceeds the relevant standard rate for welfare support of only 80 marks. The list of necessary expenditures submitted has been artificially inflated.[59]

Finally, there was the unfortunate Rosa S. of Weingarten, who had been receiving 24 marks a month as a small capital pensioner for some years. In March 1929, her support was suspended because a recent investigation of her circumstances had aroused suspicion that she was being paid, or at the very least was being given free room and board, in return for keeping house for her nephew S., with whom she had lived since 1927. To make sure that "the support granted does not serve to allow . . . S. to save himself the cost of a reasonable wage," the welfare authorities in Ulm made Rosa S. submit to a medical examination to determine whether she was physically capable of performing waged work. Rosa S. suffered from "hardening of the arteries with high blood pressure and incipient weakness of the heart muscles," but the welfare doctor still concluded that "S.'s claims that she is unable to work appear somewhat exaggerated. . . . At most, one should reckon with a 50 percent loss of the ability to work."[60] On the basis of this assessment, the local welfare authorities restored support to Rosa S. but reduced the amount from 24 marks to 15 marks. They also refused to pay Rosa S.'s recent medical bills, arguing that if "she put her labor power at the disposal of [her nephew] S. free of charge, then he should certainly pay for the doctor and medication."[61]

If pensioners possessed furniture, savings, rights to compensation for their losses in the inflation, or any other financial reserves, they might be required to sign over all or part of these assets to local welfare authorities as a condition of receiving public relief. Despite repeated warnings from RAM as well as from the social and welfare ministries of their own federal states, local welfare authorities continued to employ this tactic.[62] But this meant that sons, daughters, and even other more distant relatives were often drawn into conflict with local welfare authorities.[63] One south German welfare agency described the difficulties it had experienced attempting to recover money from the estates of deceased pensioners it had previously supported; if it did not act quickly enough, it was likely to discover that the relatives had already stripped the dead person's household of all its valuables.[64]

The pensioner's organizations acknowledged that individual families were obliged to support their elderly and disabled members if they could. But they resisted local authorities' rather one-sided interpretation of family duty. In 1928, a *DIZ* report from Bavaria claimed that "calling upon relatives who are liable often causes great hardship. . . . The family's own existence must be secure before it can be asked to support relatives."[65] The Rentnerbund also registered disapproval of state intrusion into family relationships. In 1927, *Der Rentner* complained that

this obligation for support, with its sad consequences, is one of the worst developments of recent years. Its practical implementation has had a demoralizing effect upon broad circles of the population. . . . Damage has been done not only to the pensioners themselves but also to the members of the most diverse occupations. . . . Every leader of a local organization of the German Rentnerbund knows of the sad cases, which often generate open animosities between the different family members and lead to court proceedings and the complete disintegration of the family.[66]

The *DIZ* criticized the practice of making more distant kin responsible for the support of their relatives, and it called upon relatives to reject the local welfare authorities' right to "constantly stick their noses into the family relationships of those entitled to welfare."[67] The Zentralverband also insisted that the community had a greater responsibility to its elderly and disabled members than many local authorities and welfare professionals were prepared to accept. In 1926, for example, the *DIZ* declared that "of course the individual is responsible for caring for himself and his family in the first instance; but is not the *Volk* also a large family? People gladly talk about *Volksgemeinschaft*. But when that means duties for them personally, then it is not so pleasant—what a nice *Volksgemeinschaft!*"[68]

Mitbestimmung and Local Politics

Pensioners expected national political parties as well as the central government to pressure local authorities to respect the spirit as well as the letter of the regulations governing the administration of elevated welfare. But pensioners also wanted to participate directly in the everyday administration of the welfare system by acquiring a *Mitbestimmungsrecht* similar to that already exercised by the war wounded. As the *DIZ* put it in 1925, "those entitled to welfare have the right to demand that they can adequately participate in the decision making that affects their affairs."[69] Local government authorities stubbornly resisted this demand because they believed it would infringe upon their own rights to self-administration. Revisions of the National Welfare Decree did eventually provide for a limited degree of *Mitbestimmung*. But until the end of the Weimar Republic, the pensioners' organizations continued to demand that their *Mitbestimmungsrecht* be expanded and, in particular, that they be given a real vote on decisions taken by welfare committees in place of the largely advisory role that they were generally allowed to play.[70]

Faced with intense resistance to their direct involvement in the administration of welfare, pensioners' organizations began to tell their members that they must become active in local as well as national politics. In November 1929, during important municipal elections in Prussia and some other German states, the *DIZ* argued that

> we cannot agree when we are told: You are represented in the welfare commission, where you can express your opinions and have an effect upon the shape of municipal welfare policy. . . . Welfare commissions are to a considerable extent institutions that only make recommendations to the city council; that body makes all the important and fundamental decisions. Thus, we must attempt to gain influence over the city councils. . . . We should . . . give our support to those parties who have shown that they are real advocates of our interests in the city councils.[71]

Pensioners' organizations also registered their grievances in extraparliamentary politics. The Zentralverband demonstrated in the streets of Berlin in 1925 against the "reforms" that brought the social pensioners under the administration of local welfare authorities.[72] During the Depression, protest meetings, demonstrations, and marches became even more common. In 1930, when Berlin municipal authorities decided to reduce public assistance, more than 2,000 people attended a protest meeting organized by the Zentralverband.[73] At a smaller protest meeting organized by the Zentralverband in Esslingen, near Stuttgart, in May 1931, there were over 350 pensioners present who were described as being "incensed and unsettled by the economies that the welfare recipients in the city of Esslingen would confront."[74] The Zentralverband warned that further reductions of support to pensioners could lead to "a discharge of pent-up deprivation."[75]

Like their working-class counterparts, the middle and lower-middle-class pensioners on welfare had many reasons to campaign for the reform of local welfare practices. Under political pressure from the Rentnerbund and from the bourgeois political parties, the national governments of the Weimar Republic and in particular the RAM repeatedly attempted to ensure that the small capital pensioners would receive the full benefit of elevated welfare. The provisions of the 1924 National Welfare Decree made it clear that small capital pensioners who applied for public assistance should not be made to sell off any property, investments, or furniture and other household items that they still might possess. Nor were local authorities generally to be allowed to demand that the assets still possessed by small capital pensioners would have to be made over to the welfare office as a guarantee of future repayment. But the municipal and local governments upon whom the bulk of the administration of the new *Kleinrentnerfürsorge* was imposed by the Reich after 1924 repeatedly infringed Reich directives concerning the special treatment of the small capital pensioners. In 1931, for example, the Volksrechtspartei in Stuttgart challenged a decision of the district welfare authority in Laupheim, north Württemberg. The case involved the fifty-six-year-old Anna S.:

> Since 1928—after she was robbed by inflation of a fortune of 20,000 marks—she has received *Kleinrentner* assistance of 50 marks per month, from which she must pay 15 marks rent for a very simple room. When she was granted support, she was required to sign over to the Welfare Department all her assets eligible for revaluation, consisting of state bonds, war loans, and three savings books—a total value of 1,500 marks. . . . A complaint was unsuccessful. . . . In a letter, her brother quite rightly remarks that the small capital pensioners are treated better in other districts and that the treatment she received does not conform to the intent of the Württemberg Interior Ministry's decree.[76]

In another case, a Frl. Gertrud S., born in 1882, lodged a complaint in Stuttgart against the local welfare union in 1931 because it demanded a mortgage on land she and her sisters had inherited as a guarantee of eventual repayment for all of the support she had received since 5 September 1922.[77]

The Depression gave local welfare authorities their long-awaited political opportunity simply to dismantle the elevated welfare that burdened their finances and contradicted their belief that welfare must be distributed on an individual case-by-case basis of proven need rather than as a schematic or guaranteed collective right.[78] From the beginning of the Depression, "the molelike work of undermining elevated welfare was relentless. First, the Association for Private and Public Welfare wanted to unsettle the foundations, then the Städtetag [association of municipal governments] so that elevated welfare could be made to disappear."[79] The Depression also created a political context in which local governments could roll back even the limited advances in the direction of a *Mitbestimmungsrecht* made by the pensioners' organizations since 1924. In 1930, for example, the *DIZ* reported that the Bavarian Landtag had abolished the pensioners' right to be represented on the local welfare committees and boards.[80] In the politically charged atmosphere of the early 1930s, it would be much easier to push through cutbacks in welfare support to the elderly and even to wage a broader offensive against the continued existence of elevated welfare if welfare administrators did not have to answer directly to irate pensioners' representatives. In Hamburg, where it proved impossible for political reasons simply to eliminate the *Mitbestimmungsrecht* altogether, attempts were made to ensure that the most radical voices would be excluded from participation.[81] Ironically, the new ally of the local welfare authorities was now the national state. The "presidential dictatorship" was much less sensitive than other Weimar governments to public opinion and political pressure from the pensioners themselves.

Had the pensioners been organizationally and politically united, they might have done more to reform the Weimar welfare system. As the *DIZ* put it in 1930, "the fight to develop the welfare system would have been easier if all the organizations formed by the welfare clients would pull together rather than promote the differentiation of treatment accorded by the welfare authorities."[82] The most obvious and significant division followed class lines. The small capital pensioners certainly shared many of the social pensioners' grievances against the Weimar welfare system: the pressure on relatives to contribute to the support of impoverished elderly kin and the deductions or disqualifications that resulted from working or taking in boarders, for example. Indeed, small capital pensioners sometimes described themselves as if they were the middle-class counterparts of the more working-class social pensioners. In 1924, for example, *Der Rentner* claimed that small capital pensioners were "the work veterans of the free professions."[83] But the middle- and lower-middle-class *Kleinrentner* who applied for welfare assistance really had a very different mentality than that of the mainly working-class *Sozialrentner*. The small capital pensioners expected compensation for their losses (*Entschädigung*) not "welfare." They were much more intent than the social pensioners on releasing themselves completely from the clutches of welfare authorities: "Escape the welfare system [*Heraus aus der Fürsorge*]" became their rallying cry:

> Revalorization will not bring us very much, despite all the hopes attached to it. . . . What remains for the pensioner to do? . . . Only one thing: We must . . . make new recruits to our organization, and we must stand solidly . . . behind our national leaders. . . . There is still much important work to be done . . . [such as] getting the national government to resume administration of welfare for pensioners or, better still, abolition of welfare and the maintenance of pensioners by a national government pension scheme.[84]

This insistence on escaping the grips of the welfare system altogether did not prevent the small capital pensioners from campaigning for improvements of the welfare system. But they refused to form a common front with the social pensioners, preferring instead to pressure for their own distinct status within elevated welfare and for their own special privileges and benefits, separate and apart from the *Sozialrentner*. The Zentralverband, the Social Democratic party, and even the Communist party made some overtures to the small capital pensioners, but the Zentralverband also threw itself vigorously into the competitive struggle for advantage within the welfare system.[85] Each time it appeared that some concession made to the small capital pensioners had been withheld from the social pensioners, the Zentralverband attacked not only the state and the welfare system but also the "small capital pensioners" themselves. This jockeying for positions of relative advantage within the welfare system quickly eroded any possibility of creating a united front against the state and the welfare authorities.[86]

Political, ideological, and even religious disagreements added to these difficulties. Both the Rentnerbund and the Zentralverband claimed they had no formal affiliation with any party in the Reichstag. But their political sympathies were obvious and quite opposed to one another. The Zentralverband was undeniably a working-class organization, firmly situated in the Social Democratic political orbit. The Rentnerbund, on the other hand, had very little sympathy with the politics of the left and normally found its political allies on the center-right of the Weimar political spectrum, among the politicians of the DDP, DVP, Catholic Center party, and DNVP. As they progressively became disappointed with their political options among the bourgeois parties, some small capital pensioners may have turned to the Nazi movement.[87]

But the social pensioners were themselves by no means politically united. The Zentralverband advertised the fact that it had Communist as well as SPD leaders. But the KPD saw the Zentralverband as a front for the "social-fascist" Social Democrats who had betrayed the real interests of the German working class. The Communists formed their own pensioners' organization, the Internationaler Bund der Opfer des Krieges und der Arbeit (IB), which waged a constant guerrilla campaign against the Zentralverband.[88] The Communists launched newspaper attacks against the Zentralverband leadership, disrupted Zentralverband meetings, and in general made every effort to encourage Zentralverband members to leave their organization and join the IB.[89] When August Karsten visited starkly proletarian Hamborn in 1928, he was shouted down by Communists who told Zentralverband members in the mining town that "Karsten is an enemy of the workers!"[90] And that same year, Communists also disrupted Zentralverband meetings in Stuttgart, Heidenheim (Württemberg), and Mannheim.[91] The KPD organized its own demonstrations against welfare cuts and attempted to mobilize pensioners. In 1929, for example,

> in Dresden, with the support of the agitprop group Red Rockets, a public meeting was staged in which an oppositional stance was taken . . . to the cuts in the social budget of the city of Dresden. The committee of the unemployed is very active; the IB has had 20,000 flyers produced for Dresden alone, which it distributes at the post office when the pensioners come to get their pensions.[92]

The IB also helped individual welfare clients who wanted to submit their complaints to the official grievance review.[93] And the KPD publicized the grievances of the elderly and disabled in local town council meetings. Communists submitted petitions to the Reichstag, the Landtag, and local municipal councils for very significant increases in welfare payments. But the *DIZ* saw these petitions, like everything else the KPD did, as nothing more than propagandistic gestures, meant only to serve the partisan aims of the KPD, not the real interests of the pensioners themselves.[94]

In Hamburg, which was governed by the SPD in coalition with the bourgeois parties, local welfare authorities were particularly proud of the model municipal homes for the elderly they had built.[95] And Hamburg welfare officials had also attempted to enlarge and improve the facilities of the existing local *Versorgungsheime*, where some of the poorest among the city's aged were housed.[96] But the Communist critics of the Hamburg welfare system claimed that conditions in Hamburg's homes for the elderly were so appalling that old people might well prefer to take their own lives rather than to be institutionalized. Melodramatic descriptions of the suicides of desperate old people became a stock-in-trade of KPD newspaper reporting. In 1932, for example, a *Volkszeitung* reporter visited the home of an old worker, formerly a member of the SPD, who claimed that his welfare support had been reduced because he had left the party; the old man told his visitor (in Plattdeutsch), "If I had gas in my apartment, I would have turned on the tap long ago."[97]

The Communists tried to convince aged and disabled workers of the hollowness of Social Democratic claims that "the social institutions of the Republic are already an installment of socialism." Spokesmen for the radical right, however, claimed that the "social republic" had gone much too far in its provision of social benefits for the elderly and infirm. The Nazis in particular claimed that the millions of elderly Germans receiving state welfare were a drain on state finances and an intolerable burden upon the younger, still productive members of German society. In 1930, for example, a National Socialist told the Baden *Landtag*: "It is . . . not right that millions of marks are extracted from the general public for the cripples, the infirm, and the incurable, while . . . tens of thousands of healthy people have to put a bullet in their heads because of economic distress. It is not right that healthy lives, healthy occupational groups must restrict their birth rate because of economic distress while the welfare system . . . allows the sick to increase."[98] A similar but more gruesome statement of the Nazi position on the elderly was made in a postcard sent to a Zentralverband member in 1931:

> You . . . are one of those who stuffs your belly at the state's expense. . . . We demand that you commit suicide as soon as possible. Save us the work and the bullets in the coming months, dig your own grave. Your are devouring the state. If you unnecessary people don't get rid of yourselves, then we are soon going to have to slaughter [*abschlachten*] you ourselves. Because we National Socialists are coming and we don't want any unemployed and pensioners. In the Third Reich, we can only use strong and healthy people. Everyone else has to disappear, if not voluntarily, then with violence! Make this clear to your local branch organization. Naturally, family members have to disappear as well, insofar as the women or the children are not in service or working in factories. Only people who perform productive work can live in the Third Reich. Everyone else has to go if the state is to be made healthy again.[99]

In addition to the two radical extremes of Weimar politics, the Communists and the Nazis, the Zentralverband also had to contend with a Catholic organization, the Bund christlicher Arbeitsinvaliden (League of Christian Work Invalids), which had a strong regional base in Bavaria. In 1930, the *DIZ* remarked that a few years ago, when the League of Christian Work Invalids was founded, we made it clear that this was not an attempt to protect the interests of the disabled . . . but rather to . . . splinter the organizations of the work invalids. This opinion has been more and more strengthened by the ceaseless, inflammatory articles that the Christian invalids' paper has written against us. They call us socialists and Communists . . . and think this somehow shows that we do nothing for the invalids of labor.[100]

But the Zentralverband's difficulties with Catholicism were by no means limited to its Bavarian stronghold. That same year, the *DIZ* complained about the behavior of a Catholic priest in Ober-Ursel, a small community in Saxony. In one of his weekly sermons from the pulpit, the priest "announced that in Ober-Ursel a branch of the Zentralverband . . . had been formed and demanded, quite categorically, that the men and women who had joined it must resign. . . . Whoever needed advice and information was told to go to the Christian workers' secretary in Ober-Ursel."[101]

The Zentralverband's relations with other sections of the Social Democratic labor movement could sometimes also be problematic. In 1922, for example, trade union representatives in Württemberg rejected the idea of donating an hour's wage (the so-called welfare hour) from all employed workers to needy social and small capital pensioners.[102] In 1926, the *DIZ* complained that the trade unions frequently seemed to believe that the Zentralverband "was superfluous and had no reason to exist."[103] And despite its political ties to the Social Democrats, the Zentralverband was forced to warn its members that SPD politicians who sat on town councils were not automatically their friends. In 1925, the *DIZ* observed that

the Social Democrats in the Reichstag have made every possible effort to improve the lot of the social pensioner. . . . When, here and there, Social Democratic city council members and heads of welfare departments . . . make sure that welfare payments are reduced when pensions are increased, then these people go against the national policy of their own party. These unfeeling people need to be rapped, quite sharply, across the knuckles . . . and our colleagues, insofar as they are members of the SPD, should unrelentingly make a common front in party meetings against such "unsocial" behavior. . . . Our colleagues must engage in vigorous criticism on the spot. It is not enough to send off petitions to the Reichstag and to the Labor Ministry. The target of the critique is much closer at hand and must be told the plain truth in each instance, without regard to political opinions.[104]

Gender

Important differences in the experiences and interests of pensioners were determined by their gender. Women were the great majority of small capital pensioners. Both the social pensioners and small capital pensioners who were women had to apply for welfare assistance more often than their male counterparts.[105] In 1923, the secretary of the Württemberg Rentnerbund reported that three-quarters of the 10,000 small capital pensioners on the welfare systems' rolls were women—42 percent of them were older than fifty and 23 percent were older than sixty. About half of them had incomes of less than 1,000 marks per year and had no relatives to help them. Although some of these women made a little money from renting out rooms, most depended totally "on private and public relief."[106] A study of welfare clients in Frankfurt in 1927 found that a significant number of small capital pensioners were single women without any occupation:

> Most [of them] were . . . daughters in the families of higher-level civil servants, manufacturers, hotel owners, architects, artists, and independent tradesmen. . . . From their parents who died before the war they inherited a considerable fortune in securities or houses that, in normal times, would have made it possible for them to live to the end of their days without any worries. The great bankruptcy of the Reich, which is called the inflation, let them become impoverished, so that we now find them on public welfare, which they will not escape for the rest of their lives.

A large number of women were also to be found among Frankfurt's social pensioners, but they had previously worked as "domestic servants, cooks, ladies' helpers, [and] housekeepers, as well as cleaning and washerwomen."[107]

A survey of ninety-two German cities and 105 rural counties conducted by the German Association for Private and Public Welfare in 1929 showed that only 40.0 percent of the female pensioners studied were able to survive without welfare assistance, whereas 55.1 percent of the men had been able to stay off the welfare rolls.[108] No less than 76 percent of the social pensioners living on their own who received public relief were female. Female pensioners had to turn to local welfare agencies more commonly than men did because women were systematically discriminated against by the social insurance system. Only after 1927 were all widows granted a pension after the age of sixty-five without having to demonstrate that they were physically unable to continue working.[109] Female pensioners also received smaller pensions, which they found more difficult to supplement with some form of paid employment. Although about a third of all the pensioners surveyed in 1929 still worked, "for the most part, [the women pensioners] work irregularly or by the hour as seamstresses or charwomen."

Elderly women might also try to support themselves by taking in lodgers. In Hamburg in 1929, 31 percent of pensioners who survived without public assistance had lodgers in their households, but so too did 25 percent of those who were on the welfare rolls.[110] Yet the *DIZ* complained in 1925 that local welfare authorities sometimes penalized the elderly women who tried to add to their incomes by letting out rooms:

> Generally, widows who generate a small income for themselves by renting out rooms are cut off from welfare, even though this contravenes article 8, last paragraph, of the basic regulations, which talks about income gained from work that is not to be counted when making a decision about support. . . . The widow has to put the apartment in order each day and do the necessary cleaning, and she does all this not for her own pleasure, but because she cannot live from her pension alone.[111]

To stay away from the welfare office, elderly females had to depend heavily on support from their relatives. No fewer than 31 percent of those not receiving public assistance in Hamburg in 1929 were being at least partially supported by their relatives, whereas 85 percent of the elderly who were on relief had not been able to call upon their families for any help at all. Elderly women had the advantage over men that they could at least "take care of the children, etc. and were thus often more willingly taken into the family."[112] Even if they were not directly related, an elderly woman and a younger unmarried, divorced, or abandoned women with young children might live together and pool resources; taking in an older women who agreed to look after the children might in fact be the only way that a "single mother" was able to go out to work.[113] But dependence on kin also meant that elderly women were vulnerable not only to crises in the family economy but to familial conflicts as well. In 1925, for example, local authorities in Plattenhardt, north Württemberg, described the case of Friederike E., a widow, whose daughter "lives just two houses up the street from the old woman but does not look after her because they don't get along. . . . The nurse takes care of widow E., washing her and bringing order into the house. The commune provides the necessary heating materials and the widow gets her midday meal from someone else."[114] The elderly women who did have to turn to welfare agencies often could not expect equal treatment. In 1925, the *DIZ* complained that "often the local authorities assume . . . that a woman has a smaller stomach than a man. Consequently, widows only get 2 or 3 marks from the commune to supplement their pensions."[115]

The pensioners' organizations were well aware that women formed a large part of their constituencies. And like the interest groups representing war victims, the pensioners' organizations gave some women a new access to the "public sphere."[116] Few women appear, however, to have occupied major leadership positions, especially within the mainly working-class Zentralverband. Women seem to have been more prominent in the middle-class Rentnerbund. For example, Emmy Schräder became the head of the important Landesverband Hessen-Nassau, wrote agitational pamphlets, and was a major speaker at Rentnerbund conferences.[117] A female Reichstag deputy, Frau Dr. Lüders (DDP), was a particular advocate of the *Kleinrentner*'s cause.[118] And another member of the Reichstag, Paula Mueller-Otfried, also wrote about the *Kleinrentner* question.[119] Women were active in the grass roots of pensioner politics as well; in 1925, for example, *Der Rentner* carried a report from the Landesverband Mittelschlesien about the activities of the local branch in Breslau, where

> city councilwoman Emmy Busch is a member of the main committee of the welfare office and of the commission to develop new municipal guidelines for welfare for pensioners. Recently, a smaller committee has been formed that is to consult and decide on all cases concerning public assistance to pensioners. It consists of the head of the Welfare Department, the responsible office director, the syndic of the German Rentnerbund, the lawyer Demlow, and the councilwoman Emmy Busch, etc.[120]

Women also took to the streets along with male pensioners when the Zentralverband organized demonstrations in 1925 against the new welfare decree and during the Depression when it mounted protests against government spending cuts.[121] Yet neither the Zentralverband nor the Rentnerbund seem to have been seriously interested in introducing gender into their discussions of the poverty of the aged and disabled. The cases of individual women who had been mistreated by the welfare system appeared along with those of men in the catalog of complaints publicized by the pensioners' organizations.[122] But even women activists in the pensioners' organizations do not appear to have paid much attention to the feminization of poverty in old age or to the special needs and interests of women on welfare.[123]

"Welfare Bread Has a Bitter Taste": The Case of Adolf G.

In 1937, Adolf. G. came before a lay court in Stuttgart–Bad Canstatt on two charges of slander (üble Nachrede).[124] He was sentenced to one month in prison. At that time, Adolf G. was forty-five years old. Born in 1892, he had apprenticed as a saddler and upholsterer, then volunteered to fight in World War I. In the spring of 1919, he also served with the Free Corps against the Bolsheviks in the Baltic and was awarded the Ehrenkreuz, second class. Adolf G. married in 1915 and had six children.[125] After 1925, Adolf G. was permanently unemployed. He came into frequent conflict with the Stuttgart welfare authorities. Although the extremely lengthy and detailed records of the many grievances he lodged with the Stuttgart welfare office were officially filed under the category "social pensioners' welfare" (*Sozialrentnerfürsorge*), Adolf G.'s identity and experiences as a welfare client were far more complicated than this simple category suggests. He had been injured in the war and could feasibly claim the status of a war invalid, although his were not particularly heroic war wounds; he had been kicked in the stomach by a horse at the front. But he had also suffered an industrial accident that allowed him to draw an invalid's pension as well as repeatedly to petition, usually without much success, for the additional relief that German welfare offices gave people classified as social pensioners. A somewhat weaker claim for special consideration at the hands of the welfare authorities resided in Adolf G.'s position as the head of a "child-rich" family of six children (two daughters and four sons).[126]

Unfortunately for Adolf G., these positive credentials were counterbalanced by a long history of conflict with the welfare system and by brushes with the police and administrative apparatus of the local state. In 1924, he went to prison for a month and fifteen days for assisting an attempted abortion (presumably that of his greatly overburdened wife). In 1927, he was fined 50 marks for "insulting remarks and bodily injury," and in 1933 he went to jail for three days because the police found him playing music for commercial gain in the Stuttgart streets without a license. Hitler's seizure of power brought no improvement in Adolf G.'s relationship with the authorities. In 1936, the Stuttgart police charged him with "improper statements" in letters he had written to a Stuttgart welfare office.[127] There was, in other words, a long pre-history to the charge of slander that Adolf G. faced in 1937.

In 1921, Adolf G. required his first intestinal operation, which was followed by six more. He had been denied any war-related pension, but he had until that point received an invalid's pension. However, the continued payment of this *Sozialrente*, which he appears to have been drawing from his Stuttgart welfare office, not from the Reich government, was now in danger of being blocked unless he agreed to surrender a radio receiver and antenna that he had set up in the city-owned housing where he and his family were at that time living. This he considered a great outrage, one of the growing signs that he was being deprived of his rights and was already on the road to becoming, at least in official eyes, a "human being of the second class." Among the other symptoms of this process of official degradation was the fact that he was no longer allowed personally to collect his welfare payments:

> Although it cannot be shown that my moral conduct is bad, and I am no drinker, and have not been declared legally incompetent, my wife . . . had to go and pick up the [sup-

port] money . . . every two days, and so I never had a penny in my hand. We had to buy everything by the pound. . . . Four days before Christmas, I had to deliver the [radio] headset and receiver to the Herr Oberregierungsrat so that my wife and children would not starve . . . over Christmas. . . . But I am one of the better class of welfare clients [elevated welfare], and it cannot be shown that I am work-shy.[128]

Welfare officials claimed that their action was not a disciplinary measure, designed, as Adolf G. suggested, to punish or control him; he was simply being asked, as were all the other tenants, to respect the house rules of the municipal accommodations in which he and his family had been given shelter. But Adolf G. claimed that nothing in the house rules explicitly prohibited the installation of a radio receiver in the rooms themselves. For Adolf G., the malicious pettiness of the Stuttgart welfare officials was clearly unveiled by the blatant contradiction between the fact that "public collections are taken up for blind war veterans so that they can listen to the radio, yet others of the war injured who lost their health on the field of honor are forbidden the same privilege, and their support is withheld until they comply. How does that make any sense?"[129]

Adolf G. felt that he had been labeled an undesirable and a deviant, a work-shy welfare recipient who was, as one official report put it, "a complainer who is well known to this office." His suspicion that he had been singled out by the welfare authorities for discriminatory and abusive treatment was not completely paranoid. A report filed by the municipal welfare administration in January 1926 commented rather acidly that Adolf G. had been encouraged to get a job because "as G. does not have work that brings in a wage, he tries everything possible to pass the time. So, he has bought—admittedly, for a small sum of money—an old typewriter, which he repaired himself, so that he can type his numerous petitions and complaints in several copies."[130] Despite Adolf G.'s protests, he and his family were evicted by the city of Stuttgart. The official reasons cited were "gross infringement of the house rules," but the documents dealing with this phase of Adolf G.'s life suggest that both personal and political tensions played a role in the city's decision. The administrator of this municipally owned building had clearly been at odds with Adolf G. for some time and was determined to be rid of him. Since the brother of the administrator was also a member of the city council, it was not too difficult to have Adolf G. evicted. And an undated letter in this file clearly attempted to suggest that G. had political connections with the Social Democratic or Communist parties.[131]

Adolf G. was not prepared to accept this decision passively. In a registered letter, he complained to no fewer than three higher authorities: the Labor Office in Stuttgart, the Württemberg Ministry of the Interior, and the RAM in Berlin. He claimed that there was a conspiracy by local authorities to brand him as "a so-called antisocial element" so as to justify treating him like a worthless pauper who was entitled only to the lowest form of public relief—namely, the poor law—instead of the full benefit of elevated welfare. Mocking the official bureaucratic formulations with which he was by now intimately familiar, he entitled his letter "Complaint against the Decision of the Building Commission of the City of Stuttgart against the Heavily Disabled, Child-Rich [client] G., Adolf." He also displayed a rather unusual knowledge of official regulations that was to characterize all of his future and numerous complaints to the authorities. For example, he ended this particular letter with the following statement: "I base my request on articles 119 and 55 of the constitution, on the 'national guidelines' [*Reichsgrundsätze*] of 9 December 1924 [as printed in the] *Reichsgesetzblatt* [gazette announcing new national laws], part 1, number 78, as well as on the supplementary decree of 7 September 1925."[132]

Adolf G. may have been only a crank, the well-known troublemaker that the local welfare authorities attempted to dismiss. But the discontents he voiced would have been received with firm approval by many other social pensioners and small capital pensioners, who, as we have already seen, felt unjustly abandoned by the Reich administration to the capricious and arbitrary will of the local authorities. It was against this arbitrary, "unsocial," and niggardly spirit that Adolf G. attempted to marshal the promise as well as the letter of the Weimar laws and regulations governing the administration of the new welfare system. Over the years, he was to make several interesting applications of these laws to his own particular case, but his arguments could easily have been applied to the cases of thousands of other pensioners supported by the welfare system.

By 1927, Adolf G. was firmly convinced that the local authorities were systematically attempting not only to deny him personally any rights to proper treatment but also to prove that he was an unworthy father whose children should be taken away from him. Whether or not this was a completely accurate assessment of the welfare authorities' intentions, Adolf G. was quite right to observe that an official denunciation of the moral respectability of a welfare client, which could be based on extremely insubstantial "evidence," opened the door to the progressive diminution of rights as well as benefits. He was equally correct to claim that labeling a welfare client as workshy or antisocial (equally vague categories) often allowed the welfare authorities to save money by cutting benefits, to delegitimize clients' protests, and to deny them any rights of redress.[133] At a relatively early stage, the Stuttgart welfare authorities simply warned Adolf G. that because, in their opinion, he was only trying to "make trouble," all his complaints would be useless and any further letters would only end up in their wastebasket. Fortunately, for Adolf G. and many others like him, Weimar welfare regulations prescribed higher destinations for complaints refused by the local authorities. Even in the Third Reich, disgruntled welfare clients could complain to the Führer himself, although they had little chance of receiving a direct personal reply or official intervention in their case. But to push a grievance all the way to the very top was time consuming and perhaps too intimidating for many who, unlike Adolf G., possessed neither the moral convictions nor the tenacity required for a protracted battle with bureaucracy.

Adolf G. was prepared to challenge the decisions of welfare authorities by citing the chapters and verses of complicated welfare regulations. He also disputed the officials' interpretation of a seemingly incontestable measure of welfare support, the "standard rate." In a very ingenious attempt to prove why he personally should receive a good deal more than he did in fact get, Adolf G. set about subverting the official categories employed by the welfare system. His starting point was his unusual physical condition: the many intestinal operations he had undergone had shortened his digestive tract very considerably. Because of his shortened intestine, Adolf G.'s own individual needs were quite different than those of most other welfare clients. He felt, for example, that the welfare office had blacklisted him as a client who was unwilling to try to support himself by working. Yet when he had tried to work in a factory, he lost his job because his intestinal condition caused him to go to the bathroom many more times per day than was normal: "My physical problems make it no longer possible to keep a job in a factory (three attempts). . . . I have to use the toilet often and stay there quite a while. . . . This creates constant friction with the management."

Adolf G. pointed out that his peculiar physical condition also meant that he needed to eat at least three to four times as much "as a normal person" in order to stay alive, because his body could not properly digest all that it took in. Quoting section 1 of the National Welfare Decree, which prescribed that welfare support should "assure the necessary means of subsistence," Adolf G. showed that existing official guidelines were simply unable to take into account his own special case and needs: "For the necessary maintenance of my body, I must eat three times as much, so that to assure the necessary means of subsistence I would have to receive three times the standard rate."[134] But the welfare authorities could only respond to Adolf G. in their usual stark, dry, official language; it was clear that they had no intention of even trying to understand what he was saying.

In 1930, in fact, the local welfare committee decided that from the first of June onward they would no longer pay out in cash the sum of 25 marks per month that Adolf G. had been receiving; instead, they intended to hold on to this money, which would henceforth be designated specifically for the acquisition of clothing and shoes. Adolf G. regarded this step as "just another reduction of the rights, [a form of] derision and insult to us fathers of 'child-rich' families . . . as if I were not capable of allocating the money properly; or were simply a wastrel. . . . The decision of the committee for social pensioners' welfare is . . . unfounded. . . . [It is] just persecution directed against me because of the letters of complaint that I sent to the Economics Ministry on 20 February and 25 March." But Adolf G. was not content to let the matter rest here; in fact, he tried once again to turn the table on the local welfare authorities. They claimed that the measures taken against him were responses to his "uneconomic" behavior. He attempted to show that their actions were themselves "uneconomic"; had the welfare authorities continued to give him the 25 marks in cash, he could have supplied his family with shoes and clothing much more cheaply:

> I stated above that I received a clothing allowance of 420 marks and was required to have the Hilfsverein [a voluntary association] procure them for me, which cost me 140 marks. But if I had been given the 420 marks in cash, I could have gotten a discount of at least 10 percent for paying cash, in other words, saved 42 marks. . . . These days there are also various bankruptcy auctions where, from the point of view of quality and price, I could have done much better; I could also have bought quantities of underwear . . . that has been somewhat damaged by being on display in store windows yet is of excellent quality . . . and would thereby have saved at least 120 marks. I don't want to criticize the Hilfsverein, but they did not make their purchases in the most economical way. . . . If, in the course of two years, I need to have one suit and one pair of shoes for [each of] my children, as well as underwear, can I really be charged with running an "uneconomic" . . . household and leading a wasteful life? I think not—I therefore refuse to allow myself to be kept in tutelage, so long as these charges cannot properly be leveled at me; so do not hold back anything from the payment of my standard rate. I have just the same

rights as anyone else. I therefore request that my case be reexamined, that the decision of the social pensioners welfare committee be set aside immediately; that Eugen, Sigmund, Fridolin, and Alfons be granted boots, because those provided by the Hilfsverein were pretty bad. . . . If not, then I will file a complaint with the RAM on the basis of *Reichsgesetzblatt*, number 73 "concerning the type and the extent of welfare assistance."[135]

By 1930, Adolf G. was again in conflict with the municipal properties office. In that year, he wrote to the Economics Ministry in Stuttgart:

Supported by articles 109, 155, 119, 118, 163, and 107, as well as article 7, paragraph 11, permit me, a heavily disabled father of a "child-rich" family, to file the following complaint and request. After I was unjustly driven out of the ground floor of Hallschlag 16 by the city, I moved into private housing. Scarcely had I lived here one year . . . when the house and my apartment were sold to the city. Four tenants live in the house, but the ground-floor apartment is vacant, and no one will take responsibility for cleaning the entranceway. Three years ago, when I took over management of the house, I stipulated that each week . . . one of the tenants had to properly clean the entrance, the alley, and the steps to the cellar. . . . From this time onward, there have been conflicts. Previously, nothing was cleaned.[136]

By this time, the local authorities were quite sick of Adolf G.'s complaints. A letter from a Stuttgart mayor in May 1930 emphasized that Adolf G.'s most recent complaint had been rejected as unfounded "with the observation that additional correspondence in this vein would simply no longer be acknowledged."[137] Moreover, welfare authorities told Adolf G. that he had absolutely no chance of getting the single-family house he had requested. But this could hardly have been expected to deter him. In a letter to the RAM, a copy of which he sent to the Stuttgart Bürgermeister, Adolf G. once again set out, in excruciating detail, the entire sorry history of his conflicts with the municipal housing authorities. And once again he asserted his own special needs as a sick man with an unusual digestive tract:

The Building Surveyor's Office firmly promised me that a flush toilet would be installed at the beginning of April; but so far, nothing, despite the fact . . . that I and my family must share the w.c. with two other families. . . . Because of my intestinal problems, I am compelled to use the toilet at least five or six times, often as many as eight to ten times each day, for between ten minutes and a quarter of an hour each time. It is a real tribulation to have to spend so much time in this open, drafty w.c. Last winter, my wife developed severe bladder troubles this way. The building inspector already ordered in February that the latrine must be removed, but still nothing has been done.[138]

In addition to his own troubles, Adolf G. pointed out that his present housing was a great burden to his wife, who had to do the laundry of no fewer than eight people: "The house has no washroom, no drying room, and we have six children, aged four to sixteen. Where is my wife supposed to dry laundry in the winter?" As usual, the RAM did nothing more than pass Adolf G.'s complaint on to the Württemberg Interior Ministry.[139] The Interior Ministry did make inquiries of the Stuttgart Welfare Department. But the director of that agency once again dismissed Adolf G.'s complaints, observing that the support he received already exceeded a skilled worker's monthly wage (monthly net amount, about 200 marks). Perhaps this was not enough "for such a big family," but the director firmly stated that he "was . . . nonetheless of the opinion that it really was not justified to give support from public funds that exceeded wage levels."[140]

In 1931, Adolf G. was charged with welfare fraud. Like many of the unemployed and welfare recipients, he and his family had tried to make some money by petty street trading. Adolf G. claimed that he had earned no significant income from his small business in old iron and rags or from the occasional sale of baked goods and sausages at local fairs. He also pointed out that his unsuccessful venture into petty capitalism was a desperate attempt to get free of the welfare authorities' stranglehold on his and his family's lives: "Or are we an antisocial family because we attempted to escape the conscienceless and heartless welfare system?"[141] But as far as the Stuttgart welfare office was concerned, Adolf G.'s case was, once again, simply a matter of the empirical facts and their relationship to the existing rules and regulations; as a welfare recipient, Adolf G. was required to reveal all his sources of income, and this he had not done. In addition to denying his request that the charges be dropped (he was, however, eventually acquitted), the Stuttgart welfare office decided that from now on "payment of G.'s rent will be made directly to the landlord . . . because there is a danger that G. will not keep up with his rent obligations because he has such a big family."[142] Adolf G. struck back at this affront with one of his most incendiary responses to date: a letter dated 20 December 1931 that he sent to the RAM in Berlin under the heading, "Concerning a Response to a Complaint that Borders on the Middle Ages and the Times of the Robber-Knights."[143]

Adolf G.'s anger with the Weimar welfare system was largely personal. It was his case alone that consumed his interest and energies over the years. But eventually his personal pique pushed him in the direction of certain political "solutions." What is striking, however, is the complete inconsistency of Adolf G.'s self-described political commitments over several years. Adolf G. appears to have been prepared to join just about any organization that he thought might listen to him and lend some support to his very personal war with the unfeeling welfare bureaucrats in Stuttgart. Of course, it was tactically necessary for him to defuse all charges of having been politically motivated in his attacks on the welfare system; an admission of real political or ideological conviction would only have further delegitimized his claims in the eyes of the authorities. But it is also clear that he approached politics and welfare clients' organizations in an extremely eclectic and quite instrumental fashion. He appears mainly to have been interested in getting immediate help for a specific problem:

> I . . . do not belong to any political party, but when the municipal properties office pushed me out, I joined the tenants association; the matter of public assistance for my disability led me to join the IB, and I was also a member of the Bund der Kinderreichen; but they all let me down. . . . In my distress, left to my own devices, not knowing where to turn or what to do, I sent the article to S.A.Z. [the KPD newspaper in Stuttgart], which they published. (This, however, is not the cause of the immoderate action to destroy me; I see this as more of a response to my formal request to leave the Catholic Church, made on 28 April 1926, in order to join the Protestant Church because my wife was brought up in this faith.)[144]

It is not clear from this description whether Adolf G. joined all of these various organizations at the same time or moved from one to another as each successively disappointed him. It seems likely, however, that he did approach all of them at roughly the same time, because each attempted to speak for a different element of the official identity he was trying to establish—war victim, father of a child-rich family, evicted tenant, and so on. But from a political and ideological point of view, these political commitments were wholly contradictory: The IB was clearly Communist, whereas the Bund der Kinderreichen was politically quite conservative. The blatant inconsistency of Adolf G.'s political commitments is underlined by the fact that in Württemberg, at least, there was a more radical version of the Bund der Kinderreichen that local police officials charged was a tool of the Communist party—had he wanted to join a radical organization representing child-rich families, he could easily have done so.[145]

After 1932, there is a large gap in Adolf G.'s file that extends up to 1935. But in June 1937, he appeared once more, sending off very similar kinds of complaints against the welfare authorities but now, obviously, to a very different government. He seemed to have acquired a new typewriter for the business of filing complaints.[146] Not only had Adolf G. survived the Nazi seizure of power, but he had actually been able to work for a few years at his old trade as a saddler in the Daimler factory. In 1936, he gave up this job but soon found another at a carriage works. Adolf G. seemed also to have shed the damning public reputation that plagued him during the Weimar years or the "period of the system," as he described it in one of his later letters. After 1933, he became a member of the Nazi party, the Kriegsopferverband (the National Socialist War Victims Association), the Arbeitsopfern, and, finally, for good measure, the Baltikum Kämpfer and the Kyffhäuserbund.[147] But Adolf G. quickly squandered this newfound respectability. Between 1935 and 1936, he was ejected from all of these organizations. In 1936, he lodged a charge with the Stuttgart public prosecutor alleging that not only the Economics Ministry but even the Kriegsopferverband had withheld and even falsified documents that were vital to a complaint he had recently filed against welfare authorities. Adolf G. claimed that he "was described in [a ministry] document . . . as a 'second-class human being,' who should be happy 'to get any public assistance at all.'"[148] He believed that it was these phrases that had not only led to a recent reduction of his welfare support but also caused his exclusion from all of the Nazi organizations he had joined since 1933. Adolf G. tried to appeal directly to Hitler. In his letter to the Führer, he began by lavishing praise and good wishes upon Hitler for all that he had achieved in the name of the German people. But then very quickly Adolf G. shifted into the only tone of public criticism now permissible—an attack upon the corruption of the little Führers, Hitler's underlings:

> May Almighty God protect our esteemed Führer in the New Year and allow him to detect all duplicity, so that his name and his person will not be misused as a disguise for forgery and the destruction of documents, so that his name, his person, his escutcheon remains bright and clean in the eyes of the humble population by showing that he is the guarantor of the law, for the entire German people, and not just for the middle classes [*Bürgertum*].[149]

But Adolf G. still could not produce the crucial documents. And far from helping him, his letter to Hitler was taken into evidence in his trial. He was convicted of the charge and sentenced to prison. Offered the chance to retract his charges, Adolf G.

repeatedly refused. Even if he lost everything else, he felt that he must retain his honor. And, perhaps, after all, Adolf G. had finally achieved a certain Pyrrhic moral victory. For in February 1937, the local welfare authorities to whom Adolf G. had fired off so many of his complaining letters in the preceding twelve years, admitted rather wearily that

> the two-day period of detention ordered against Adolf G. for improper remarks in his written, official exchanges with the welfare office . . . appears to have exercised no deterrent effect. . . . In general, one can say . . . that G. is one of those types of people who has always believed that the courts and all the public authorities stand at his disposal; he finds nourishment, so to speak, in litigation and case-file documents. This type of person has no consideration for the other *Volksgenossen* [national comrades]. For years now and just for the pure pleasure of engaging in litigation, he has laid excessive claim to the time and labor power of every public agency he can find by filing totally unfounded complaints and petitions and has charged the officials who have in any way been involved with these matters with serious infringements of the law. Unfortunately, current national laws offer only an extremely limited opportunity to take action against such elements, which is the reason why the "eternal complainers" can continue to make trouble.[150]

The case of Adolf G. demonstrates that the popular politics of welfare could assume at least two different forms. The pensioners' organizations used rather traditional political, agitational, and organizational methods, derived from the models of the labor movement and the bourgeois political parties, to promote the collective interests of a rather unorthodox and relatively new constituency: elderly or disabled pensioners. But individual pensioners like Adolf G. also engaged in a very different kind of "everyday politics." Adolf G. was not an apolitical man; indeed, over the years, he joined a bewildering variety of political organizations and interest groups. But at the same time, Adolf G. devoted his energies to a highly individualized "micropolitics" of power and rhetorical self-assertion. At first sight, this politics may not appear to have been very rational. In a straightforwardly instrumental sense, it was in fact counterproductive: Adolf G.'s numerous, unrelenting challenges to the power, authority, and even competence of the local welfare authorities never gained him any concrete material advantages and only served to marginalize him as a welfare client. What this politics did have to offer Adolf G., however, was the chance to reconstruct the personal "honor" (*Ehre*) and dignity that he felt the welfare system had systematically attempted to destroy. These sentiments were not unique to Adolf G. alone. But attempting to harness them to the cause of collective action was a difficult enterprise. Certainly, the pensioners' organizations used every opportunity to publicize the insults to the honor and dignity of the *Rentnerstand* (pensioners' estate) that contact with the welfare services all too frequently involved. But for Adolf G., honor was a very individual matter, and he was in fact quite prepared to reassert his own respectability by calling into question the morality of other welfare clients. Answering the charge that he had failed to declare his income from street trading to the welfare authorities, Adolf G. protested:

> I was of the opinion that bread earned honestly, with difficulty and pain, would taste better than bread got by begging. . . . I am not the only one who has tried to make a little money on the side, above and beyond what we get in public assistance. I know an old

woman in the neighborhood who supports an unmarried man, trades in vegetables, and for the past half year has kept a white horse in a local stall, even though she's been on welfare for years. I could describe a whole string of cases like this one. . . . I know cases where people [who] are given food and clothing as well as money put their children in a home and go out whoring every night.[151]

Adolf G. refused to name names because he "was not a Judas." Other welfare clients had fewer scruples. Especially during the Depression, when the welfare system was swamped with clients and its resources were strained beyond belief, a denunciation might help the informer to curry favor with the authorities, and it would certainly eliminate some of the competition.[152] The pensioners' organizations attempted to establish greater collective rights in place of *Individualisierung*. If they had been more successful, all welfare clients and not just the pensioners alone would have benefited. But the pensioners' efforts were sabotaged not only by the devastating effects of the Great Depression and by all of the obvious divisions within their own ranks. The dissonance between their formal politics and Adolf G.'s politics of everyday life also played an important part.

CHAPTER SIX

Weimar Women on Welfare

Until the Great Depression and the fiscal policies of the presidential dictatorship dumped millions of unemployed males onto local welfare rolls, the majority of the Weimar welfare system's clients were women. A variety of causes brought Weimar women into contact with welfare authorities. Economic need was a major factor, but the economic distress of women was often caused by quite noneconomic events— divorce, abandonment, or the death of a husband, for example. And the economic needs that brought women to welfare offices usually had some basis in their disad- vantaged position in the labor market and their unequal power and legal status in marriage and divorce. Women with young children usually found it difficult if not impossible to support themselves with full-time, paid employment away from the home. Women who became unemployed usually did not receive the same unemploy- ment benefits as men.[1]

At the same time, there were equally gendered "pulls" bringing diverse categories of women into the welfare authorities' network of surveillance and control. The ex- perience of wartime deprivation and population losses, the enfranchisement of women, and the political ascendancy of Social Democracy after the German Revolution all made the "protection of motherhood" a major concern of the new state welfare sys- tem. This public commitment (which was shared, albeit in different ways, by all points on the political spectrum) prescribed welfare practices that brought specific catego- ries of women—pregnant women, nursing mothers, and especially illegitimate or single mothers—under the intense scrutiny of welfare and youth authorities. And even the more general everyday practices of Weimar welfare authorities were infused with an intense concern for the preservation of the German family, which translated into a gender-specific focus on the character and behavior of women.

"Protecting" Mothers and Children:
The Contradictions of Maternal and Infant Welfare

Perhaps the single largest group of women whose lives were touched by the Weimar welfare system were pregnant and nursing mothers. After World War I, the German family seemed no longer able to ensure cultural or even biological reproduction of the healthy and productive postwar generations that Germany would require to overcome the devastation of "total war." In 1920, a Catholic Center party city council woman in Düsseldorf warned that one of the welfare system's most urgent priorities must be the provision of comprehensive care for mothers and children, "so as to heal from within our economically, physically, and morally shattered people. Everywhere that private welfare activities are insufficient, the municipality must step in to help, in order to prevent developments for the life of our people that would be unhealthy." Preventive care was especially important in this area, because the damage done when children were young could not be made good again later: "If we look at the family as the germ cell of the nation, then all our efforts must be directed toward strengthening it and filling it with the proper spirit."[2]

Although social workers "sought to impose the gendered obligations of breadwinning for men and household management for women," in practice women and children received most of the female social workers' attentions. These interventions into family life created profoundly ambiguous effects for women because, as Jane Lewis observes, "the notion of 'women's mission to women' relied on the idea that women were both cause and cure of social ills."[3] Weimar welfare experts claimed, for example, that most ordinary women lacked the scientific knowledge of child psychology, household management, and health care that was required to practice the "profession" of motherhood competently in the modern age: "Broad sections of the population . . . have still not understood that the study of psychology and knowledge of biological interconnections are required in order to be capable of performing this most difficult of all professional work."[4] The professional social worker would supply this "expertise."[5]

Pre- and postnatal health care programs appeared to offer the social worker a "neutral point of entry, assuring access to those groups in the population who most need preventive and reconstructive work."[6] In Hamburg, the civil registry office reported all births to social workers employed by a private organization, the Hamburg State Central Organization of the German Alliance for the Protection of Nursing Infants and Small Children, who made an initial visit to the mother to decide whether to keep the newborn under observation. If the mother did not take her new baby for a medical examination at one of the city's "mothers' advice centers" at least every two months during the first year of its life, she could expect to receive further visits from the social worker. Health visitors were also required to make sure that mothers who received "nursing money" (*Stillgeld*) under the provisions of the Law on Maternity Benefits of 1919 were, in fact, breast-feeding their babies.[7] The doctor's inspection of the newborn focused upon the child's physical development. At each visit, the doctor weighed the child, recorded the results in a case file, and gave the mother nutritional advice. The doctor made the mother aware of any health problems and told her how to deal with them but did not provide actual treatment. For that, the mother had to go to her own doctor.

The financial support provided by the Hamburg welfare department allowed the State Central Organization to increase the number of its health visitors from 10 in 1917 to 108 in 1927.[8] By the mid-1920s, the number of follow-up visits during the infant's first year of life had risen, on average, to 10.8. In 1919, 55 percent of all mothers of newborn infants in Hamburg presented their children for inspection by the doctor; by 1925, this figure had increased to 67 percent and by 1933 to 89 percent. Mothers came to the Hamburg advice centers an average of five or six times. By 1928, there were no fewer than 6,159 municipal and 3,617 private maternal, infant, and child welfare clinics in Germany as a whole.[9] After the onset of the Depression, however, "the female social workers were increasingly set to work in economic welfare, because of the rising mass unemployment."[10]

Benefits and Costs

The representation of motherhood as a profession was certainly used to claim improvements in the status and material conditions of wives and mothers. But attempts to rationalize and modernize reproductive behavior, child rearing, and domestic labor also produced, as Karen Hagemann puts it, a "therapeutic siege" of the working-class family. In 1922, for example, a south German welfare officer suggested that "it would be the ideal situation if the Youth Office . . . could provide a helper for every mother and child."[11] In 1929, a Hamburg social worker claimed that "the more intelligent women, who are in a better social situation, find it relatively easy to decide to seek out an advice center and have a much greater insight into the necessity of taking the appropriate precautions for the birth of their child."[12] But other women were reluctant to conform to the dictates of a knowledge whose benefits (for them, if not for their children) were far from obvious. Hagemann observes that many working-class women in Hamburg were

> skeptical about the recommendations made by "modern infant-care." The behavior proposed to them was foreign. It contradicted their human feelings, made greater demands on their labor power and their nerves and, in addition, cost more money. . . . They experienced the social worker's home visits as a burdensome form of surveillance. . . . The reduction of work that family planning and birth control had achieved was again increased by the increased demands of [modern] child care.[13]

Indeed, maternal and infant welfare campaigns appear to have been least successful in reaching precisely those women whose children were most at risk—that is, the poorest mothers living in the worst housing. In 1929, a Hamburg school doctor complained that the parents' meetings to which he spoke were not well attended and that his advice on child care did not reach the right ears because "it was really only the most orderly people who showed up regularly."[14] The advice dispensed by the maternal and infant welfare centers was often simply irrelevant to the actual living conditions of these women. At a meeting of the Red Women's and Girls' Union in Berlin-Wedding in 1926, one woman suggested that poorer working-class mothers, living in overcrowded urban tenements, found the advice offered by child welfare experts to be simply absurd: "Light, air, and sun? I should probably just tie a strip of cloth around my infant's belly and hang him out the window; otherwise, there is precious little light, air, and sun for us proles!"[15]

Many of the women who did participate in pre- and postnatal health programs expected economic assistance as well as advice. In 1925, a rural health visitor in Schleswig-Holstein remembered that during the inflation it had been necessary to offer women "biscuits, sugar, infants' linen at significantly reduced prices and, when necessary, completely free." She claimed, however, that now "that large numbers of people are convinced of the value of the mothers' advice centers, we no longer need these means of publicity."[16] Yet in 1926, an article in a Social Democratic journal of municipal affairs complained that in rural areas, there were still many "imprudent mothers, who just cannot see the value of a continuous inspection of the child's weight and health. Economic need and the inadequate earnings of the husband soon compel the mother to return to work, and she is often forced to leave the infant in the care of her older brothers and sisters or other relatives, who are not as concerned for the child's welfare as a caring mother would be."[17] In 1930, a Hamburg newspaper reported that "the Hamburg health authority has for several years maintained seven advice centers for pregnant women. . . . Unfortunately, attendance has not lived up to the expectations that led the Health Office . . . to set up these . . . centers."[18] Maternal and child welfare programs did offer very real benefits (including, perhaps, the survival of one's children). The least tangible but not necessarily the least valuable benefits came in the form of advice on how to feed and care for infants, how to raise children, legal advice, and so on. Yet women were certainly more likely to welcome this advice if it was accompanied by tangible, material support. Before the war, only pregnant women who were insured through a sickness insurance fund (*Krankenkasse*) received any financial support in the period just before and immediately after the birth of their children. During the war, however, this coverage was extended. The 1924 decree regulating the operation of the Weimar welfare system allowed women who had no claim to the maternity benefits (*Wochenhilfe*) paid through the sickness insurance funds to receive a rough equivalent called *Wochenfürsorge* that would be paid out by local welfare authorities on the basis of a means test. Both *Wochenhilfe* and *Wochenfürsorge* payments were meant to draw pregnant and nursing mothers into a medical surveillance network; to collect their maternity benefits, women had to present themselves at district maternal and infant welfare centers, where they would also be given medical advice about their pregnancy.[19] Women were to be instructed about the importance of breast-feeding and about "proper" infant and child care more generally.[20]

Yet the material benefits were themselves rather limited, never sufficient to allow a single woman not to work during the last weeks of pregnancy and the first few weeks after the birth of her child.[21] At best, the money paid provided a useful supplement to a family income. Maternal and child welfare programs were meant to function as pronatalist population measures, which meant reaching the largest possible number of potential clients. But under the mounting pressures of financial crisis, they were increasingly administered as forms of public relief, subject to a means test. In 1925, the news service of the German Association for Private and Public Welfare reported that "handing over the maternal welfare services to the local authorities has by no means been greeted uniformly with enthusiasm. Some fear that the local authorities will . . . not pay enough attention to the role these services are meant to play in support of our population policies but will instead simply look at them as another form of poor relief."[22] These were not unfounded fears. In 1926, the Hamburg socialist newspaper commented, for example, that "in a whole series of cities, the money given to mothers has been deducted, at least in part, from the unemployment support payments."[23]

Many women clients also wanted to use the benefits that maternal and infant welfare programs did provide for quite different purposes than those that the welfare professionals and administrators had intended. Social workers in Hamburg complained that female clients wanted the money awarded as a premium for breast-feeding given to them in one lump sum so that they could pay off old debts or make new purchases. In 1928, Hamburg welfare authorities reported that they preferred to give out milk instead of money because it could be expected that cash payments would not be put to the proper use.[24] Yet even these forms of payment in-kind did not prevent what welfare authorities regarded as the misappropriation of maternal and child welfare benefits. In Hagen, for example, local welfare authorities warned social workers that they would have to prevent pregnant women who were given extra food from sharing it with their families.[25]

The cost of the limited financial support as well as the other benefits (medical advice, for example) provided by pre- and postnatal clinics was submission to official surveillance, which brought with it attempts to interfere in the personal lives of pregnant and nursing mothers, to discipline and control their behavior, sometimes with quite undesirable results for the women involved. Social workers tried, for example, to persuade women that they should not work while pregnant or nursing, even though these women clearly needed this income in order to survive. In Düsseldorf, social workers were actually told to give the police the name of any pregnant women who continued to work during the period just before the birth of her child.[26] In many German cities, civil registry officials were routinely required to inform welfare authorities of the birth of all children who might be in need of a social worker's attention.[27] Welfare authorities were also well aware of the need to draw midwives into their surveillance network. In Gelsenkirchen, for example, the midwife was to provide a full description of the social relationships within the family on the day the child was born. For every case reported, the midwife received 20 marks.[28] In Freital in Saxony, a local doctor suggested that all midwives be made employees of the municipality because midwives had set up their own "weighing hours" in competition with the public advice centers:

The present system forces the midwife to be very concerned about making a sufficient income. Therefore, it is not at all surprising that the most enterprising attempt to increase their incomes by other means. Sometimes they do this by taking over a franchise for the sale of baby foods or tonics. From the recent Rad-Jo trial we have learned that when midwives sing the praises of Köstritzer black beer for nursing mothers or Kusekes child flour as nourishment for infants, then there is usually a financial motive in the background. It is pretty obvious that such recommendations are not in the best interest of public health. Nowadays, however, there is also a very great danger that the midwives will attempt to make money outside of their immediate area of responsibility. Of all the lay health experts, the midwife is the only one who really has a professional knowledge of the female reproductive organs. It is to her that ordinary women turn when faced with an unexpected and unwanted pregnancy. . . . Most midwives will surely shrink back from giving an abortion. But not all can resist the temptation of the money involved.[29]

The protection of motherhood frequently translated in practice into an intrusive policing of mothers. Yet working-class women and especially the mothers of illegitimate children received more attention from welfare authorities than wealthy and middle-class mothers, who were often exempted from surveillance and control altogether because, as Hamburg youth welfare authorities put it in 1918, "the well-to-do circles can easily obtain for themselves the necessary advice. Social workers make hardly any house visits in the more distinguished neighborhoods of the city."[30]

If a social worker did in fact visit a middle-class family uninvited, she might provoke an indignant reaction, such as the following letter sent by Kurt A., the father of a newborn infant, to the Düsseldorf welfare authorities in 1932:

On the thirteenth of this month [January] a "sister" [*Fürsorgeschwester*] appeared at my house in the course of the morning and asked to be allowed to see the child born on 16 February 1931. My wife was very surprised by this strange request but permitted the sister to attend to her duties. As much as I fully believe in the necessity of having the *Fürsorgeschwestern* and think their activities are important . . . I do, nevertheless, believe that certain limits must be set upon their activities. Raising children to the proper state of physical and social fitness is the highest duty and the natural right of parents. If it appears that this responsibility is in danger of being improperly performed . . . then the state has the right to intervene. If it had been the case that something unpleasant had been heard about us, about our capacity and suitability for raising children . . . then the social worker would have had the right and the duty to concern herself with the child. But I find it quite unjustified that without any real reason and without having previously checked our reliability, an examination of the child was undertaken. I find it hard to believe that the law would support the *Fürsorgeschwester* in this instance; but even if it does, then one has the duty to push for a change in the regulations. Such a form of examination and investigation cannot be reconciled with the spirit of freedom with which the constitution of our nation breathes. Nor have any of my friends or acquaintances ever experienced such a visit.[31]

On 19 February 1932, the city's chief medical officer addressed an extremely apologetic letter to Kurt A. It seemed, or so the authorities now wished to claim, that the family care social worker had never intended to visit his home. Rather, a mistake had been made when cases were selected from the list of recent births. Kurt A.'s name had been taken down when it should have been the name of the next family in the list. Whether or not this explanation was actually true, the authorities now wanted to dispel any suspicion on Kurt A.'s part that the female social worker had ever harbored any doubts about his or his wife's reliability as parents. The doctor hoped that Kurt A. would be satisfied with this explanation and that the regrettable error could now be forgiven and forgotten.[32]

The child, not the mother, was the primary focus of the welfare state's commitment to the protection of motherhood.[33] Women found it difficult to claim an official identity independent of their relationship to children the state wished to protect.

The rights of mothers were defined and limited by the state's concern for the well-being of their children. And the needs and interests of women and children recognized by welfare experts were derived from ideological representations of normal motherhood, of the normal family, and of the normal child.[34] Welfare experts accepted as legitimate only those needs and interests that contributed to the production of "normality"; other needs were refused or simply ignored.

Working mothers desperately needed child care. In 1924, for example, one observer remarked that "women's work should have declined after the war, but our statistics indicate quite the opposite. . . . Compared to 1918, the level of women's wage work has remained the same, but there are now less than half the number of day-care centers [that there were during the war]; that means that a far larger number of children have to go without supervision while the mother works."[35] In the late 1920s, another commentator reported that "female employment has continued its permanent increase in the past decade. . . . Infants are locked in and left by themselves at home—there is really no question of being able to use the few existing nurseries. Small children and older children of school age are simply sent out onto the streets."[36] In 1928, tenants of the Praunheim Siedlung in Frankfurt petitioned the city council for their own *Kinderhort* because "a large number of the women who . . . live here . . . are employed and have to take their children to the kindergarten in the inner city. In addition, there are many women who, although not employed, cannot use the central laundry house because they are not allowed to bring their children with them, yet there are no other facilities where they may be left."[37] But the expansion of public child care was not a priority for financially hard-pressed local governments. Nor did female social workers think they should make it too easy for working-class mothers to put their children into the few existing municipal child care facilities. In 1930, a Hamburg social-work director cautioned her subordinates "not to send the children of unemployed parents to [day care centers] without compelling reasons, so that families that already have nothing to do should not further disintegrate. Neglectful parents should not be encouraged in their complacency."[38]

The protection of motherhood also focused welfare authorities' attention upon female sexuality.[39] Pre- or extramarital sex threatened the moral integrity and the reproductive abilities of legally sanctioned marriages by spreading sexually transmitted diseases that caused infertility. In the Wilhelmine Empire, controlling sexual disease was primarily a matter of policing prostitution.[40] But persistent pressure from bourgeois feminists and Social Democrats eventually produced a Sexual Diseases Law in 1927, which ended police regulation of prostitution and required all persons, whether male or female, who were infected with a venereal disease to seek adequate treatment under the supervision of the local health authorities.[41] In practice, women were more often subjected than men to the controls created by the 1927 law. Indeed, the numbers of women who could be subjected to state control under the provisions of the Sexual Diseases Law was actually greater than under the old system of police regulation. Under the act, not only professional prostitutes but also any female suspected of "promiscuous" sexual activity (*Männerverkehr*), even if she earned nothing from it, could be made to undergo a medical examination. A special welfare agency—the Pflegeamt—patrolled the streets, railway stations, and bars in search of juvenile runaways, older homeless women, and other "endangered" females who were thought to be at risk of falling into a life of prostitution.[42] Although many medical experts acknowledged that promiscuous men also spread venereal diseases, health and welfare authorities were more worried about female than about male sexuality. Youth welfare authorities claimed, for example, that the "endangerment" of boys and girls exhibited quite different, gendered symptoms. Sexual activity appeared to indicate deficiencies in young girls' characters that, if left unattended, would prevent them from becoming good mothers in later life. So while boys were sent to reform schools because they stole, committed other petty crimes, or ran around in gangs, girls were put into reformatories because they were suspected of engaging in promiscuous sex or, indeed, any sexual activity at all.[43]

The Protection of Illegitimate Mothers and Their Children

Throughout Germany in the late nineteenth century, the fate of illegitimate children who died in infancy at a much higher rate than their legitimate counterparts aroused public sympathy and concern. It was argued that the guardianship of illegitimate children, exercised mainly by the mothers themselves, would have to be placed in more competent—which increasingly meant more "professional"—public hands. The Youth Welfare Law of 1922 made the newly created youth offices responsible for exercising a so-called professional guardianship over all illegitimate children. Its main tasks were to make contact with all unwed mothers so that they could be informed of their legal and social rights; to ensure that illegitimate children would be born and continue to remain healthy by placing the mothers and the children under medical surveillance; to promote the "education in motherhood" of the usually young and working-class women who had given birth to illegitimate children; and to press the legal claims of the child for support against the father in the first instance but also against all other legally responsible relatives.[44]

Weimar youth offices did not encourage young women to keep their illegitimate children, preferring instead to place them in foster homes (unless, of course, the couple could be induced to marry). But this did not end mothers' financial responsibilities for their illegitimate children. Foster care had to be paid for, and local youth welfare authorities refused to foot the bill themselves. Youth welfare authorities developed quite elaborate methods of tracking down unwilling fathers and forcing them to pay.[45] But it was extremely difficult to derive the necessary revenue from this source alone.[46] The mother of the child was herself the next person legally responsible for child support. So mothers who had applied to a youth office, indeed, who had been officially encouraged to seek aid—were frequently confronted with the bitter irony of becoming the targets of legal action undertaken by the welfare authorities.

In December 1930, for example, Frida K., a single worker in Ludwigsburg, near Stuttgart, appeared in the Youth Office to answer charges that she had failed to provide properly for the support of her illegitimate male child born in 1929, who was now in foster care. She argued that she had at least bought some clothes for her son and claimed that "I would very gladly pay the 15 marks a month [that the Youth Office was demanding] if I were only in a position to do so. But during the whole summer, I was unable to work full-time." Frida K. earned only 20 marks a week, from which she had to find 22 marks per month for her rent. She claimed that her income did not allow her to eat a proper midday meal.[47] But the Youth Office would not listen. In 1931, it demanded a temporary garnishment of her wages. The unfortunate Frida K. was one of thousands of mothers of illegitimate children for whom the promises of the Weimar constitution and of the Youth Welfare Law must have appeared rather hollow. The protection of illegitimate children was translated into welfare practices that undoubtedly baffled, puzzled, and perhaps enraged many unmarried mothers. One of them, Lizette K., testified before the Youth Office in Besigheim in November 1930 that although "I clearly understand that the Stuttgart Welfare Department has already paid out 300 marks for my child; nonetheless I cannot understand why it has not been possible to get this money from the child's father."[48] However, mothers were not the only relatives of illegitimate children who were directly affected by these practices. If neither the father nor the mother would or could contribute to the illegitimate child's support, then youth offices would not hesitate to go after other relatives, in particular the child's maternal grandparents. In 1931, the Youth Office in Heilbronn prevailed upon local authorities to serve a support order on the grandfather of an illegitimate child. The grandfather then declared that instead of paying he would take the child into his own household; precisely what the Youth Office had hoped would happen.[49]

The search for remuneration pushed deeply into family economies and family relationships. In January 1931, for example, the single servant girl Emilie F. took her newborn illegitimate son, Robert, to the municipal infants' home in Heilbronn. In August 1931, the local Youth Office pressured Christian F., the child's grandfather, for a financial contribution, even though, as he put it in his letter of complaint, "my daughter Emilie left home four years ago and has broken off all relationship with us."[50] Relentless, the Youth Office pointed out that Christian F. had a house and a small vineyard. In addition to the income from his job at the Württemberg Portland Cement Works in Lauffen, he also received some money from his two sons, who still lived at home. After making inquiries at each of the son's workplaces, the Youth Office decided that "the father can demand from these children, who earn a good wage, that they provide completely for his subsistence, and therefore it can be maintained that he [in turn] must pay the 20 marks [per month for his illegitimate grandchild]. . . . The local [administration] has issued support judgments against grandparents whose income situation is by no means as favorable as that of this family F."[51]

The parents of irresponsible or intransigent natural fathers enjoyed no immunity from Youth Office actions in search of child support. In September 1930, the Besigheim authorities reported that Eugen G., a tailor in Bietigheim, had not yet paid "one pfennig of support" for his illegitimate child, commenting that although "it's true that G. is at present unemployed . . . this doesn't at all prevent him from attending every conceivable form of public amusement, e.g., the sheep run [*Schäferlauf*] in Markgröningen. Therefore, he simply must have some money." Though it could find no way to squeeze money out of G. himself, the Oberamt was pleased to report that because Eugen G.'s father "has legally obligated himself as the . . . guarantor for his son's [financial] responsibilities, we can get something out of him. G. Sr. works at the German Linoleum Factory."[52] In a rather unusual case, youth welfare officers who had failed to get child support payments from an auto mechanic who had just inherited a house summoned all his tenants to the Youth Office and made them sign an agreement to pay at least 4 marks weekly directly to the Youth Office.[53]

These were not the only unwelcome intrusions by child welfare officers. Whether the illegitimate child stayed with its mother or was put into a succession of foster homes, both the child and the adults responsible for it were subjected to surveillance lasting until the child achieved legal maturity. This official observation (*Über-wachung*) was meant to ensure the physical health and well-being of the child, but it also policed the moral behavior of both mother and child. Thus, in 1930, the Youth Office in Besigheim wrote to the Oberamt that one of its charges, the nine-year-old Gertrud H., living with her mother, who had two other illegitimate children, "was very badly looked after. We therefore asked her and her father to present themselves to discuss how this situation could be improved. Neither of them appeared, nor did they so much as offer an apology for not appearing. . . . We therefore wish to inform them that if they do not present themselves the next time, they can expect that charges will be laid against them and that they will be forcibly transported to our office by the rural police."[54] The same Youth Office declared that it wanted to have a "serious talk" with the mother of another illegitimate child, even though this "girl" was now almost nineteen years old, because she "is living a very light-headed and irrespon-sible life that her mother only seems to encourage."[55] It is perhaps not surprising to find a Berlin social worker in the Prenzlauer Berg district complaining in 1929 that "often people are suspicious of the surveillance by the Youth Office, and they fail to understand why it is necessary. It is especially the mothers of illegitimate children . . . who do not understand when suddenly the Youth Office makes known to them that it has a right of inspection."[56]

Foster Children

Foster parents were to be carefully selected by youth welfare authorities. Illegitimate and other children placed in foster care were to be kept under Youth Office surveil-lance until they reached maturity. Yet the Weimar conditions of supply and demand in the foster care market weakened Youth Office control over foster parents. Youth welfare authorities preferred to place foster children in "respectable" working-class or lower-middle-class homes. But the poorer members of the German working class more often presented themselves as candidates.[57] The money to be earned was not the only motive for looking after foster children, yet economic factors exercised an undeniable (and from the Youth Office's point of view undesirable) effect on the supply of foster parents. In 1932, one commentator remarked that "we regularly observe . . . that in periods of growing unemployment . . . there is an increase in the number of places offered for foster children, whereas during economic upturns, when workers earn money, are able to lead a more ordered existence, and should thus be able to provide a suitable foster home, there is, in fact, a shortage. . . . These ups and downs are, in addition, influenced by the condition of the housing market, i.e., rent prices."[58] The shortage of suitable foster parents made it hard to discipline their be-havior. Youth welfare authorities insisted, for example, that strict limits be placed on work done by foster children, but especially in rural areas "the motive for accepting a child . . . is often the wish to have an unpaid worker."[59]

Youth offices tried to improve the quality of foster care by inviting foster mothers to "mothers' evenings" where they would be introduced to modern standards of child care.[60] But these meetings had a limited effect; in Hamburg, the Youth Office did not have enough money to organize mothers' evenings in each welfare district, and it could not compel foster mothers to attend. Only the "more intelligent and experienced . . . foster mothers" actually participated.[61] Mothers' evenings preached to a relatively small circle of the already converted.[62] Negligent foster parents could be fined, even taken to court.[63] As a last resort, children could be removed from a foster home. But these steps were admissions of the Youth Office's inability to educate foster parents, and they could poison the relationship between social worker and client. When Hedwig Stieve tried to take a foster child away from its uncle, the man threatened to shoot her.[64]

Abandoned, Divorced, and Widowed Women on Welfare

Contemporary studies of women on welfare showed quite clearly how economic relationships and pressures were filtered through and mediated by personal and emotional relationships, and how these in turn were affected by economic circumstances. For example, unemployment and economic hardship contributed to the dissolution of marriages, which was frequently disastrous for women who had been off the labor market for many years and suddenly had to combine some form of paid employment (hard enough to find in itself) with child care. The housing crisis in Weimar Germany also added to these single mothers' problems. It was frequently impossible to find another dwelling, except as a subtenant, which brought with it further hardships and deprivations, such as lack of access to cooking facilities.[65] Alternatively, abandoned, divorced, or otherwise single mothers might stay where they had lived with their husbands, although this, too, could sometimes lead to completely untenable emotional situations if, for example, the man retained some legal rights to the accommodations. But if these women remained in their original apartments, they were normally forced to take in boarders so as to cover the rent or to bring in additional income. Contemporary social observers agreed that this situation was similarly untenable because it severely disrupted any family life that remained and made more work for the woman, usually at the cost of her health.

If they attempted to find jobs, these single mothers frequently experienced extreme difficulties. Middle- and lower-middle-class women who had not worked before marriage lacked marketable skills or training. But even women who had been employed before their marriages or before the birth of their first child found that they were severely disadvantaged in the labor market—skill requirements had changed since they had last worked, and they were often no longer physically capable of performing the jobs they tried to get. In addition, single mothers seeking paid employment felt the ironic effects of one of the achievements of the Weimar social state: If they tried to improve their market position by working more cheaply than their competitors, these women found that the agreements governing wages and working conditions in many industries prevented employers from hiring them at less than the state-regulated wage. As a result, single mothers were frequently forced into low-paying, marginal jobs (i.e., as cleaning ladies, in low-paid laundry work, etc.).[66] Often, they were unable to work full-time because they had no one to look after their children. So the poverty of single mothers became a viciously repetitive cycle.

Yet despite the fact that finding any kind of work was often impossible and that in order to work outside the home single mothers needed some kind of public or private day care, local welfare authorities increasingly insisted that single mothers get jobs rather than allowing them to live on public support.[67] Single mothers could sometimes improve their economic situation by forming a joint household with another woman, usually an older widow (who might or might not be a relative). The older woman contributed a part of her pension to the household economy and looked after the children while the younger mother worked.[68] But the advantage of this arrangement was increasingly undermined by local welfare authorities, who insisted on expanding the responsibilities of relatives for the support of their indigent kin. Living with an unemployed sister, a mother on a small pension, or even with a nonrelative increasingly produced a reduction of public support.[69]

"Housing Welfare"

The Weimar housing crisis made it quite clear, if it had not been apparent before, that the unpaid domestic labor of women was essential to the maintenance of the family and the reproduction of German society. Intense overcrowding, clearly inadequate cooking, cleaning, washing, and sanitary facilities, the refusal of landlords to undertake even the most necessary repairs, together with the effects of food shortages, inflation, and increasing unemployment, all made it difficult, sometimes impossible, for many women to secure the basic survival of their families. As a Communist newspaper put it in 1921, "The proletarian mother and housewife . . . and the single working woman suffer the most under these conditions."[70] With time, the conditions under which women's reproductive labor was performed might be improved by moving families from overcrowded, unhealthy rooms to the better quality housing that started to go up after the middle of the 1920s. But the new housing programs of the Weimar period never managed to erase the basic housing shortage, let alone provide better general housing conditions for the great majority of Germans. A select minority of working- and lower-middle-class families did escape to the new housing estates. But the 1927 annual report of the Hamburg Agency for Housing Care (Behörde für Wohnungspflege) explained that

> people of moderate means, who by no means belong to the typical lower classes of the big city . . . are not in the position to manage the rents for new housing that are common nowadays. . . . The new housing with rents of about 540 marks (sixty square meters at 9 marks per meter) does not benefit them. The average income of an unskilled worker is about 1,500 marks per year, that of a skilled worker 2,100 marks. From these incomes, no more than 300 to 400 marks per month can normally be allotted to rent. As a consequence of the contemporary social distress, the maximum that can be spent on housing has been pushed down, not only for the unemployed but also for many of the self-

employed in the lower and middle strata of the population who are fighting a desperate
struggle for their bare existence. For them, the new housing is completely impossible,
especially as there are often additional expenses for traveling [to work].[71]

Most tenants were stuck in housing that had been put up before the war and was
beginning to deteriorate rapidly in the 1920s.[72] Karen Hagemann observes that "the
average workers' family in Hamburg lived . . . in a crowded, comfortless two- or three-
room dwelling . . . in an old tenement in a working-class neighborhood."[73]

To improve the general level of "housing culture" (*Wohnkultur*) in the old, overcrowded, and frequently dilapidated houses where most people lived, it was not
enough to enforce building codes and rent controls. Municipal housing offices must
also undertake "housing welfare" (*Wohnungsfürsorge*) or "housing cultivation"
(*Wohnungspflege*) activities among tenants so as to encourage and to educate them
to cope with their circumstances. The efforts of the *Wohnungspflege* were to be addressed primarily to working-class women:

> Her occupation as housewife and mother binds her intimately to [the home]. . . . She
> does not have the same opportunity to participate in public life. . . . Consequently, she
> is much more deeply and directly affected by all of the . . . drawbacks of the dwelling
> than the man. . . . The women is normally much more strongly interested in [the family's]
> housing. Every intervention in favor of a better standard of life must therefore be aimed,
> first and foremost, at the woman. . . . [From a more practical viewpoint, it is also true
> that] the housing welfare agencies will almost always find the woman, but only very
> rarely the man, at home [when they make their inspections].

Women were also to play an important role as both professional officials and voluntary inspectors in the *Wohnungspflege*. Working-class housewives were thought to
be more likely to trust other women, even if they came from another class, than men,
when it came to the kinds of questions that housing welfare was supposed to address:
"It would create a very comic picture if a male housing inspector were to demonstrate how one prepares vegetables for cooking or how windows can be cleaned
without cloths. But without such practical demonstrations, you get nowhere in housing welfare. Precisely for this reason, it is difficult for a man to be seen as an authority in household matters."

The female housing inspector was depicted as "the gender comrade and the woman
who knows the circle of work and worry of the one who must wrestle with all the
disadvantages and inadequacies of a dwelling: the housewife. As a result of her nature, enhanced by traditional practice . . . [the female inspector] has a pronounced
aptitude for accomplishing the tasks of physical and psychological care." Yet female
housing inspectors sometimes "met with an unfriendly, even rough reception. . . .
On occasions they were even shown the door." In Munich, right after the war, "female housing inspectors encountered lamentable treatment in a whole string of cases.
The female inspector's visit was felt to be an unpleasant surveillance. . . . People
refused to answer the questions . . . posed. . . . This behavior was seen as [the result
of] the 'revolutionary ferment amongst the population.'" Yet even the "return of more
orderly conditions" did not necessarily bring with it an "understanding and appre-
ciation of social institutions," especially when "a female housing inspector . . . does
not react with a warm heart to the distress she has been called to alleviate and re-

move." She might then quickly come to be seen more as an unwelcome "inspector" (*Kontrollbeamte*) than as a "teacher of the people" (*Volkserzieherin*).[74]

In Düsseldorf, a *Wohnungspflege* was set up under the Prussian Housing Law of 1918. Although it had the same police powers as the Housing Office, the *Wohnungspflege* did not enforce housing regulations. Physical defects in the housing could be reported to the competent authorities, but the *Wohnungspflege*'s real responsibility was to deal with the "human defects" that contributed to housing problems: "Looking after housing also involves taking care of human beings. What good is a nice home if the people who live there do not understand how they should use it, if they are not physically and spiritually well?"[75] The *Wohnungspflege* was to teach tenants, specifically housewives, how to make the best use of the rooms they had, how to set up beds, how to air rooms, and how to clean them. It was also supposed to offer "economic and 'social-hygienic' advice with regard to . . . proper household management and any other issues that may be relevant to the well-being of the family."[76]

In Hamburg, the Behörde für Wohnungspflege, which had existed since 1898, engaged in "continuous detail work in the enlightenment and education of families, especially of housewives, toward the goal of good and healthy living habits. The housewives are taught the basic concepts of hygiene and handling of living space."[77] The agency's primary goal was to convince working-class women that "with careful treatment, even an inferior dwelling could be made more bearable, which through inappropriate and neglectful occupancy would quickly sink to the level of being uninhabitable."[78] Most of this educational work was done on a voluntary basis; in the mid-1920s, the agency employed only thirteen technical officers (*Aussenbeamte*) and four housing social workers, who were supported by thirty-four volunteers. Beginning in 1921, women were admitted to both paid professional and voluntary work in the agency, and by the mid-1920s about 38 percent were female. The agency lacked the personnel to inspect a large number of working-class households, so visitations inevitably came to concentrate upon "households 'with bad habits and bad use of the housing' in the older districts inhabited by workers." The agency also distributed educational publications such as, for example, a small brochure produced in 1926 that "was supposed to enlighten tenants about their responsibilities for the hygiene and cleanliness of the dwelling with the help of 'unpretentious rhymes' as well as 'colorful and friendly pictures.'"[79] The Hamburg housing welfare agency did, however, have to admit that

> poor housing conditions often make any really effective help difficult. . . . Often babies must be raised in the same room in which people live, cook, work, and sleep. Consequently, much of the effort to improve the health of the people . . . is rendered illusory. Just as bad as the damage done to health are the moral effects on youth caused by overcrowding, the lack of separation of the sexes, and the presence of boarders who are not relatives.

One housing expert acknowledged, for example, that frequently repeated admonitions to provide separate beds for male and female children were "worthless so long as crowded housing excluded their implementation. The fight waged by the housing care agencies against taking in lodgers can have no permanent success as long as . . .

[there are no] homes for single people to provide alternative lodging." Housing welfare agencies did sometimes provide material assistance that would allow families to improve their housing conditions. A supplementary benefit from the welfare office might permit a family not to take in lodgers and hence have more room for themselves. A small loan might help a family to buy the basic household items that so many of the poorest German families seemed to lack. Women might be much more inclined to heed the advice not to do their laundry in the kitchen "if the landlord repairs the damaged flooring [in the washroom]."[80] Yet the Hamburg housing welfare agency also insisted that tenants contributed to their own material problems: Often, overcrowding was "only caused by the excess of household items from which no one will part, produced by the joining together of two families, or by the fact that one room is kept as the 'good front parlor' and basically not used." Sometimes overcrowding could be reduced by convincing the families to part with some of their possessions, by finding one of the grown children a place in another household, or by taking the younger children into a day nursery. But insufficient beds, not enough space to set up extra beds, and the presence of prostitutes as lodgers in some of the poorer families continued to be problems.[81]

The primary emphasis of housing welfare activities remained education, not material assistance. In order to "introduce the idea of housing hygiene and of rational housekeeping to broader circles of the population" and to show "how, with the simplest means, even old housing can be made more hygienic and used more rationally," the Behörde für Wohnungspflege joined with a number of organizations to sponsor a lecture series in January 1928. The speakers included Hildegard Margis of the National Association of German Housewives (Reichsverband deutscher Hausfrauenvereine), Berlin, who lectured on "improving old housing from the standpoint of housekeeping" (with slides), and an architect who offered advice on "equipping old housing with cheap household items" (also with slides).[82] Oberbaurat Brandt used slides to demonstrate relatively inexpensive ways to add heating, washing, and bathroom facilities to older buildings. But he also emphasized "that the tenant, especially the housewife, can . . . contribute a great deal to the improvement of the dwelling by treating it rationally: good lighting, light-colored . . . carpets, cleanliness, ruthless removal of all unnecessary household items and 'junk.'"[83] It is not clear exactly who attended these lectures, but with an entrance fee of 1 mark for one lecture or 2 marks for the initial series of three, there were probably not large numbers of housewives from poorer families in the audience.[84] In cooperation with several of Hamburg women's associations and with the support of the health, youth and welfare offices, the Behörde für Wohnungspflege organized another lecture series with the title "The Reform of Old Housing" in January 1928 that included a talk on how to outfit a home with cheap household equipment.[85] The Prussian Ministry of Culture considered this kind of knowledge so important that it issued a decree in 1931 directing that "henceforth, in all girls' schools, the closest possible attention will be given to housing care and housing culture. The cultivation of good housing habits contributes to the economy by maintaining the stock of housing, and it also serves the health of the nation."[86] Some women certainly found the advice disseminated by housing welfare agencies helpful in their daily struggles with the deficits of Weimar housing. But others doubted the benefits of this instruction: "The individual housewives, who were being lectured on their duties in the household and who were being trained for a 'good and healthy housing culture,' found that following these suggestions frequently meant more work; on these grounds alone housewives were probably skeptical, even hostile [toward this advice]."[87]

Female Social Workers and Women Clients

Women welfare clients' relationships with the Weimar welfare system were mediated and complicated by their dealings with the female social workers who examined their individual cases. Fearing that the breakdown of women's "reproductive labor discipline" would threaten the continued existence of families on welfare, social workers paid close attention to the way that women clients performed their allotted roles as mothers and homemakers. In the mid-1920s, a social worker in Cologne contrasted the impressions she drew from two household visits. In the first case,

> the home visit certainly presents a very sad picture but at the same time a real challenge to reform these conditions. . . . In particular, the wife must . . . be advised on an ongoing basis about the care and education . . . of her children. . . . This means that home visits should be made as often as possible. It would be best if some diligent housewife could take the women under her wing, show her how to manage her household, and put pressure on her to bring in some money by getting waged work. In a pedagogically appropriate manner, the [clients'] will to help themselves must be awakened. They must be disabused of the idea that public relief is a natural right to be claimed without putting any effort at all into the "healing" of one's own circumstances. [On the other hand,] a quite different picture . . . is revealed by the domestic circumstances of a thirty-five-year-old woman who comes from a better class of people but who has been abandoned by her husband. She has to struggle very hard so that she and her children can manage at all. . . . [but] order and cleanliness prevail. . . . She is very eager to work, will do everything for her children, asks only for temporary help in order not to be driven to complete despair. Her attitude shows that welfare work with her will not be fruitless but will be accepted with a thankful heart."[88]

Women welfare clients might resent this surveillance of their everyday lives if it was not accompanied by any significant material benefit. In 1931, for example, a south German newspaper carried a story about the grandmother of an illegitimate child in Zuffenhausen (northern Württemberg): "From time to time, a 'sister' from the youth welfare office came to the house and always had something to bleat about [*meckern*]. The grandmother was naturally incensed and finally ordered the sister out of the house with these words, 'So long as I do not get any money for the child, then you have no reason to come snooping around in my house."[89] A left-wing social policy journal tried to play on such resentments:

> The snooping around about the most intimate family matters appears to be going even further; it has been proposed that the social workers will instruct families in the making of their own clothes, give them tips on economical shopping, pressure them to sublet rooms, encourage women to bring in more income by washing their lodgers' clothes or preparing their meals and God knows what else. . . . The old poor-law guardians of earlier times did snoop around in the clothes closets . . . but it is the particular achievement

of the [present system] that it seeks to dictate how the proletarian wife will run her household."[90]

But tensions between women welfare clients and female social workers involved more than material grievances. To the battles over material benefits were added conflicts about less tangible but equally important issues, such as the autonomy and reputation of women welfare clients as wives and mothers. Women welfare clients might dispute the (usually single) female social worker's competence to judge them as mothers and to offer advice that was not based on everyday experience and common sense. In 1928, a Hamburg welfare official insisted, for example, that women welfare clients were "quite disinclined to accept the advice of a social worker whose merely theoretical knowledge . . . provokes feelings of resistance."[91]

Social workers' claims to be the sympathetic allies of women on welfare in their daily struggles for survival could sometimes sound rather hollow when measured against the everyday practice of social work. A reader's letter to the Hamburg Communist newspaper, published in January 1929, described how a female social worker visiting a woman welfare client who received 15 marks a week in support for herself and her child "inquired very thoroughly about my circumstances." In passing, the social worker remarked that "it is quite cold and also very damp in your room. You need to heat it," even though she knew that the welfare office only gave the woman two hundred weight of coal per week; properly heating her room would have required at least four hundred weight. In the same breath, "the sister asked whether I couldn't perhaps take in a subtenant [in the damp room]."[92] In 1932, another welfare mother wrote to the Cologne Communist newspaper complaining that "a few days ago, I went to the social worker, Frl. Z., to get a milk coupon for my fourteen-month-old child. In an uppity tone, she told me that my child was too old for milk . . . and she had the indecency to inform me that I had probably neglected my child and not looked after it properly. . . . Isn't it a scandal that we have to be spied upon and harassed by such ladies who themselves have not the least idea of life and who are paid a good salary? And the people in charge are puzzled when we sometimes lose our patience in the [welfare] office!!!"[93]

Rejection of the social worker's competence as a social mother was, however, not anchored in any single language of formal politics. Although the complaint quoted above appeared in a Communist newspaper, similar strains of argument appeared in a letter sent to Cologne Oberbürgermeister Adenauer, by Frau Alexander H., a Catholic, "female academic and daughter of [a] now dead, but well-known Viennese trial lawyer." Her husband, the scion of "a very old, very rich Duisburg family," had left her to live with his mistress in an expensive boardinghouse on the Ringstrasse. While he bought jewelry for his mistress and entertained her with luxurious trips to Hamburg, his wife had to get used to the unfamiliar taste of poverty and homelessness. Frau H. admitted that her husband's well-to-do family was prepared to help her, but only if she agreed virtually to sign over her rights to her child. "Because I am a Catholic and my husband's family is Protestant . . . they want to exploit my unhappy situation and demand that my child be sent to a Protestant religious foundation in Kaiserwerth before they will give me any help at all. If I agree, then I am to receive 300 marks a month. I didn't agree to this proposal and kept my child with me instead."

Bitterly, Frau H. complained that the social worker in charge of her case had refused all financial help: "After starving for six days, I went to the social worker at the Deutz district office . . . with the request that she help me and my child. But she just told me in a cold-blooded manner . . . that I would receive no public support because my husband's family had already offered me 300 marks a month that I had refused."

Frau H. directed her anger not only at this individual social worker but also at the state that could permit her, a German mother, to be subjected to such mistreatment:

> Do we now live in such barbaric times, does the state really pay such women to give advice so that they can indeed say to a poor, starving mother that no one can help them because they can get money by giving up their children. . . . Does that mean that every mother in Germany who finds herself in distress must first sell off her children? . . . I do not want to burden you with my sad case alone; rather, I write in the name of every mother who might find herself in my position. . . . If my husband had been a poor worker, he would long since have been sitting in the local workhouse, but the welfare office appears to have a colossal respect for "distinguished" gentlemen sporting monocles who let their families starve on the streets. . . . Otherwise, the welfare office in Deutz would have long since found some way to make my husband live up to his responsibilities to his wife and child. If the welfare office in Deutz continues to act according to these principles, we will soon see a thriving business in religious blackmail.[94]

This one woman's protest turned the official rhetoric of the protection of motherhood against itself, exposing to public ridicule the language of public parenthood employed to legitimate social work and the child welfare services. Similar strategies can be observed in some collective protests by women. In 1932, for example, two women's committees in Hammerbrook warned an official of the welfare office that they would bring their children into the welfare office district branch and leave them there if they did not get the clothing, potatoes, and fuel they needed.[95] Yet women's experiences with the Weimar welfare system did not translate directly into collective action or participation in formal political organizations. The women who confronted the Weimar welfare system were in no sense a homogeneous group, nor was the treatment they received at the hands of welfare authorities uniform. The wives and mothers whose welfare Koven and Michel's maternalists wanted to promote were certainly not the only female clients of the Weimar welfare state. A visitor to the welfare office of any large German town in the mid 1920s would certainly have found women whose identities as mothers had brought them into contact with the welfare services (although their interests were by no means homogeneous): pregnant women and nursing mothers, women with illegitimate children, foster mothers. Yet standing in the same lines were other women who had been discriminated against by the unemployment, health insurance, or state pension systems: divorced and abandoned women, unemployed female workers, war widows, and genteel ladies from the property-owning classes, now dispossessed by inflation. In addition, there was the occasional former prostitute whom the state welfare system was attempting to rehabilitate. Nor, indeed, was gender the only factor that shaped female clients' identities and interests; an unemployed, young, single, childless, working-class woman had little in common with the aged, propertied widow whose assets had been destroyed by inflation. Private capital pensioners, the majority of whom were women, found it a terrible indignity that "we members of the pensioners' estate [*Rentnerstand*], who have become gray as a result of strenuous work and great parsimony, should be set on the same level as petty thieves and work-shy riffraff," as the Detmold branch of the Rentnerbund put it in 1924.[96] It is therefore impossible to speak of "women and welfare" in unproblematic, collective terms; rather, we need to distinguish a variety of quite different types of gendered encounters with the welfare state.

The intervention of the welfare services into families and neighborhoods also facilitated—indeed, encouraged—the expression of divisive conflicts, passions, hatreds, and feuds produced by the frictions of everyday life in working-class neighborhoods, tenement blocks, and courtyards. In 1932, for example, a well-known social-work handbook contained the following interview with a neighbor and landlady, drawn from an actual case file:

> Recently, Frau N. has been running around at night and comes back home quite drunk. The children are totally neglected. They have lice in their heads and on their bodies. If I didn't have to worry about the unpleasantness to which I would be subjected, I would already have written telling the welfare services to take her kids away from Frau N. Now it appears that some of the other tenants in the building want this to be done. Frau N. also badly neglects cleaning the apartment. If it wasn't for the fact that the rent control office ties my hands, I would have evicted her long ago. And this family is not really so poor after all. Certainly, they can manage to buy things that I cannot, and I have only one child.[97]

Denunciations might express sincere moral disapproval of the way a neighbor was treating his or her child or a husband his wife. But denunciations also allowed women to use the welfare services to voice all sorts of other grievances against their neighbors, relatives, or husbands.

Women's struggles to renegotiate their relationships with the welfare system commonly found expression in "cultural" transactions between a single client and a single welfare official. In any instrumental sense, overt protest against the Weimar welfare system, whether individual or collective, whether explicitly political or intensely personal in language, was generally counterproductive. The Weimar welfare system gave its clients the legal right to complain and provided appropriate administrative channels for a review of the details. Yet the many thousands of welfare recipients who did make complaints along officially prescribed channels frequently discovered that their protests produced few results. Anyone who stubbornly persisted in voicing their grievances, once the official review procedure had run its course, risked being branded a professional complainer, who would eventually be ignored or, worse, cut off from all benefits. It was a very difficult task to avoid this marginalization or exclusion and yet at the same time attempt to (re)assert one's own dignity, autonomy, and rights as a human being and as a citizen of the Weimar Republic. Given the constraints of the Weimar welfare system, the real "heroes of their own lives" to borrow the title of one recent American study of child abuse, may well have been those women who understood how to cultivate the "correct" relationship with the social worker by presenting the appropriate image, by manipulating the official language and ideology of motherhood to their own benefit.[98] What I have in mind is beautifully captured by Ruth Fischer's semifictional description of the "two Annas":

> And so with time there were two Annas. One was the "official Anna" [die Behörden-Anna], the woman with no husband and with six small children who sat there at many

official desks and had to make it very clear to the welfare officers that without support she and her children would surely starve. Welfare Office, Youth Office, private charities, Labor Office, Housing Office . . . all of these knew this one Anna quite well. . . . She needed this, she needed that, she must have it, otherwise there would be a disaster. And always she had several quite blond, very cleanly washed and properly dressed pretty little children with her, the illustration of her complaints. That was the "official Anna," Anna with a mask, Anna the mime, a woman who inside was really boiling over with rage because of this comedy she had to play, mother of six little children. . . . But the "everyday Anna" was quite different. She worked liked a slave, this real Anna. She could not live and had no intention of trying to live on only the money the welfare gave her.[99]

The two Annas were certainly not alone. A letter sent to social worker Emilie Zadow claimed that a woman welfare client was giving other women lessons on how to represent themselves to the social worker. Her strategy was quite the opposite of Ruth Fischer's Anna: "If you dress your kids properly and have covers on the beds, all your complaints will be useless. You must allow only a pot and two cups to be seen, and everything must be tattered and patched, and you should always begin to sob whenever a stranger comes to the house."[100]

Even when the actions and words of welfare clients were saturated with submission and conformity, there was often still present a tone of subdued—indeed, quite subtle—self-assertion. For example, female social workers placed great emphasis on the importance of creating a personal relationship with their clients and stressed the need to support and encourage sympathetic personal and human ties in German society as against mechanistic, abstract, and bureaucratic relationships.[101] Women welfare clients were sometimes able to use this intensely personal and affective language to challenge welfare practices. In the mid-1920s, the Nuremberg welfare office decided on an administrative reorganization that would have made Hedwig Stieve's clients, all of whom were foster children and foster mothers, the charges of another social worker with broader responsibilities for a variety of different types of welfare families. In her diary, written over a five-month period in 1924–1925, Stieve shows that she had cultivated quite intense personal—indeed, emotional—relationships with her clients: "I am really so attached to these people, many of whom I have known for years. They are quite right to complain because I have to say good-bye to them, and I have already promised some of them that now and then I will visit them again. Many of them really dislike the idea that now a 'stranger' will want to know about their personal circumstances." In her discussion of the transition in Nuremberg from the older system of "special care" for different categories of welfare clients to a more generalized and more anonymous system of "family care," Stieve presents a wonderful small drama, played out between her and one of her clients, that shows just how creative women welfare clients could be:

The foster mother H. came by the office today to discuss some matter. She burst into my room, coarse and noisy, as is her way, hiking along in her boots directly for me. . . . [But I had to tell her that] "from now on you will have to discuss your problems with the lady over there." For a while she just stood there with her mouth open, then very cautiously she turned her head in the direction of Fraulein F. [her new social worker], and then she looked back at me. "What," she screamed, "you are not coming anymore? But I just won't have anything to do with anyone else!" She turned and began to stomp toward the door. But then she stopped for a minute, turned back toward the room, and by way of explanation for her response informed all of those present: "Look here! You have to understand that I just can't stomach those other 'subtle' ones; but you and I, well, we knew how to speak plain German to each other, and I really liked that." And then she swung abruptly around again and, with her head held very high, she disappeared into the street.[102]

CHAPTER SEVEN

The State as Parent?

Youth Welfare and German Families

The Youth Welfare Office and *Volkserziehung*

All branches of the Weimar welfare system claimed to dispense *Volkserziehung* (popular enlightenment) as well as material benefits. But the educative function of welfare was most insistently and repeatedly invoked in Weimar youth welfare offices.[1] Youth offices were the main institutional agents of the 1922 Youth Welfare Law, a political compromise between the bourgeois private charities, who wanted to defend their very considerable realm of child and youth welfare activities, and the Social Democrats, who argued for a state monopoly of welfare functions.[2] The 1922 law obliged the youth offices to include "men and women experienced and approved in youth welfare work" who were to be "nominated . . . by the private associations devoted partially or wholly to the promotion of welfare or of the youth movement."[3] Much of the actual work done by youth welfare offices was contracted out to private welfare agencies. This created a new terrain of social and political power where the socialist Arbeiterwohlfahrt, the Catholic Caritas, and the Protestant Innere Mission fought one another for state funds and for religious and ideological control over welfare clients. Social Democrats insisted that German workers should be allowed to participate directly in the administration of the child welfare system rather than remaining its passive "objects."[4] But Caritas and the Innere Mission were intent on blocking this "godless," secular, socialist influence on youth welfare work.[5]

Socialists and nonsocialists disagreed about state intervention into German family life. Weimar socialists argued that industrialization, the spread of the capitalist market economy, and even the growth of the commercial mass entertainment industry had already begun to deprive the German working-class family of most of its vital functions and internal cohesion. Consequently, Social Democrats were less troubled than nonsocialists by state intervention into what they thought was an already weakened family structure.[6] Religious spokespersons found the intrusions of state welfare agencies more problematic; in 1929, for example, the report of the annual meeting of Caritas warned "against a development of the youth offices, which . . . to an increasing degree place decisions about the welfare . . . of minor children in the hands of 'political' agencies, among which, unfortunately, the youth offices must often be counted, while at the same time weakening the influence of the parental home. . . . [This] will also increasingly reduce the parents' sense of responsibility toward their children."[7] Catholic and Protestant welfare organizations also doubted that the specifically educational character of child and youth welfare would be compatible with the institutional forms provided by state agencies. The religious charities viewed welfare work as a "charismatic" relationship, not a "functional-rational" one. The youth welfare worker would "save" the endangered child by the force of his or her personal example and influence. In the process, the gap between the classes, produced by industrialization, urbanization, and, not least, Marxism, could be bridged; the practice of welfare would contribute to the construction of a *Volksgemeinschaft*.[8] For many who shared these views, the state form of welfare too often threatened to degenerate into merely formal "bureaucratism": the orderly, anonymous, rational disposition of cases according to abstract, impersonal criteria, a pure *Richtsatzpolitik*, dispensing material benefits but providing no real educational care.

Correctional Education

Of the "therapeutic measures" that a Weimar youth office might prescribe, "correctional education" (*Fürsorgeerziehung* or *FE*) was the most severe. A court order for *FE* required that the youth in question be removed from his or her family and placed in foster care or in a reformatory. Unlike a prison sentence for an adult, *FE* was of unspecified duration. The District Court (Amtsgericht), sitting as a "Guardianship Court," granted Youth Office petitions for *FE* orders if it could be established that a condition of *Verwahrlosung* existed within the child's family. *Verwahrlosung* had, at best, an amorphous and arbitrary definition that allowed youth welfare authorities considerable powers of discretion in labeling "aberrant" and potentially "dangerous" behavior.[9]

Verwahrlosung was thought to be both symptom and product of the parents' inability to do their job properly. Hence, an *FE* order was directed as much against the parents as against the child. Correctional education drastically abridged parental, especially, patriarchal, rights. Parents no longer determined how their children would be raised or what education they would receive. While their children were in *FE*, parents lost the earnings that sons or daughters would otherwise have contributed to the family income. Yet parents were still legally responsible for the economic support of their children and were even expected to contribute to the costs of their reform school "education." A vitriolic note sent to local welfare authorities in 1929 by a south German father illustrates the hostilities that *FE* could produce: "The so-called welfare means nothing to me or to him [the man's son]; we both snap our fingers at it. . . . Even if it lasts another 199 years, it will still be nothing more than a rank swindle. . . . [The fact that] my son, Otto, was not released [from *FE*] was an act of revenge, to make me angry, simply because I will not pay the 500 marks [that the Youth Office demanded for Otto's support]."[10]

Most of the reformatories to which "endangered" children were sent were run along authoritarian lines by private charities.[11] Popular distrust of *FE* was deepened by several widely publicized revolts by inmates against conditions in these homes and by Social Democratic and Communist campaigns against the abuses associated with "correctional education."[12] Occasionally, entire families united against the authorities: In the 1920s, Margarete Kahle reported, for example, that some young girls who were supposed to be sent to a reformatory "were hidden [by their families] or received information about how to make good their escape. . . . The relatives promised to do everything possible to 'free' them and poured threats and curses on the heads of the female officials who came to take the children away."[13]

Marcus Gräser is undoubtedly right to conclude that "the origins of correctional education in the criminal law, but above all the knowledge that a reform school education was of little use, meant that the majority of lower-class youths and their parents viewed [*FE*] as a threat, not as a form of help."[14] This did not, however, mean that all parents and all children simply resisted correctional education. The relationship was in practice more complex. Parents might, for example, try to use correctional education to discipline their children. In 1922 Gottfried E., a married unskilled worker living in Kongen in the Oberamt Esslingen, asked local authorities to send his son from his first marriage to a reform school because "he is not engaged in any sort of employment. I have to support him completely. He already has several convictions for theft and disturbing the peace at night. . . . He presents a very bad example for my other children. He has also repeatedly threatened to murder us."[15]

The parents of Marie W., who was born in 1911 in Frickenhausen, seemed to agree with the authorities that the girl was "very seriously endangered," and they actively supported the Nürtingen Youth Office's efforts to have her committed to a reformatory.[16] Marie W. had a long record of stealing. She was now also thought to be infected with a sexually transmitted disease.[17] Nürtingen youth welfare authorities described her parents as "orderly people, but they have done a completely inadequate job of raising their daughter," an assessment that the father and mother did not dispute.[18] After the girl ran away to Mannheim in the spring of 1928, her mother "repeatedly . . . asked the Youth Office to do everything it could to find out where the girl was and to ensure that her daughter, who was not doing well at home, be sent to a reform school."[19] But Marie W. insisted that she had run away, not because she was "crazy for men [*mannsüchtig*]" and an "irresponsible young thing,"[20] as the Youth Office claimed, but "because my brothers [from whom her parents had clearly not protected her] made my life such a mess."[21] Marie W. insisted that she had not, as the youth authorities charged, had sex with Walter V. in the zur Alpenrose pub, or with one Paul T. from Egg, or with Otto K., a twenty-two-year-old "civil servant in the post office" in Essen with whose parents she stayed for a time, although she did admit that she "certainly did have sex with him earlier, while he was still in Nürtingen."[22] A much more compelling reason for her flight from Oberensingen was the abuse (possibly including sexual abuse) to which she had been subjected by her older brother: "As long as my older brother was in Oberensingen, I certainly would not return voluntarily. But now he is gone, and I would gladly stay with my parents."[23]

This explanation of her behavior did not prevent Marie W. from being sent to the Protestant reformatory at Oberurbach, from which, however, she escaped, though pregnant, in November 1928.[24]

In other cases, youth welfare services were drawn into disputes between the parents. Eugen F., son of a Nürtingen cabinet maker, was not only, as one report observed, "at the mercy of his every mood" but also at the mercy of his divorced parents' conflicts with each other. Eugen F. was born in Nürtingen on 15 June 1910. His parents divorced in August 1921, with blame (*Schuld*) being allocated to both parties.[25] In September 1925, he ran away from his apprenticeship, claiming that the wage he received—1 mark per day—was too low.[26] In February 1926, he started another apprenticeship with a master baker in Augsburg, but on 29 April he took flight "after embezzling 29 marks 40 pfennig." On 4 May 1927 he was picked up by the Munich police.[27] After having run away several times from one reformatory, Eugen F. was transferred in May 1927 to the St. Konradihaus in Schelklingen. In August 1928, his mother wrote to this reform school, asking that her son be released. The director reported that Eugen F. was learning to become a bookbinder and seemed to be doing well at this trade, "but his friends envy him being in this position. From a false sense of honor, he gave in to the bad feelings around him, and let himself be misled by some of his friends into running away. . . . [After one of his escapes], he wandered aimlessly from his mother in Stuttgart to his father in Nürtingen. He simply did not know which one he should side with. He appears to have come under bad influences in Stuttgart." At this time, Eugen F. took a temporary job as a dishwasher in a restaurant, which, however,

> did not satisfy the not untalented lad. So, he went to the Caritasverband, whose secretary found him a place in the [protestant shelter] in Stuttgart. There, as he told me in a letter, F. met "one of the lowest types, [who] talked me into running away . . . to the Rhineland on a motorcycle (which his friend also let him drive). [The friend] talked of breaking into houses and of murderous deeds, which, however, I firmly refused, because I am too good-natured to do such things." . . . The youngster now regrets his flight. . . . What causes concern . . . is his weak will and lack of energy. . . . He has the best of intentions and makes the nicest resolutions. But he lacks the strength to keep his promises. Without even thinking about it, he . . . allows himself to be driven by his moods. The young boy understands quite well that he is no match for the dangers of his environment. He needs the support and discipline that an institution provides. If he were now to be released from the reformatory and from *FE*, he would quickly become wayward once again, as the last weeks have clearly demonstrated.[28]

From this point on, Nürtingen youth welfare authorities increasingly found themselves embroiled in the struggles between Eugen F.'s divorced parents. His mother and the unemployed man she now lived with intimated to Eugen F. that his father had an "immoral" relationship with his sister. The Nürtingen youth welfare authorities found this allegation "absolutely irresponsible, indeed, vile, because not a single one of these claims has been proven." As far as they were concerned, the mother was the real problem; in their opinion, both Eugen F. and his sister "appear to be hereditarily tainted by the mother," and for this reason, along with the poor housing conditions in which the mother now lived, "a permanent reunion of the young boy with his mother should be prevented." But Eugen F.'s father appeared to have been intimidated by the charges against him and his sister:

> He believes that his son should be left peacefully where he is, for the time being. . . . I have the impression that the father has expressed this wish mainly because he is afraid that his former wife and his son will immediately blame him if the boy is returned to the reformatory. . . . One could attempt to leave the youngster in his present workplace . . . but [I] do not believe that the weak-willed, unstable lad can resist the temptations of the big city, and I fear that this attempt will quickly go awry.[29]

In 1926, Eugen F.'s father had requested that the boy's sister, Aloise, born in 1908, also be taken into *FE*: "From time to time, the girl has apparently stayed with her mother, who lives together with a lover. . . . This abode appears in no way to serve the girl's well-being."[30] On 22 April 1925, a provisional order for *FE* had been issued against the girl "because, without any good reason, she has repeatedly changed her place of work and avoids any regular employment."[31] But Dora R., a police social worker in Stuttgart who was asked to report on Aloise F., did not believe that *FE* was warranted. By 11 January 1926, Aloise had been in service for eleven months "with the family K.," who seemed quite satisfied with her work; "she has not been running around and makes a completely orderly impression. She does not go to her mother often." Aloise had, indeed, recently been hospitalized, but not for a sexually transmitted disease, as the Nürtingen Youth Office evidently feared; she had instead been diagnosed with scabies, "which she appears to have picked up in her previous job."[32] In a second report, the police social worker affirmed that "Aloise F. has maintained herself well . . . in her position with Frau K. and performed her work diligently." But, unfortunately, the girl "could . . . not be kept from continuing to search out her mother." In order to remove the girl from the mother's direct influence, "we placed her, yesterday, in a position in Oeffingen, near to Fellbach."[33] This move clearly unsettled the young girl. In early March, without permission from her employer, Aloise ran away to her mother, claiming that she could not stay at her new job "because it was too lonely for me there."

   In April 1926, the police social worker reported that, according to Aloise F.'s mother, the girl "goes out every night, despite the curfew. . . . She appears to be running around with boys. She is also unable to work. When the mother was very ill, the girl did nothing to help. Herr F. then sent her to the Labor Office, which gave her a domestic position for four weeks with the local architect K." The police social worker now revised her previous assessment: Aloise F. must be put in a reform school "to protect the girl from the influence not so much of her mother but of the city, to which she keeps coming back to have contact with young men. In this regard, she appears to be severely endangered. Recently, she has not come very often to her mother, who forbids her to continue with this conduct."[34] Toward the end of April 1926, one of Aloise F.'s parents (it is not clear from the record which one) petitioned for her release from *FE*. But when questioned about Aloise F.'s conduct, all of the people she had worked for over the past two years "unanimously agreed that, after her initial probation, F. showed herself to be disorderly, dirty, lazy, mendacious, and, recently, quite crazy for men. She simply cannot muster a firm will against the influences of

the big city and more recently, according to a report from the Stuttgart police head-
quarters, against the possibilities for intercourse with men. . . . To prevent [further]
moral and physical dissolution, she must be confined to an institution." The Nürtingen
Youth Office insisted that "F.'s . . . mother, who gave birth to five children before
she was married and who has lived for years with a man to whom she is not married, provides no good example for the endangered girl, [but] the father and the
aunt in question have a good reputation here."[35] In May 1926, the girl was sent to
the Untermarchtal reformatory.[36]

Yet in August 1928, the father reversed his previous position and petitioned that
both children be released from *FE*.[37] Three days later, Eugen F. ran away from the
St. Konradihaus, first to his father, "then, again, to Stuttgart where, however, his
mother would not take him in. . . . He then returned to Nürtingen, from where his
father returned him to the reformatory on the nineteenth of this month."[38] The regional welfare authorities would have preferred that both children remain institutionalized for an indefinite period: "It is regrettable that such tainted human beings
must simply be left to their fate, and thus their downfall, when they have reached the
age of maturity. The influence that the mother and her current husband exert upon
the children has a damaging effect."[39] Yet Eugen F.'s next escape attempt, "without
any reason," in late January 1929, convinced the director of the St. Konradihaus that

> F. is an irremediable psychopath. He is unpredictable and unreliable. He can be docile,
> diligent, and content. But if something does not go the way he wants, then he falls into
> brooding and hatching schemes; or, as he puts it, he "studies" and ends up in such a
> mood that he tends to take flight. He does not shrink back from anything. . . . He [always]
> has an eye on motorcycles, on which he hopes to escape. . . . F. is completely weak willed
> and unstable. We do not have much hope for him.[40]

After a number of additional escapes, Eugen F. was released from *FE* at the age of
twenty-one on 15 June 1931.[41] His sister was released in April 1929, after which she
went to work as a "temporary maid with the homeowner B. in Nürtingen."[42]

From "Hard" to "Soft" Interventions:
"Protective Surveillance" (*Schutzaufsicht*)

Parents and children could find ways to use correctional education to pursue their
own interests, but this did not make *FE* a popular institution: "A regular demand for
these measures of the welfare state did not develop."[43] The coercive aspects of *FE*
contradicted the youth welfare authorities' larger aim of making the Youth Office a
"people's" agency, whose help and advice German fathers and mothers would seek
voluntarily.[44] These counterproductive effects of *FE* encouraged youth offices to
replace it with other, less coercive educational measures whenever possible. Weimar
youth offices began to explore the possibilities of "softer" interventions into German
family life such as *Schutzaufsicht* (probation).[45] Under the provisions of *Schutzaufsicht*, an endangered child remained in the family and was given a "helper" by the
Youth Office. Youth welfare authorities hoped that *Schutzaufsicht* "should make it
possible to avoid *FE*."[46] But *Schutzaufsicht* required dedicated, trained personnel who

were not easy to find.[47] Nor was it clear what forms of "treatment," beyond the force of moral example, could actually be used to make a *Schutzaufsicht* work.

A properly exercised *Schutzaufsicht* was a significant intrusion into the everyday lives of young people and their families.[48] But *Schutzaufsicht* was, if anything, more vulnerable than *FE* to parents' refusal to cooperate: "People will always find ways and means of lying to the helper, of deceiving him, and, in the end, of laughing at him behind his back." When this happened, the youth welfare authorities had no other alternative but to proceed to the harsher measure (*FE*). Indeed, parents and children had good reason to fear that a *Schutzaufsicht* was often the first step on the road to reform school rather than a real alternative to it.[49] In 1926, for example, Erwin Fr., son of a Catholic wood sculptor, born in 1913 in Kirchheim-Teck, came to the attention of the Nürtingen Youth Office because he was alleged to have stolen a watch, money, and some chocolate from Konrad Z. in Kirchheim.[50] Erwin Fr. and some of his friends were also reported to have repeatedly stolen from an eighty-two-year-old widower.[51] According to Pastor Blum in Kirchheim, Erwin Fr. "is almost impervious to any improving influences and to the positive stimulus of religion. When he was still at school, he was viewed as lost to his church. The parents have failed completely in the religious-moral education of their son."[52] Both the local teacher and the pastor expressed concern that Erwin Fr.'s father "does not appear capable of properly raising the boy. [The father] apparently has nervous problems and punishes the boy too harshly when he learns of something [the boy has done]. Consequently, the members of the family generally keep him in the dark." But the Youth Office was reluctant to put Erwin Fr. into *FE* because the boy had not yet finished his apprenticeship with a local cabinetmaker and because his father, a social pensioner who suffered from "severe physical injuries," clearly relied upon the son's earnings. Instead, the Youth Office asked that Erwin Fr. "be taken into *Schutzaufsicht* so as energetically to fight the danger of *Verwahrlosung* and to return him to the correct path."[53] This milder measure clearly did not work. In June 1930, local authorities asked that Erwin Fr. now be taken into *FE*. He had stolen some money, which he "used to take a trip to Stuttgart, to go to the movies and eat snacks alone, but also, in part, with his friends."[54] One of the helpers responsible for supervising Erwin Fr.'s behavior during the period in which he had been under *Schutzaufsicht* testified that

> he manifested a bashful, withdrawn character that I did not like. I . . . had the impression that Fr. did not want you to see all his cards. . . . During the time that he was at school, I spoke with the father again; I came to the conclusion that he was troubled by his son. Fr. . . . very often found his way to the cinema. I have the impression . . . that Fr. . . . wanted to treat himself and procured the money for this purpose by criminal means. Perhaps he has a proclivity to theft. There can certainly be no doubt that Fr. understands what he is doing. I would petition for *FE*.[55]

The juvenile court convicted Erwin Fr. of "grand larceny" on 5 August 1930 (he had stolen 25 marks, 30 marks, 15 marks, and 2 marks on separate occasions from the same people) but put him on probation for four years. Two years later, the Konradihaus, to which Erwin Fr. had been sent, reported that further educational measures would be useless; in their opinion, the boy was "beyond reform" (*schwer erziehbar*) and should, instead, be released and sent off to the "labor service"

(*Arbeitsdienst*), a recommendation that both Erwin Fr. and his parents appeared to support.[56]

School Health Care

Correctional care and *Schutzaufsicht* dealt with "problem" children and families. Forms of preventive care, such as school health inspections, tried to ensure that "normal" children and families would not become problem cases.[57] The advocates of preventive care insisted that "prevention is not only easier but also cheaper than healing."[58] And health experts warned that "the adult only engages properly in health care . . . if the ideals of cleanliness and a healthy way of life have been kept constantly before his eyes when he was a child, if not at home, then in the school."[59]

School health programs combined social with medical surveillance. If the examination of the child's body at school suggested that its health and welfare were being neglected at home, a social worker visited the family to ensure that the parents (but especially the mother) followed the doctor's advice about nutrition and hygiene.[60] Many parents cooperated with school health programs and even demanded that they be made more comprehensive. A meeting of parents at a Berlin school in 1926, for example, called for full-time school doctors, free treatment, and free medicine.[61] In 1932, a Hamburg school doctor reported that "the complaints of teachers and parents about the inadequate provision of school doctors has increased. . . . Many children have not been examined by a school doctor for three or more years."[62] But other parents and children were indifferent, sometimes even hostile, to the aims of school health programs. In 1928, evening health lectures were canceled in one Hamburg school district because the school administration felt there was insufficient interest among parents.[63] A Hamburg school doctor complained in 1929 that the parents' meetings to which he spoke were not well attended and that his advice on child care did not reach the right ears because "it was only the more orderly people who were present."[64] Another school doctor complained that

> it is only before the elections to the city parliament that there is a strong demand in meetings of parents for reports on the health of the children. My fears that these evenings would be used for agitation against the current welfare system were certainly justified, but I was, for the most part, spared sharp attacks either because the more reasonable parents resisted the agitators or because the school director nipped all such attempts in the bud, which was certainly the right thing to do.[65]

In 1928, a doctor responsible for examining students at several vocational schools (*Berufsschulen*) located in working-class districts of Hamburg complained that "if the examination was made known two days in advance . . . only a third of the students would show up, even in otherwise well-attended classes. . . . Of those who did appear, there were still a few who refused to be examined. . . . In individual classes, there is a passive or even an active refusal to be examined, in most instances caused by the 'spiritual' leader of the class."[66] This resistance did not prevent school medical examinations from taking place; but it mocked the school doctor's pretensions as an "educator of the people" (*Volkserzieher*).

The school health system provided certain material benefits, but on terms not always palatable to parents or children. School health services did not allow doctors to treat the illnesses whose symptoms they uncovered. School doctors were supposed to refer children with health problems to their regular family doctors (*Kassenarzt*) or, if the family was not properly insured, to the welfare doctor.[67] Doctors were supposed to "prescribe" free school meals on strictly medical grounds, but, especially during the Depression, many parents, some teachers, and even some doctors came to feel that economic and social considerations should also play a role in determining which children were given free school meals.[68] In 1932, for example, a Hamburg school doctor suggested that "the policy that now only those children receive school meals whose breadwinner is completely unemployed should be reviewed. Nowadays, there are many children whose parents earn no more than the unemployed receive [in public assistance] . . . but who are not allowed to participate in school meals programs simply because the family is not on welfare. I think other guidelines should be followed here."[69] In the spring of 1933, another school doctor in Hamburg suggested that "the children of people who are not working full time are often no better off than the children of the unemployed, [and] should be included in the regular examination of children for school meals programs."[70]

School health services also offered rest cures in the countryside. But for some families, the economic or emotional costs of sending their children away to the countryside outweighed the health benefits.[71] Parents of older children were particularly concerned about the loss of family income.[72] During the Depression, one Hamburg school doctor complained that "a whole string of students whom I had recommended for health cures refused my offer, with the explanation that they might possibly pay for this 'vacation' with the loss of their jobs."[73] Another school doctor bemoaned the fact that "it is precisely the children who need a health cure the most who often cannot go, because the parents cannot afford the financial contribution that is required or cannot buy the children the things they need for the trip."[74] Children on cures sometimes had to endure primitive conditions, especially if they stayed on farms rather than in rest homes. A 1925 survey showed that Berlin children on rest cures had to sleep in mangers or stalls, as well as in beds shared with maids or servants.[75]

School health programs might also challenge a family's pretensions to respectability or a woman's reputation as a good mother. Some mothers refused to believe their children were infested with lice.[76] In 1929, a school doctor ordered school meals for the obviously undernourished child of a lower-level civil servant who was trying, unsuccessfully, to feed five children on his small salary. But "on the very next day, the mother came to me, very upset and annoyed, to ask why school meals had been prescribed? She wasn't letting her children starve, etc. I calmed her down; the child was not given school meals and continues to be undernourished."[77] Finally, school health programs gave private welfare organizations an opportunity to exert political and ideological influence over young children. In 1925, the "parents' councils" (*Elternbeiräte*) of a group of Catholic schools in Cologne were drawn into a conflict with the local Arbeiterwohlfahrt in 1925 when they discovered that "the municipal school administration had instructed the headmasters of all elementary schools to give the Arbeiterwohlfahrt the names of 800 children whom this organization should send [on health cures] during the school holidays." These Catholic parents were mistrustful of "an organization . . . that uses every opportunity to advertise for secular schools and education. . . . We Catholic parents do not want our children to come into contact with a welfare organization whose views on education diverge so fundamentally from our own."[78] The parents also pointed out that in most of the city's Catholic schools, the parents' councils and the parish Caritas committee were already doing quite enough to provide holiday excursions and other activities for Catholic children. Social Democrats voiced similar complaints against the Catholic Caritas organization.[79]

Policing Child Labor

In the Weimar Republic, child labor was still controlled by a special branch of the police (*Gewerbepolizei*) that was supposed to enforce the 1903 Child Labor Law. But Weimar youth welfare experts insisted that child labor was really a welfare problem. Work damaged children's health and interfered with their proper education. Working children were also exposed to "moral dangers" that supposedly led them into delinquency; it was suggested that children often went to work so that they could buy sweets, purchase cigarettes, or attend films, all regarded as symptoms and causes of *Verwahrlosung*. Child labor was taken as a sign of deeper educational and disciplinary defects in the family, which only the youth welfare authorities could address by means of "a positive promotion of the child's education." Unlike the police, youth welfare authorities could take action even when the law had not actually been broken. They could "enlighten," "educate," and reform the misguided or selfish parents who were the real causes of the problems, and they could reinforce their advice with the special powers available to the Guardianship Court.[80] Youth welfare experts insisted that the main causes of child labor were parental ignorance and selfishness, but they were not blind or insensitive to the economic reasons that encouraged parents to send young children to work.[81] Welfare authorities understood that the success of their campaign against child labor depended to no small degree on the provision of supplements to the incomes of poor families in the form of clothing, shoes, or school meals. But youth welfare experts insisted that economic aid must always be combined with the appropriate educational measures."[82]

The 1922 Youth Welfare Law gave youth offices the right to be consulted about applications for child labor permits. Youth authorities used this opportunity to educate parents about the dangers of child labor and to persuade them not to send their children out to work.[83] An application for a child labor permit could invite unexpected, detailed, often lengthy examination of the parents' economic circumstances and moral character. Permits could be refused because the welfare authorities detected a threat to the child's health and welfare, even though the work itself was not legally prohibited. In 1928, for example, the Youth Office in Düsseldorf objected to the moral effects on twelve-year-old Helmut R. of his job as a messenger for a local merchant. The Youth Office claimed that the schoolboy "is given tips when he is working that allow him, without his parents' knowledge, to go on [various] day trips and excursions. Here there is very certainly a threat to the child's moral development."[84] Helmut R. was required to return his work permit to the police.[85]

The Düsseldorf Youth Office based its objections to another application for a work permit on the moral character of the child's parents rather than on the dangers of the work itself:

> The widow B. . . . lives with a divorced man, named P., who is already well known to the municipal Family Care Agency as a work-shy human being. Most of the day, he lies in bed, smoking cigarettes. Frau B. draws a pension because her husband was killed in the war. She also makes some money as a cleaning lady. From this income she appears to support not only her child but also the (aforementioned) Herr P. The child, who looks pale and weak, should . . . not be allowed to help support the "good-for-nothing" P., even though the proposed employment with a butcher would improve the young boy's nutrition.[86]

But Weimar youth offices clearly had trouble convincing parents that the physical, mental, and moral well-being of their children was more important than family income.[87] Recalcitrant parents could evade Youth Office control by a simple conspiracy of silence. In the Depression, child labor moved into the shadow world of the unofficial economy (*Schwarzarbeit*).[88]

"Public Parenthood"?

Christopher Lasch, Jacques Donzelot, and Philippe Meyer have all argued that the twentieth-century welfare state has invaded and colonized the family, replacing its private powers with a "patriarchy of the state."[89] These authors lament the passing of private patriarchal powers into public hands. Some feminist historians think, however, that women benefited from this state-sponsored dissolution of unrestrained patriarchy within the family.[90] In her study of family violence in America, Linda Gordon argues that campaigns against child abuse provided immigrant and working-class women with support in their attempts to resist oppressive patriarchy.[91] Other feminist historians have, however, argued that state social policy and welfare practice in the twentieth century reinforced or reimposed female subordination to and dependence upon males.[92]

I would argue that the construction of welfare states created profoundly ambiguous effects for both women and children that cannot be understood simply in terms of losses or gains; as Jürgen Habermas puts it, "From the start, the ambivalence of guaranteeing freedom and taking it away has attached to the policies of the welfare state.[93] Some children were rescued from parental abuse. Some women were saved from their wife-beating husbands. Yet at the same time, "the fact that there were battered children in some working-class families was used to justify the inspection of all working-class families to make sure their children were not battered."[94] "Clients" of the welfare state might escape familial oppression only by accepting a new dependent status as subjects of a "tutelary complex."[95]

Advocates of the Weimar welfare project insisted that it was a more effective way of treating social problems than the coercive technologies of power employed by the Wilhelmine poor law and the police. *Fürsorge* would rely not upon compulsion but upon consent; this was the justification for seeing it as the provision of "protection" and "care," rather than the exercise of force.[96] Women's organizations and female social workers insisted that Weimar social work was defined by the gender of its practitioners: "Men use fear and force against individuals to insure public order and health." Women, in contrast, use "preventive, protective, and healing approaches to helping individuals and thereby serve the welfare of all."[97] Yet the break with the practices of the nineteenth-century poor law and with contemporary male police work was not as complete as welfare reformers, Social Democrats, and feminists liked to think. Eckart Pankoke points out that

> this area . . . always had its roots in the tradition of thinking about the policing of state order—even when the transition from "repressive" to "preventive" forms of intervention dissolved the "police" concept, heavily loaded with repressive connotations, with formulas oriented more toward prevention, such as "protection," "care," and "welfare." It is in this sense that preventive administrative tasks such as "welfare," "social welfare," "protection of youth," "youth welfare," and "family aid" developed out of the older state policing complex.[98]

Consequently, the attempts to give youth welfare work a new popular legitimacy did not remove the taint of repression. As late as 1927, for example, the director of the Hamburg Youth Office admitted that "the Youth Office is still . . . a bogey-man; the justifiable distaste for the 'Discipline School'—which, as is well known, was done away with in 1905—. . . still has an effect. . . . [Our] reformatories . . . are run in a pure spirit of education and welfare—but we must continuously plead for the trust of the parents, without which our educational task is very difficult, even hopeless."[99]

The contradictions of Weimar child welfare work were, however, produced not only by these continuities with the past but also by the inherent ambiguities of youth welfare's "modern" and "progressive" programs. Compulsion and consent were inextricably combined in all the Youth Office's practices. Even the most "voluntary" forms of child welfare opened the door to potential or actual coercion. Once the gaze of the Youth Office was fastened upon a family and its children, there could indeed be no guarantee that intervention would not escalate from the softer, more advisory forms to the harder, more coercive ones:

> Through personal visits and individual involvement, the helper attempts to have an educational effect on the parents, so that any disorders or dangers to the child can be reduced or eliminated within the family. Any resistance or restraints put up by the parents are to be overcome with the help of the Guardianship Court; but, as a last resort, to rescue the physically, spiritually, or morally endangered child, there is always "correctional education" [*Fürsorgeerziehung*].[100]

On occasion, the social worker might even call upon the police to apply direct force; Hedwig Stieve was certainly not the only social worker to ask a police constable to accompany her when she removed a child from a recalcitrant family.[101]

The "policing of the family" carried out by Weimar youth offices was in many ways broader and more intrusive than normal police practices because it was triggered by amorphous, arbitrarily defined threats of endangerment. Parents might themselves seek help and advice from the Youth Office. Yet even without their consent or knowledge, many parents and children were reported to the youth welfare authorities by private charities, by local moral authorities (such as pastors), and by concerned or vengeful neighbors. Only compliance or a convincing simulation of cooperation with the "therapy" prescribed by the social worker might eventually free "endan-gered" children and their families from the welfare gaze. This makes it impossible to pronounce with any confidence upon the relative effectiveness of youth welfare prac-tices: Were children really rescued? Were families actually reconstructed and re-formed? Or did parents and children simply learn how to present the images that would make them less interesting to youth welfare authorities?

An Epilogue: Two Case Histories

A case history, used as a teaching device in Siddy Wronsky and Alice Salomon's 1926 social-work handbook, demonstrated how youth welfare work was ideally meant to function. In 1920, a concerned (or interfering) neighbor reported that the sixteen-year-old Else H., daughter of a Protestant pipe fitter and his Catholic wife, "has been gallivanting around by herself," a clear indication of incipient *Verwahrlosung* so far as the authorities were concerned. In October 1920, the Youth Office gave the direc-tor of the Catholic young women's club a *Schutzaufsicht* over Else H. This produced no improvement in her behavior; indeed, in November 1920 she ran away from home once again after stealing money from her parents and a pair of shoes from a neigh-bor. A series of similar incidents led to the imposition of *FE* in early 1921 "so as to prevent complete moral degeneration." Although her parents were judged to be "re-spectable people," they appeared to be totally incapable of controlling Else H. But her stay in the St. Cecilien-Stift home for girls produced a remarkable transforma-tion. In 1923, she was allowed to leave the home because "she makes a good, mod-est impression. Indeed, she was very happy in the home." Toward the end of that same year, a female "helper" for the federal state Youth Office reported that "since September, Else has been working as a domestic servant. In her new position, they are very happy with her work; she is willing, diligent, and home loving. She seldom goes out and then only to visit her parents or the St. Cecilien-Stift. She returns promptly from these trips. A helper is aiding Else in the disposition of her earnings. She appears to be healthy, both physically and spiritually."[102]

Else H. was one of the welfare system's success stories. In contrast, the family life of the Württemberg shoemaker Gottlob T. was the kind of nightmare that haunted the imaginations of Weimar welfare authorities. By the end of the Weimar Republic, the local Youth Office in Nürtingen had compiled extensive case files on all four of the children in this family—Anna, Klara, Elsa, and Heinrich—and had prescribed some form of educational care for each of them. The family first came into the case files of local welfare authorities in 1926, when Anna T. was taken into the hospital in Ebingen "because of an apparent sexual disease." Although at this time Anna T. was only fifteen years old, "by her own admission . . . she had already had sex sev-eral times with various boys."[103] The District Court concluded that Anna T. was "morally very neglected" and sent her to the St. Konradihaus reformatory. Just three years later, Klara T. appeared to be following her older sister's path. Admittedly, her delinquency was not sexual; instead, she was charged with having stolen money from a woman "from whom she received her midday meals."[104] Just as worrying to the youth welfare authorities as anything the young girl had actually done was the allegedly "deceitful essence" she exhibited. Investigation of the family circumstances showed that they were "as bad as you might expect": Both parents were unemployed, and in fact they and the three younger siblings depended solely on the young Klara T.'s earnings. Welfare authorities were consequently reluctant to put the second sister in a reformatory and were in any case skeptical that such educational measures would be successful, since *FE* had already failed to redeem Anna T.[105] Anna T. had earlier been released from the reformatory, but instead of being allowed to return to her family, she was put into domestic service. Rather than settling in to this new work, she ran away a number of times. In July 1929, the Youth Office in Reutlingen reported that Anna T. was in the custody of the local police. A story printed the following August in the *Nürtinger Tageblatt* explained that

> the local lay court has sentenced the twenty-two-year-old cabinetmaker Otto L. from Rommelshausen to sixteen months in prison for the abduction of a minor. . . . The accused was unemployed at the time of the offense. He had originally been introduced to the nineteen-year-old Anna D. [*sic*] by his fiancée [when both girls were inmates] of the Oberurbach reformatory. He later went to visit [Anna] at the house of her foster parents, the miller S. and his wife in Wolffolden. There, he understood Anna . . . to say that she would run off with him. They then both went to Waiblingen, to his fiancée, and, later, to his parents' home.[106]

By November 1932, both Anna T. and her sister Klara were reported to be engaged in prostitution in Stuttgart. But the authorities were beginning to feel that the real problem was not so much Anna T.'s "bad influence"; even more serious was the girls' mother, who was assessed to be "equipped with an inferior genetic inheritance."[107] These various family deficiencies were not, however, thought at this time to be so overwhelming as to make any educational measures completely futile, and so Klara followed her older sibling's earlier path to a reform school in 1932. In December 1934, Klara T.'s parents asked that she be allowed to return home. As Klara was now already nineteen years old, the youth authorities could no longer legally keep her in the reformatory, but they insisted that she be placed in domestic service instead of returning to her parents.[108]

Faced with what appeared to be an endless cycle of the reproduction of delinquency that it seemed completely powerless to halt, the Youth Office resolved not to allow the "deficient" genes that they thought were the cause of this aberrant behavior to be passed on. The radically altered legal and political context provided by Hitler's seizure of power in 1933 gave the Nürtingen Youth Office an opportunity to close the file on the bothersome Anna and Klara T. and, additionally, on their younger sister Elsa. On 14 November 1935, the Nürtingen Youth Office informed local health authorities that

> on the occasion of our petition to the Nürtingen District Court . . . which requests that Elsa T., born 28 Nov. 1920, be put under an order of "correctional care," the Youth Office asked that an investigation be undertaken to determine whether the grounds exist for the sterilization of Elsa T. and her two sisters. The proceedings were successful, and Elsa T. was sterilized on the fifteenth of last month. . . . I would also like to know the outcome of the petitions for the sterilization of Anna and Klara T., who are supposed to have married in the meantime.[109]

On 29 May 1936, the municipal health authorities asked the State Health Office for Anna's records to prepare a case against her according to the provisions of the new Nazi Law for the Prevention of Hereditarily Diseased Offspring. Even though the two sisters were now in their twenties and both were also married, the Nürtingen youth welfare authorities regarded their bodies as threats to the genetic/racial purity of the *Volksgemeinschaft*. In February 1937, Anna T's. case was taken before the Genetic Health Court (Erbgesundheitsgericht) in Stuttgart. She was presented as a candidate for forced sterilization "on the grounds of inherited feeblemindedness."[110] There is no record of a final decision on her or her sister Klara, but there is little reason to believe that either of them escaped a fate shared by more than 320,000 German men and women in the years between 1933 and 1939.[111]

The Weimar Welfare State's Last Crisis, 1929–1933

By 1932, the permanent constituency of the Hamburg Welfare Department was 7.7 times larger than it had been in 1925. The total numbers of people receiving any kind of cash support had increased 12.9 times and represented 22.4 percent of the total population of 1,086,734 people living in Hamburg in 1933.[1] The largest single group among the Welfare Department's clients were the "welfare unemployed" (*Wohlfahrtserwerbslosen*).[2] In July 1928, 13.1 out of every 100 welfare clients were welfare unemployed. By July 1929, this had risen to 21.4, by December 1930 to 36.1, by January 1932 to 49.7, and by December 1932 to 61.3.[3] The massive increase in the numbers of the city's welfare clients caused primarily by the influx of the welfare unemployed had in no way been matched by an expansion of the Welfare Department's personnel: In 1925, the department had 726 full-time officers; by 1930, this number had grown only to 1,006. The number of voluntary workers had increased in the same period only from 2,412 to 2,650, which meant that one volunteer had 5.7 cases to look after in 1925 but 14 cases in 1931. Yet despite this relatively small increase in the size of the welfare bureaucracy, the costs had skyrocketed. Whereas in 1913 Hamburg had spent only 3.8 percent of its budget on welfare, by 1930 it was laying out 17.1 percent. In 1913, welfare had cost each citizen of the Hansestadt 5.64 marks, but in 1928 this had risen to 38.15 marks, and in 1931 it was 58.40 marks.[4]

The Crisis of the Local State

By 1933, German municipalities were caught in the vise of a mounting contradiction: "The number of people [they] had to take care of increased, yet at the same time the municipalities' ability to provide financial assistance receded—to a really quite shocking degree." The Social Democratic city council member in Frankfurt who made this observation suggested that the German welfare system had in fact returned to the "alms economy" of the prewar years. The growth of the social insurance system had originally been intended to unburden the poor-law system; now, the direction of this movement was reversed. As successive emergency decrees eviscerated the social insurance system, many of its most important former responsibilities were passed back to the local welfare systems. The financial situation of some German cities was no less than catastrophic. In Duisburg-Hamborn, for example, welfare costs were 3.2 million marks, but the city had only taken in 1 million marks in tax income. In Bochum, tax revenues were 18.6 million marks, but welfare expenses had reached 22.5 million marks. These immense and growing deficits simply could not be dealt with by further reduction of the levels of relief—indeed, that response would only generate extra costs to municipal welfare systems in the form of additional requests for rent support and mounting health costs.[5] Local authorities were hamstrung in their attempts to deal with the mounting welfare crisis by the financial constraints forced upon them by both the national and the federal state governments.[6] The Brüning regime was determined to make the municipalities absorb more of the costs of supporting the unemployed.[7] The mechanism for doing this was quite simple: As municipal welfare systems were responsible for assisting the unemployed whose insurance benefits had run out, the Reich government only had to reduce the length of time that the insurance system paid benefits and exclude certain categories of the unemployed. By 1933, the Reich government had managed "very successfully" to shift the primary burden of unemployment relief to the local state; at the beginning of 1933, the unemployment insurance system paid benefits to only 900,000 out of the total of 6.1 million officially unemployed.[8] The Reich government did provide some financial contribution to the municipalities for their massively increased welfare expenses for the welfare unemployed, but in return for these always inadequate supplements the national government imposed restrictions and conditions on local welfare practices, progressively eliminating any remaining space for independent action and for left-wing political influence on the administration of welfare.[9]

During the Depression, the national government used its emergency powers to force local authorities to reduce their standard rates of support.[10] Under the Second Emergency Decree of June 1931, for example, "financial aid from the national or state government was only provided 'if the standard rates did not exceed the necessary and appropriate amounts.'"[11] Organized welfare interests, such as the German Association for Private and Public Welfare, were certainly not happy with this invasion of local "self-administration" and continued to support individualization against schematization. But they were not, in principle, opposed to welfare cuts, because as Wilhelm Polligkeit put it, "in the past, the local standard rate has often exceeded what is necessary as a result of party-political influence."[12] After 1931, no welfare district in Germany increased its standard rates, and many began in practice to reduce the levels of support, even when the official standard rates remained undisturbed, supporting these actions with the argument that public assistance must keep pace with the decline in wages for the employed. Often support in-kind was substituted for monetary relief.[13] Reducing the standard rates was justified with reference to the overall decline in the cost of living during the Depression but was not based on any detailed study of the actual expenditures of the unemployed or welfare clients and also ignored the fact that rent, which constituted one of the major household expenses, continued to rise, not decline.

From April 1929 to August 1931, the cost-of-living index dropped some 13 percent. Support levels in the Rhineland-Westphalia industrial region were reduced, as shown in Table 7. For married couples, this was a reduction, between 1928 and 1932, of 18.4 percent, and for single persons, living alone, of 21.8 percent. Elderly people living with relatives who were legally responsible for contributing support suffered a 49.7 percent loss. Single people were also subjected to severe restrictions; in some municipalities, they were not paid the amount earmarked for a head of household if they were listed as boarders or lodgers, "although the distress of these people . . . is even greater than in many families." With these reduced amounts of money, welfare clients were expected to buy all their food and clothing. And one-sixth of these regular grants were supposed to cover rent; if the rent exceeded this amount, rent supplements might still be granted, but only up to 30 marks for small families and 40 marks for larger families. Welfare clients would still receive grants of potatoes and coal during the winter months, although here, too, the amounts were limited. In Bottrop, welfare authorities calculated the amount of money required to buy a set ration of various foodstuffs at current prices, to which a small sum was added for other necessary household purchases. Single people with their own households received 100 percent of this amount, single people living with relatives 80 percent, children over fourteen years of age 80 percent, household heads 90 percent, wives 80 percent, and children under fourteen 60 percent. Rent was paid directly to the landlord. Municipalities in Rhineland-Westphalia wanted to be relieved of the added burden of providing supplementary benefits for those receiving unemployment insurance payments (*Alu*) or crisis support (*Kru*), which fell short of the officially prescribed levels for welfare clients. Indeed, welfare departments in some municipalities refused to pay these supplements if the difference was less than 10 marks. Others set minimum welfare support levels lower for those on *Alu* and *Kru* than for regular welfare clients.[14]

Another way for local authorities to reduce their welfare costs was to subject existing cases to more rigorous scrutiny, with the result that many longer-term welfare clients suddenly discovered that their support had been drastically reduced or cut off

TABLE 7. Standard Rates of Support in Rhineland-Westphalia in 1931

Category	Westphalia	Rhineland	1928 levels (Gelsenkirchen)
Married couple	51 marks	54 marks	62.50 marks
Single person, own household	34 marks	36 marks	43.50 marks
Elderly person in household with responsible relatives	17 marks	18 marks	33.80 marks
Minor in household with responsible relatives	12.50 marks	14 marks	15.50 marks
Single person in household with others not legally responsible	25 marks	27 marks	33.80 marks

Source: "Die Handhabung der öffentlichen Fürsorge im rheinisch-westfälischen Industriegebiet," *Arbeiterwohlfahrt*, 1932, p. 50. On 1 May 1924, the rate for a married couple on general welfare was 32 marks, on 1 August 1924, 39 marks, on 1 December 1925, 48 marks, and on 1 November 1927, 57.60 marks. Ibid., p. 53.

altogether when they most needed it. In 1932, for example, the cases being looked after by the volunteer workers in one Hamburg welfare district (which represented some 50% of the total of 700 cases) were examined by one of the city's *Berufspfleger*. He found that it was possible to save the district some 450 marks by cutting off five people altogether and by reducing support in another 156 cases.[15] In welfare district VI, subdistrict 164, a number of cases had to be "double-checked several times because of the district's generous attitude."[16] Support might be reduced or terminated for any number of reasons: faked addresses, increased earnings by family members, higher income from subletting rooms than originally reported, higher pensions, unreported joint households, or because the reasons for exceeding the standard rates were no longer valid.[17]

Annemarie Hermberg tried to demonstrate the significance of these cuts for people on welfare by comparing the income of the unemployed and welfare clients in 1931 with the earnings of employed workers surveyed in a 1927 study. She estimated that an employed worker with an income of 2,500 marks in 1927 spent as much on food alone as an unemployed person who received 1,000 marks per year in 1931 had at his or her disposal for all household expenses. Indeed, those on relief in 1931 had an income lower than the lowest level among employed workers in the 1927 study. By comparison with 1926, the cost of living had dropped by about 3.8 percent. Food was 14.0 percent cheaper and clothing 24.7 percent cheaper. But rent, heat, and lighting were actually now more expensive. Rent formed a higher proportion of the expenditures of families on welfare but was not fully compensated for by rent supplements and the occasional supplement for heating. Moreover, the costs of the foodstuffs that formed the bulk of poorer people's diets—bread, potatoes, margarine, and sugar—had either not declined significantly or in some cases actually increased. This showed, according to Hermberg, that although the official cost-of-living index had dropped some 14 points, this index could not be applied without adjustment and without more detailed knowledge of the actual expenditures of people on welfare. Rather than cutting the levels of support, welfare departments should provide additional supplements to the income of the unemployed and other welfare clients in the form of bread, potatoes, and coal, as the SPD and the trade unions were demanding.[18]

"Family Values" in the Depression

The increasingly massive assault on the living standards of German families during the Depression inspired a Protestant commentator to warn that "whether or not our people survive the distress and dangers of this historical epoch will, in the end, be decided by the German family's powers of resilience. The family must carry the largest part of the burden, which the welfare system can no longer manage. . . . That we can dare to make such drastic cuts at all is a 'blank check' of our faith in the strength of the family." Yet other religious and conservative observers feared that German family life had already been seriously weakened by "the mental currents and the spiritual jolts of our period,"[19] as well as by the general "moral-religious uncertainty" of the 1920s.[20] Existing social policies appeared to have failed to provide "the special protection of the family by the state" promised in the Weimar constitution. The legal

measures taken by the Weimar state had, in fact, produced exactly the opposite effect: tax legislation; regulation of wages and salaries; child support benefits; regulations concerning pension, sickness, accident, unemployment, and welfare benefits;
housing and educational policy; and even regulations governing garnishment of income (*Pfändung*) all had consequences "hostile to the family."[21] One observer pointed
to the contradictions that were the inevitable result of social policies that attempted
to protect the family by constructing individual subjects and identities:

> Article 119 of the Weimar constitution gave this goal a programmatic formulation: "It
> is the task of the state to keep the family pure and healthy; the social promotion of the
> family is likewise the task of the state and the community." But at the very same time,
> the constitution provided for a whole range of social welfare measures that applied, above
> all, to the individual and especially to the mother and the child and that intervened into
> the family to undertake corrections or to supplement its role. . . . So the question can
> well remain open whether this whole system has not, perhaps . . . contributed to a weak-
> ening of family responsibility. . . . Against the atomizing tendency of public assistance
> aimed at the individual, one can pose another "organic" way of thinking oriented [more]
> toward *Volk* and family.[22]

This rhetoric furnished local governments with a moral rationale for passing state
spending cuts along to individual families, allowing them to claim that they wanted
to reinforce family bonds.[23] In the Rhineland and Westphalia, for example, relatives
were held strictly to account for the support of their needy kin. Norms were established that dictated that relatives would be allowed a certain amount of income for
their own support (150 marks for a married couple, 20 marks for each child), but
then half of all income above this amount would have to be given to relatives on
welfare, if a legal obligation could be established. In Gelsenkirchen, the courts set
the amount of the exemption somewhat higher, but a court decision in Essen reduced
this "subsistence exemption" to 120 marks for a married couple.[24]

Welfare authorities' readiness to subsume the identity of each individual case in
that of the family, even when this was only a "fictive family" that the Welfare Department had itself created in order to save money, could easily make welfare authorities' pronouncements about the sanctity of the German family appear cynical or
simply ludicrous. Guidelines laid down for the city of Berlin in 1931 declared, for
example, that "all the individuals present in a household constitute a 'community of
need,' even when they are not legally required to assist one another." In Düsseldorf,
the Welfare Department decided that "when determining the amount of support, all
the people in a common household will be treated as a family unit, regardless of
whether they are or are not related to each other." The Düsseldorf regulations also
insisted that "leaving or dissolving this family unit with the intention of getting an
increase in the amount of relief for oneself or one's dependents has no effect upon
the determination of the level of support."[25] In 1932, Hamburg welfare authorities
went even further, insisting that if all the members of a household were on welfare,
they were to be treated as a "closed family unit" for purposes of determining support.[26] The Hamburg Welfare Department also attempted to cut its costs by insisting
that young people not be given support that would allow them to live away from
home.[27] No attention was paid to the economic or emotional stress that children's
forced return home may have placed on them or their families.[28] In 1933, the Social

Democratic municipal journal, *Die Gemeinde*, complained that in Zwickau welfare authorities were exploiting the family feelings of their clients "to give a bankrupt system an additional lease on life."[29]

The way welfare authorities treated German families during the Depression generated intense criticism, even in the ranks of the religious welfare interests. In 1932, Bertha Finck attacked the dangerous shortsightedness that informed state spending cuts: "To balance the budget, the suffering German family is asked to make one sacrifice after another. The amount of welfare is now dictated not by the amount of distress but by the available financial means."[30] A Catholic commentator agreed with Finck's remarks and pointed out that successive emergency decrees had deprived German families of the financial assistance previously provided by health and accident insurance, public housing, and other supports at the same time as their own economic resources were being severely depleted by the ravages of mass unemployment.[31] Other religious and conservative welfare experts felt that the notion of a fictive family challenged the moral foundations of real families.[32]

Violence in the Welfare Office

Having to "process" literally hundreds of individual cases each day during the Depression, the larger urban welfare offices depended upon the passive submission by welfare clients to the slow-grinding administrative machinery of the welfare system, which required them to endure protracted periods of waiting in welfare office lines. Yet these same lines could subvert the official need for quiet, order, and discipline because they provided the opportunity to construct an informal "counterpublic" (*Gegenöffentlichkeit*), which permitted communication and the formation of (at least temporary) solidarities among welfare clients. Welfare officials were well aware that it was often quite dangerous to bring together in the public space of the local welfare office so many disgruntled, often desperate people. In 1931, a social worker at the district welfare office in the Immermannstrasse in Düsseldorf reported:

> When I came in today, at five minutes to eight, people had pushed into the waiting room and were standing, pressed up against one another, head to head, right out into the corridor, even on the landing, right up to the entrance. It was impossible for anyone to move forward or backward. . . . By using every ounce of my strength, I was able to open up a small path to the office, although some of my clothing was ripped or got dirty in the process. After about an hour, I wanted to go out into the neighborhood, but it was impossible to open the door from the inside so that, in the end, so as not to waste even more time, I had to jump out of the window onto the street. At about ten o'clock, one of the young trainee assistants also wanted to go out into the district; she was also unable to get the door open and ended up going out of the window, too. Just before eleven o'clock, the courier . . . came with the files. With a lot of effort, he finally managed to get into the office but was not able to get out again. No amount of banging or shouting was enough to get him out; from outside the door, the people yelled, "Stay where you are! We are not letting you out." The courier had to put down his files and use all his physical strength, helped by one of the social workers, finally to get the door open. But this produced such a tumult that it almost came to blows. The supervisor on duty was powerless to do anything. . . . At eight o'clock this morning, I had already placed an

urgent phone call to the district office [*Kreisstelle*] asking for help. . . . For the whole of last week there have been days when it was almost impossible to get into the office, even though there were no office hours scheduled for these days.[33]

During the Depression, personnel were transferred from other branches of local administration to deal with the explosive increase in cases, even though these officials were completely unfamiliar with the workings of the welfare system.[34] Clients could easily feel that they were being mistreated by these harried, overworked, often inexperienced officials.[35] The Social Democratic *Hamburger Echo* warned that even "the smallest . . . remark of an official, which is simply ill considered though . . . perhaps not intended to be harsh, can produce an explosion."[36] Yet in 1931, a Hamburg welfare official had to warn that "the German language disposes of sufficient suitable phrases to describe the antisocial and unworthy behavior of the clients in an unobjectionable manner without resorting to derogatory words of abuse. One can just imagine what impression such reports would leave behind if these documents had to be shown to the Senate in the investigation of a client's complaint."[37] A year later, a local police official reported that he had received complaints from clients about the "arrogant and highly inappropriate conduct of the personnel in the district welfare office."[38] A contributor to the liberal *Hamburger Anzeiger* complained that "especially when dealing with the young, female welfare officials, I have encountered an absence of social feeling that can go as far as complete insensitivity. . . . I have often seen women grimacing with rage or . . . completely in tears after having been interrogated by one of their own gender. And we are supposed to believe that the inherited gentleness of their sex makes women especially well suited for this profession!"[39]

The physical conditions in many welfare offices made the time spent there extremely unpleasant for both clients and welfare officials. In 1922, a Cologne newspaper complained that

> when one enters . . . the district office in the Pinstrasse, one has the impression that this is not a municipal building but the lodging of a junk dealer. . . . The primitive furnishings [give] the people coming here for help the feeling that "this is meant to be good enough for the poor." But even the officials . . . receive the impression that their work is not highly valued. . . . Several people must be questioned at the same time so that their most intimate family details are discussed in the presence of complete strangers.[40]

In 1926, the Hamburg Communist newspaper, the *Volkszeitung*, drew attention to similar conditions in local district welfare offices.[41] Although Hamburg welfare officials proudly described the modern facilities of the new welfare district offices that began to be constructed in the late 1920s, they had to admit in 1928 that "with few exceptions, the welfare district offices are [still] poorly housed."[42]

Even after a long wait under intolerable conditions, applicants might simply find that their request had been rejected outright or reduced in scope. The onset of the Depression brought a flood of challenges to welfare office decisions. In Berlin, the number of complaints went from 1,554 in 1928/29 to 2,098 in 1929/30, an increase of some 35 percent. Berlin welfare authorities attributed the bulk of the new complaints to "the massive increase in the numbers of the welfare unemployed."[43] By September 1932, when Hamburg welfare district offices were having to handle between 7,000 and 10,000 cases, compared to their previous workload of between 2,000 and 3,000, the numbers of complaints were so great that welfare district offices could not deal quickly with all of them, and clients were becoming "quite embittered."[44] A considerable number of applications for support and letters of complaint now appeared to have been written "by a third party or with a typewriter." Most of these were probably prepared by the various organizations claiming to represent welfare clients, although "in one individual case . . . someone had been paid a relatively large sum of money to write the request."[45] By 1932, Hamburg welfare authorities were convinced that "it is gradually coming to the point that basically everyone lodges a complaint. Agents are being sent into the public buildings by the different political parties to collect complaints. Often enough, it appears that these people compose and type the letters of complaint." The Hamburg Welfare Department also complained that it was being drawn more and more into political conflicts. When the newspapers printed criticisms of welfare practices (which were not, however, always based in fact) these public attacks "make a strong impression on welfare clients. . . . The Welfare Department must increasingly respond to . . . complaints and queries, including those that are politically motivated, as quickly and as carefully as possible, so as not to allow false impressions of the department to develop."[46] Yet despite all of this pressure, the chances of having an unfavorable ruling overturned appear to have been rather slim. In the administrative year 1929/30, for example, 78 percent of the complaints filed in Berlin were rejected.[47]

Impatient with the dilatory and apparently futile official complaints procedure, some clients resorted, instead, to more direct action, engaging in verbal and even physical attacks upon welfare officials to make their grievances heard. In 1930, the *Hamburger Anzeiger* claimed, for example, that

> when the money does not begin to rain down, as expected, then there is a row. . . . In November, a married couple engaged in a nasty attack upon [a welfare] official that degenerated into a wild scene that even continued on the street after the police had taken the couple into custody. . . . A second case in January . . . involved a thirty-year-old worker . . . who had become jittery after a long wait. . . . When he was given just 3 marks as an advance . . . he suddenly attacked the cashier, who had nothing at all to do with the decision, threw him to the ground, and beat him so severely that he could not work for the next three days; in addition, he destroyed a chair . . . broke a table, ripped up . . . files, and then . . . left. The court went easy on the man, who had no prior record, and let the matter rest with a five-week jail sentence for bodily harm and damage to property.[48]

Disturbances like these, which became fairly common during the Depression, had already begun, sporadically, to disrupt the daily bureaucratic routine of welfare offices during the 1920s. In 1923, for example, Hamburg welfare officials complained that unemployed workers who had been excluded from the Labor Office because they had physically attacked officials there were sent to a welfare office, where they likewise "not only endangered . . . the health and the lives of the officials, but also created unbelievable disruptions of the office's work."[49] In 1926, a Hamburg welfare official reported that "recently a lot of rabid people are reported to have appeared in the welfare district offices who often create severe rows. Several of the personnel have reportedly been threatened and hit."[50] In 1927, a district welfare office director complained that

hardly a day goes by without a row, which can often better be described as a disturbance. . . . Many of these people, preeminently the single ones, declare, as soon as they
have filed their applications, that they will not leave the building until their often quite
extensive "demands" are met. They themselves say that the police should be called. . . .
They think they can get somewhere with this behavior and explain that "you just have
to make a real disturbance, then you will get everything you want." . . . These . . . outbursts are often reinforced with the banging of fists on tables and with threats.[51]

Welfare district office VI (Barmbeck-Nord) claimed that "the clients generally engage in disturbances when they do not immediately receive support."[52] Moreover,
"when such disturbances take place in the waiting room, the other members of the
public who are in the building take up the same tone, which makes the further processing of cases a great deal more difficult for the officials."[53] The director of district IX (St. Georg) reported that "threats . . . are quite common."[54]

Many of these incidents were produced by individual clients acting on their own,
but some appear to have involved groups of clients with political motives: "We have
observed that when a certain party has held a meeting on the previous evening, the
applicants from this group are much more aggressive . . . the next day. . . . Clearly
. . . they have come to some agreement among themselves."[55] And in 1929, district
office II reported that

it is above all the young . . . welfare unemployed . . . who have been incited the most.
So, for example, a young applicant, angry at being turned away . . . struck the welfare
official in the face a couple of times. Another client, who had earlier been banned
from the building, took part in the . . . subsequent brawl and the attempts to work up
the people waiting in the welfare office. . . . We later discovered that "reinforcements"
had been sent to the district office. . . . Not only were various young people hanging
out in front of the door . . . waiting for the first rowdies to be taken off to the police
station but . . . every known agitator . . . in the district was also present at this under-
taking, including certain of the Communist leaders such as Levy and Göcken, the first
of whom came and listened at my door as an agitated discussion was taking place, to
find out how things were going.[56]

In their attempts to contain violence in the welfare office and to deal with the individuals and groups who provoked confrontations, welfare officials found that they
could not always count on the unquestioning support of the police. In 1930, for example, welfare district office X complained that the police had told a client that the
officials, who still had their salaries, should be more understanding of the plight of
the unemployed. The district office suggested that the policeman stick to his job and
leave the practice of welfare to them.[57] Apart from any sympathies for welfare clients that individual police officers may have felt, it was clear that they did not enjoy
being summoned frequently to welfare offices to eject troublesome clients, some of
whom kept coming back several times in the same day. Welfare officials wondered
why the police could not hold people involved in incidents longer.[58] Welfare officials also complained that the courts were not doing enough. Clients who had engaged in violence or who caused disturbances frequently received only probation
"which, in these circles of the population, is often seen as a type of acquittal. Other
clients soon learn about the verdict and flout it triumphantly in the faces of the officials, whose authority is thus severely damaged."

With over 1,000 people a day showing up at some welfare district offices during the Depression, the dangers of failing to deter or to control confrontations were obvious: "Political agitators, troublemakers, and psychopaths use these gatherings to incite the public against the agency."[59] In December 1932, welfare district office VI reported that it had been virtually besieged by crowds of unruly welfare clients:

> At about 10:30 in the morning a lot of people quickly assembled in the waiting room. . . . Several women and men suddenly pushed their way into the anteroom to my office, where they presented their long-standing demands for more money, more clothing, and more fuel. The police arrived immediately, but as they were trying to push the people out of the room, they were attacked and had to make use of their rubber truncheons. It appeared that the police would not be able to restore order, so I summoned the riot squad. Soon after it arrived, peace was restored. But instead of having the building cleared, I . . . received a deputation of three people and listened to their wishes. I then tried to make it clear to the deputation that such demonstrations were not appropriate, and I requested that they direct their supporters to present their wishes, calmly and unemotionally, to the district subcommittees of volunteers. . . . In subdistricts III, IV, VI, and VII petitions could be processed peacefully, but in subdistricts I, II, and V things were quite stormy. . . . Because of this constant agitation, the processing of cases can be expected to be quite unruly in the next few days; the police authorities will strengthen the watch posted here to ten men, half inside the office, the other half on the street in front of the building. . . . Moreover, clients who have come to apply only for support in kind will be given a questionnaire that they can fill out at home and return later. As soon as the waiting room is full, no one else will be allowed to enter.[60]

Out in the neighborhoods, the volunteer workers were also exposed to the threat of violence: "The numbers of cases are mounting . . . in which the clients' vulgar, boisterous, abusive behavior . . . makes the volunteers' work more difficult and even disgusting." One *Pfleger* had resigned in 1931 because "a client created such a spectacle in the volunteer's shop that a crowd began to form in front of his door, yelling all manner of abuse." Others might soon follow his example because, "for a tradesman, these kinds of incidents are just impossible."[61] The welfare district asked that a flyer be printed, explaining to welfare clients that the periodic meetings of all volunteer workers in the district, not the individual *Pfleger*, decided how much support each client would receive, and that these decisions were in turn constrained by the guidelines issued by the central welfare office, which only the welfare committee of the Hamburg Senate had the power to exceed. It was therefore pointless for clients to attempt to put pressure on any particular voluntary worker.

Welfare officials wanted to dismiss violence as either the isolated irrationality of a few deviant individuals or a political provocation organized by Communist hotheads to use the welfare office as a stage for their radical propaganda. But these assertions ignored the real meanings and consequences of violence in the welfare office.

Violence as Body Contact

Violence temporarily dissolved the physical and symbolic distance that normally separated and protected welfare officials from their clients. The remarks of a Hamburg welfare official in 1926 suggest that intimate bodily contact with welfare clients could be experienced not just as physical pain but as contamination or pollution: "The welfare official's hands regularly become quite filthy from dealing with a public, drawn from circles in which cleanliness is not one of the stronger characteristics and whose personal documents are covered with smaller or larger amounts of filth."[62]

Violence committed by or against women, which confused dominant notions of gender difference, was particularly unsettling.[63] In 1923, for example, a conservative Hamburg newspaper was outraged that "an unprecedented scandal took place in the offices of the Welfare Department in the ABC-Strasse. A number of soldiers' dependents, mainly women, banded together in the building on the obvious orders of the Communists. When President Martini saw that this was going on and asked what they wanted, one of these female persons gave him the answer 'How about a rap on the snout?'"[64] Female social workers frequently had to visit rough working-class neighborhoods but assumed they would be protected from the threat of physical violence by their gender. Emilie Zadow was particularly proud of her ability to work, unharmed, with the Gypsies living in an encampment on the outskirts of a large German city where male representatives of the state were hesitant to venture:

> Some welfare office investigators would not dare to do their job in the Hasenheide without a rubber truncheon, and one guardian of orphans even applied for a revolver. . . . When the police feel obliged to intervene—and that happens on a daily basis—then one officer seldom goes alone. In the big municipal school that the Gypsy children attend, there are always a couple of teachers who want to be transferred because "this rabble is sending them to an early grave." Irritation and annoyance everywhere you look.

For Zadow, however, "the key to this world is called 'love.'"[65] Yet female social workers were certainly not immune to the threat of violence. During the Depression, the welfare authorities in Hamburg refused to allow welfare clients to submit their applications for support directly to female social workers because "given the current mood of the population . . . the individual female social worker would be blamed and possibly subjected to threats if an application was refused."[66]

Memories of Violence

Memories of past violence haunted subsequent confrontations. In October 1923, for example, during the Hamburg Communist "uprising," welfare district offices VI, VII, and VIII, all in neighborhoods where fighting was heavy, reported that "their work was greatly disturbed. . . . Welfare district X had to pay out support to its clients under the protection of the security police."[67] Nine years later, an official's reactions to a demonstration by welfare clients in district office VI was deeply colored by his recollections of that earlier, political violence: "This was the Communist trouble spot in the autumn of 1923."[68] Another report suggested that "the main contingent of the troublemakers . . . comes from the area of Vogelweide, Holsteinischer Kamp, Volksdörferstr. . . . These are probably the same elements as those who were active in the

1923 disturbances."[69] But the reactions of welfare clients to violence could also be influenced by their past experiences. In 1930, a client required by the welfare office to earn his support by means of "work relief" (*Arbeitsfürsorge*) was attacked in front of his house by other "relief workers" because he refused to join them in a strike. This recent experience of violence brought back memories of the pain he had suffered years before in a different context: "If I receive my support payment, I want to keep on working. I am against the strike. I have had enough of such matters because, as a schoolchild, I was wounded by machine-gun bullets in November 1918."[70]

Violence as Melodrama

Violent incidents were played out in front of an audience—the other clients waiting in the welfare office—who could not be expected to remain passive observers and whose reactions were, indeed, quite unpredictable. In December 1932, for example, welfare district office X reported that the office staff recently had to take a knife away from one of its clients: "The people in the office became upset at this incident when someone yelled that 'here the clients are beaten up!'"[71] Certain confrontations appear almost to have been staged to achieve a theatrical effect. In February 1930, for example, a barber was denied a supplement to his support. Refusing to leave district office IX, he suggested instead that, "so far as I am concerned, you can . . . call the police. I'll just wait here." The police were summoned but did not arrive until about an hour and a half later. In the meantime, the barber sat in the waiting room where he proceeded to "talk a lot with the other clients and to direct ironic remarks at the officials whenever they came into the waiting room." Then he returned to the welfare official's office and demanded at least another 5 marks. When the official said that he could not do this, the barber responded, "Why don't you just say that you don't want to?": "He engaged in the most extreme slander of the officials. Then he drew a straight razor out of his bag and asked, 'Do you know what is going to happen now?' . . . 'I am going outside one more time. If, when I return, I still am given nothing, then you will see what will happen. This isn't over; there is a sequel!'" When the police finally arrived, the barber claimed, however, that "he had not threatened any official with the razor and had only meant to suggest with his statements that he would slash his own artery."[72] How welfare clients would react to such performances could not easily be predicted. But welfare officials began increasingly to fear that any single violent incident might ignite a mass disturbance. As a report from welfare district office VI put it in 1927, "by responding energetically, we have managed until now to contain the effects of such outbursts, but it is difficult to shake the feeling that one fine day it will come to a big disturbance."[73]

Representational Struggles: The Public Discourse on Violence

The melodrama of violence in the welfare office was also presented to the readers of Hamburg's daily newspapers (especially the Social Democratic and Communist press) in reports that strove less for a dispassionate, factual narration of events than for a politically inspired representation of violence. This does not mean, however, that the descriptions of violent incidents and violent clients that have been preserved in the official files of public welfare offices can simply be regarded as straightforward "facts," different and distinct from the politically inspired representations that circulated in the daily press. The official records of violent incidents were also representations of violence generated by and at the same time reaffirming welfare officials' own images of the "normal" and the "deviant" welfare clients and of the appropriate relationship between welfare officials and welfare clients. Normal clients were expected to submit themselves peacefully to the administrative routine of the welfare office; clients who disrupted this routine were, thus, by definition, deviants whose abnormality could be dismissed as a reflection of external political manipulation or of unusual individual psychological problems. This mode of representation allowed welfare officials to disregard the reasons why otherwise quite "normal" welfare clients might resort to violence. The official discourse on violence also rejected, by ignoring, the competing representations of both clients and welfare officials that circulated in the daily press and the public political sphere more generally.

The competing voices in this public discourse on violence expected to alter the balance of symbolic power within the welfare system by discrediting either welfare clients or welfare officials.[74] In 1930, for example, the Hamburg Social Democratic newspaper charged that Communist descriptions of violent incidents were largely fabrications designed to incite further unrest among welfare clients:

> "Loutish Behavior in the Welfare District Offices" . . . so run the bombastic titles of articles every day in the *Volkszeitung*, with the result that among the mainly still quite young clients in the individual district offices, one can observe truly boorish behavior. The welfare officials . . . including the volunteers . . . are slandered and attacked in an unheard-of manner, frequently even physically attacked. . . . Often, it is mentally inferior people who cause these scenes and then send false reports to the *Volkszeitung*, which it publishes. . . . Often . . . the reports of the so-called worker-correspondents originate in the editorial office of the *Volkszeitung*.[75]

Hamburg Communists not only rejected these accusations but also attempted to turn the tables on the Social Democrats by claiming that certain welfare officials had actually attacked defenseless clients.[76] In 1930, for example, the *Hamburger Volkszeitung* published a "letter from a worker" who claimed that

> a short while ago, I went to the welfare office in the ABC-Strasse. It was my intention to pick up my support. In room 37, I got into a verbal exchange with the official, who held his fist in my face and started to get ready to hit me. In a flash, the door was closed. . . . Four other officials jumped all over me. . . . I was choked around the neck, and they trampled my body with their feet. At the same time, my arm was twisted. When the clients waiting outside heard all the noise, they quickly knocked the door asunder. Then the police came and took me to the station.[77]

Similar representations and counterrepresentations of violence circulated in the debates of the Hamburg city parliament (Bürgerschaft) that, in turn, were reported in the daily newspapers. In November 1930, for example, the *Hamburger Volkszeitung* observed that the growing number of scandalous incidents in the offices of the Welfare Department gave the Communist [parliamentary group] the opportunity in the last meeting of the Bürgerschaft to condemn . . . the harassment and brutalization of welfare clients. The 30,000 mark Senator Neumann claimed, without providing any evidence, that [these] incidents . . . can all be traced back to the incitement of the Communists. . . . The Senator asked whether "he should allow officials to be mishandled by twenty-two- and twenty-three-year-old males . . . who come into the offices, already supplied with pepper, which they throw into the officials' eyes, before any discussion has taken place. These people have been sent by the Communists to stage a brawl." It is the most cynical impudence for the "social-fascists" to claim that the beatings [of clients] . . . were no more than the "necessary defensive measures." People talk a great deal these days of the "justified outrage felt by the officials." But these men who have engaged in the crassest betrayal of the workers cannot really fathom the outrage of the starved proletariat.[78]

Welfare clients and officials who read the newspapers carried these competing images of violence into their daily interactions with one another. Even if they had not observed or experienced violence at first hand, welfare officials and clients may well have feared that the "other" who faced them in the welfare office could turn out to be the type of violent and dangerous figure described in the newspaper reports.

Through the use of violence, welfare clients attempted to exert at least some measure of influence over the daily administration of welfare. Physical violence made a symbolic statement about the client's refusal to submit passively to the "soft violence" the welfare system administered to the bodies of its clients on a daily basis.[79] Clients (those who witnessed, as well as those who were directly involved in, violent incidents) might also enjoy the official's physical pain and emotional anxiety.[80] Occasionally, violence appears to have been accompanied by almost apocalyptic visions of a final reckoning with the welfare system and, perhaps, with the Weimar Republic. In 1931, for example, "the welfare volunteer, Frau D. reported that her husband . . . who is active as a volunteer in district 17 . . . was attacked in front of his house by a welfare client who told him that 'now all of the agencies of the Welfare Department will be swept overboard.'"[81]

The threat of violence caused some welfare officials to arm themselves with surplus police clubs or to sign up for judo lessons.[82] But others may have been encouraged by their fear of violence to be more generous with their clients, to treat them with greater civility, or perhaps to process their applications faster. Whether physical violence influenced welfare officials to be more responsive or more resistant to clients' needs and demands, memories of past physical violence, sometimes painfully inscribed on the bodies of welfare officials and their clients, combined with fears of future violence to influence the many thousands of interactions between officials and clients that took place in the welfare offices. By the early 1930s, "the personnel in the district offices set to work each day with feelings of utmost insecurity."[83]

CHAPTER NINE

Hungry and Homeless in the Depression

The threat of widespread hunger after 1930 evoked painful memories of the food shortages during the war and the inflation.[1] The physical condition of the youngest students in Hamburg in 1932, for example, reminded a school doctor of "the situation at the end of the war, after three years of food rationing and hunger."[2] Wartime food shortages, the continuation of the Allied blockade after the armistice, postwar transportation problems, the dismantling of state rationing, and the effects of soaring inflation had produced a decade-long deterioration of nutrition.[3] Alf Lüdtke suggests that the constant anxieties experienced during these "hunger years" between 1914 and 1924 were probably "not 'disposed of' when the immediate torment of distress markedly diminished after the end of 1923. It may well be that these experiences and memories had long-term consequences, that they continued to be 'preserved' and were passed on to children, relatives, or neighbors in stories but also in silent gestures."[4] Even after the stabilization of the currency in October 1923, "the amount and the quality of the daily diet did not by any means improve equally for everyone."[5] Surveys taken in 1925 and 1926 of "families of lesser means" in Hamburg showed that they were often forced by the expense of "the more nutritious . . . foodstuffs" to resort to substitutes: "margarine in the place of butter, less meat, more potatoes, etc."[6] During the entire interwar period, the diet of many working-class households continued to be quite meager, especially for women and children.[7]

Between 1914 and 1924, many Germans—women, especially—had been forced to revert to a "subsistence economy" for their food and other basic necessities.[8] In the Ruhr, miners and their families had to grow their own food. Some stole food from farmers' unguarded fields. In Hamburg, "for obvious reasons, the breeding of small animals during and immediately after the war assumed dimensions unknown before the war."[9] The hungry also came to rely upon the food provided by so-called war kitchens (*Kriegsküchen*). Yet Germans found the war kitchens and their much less extensive peacetime successors, so-called *Volksküchen* or *Notspeisung*, to be inadequate and quite literally "distasteful" remedies for mass hunger.[10] It was generally agreed that "the experiences of the war and the inflation period [certainly] did not speak in favor of '*Massenspeisung*' [the mass provision of meals]." During the Depression, these negative associations attached themselves to the public meal programs offered to the indigent and unemployed.[11]

Memories of the wartime experiences repeatedly resurfaced in discussions of public meal programs after the war, even though these were more restricted in scope and intended either to improve the nutrition and health of school-age children or to provide warm meals for certain limited categories of needy adults: pensioners living on their own, for example, or the unemployed. In 1921, Düsseldorf's Independent Socialists (USPD) filed a petition "that emergency kitchens be set up on a large scale." A USPD city council member made it clear, however, that the meals offered "must really be edible, unlike the food during the war, which the livestock refused to eat."[12] Even the German Communist party, which included a demand for "communal eating facilities" in its municipal program of 1923, admitted that the wartime experience had created a popular aversion to communal kitchens, although it thought this could be overcome "by means of suitable propaganda and, above all, by providing appetizing food."[13]

Although city governments were often unwilling to reestablish their own public kitchens after the war, they did subsidize private initiatives. In Düsseldorf, in response to the increasing unemployment produced by the inflation and the Ruhr occupation, emergency committees composed of local tradesmen and other concerned citizens began to set up soup kitchens. The Social Democratic Arbeiterwohlfahrt, the free-trade unions, and the welfare committee of the Christian trade unions also provided meals for the needy.[14] The municipal welfare office exercised a loose directing and coordinating function with regard to these private, charitable undertakings. Initially, this postwar *Volksspeisung* was not meant to be outright charity; the 1925–1926 guidelines emphasized that food was to be given out only upon receipt of coupons purchased for 10 pfennig per portion. By February 1927, however, the great majority of the more than 42,000 portions of food distributed were provided at a reduced rate or without charge.[15]

Public kitchens were intended primarily for needy single people "who did not have their own households."[16] Welfare officials worried that families would fall apart if they received their meals at public kitchens and "the last form of activity for the unemployed household falls away."[17] But increasingly, exceptions to these general rules had to be made because it was obvious that large numbers of families, not just single people, lacked the means to feed themselves properly.[18] Welfare authorities were also nervous about the political dangers of "accumulating flash points of mass dissatisfaction. It is thus intended to limit the distribution of meals to single people, specifically the long-term unemployed, especially the welfare unemployed and the recipients of crisis support."[19] In Hamburg, these anxieties were confirmed by a riot, set off in 1932 by a proposed increase in the price of the food served at one of the city's district soup kitchens.[20] A Social Democratic observer claimed that, to provoke the people who ate at this kitchen, Communists had thrown fish heads into the soup, which they then displayed in the front window of the *Volkszeitung*'s editorial office with the following sign: "Unemployed workers, take a look; this is the kind of muck that the SPD Senator Neumann dares to set in front of you!"[21]

Fearing that public kitchens promoted "an undesirable separation of the family from its own household," welfare agencies preferred, whenever possible, to distribute unprepared food that wives could cook at home.[22] Welfare authorities acknowledged that unemployed families often depended for their survival upon the energy and ingenuity of housewives. As one social worker in Hanover put it in 1932, "Without their thriftiness, their artifice, their ability to divide up the little they have and get the best use out of it . . . the situation of the unemployed would have been much, much sadder."[23] Yet that same year, a committee of women's organizations in Düsseldorf lamented that "against their better judgment, the housewives and mothers are forced to give preference to the cheapest foodstuffs" because many families now had to devote between 30 and 50 percent of their much-reduced income to rent.[24] This decline in nutritional standards, which posed a dangerous threat to the health of the nation, made it imperative that social workers not leave women to their own devices. Women welfare clients in Düsseldorf who wanted food from the welfare office were required to submit to instruction by a social worker on the best way to prepare the food they received.[25] Düsseldorf's social workers understood that their educational efforts would probably run into some opposition in working-class neighborhoods. "Therefore, the director has explained the goals of these 'household hours' to the population in district meetings or at sewing evenings."[26] Social workers could also use their regular visits to make sure that their advice was being followed. In Hanover, for example, a social worker lectured one of her women clients on the advantages of eating vegetables: "She did not seem to know that white cabbage costs only 6 pfennig a pound and that with one pound of cabbage, two pounds of fried potatoes, and a little flour and fat, you could make the midday meal for two people with normal appetites at a cost of only 16 pfennig."[27]

Doctors, nutritionists, and welfare experts devoted a great deal of attention to the task of establishing the quantitative caloric minimums required to keep people on welfare alive and healthy.[28] In 1930, for example, the Hamburg Communist newspaper reported on a series of articles written by a Dr. Baumann in neighboring Altona, which claimed that existing levels of support payments made by the city's welfare office, exceeded the amounts required for "scientifically" established nutritional standards: "We must employ such caloric computations in the calculation of the standard rates, because they offer the only objective point of departure."[29] The *Volkszeitung* offered its readers a table in which Baumann was alleged to have set out what he thought were the necessary minimum weekly food requirements for both a child and an adult (see Table 8). On the basis of these figures, existing general guidelines for support payments in Altona—9 marks per week for an adult, 15 marks for a married couple, and 3 marks for a child—certainly appeared more than adequate.[30] Indeed, according to Baumann's calculations, they could easily be reduced to less than half of their present levels and still provide the basic necessities of life for people on welfare.

Like the nutritional experts and the welfare authorities, welfare clients were intensely interested in the amount of food that welfare support allowed them to consume. The fact that the welfare officials who decided just how much a welfare client

TABLE 8. Dr. Baumann's Estimate of Minimum Weekly Food Requirements

Amount	Food Item	Calories	Current Market Price (Marks)
1,800 grams	Rye bread	4,320	0.50
250 grams	Rye flour	850	0.11
250 grams	Barley	875	0.14
3,000 grams	Potatoes	2,700	0.36
1,500 grams	Vegetables	300	0.12
25 grams	Margarine	921	0.20
250 grams	Sugar	900	0.16
1 liter	Milk	325	0.26
Total for a child aged 6 to 10 years			
Weekly		11,191	1.85
Daily		1,599	
500 grams	Rye bread	1,200	0.14
250 grams	Rolled oats	938	0.15
1,000 grams	Potatoes	900	0.12
2,000 grams	Vegetables	400	0.24
250 grams	Frozen meat	625	0.17
250 grams	Bacon	1,688	0.66
250 grams	Margarine	1,847	0.40
500 grams	Rice	1,725	0.29
Total for man or woman			
Weekly		20,514	4.02
Daily		2,931	

Source: "Dr. Baumanns Kalorienberechnung . . . ," *Hamburger Volkszeitung*, 2 Sept. 1930.
Note: The figures presented in the second part of the table appear to list not an adult's total weekly caloric needs but only the additional calories that an adult requires beyond those thought necessary for a child. To arrive at the total calories and cost for an adult man or woman, Baumann appears to have combined the second set of figures with those estimated for a child in the first part of the table.

could eat at public expense were themselves well fed did not go unnoticed. In 1932, for example, one social worker in Hanover described how, during a house visit, a family "became very impudent and insulting . . . and grumbled about 'well-fed officials.'"[31] But hunger meant more than just a lack of food; one could even be full and yet still continue to hunger after the special treats, tastes, and pleasures one could no longer afford. For hungry families and individuals, food could not be reduced to the abstract calories required for the daily continuation of human life; food was also a source of pleasure and a symbol of status. What often mattered just as much as the amount of food was the (growing) discrepancy between the food that could be eaten and memories of specific meals or individual dishes enjoyed in the past but now no longer accessible. Weimar nutritional experts complained, for example, that working-class families spent too much money on white bread and rolls and did not eat enough of the cheaper, "healthier" rye bread.[32] The food budgets drawn up to show that a welfare client could eat "properly" on the amounts of support provided by the welfare system normally included rye bread as a staple of the weekly diet. Alf Lüdtke points out, however, that eating white bread was a more pleasurable experience: It was more easily digested than rye bread, and the crusts of white rolls produced a

particular feeling of satisfaction. No less important, perhaps, was the symbolic significance of white bread, which gave families on welfare a sensual reassurance that
they had not yet been completely "declassed." Popular ideas about the importance
of other food items—"fat" (especially "real" butter, not margarine), meat, sugar, and
coffee (rather than chicory)—were seldom, if ever, reflected in the food budgets drawn
up by the nutritional and welfare experts. In 1932, the Hamburg Communist newspaper published what it claimed to be a letter from an unemployed man who, like
many others, ate at the Schaartor meal hall. On Saturday, this soup kitchen offered
its patrons "cabbage soup. Two to five old potatoes in a thin, gelatinous . . . fluid . . .
pieces of meat small enough for a sparrow, each weighing ten to thirty grams." The
correspondent decided to skip the Monday meal, a "bean soup," which could not be
distinguished from the "potato soup" offered on other days but which "from its taste
should really be called soda-soup." On Tuesday, "the soup calls itself rice broth,
containing few potatoes but all sorts of indefinable items. My wife estimated the entire
cost of such a soup at not more than 10 pfennig. But as a welfare client, I must pay
40 pfennig for it." On Wednesday, there was "carrot soup with fried sausage," which
sounded appetizing, but in reality "you could hardly eat it. Large amounts just sat
there, untouched. I would have been interested to know just what sorts of carrots were
used."[33]

That same year, another unemployed worker in Hamburg described how he had
managed, at least temporarily, to enjoy the kind of sensual pleasure denied him by
the food he could normally afford to eat:

> Yesterday afternoon about three o'clock, I was starving. As I had . . . to sign on at [the
> Labor Office at the] Johanniswall, I went to eat afterward at the restaurant in the Trade
> Union Building. The menu there was as good as any in an expensive restaurant. . . . When
> you are really hungry, you don't ask about prices. So I ordered hare with chanterelle
> [mushrooms] and apricots. . . . As I was finishing dessert, the waiter wanted to settle
> up. . . . I asked the waiter to please introduce me to his boss. . . . The manager came,
> and when I made my situation clear he got nasty and began talking about a thrashing
> and the police . . . then he called his bouncer up from the cellar . . . who brandished his
> fist in my face and bellowed, "You scoundrel, we'll give you such black eyes that you
> won't be able to see." . . . [When] I made clear to them the role they were playing . . .
> they began to get embarrassed and refused to do their boss's dirty work. I was able to
> leave the [union] facility unharmed . . . I want to advise the SPD worker who complains
> about the miserable welfare food to give the [union] kitchens a try; it is really good there.[34]

The longing for a good meal that drove this unemployed worker to risk a beating
or imprisonment may have made other welfare clients receptive to attacks upon
welfare officials that described the quality, as well as the quantity, of food they were
still able to eat. In 1930, for example, the *Hamburger Volkszeitung* chronicled a visit
by local welfare officials to the

> homes operated by the federal state insurance organization [*Landesversicherungsanstalt*]
> . . . in Gross-Hansdorf. . . . The participants included the boss, Herr Neumann, the . . .
> heads of the district volunteers, as well as leading functionaries in the Welfare Depart-
> ment. This group of 300 people was at the [home] scarcely half an hour when they took
> a break for coffee. At five long tables set up in the gymnasium, a large number of young
> female helpers had lots to do, making sure they took care of the . . . needs of these top-

level welfare officials. . . . In Volksdorf, the tour was interrupted, the entire company went into the Hotel Stadt Hamburg to take lunch . . . paid for by the Welfare Department . . . as well as to use the 1 mark for drinks given to each person.[35]

By comparison with the delicacies that Hamburg welfare authorities enjoyed on this outing, the food they provided to Hamburg's needy schoolchildren was sometimes unappetizing, as Hamburg's social-work directors themselves had to admit in a 1927 meeting: "A lively discussion developed about the monotony of the school meals . . . which caused a big turnover among the children, who very quickly developed an aversion. . . . Some of the pensioners have also complained about the food."[36] School meals were provided at a moderate cost (12 pfennig per day), and in cases of real economic hardship the welfare office paid for them. But throughout the mid-1920s, Hamburg's social workers complained about the fluctuating usage of school meals programs.

Despite their unattractive features, school meal programs and public kitchens became important components of many families' strategies for survival during the Depression. Welfare officials continued to insist that "provision of meals can only be approved as a health measure; as a form of economic assistance, it is to be utterly rejected." Yet by 1929, it was already becoming clear that "in just about every welfare district office, the granting of free meals plays a very large role as a form of . . . additional food for those in need [welfare clients, the unemployed receiving *Alu* or *Kru*, etc.]." In welfare district I, even unemployed fathers, as well as some single people, were admitted to the meals for mothers and children. The welfare kitchens were also opened to children whose families lived in such poor housing that "they have absolutely no cooking facilities," and several welfare district offices gave children a warm breakfast "to ease the burdens of 'child-rich' mothers."[37] In 1931, President Martini of the Hamburg Welfare Department continued to insist that "the Welfare Department is fundamentally against *Massenspeisung*." Yet he was also forced to admit that "taking account of the shortage of resources for supporting the needy, *Massenspeisung* is necessary."[38] A Hamburg doctor reported in 1932 that at schools in Barmbeck, where 60 percent of the parents were unemployed and many had been without work for several years, "there is an increasing demand for the midday meals of the Wohltätige Schulverein [a voluntary association]."[39] In the spring of 1933, the same doctor reported that the demand for school meals was particularly high at schools with a large percentage of unemployed parents, "especially where the meals are distributed either in the school itself or somewhere nearby."[40] In 1932, Hamburg Communists demanded "immediate improvement of the food, free distribution to every unemployed person and welfare client."[41] That same year, *Der Arbeitslose*, a paper for the unemployed, exhorted parents in all school districts to hold meetings at which they were to raise demands for "adequate school meal programs, shoes, and clothing" for every child.[42] And a delegation of the "wives of welfare recipients" in Hamburg demanded "public kitchens . . . to provide free meals for all those receiving welfare as well as for their families, under the supervision of the committee of the unemployed."[43] Meal programs that tried to restrict their efforts to young children could not be sure that members of the child's family would not also appropriate the food. In 1931, for example, Hamburg social workers complained that "some children take the food home from the school kitchen and probably don't get any of it. It must be insisted that the food be eaten in the school meal room itself."[44] Social workers cautioned against providing cash supplements for food for children because "with very few exceptions the money will definitely not do the needy child any good. It is better to grant milk, meals, or foodstuffs."

This did not mean that public kitchens had shed the negative associations produced by wartime and postwar experiences. Even though public meal programs originally intended primarily for children were now beginning to feed adult men and women as well, they continued to serve food that adults found unpalatable. In 1929, for example, social workers reported that, in welfare district II, "the food distribution center in the gymnasium on the Seilerstrasse is so unpleasant and the food . . . so unpalatable that the mothers do not want to go there with their children." In 1932, Hamburg social workers reported that even though the food in one public kitchen was carefully prepared, "the people are apparently not able . . . to get used to food that is cooked . . . for small children. . . . A number of women gave back the meal tickets, saying that the food was too soft for them."[45] Food from the welfare office also continued to bear a certain stigma.[46] An offer of food at a soup kitchen still served as a "means of clarifying . . . [the client's] circumstances. . . . If the food offered is refused, it has to be assumed that the distress is not as severe as the client has portrayed it."[47]

Some welfare clients tried to supplement their diets by growing their own food in allotment gardens. The demand for allotments had increased considerably after World War I "because of the poor food supply." In the middle years of the Weimar Republic, when "agriculture and trade could supply the urban population with adequate food at reasonable prices," interest in growing one's own food declined, only to increase again during the Depression.[48] In Hamburg, the number of allotment gardens, located largely outside the city and tended primarily by women, increased from 4,200 in 1917 to 47,422 in 1933. And despite municipal prohibitions, many working-class families also raised rabbits or poultry on their apartment balconies or in the courtyards of their buildings.[49] In Duisburg, the city government set up an office in 1919 that attempted to make allotment gardens available at reasonably priced leases to lower-income and unemployed citizens. Because the city of Duisburg could not provide enough land to meet the demand, this Kleingartenamt (which was incorporated into the Welfare Department in 1921) supported the construction of new allotment gardens with financial subventions as well as free seed and other necessary materials. The city also organized instructional courses for allotment users. In the Depression, Duisburg and other German cities made use of interest-free loans provided by the Reich government after 1932 "for the construction of small gardens for the unemployed and part-time workers." Between 1930 and 1932, Duisburg tripled the amount of allotment land in the city. As the levels of public welfare relief declined, "one's own allotment garden . . . formed the basis for survival."[50] But the partial or complete reversion to a nonmonetary "subsistence economy" could shade over into outright theft from farmers' fields. In 1932, for example, a Cologne newspaper reported that

> fodder and clover were stolen, especially in the vicinity of cities and industrial sites, often as a consequence of the increase in breeding goats and rabbits. . . . Even the seeds just planted for beans and potatoes and the fertilizer just spread are no longer safe . . . especially near allotment gardens. . . . Vegetables, early potatoes, and fruit . . . have been

stolen in broad daylight and in great quantities. . . . It is often not possible to ward off these attacks because . . . the transgressors, working in gangs . . . do not shrink back from using violence . . . and threats with weapons. . . . The police . . . cannot be counted on to help because the tense political situation in the cities, along with their other police duties, makes it difficult to send men to increase protection of the fields. . . . In some . . . areas, hundreds of *Zentner* of fodder, vegetables, potatoes, and fruit have been stolen . . . and a portion of these stolen goods . . . ends up in the street trade.[51]

Clothing

Pinneberg tried to speak; Pinneberg looked at the policeman; his lips quivered, and he looked at the bystanders. A little group was standing round the window, well-dressed people, respectable people, people who earned money. But in the mirror of the window still stood a lone figure, a pale phantom, collarless, clad in a shabby ulster and tar-smeared trousers. Suddenly Pinneberg understood everything; in the presence of this policeman, these respectable persons, this gleaming window, he understood that he was outside it all, that he no longer belonged here and that he was rightly chased away; he had slipped into the abyss, and was engulfed. Order and cleanliness; they were of the past. So too were work and safe subsistence. And past too were progress and hope. Poverty was not merely misery, poverty was an offence, poverty was evil, poverty meant that a man was suspect.

—Hans Fallada, *Little Man, What Now?* (1933)

The life of the little employee, Pinneberg, is . . . ten times better and more ordered than the lives that our clients can lead.

—"Pinneberg muss stempeln,"
Jugend und Volkswohl (Hamburg), 8 Jg., Nr. 4, Dec. 1932

Like food, clothing had symbolic as well as practical significance. Clothing was central to the story of a commercial clerk in Hamburg who had been dismissed because of lack of work at the end of September 1926. In a letter published in the *Volkszeitung* in 1927, he described his desperate attempts to resist downward mobility: "I could have gotten work on several occasions, but at a ridiculous wage. . . . Naturally, I refused to let myself be exploited in this fashion, and so I am partially responsible for my own joblessness." After several months of unemployment, this clerk's clothing became so threadbare that no employer would even consider allowing him to work in an office again. In October 1927, the Labor Office gave him the "happy news" that his unemployment benefits had run out and he must now apply to the welfare office. Here, after "endless interrogation and scrupulous examination of his case," he received just 6 marks cash and a note that he would be given a job in the shipyards: "But how was I to do this work, with my one suit of clothes that the wind could whip right through and my tattered boots. . . . Once I was healthy and strong, now I am a sorry sight, and the only thing that keeps me going is the hope that one day the working class will settle scores with the capitalist gang."[52] Welfare authorities recognized the symbolic as well as material significance of clothing when they required applicants to perform "obligatory labor" (*Pflichtarbeit*) as a test of their "willingness to work": "Only jobless salaried employees [were] spared the requirement of demonstrating their will to work by performing *Pflichtarbeit*." In 1925, after the salaried employees' unions protested that "the physical labor required damages the health of the person in question and . . . their clothing and shoes, thus destroying their chances of being rehired," the RAM instructed the labor exchanges to take into account "the special position of the salaried employees" when assigning *Pflichtarbeit*.[53]

If clean and in good condition, clothing was a sign of respectability, of being employed; if torn, dirty, and worn, it was a symbol of destitution and despair. Ragged clothing or worn-out shoes were often the first signs of need to bring potential clients to the attention of the welfare authorities. A Hanover social worker explained, for example, "I did not know the family T. until the son, Norbert, came to my attention at an inspection of shoes in the Bürgerschule 55; his boots were completely tattered and beyond repair. In the meantime, I got the welfare office to allow the boy a suit for confirmation and a pair of boots. A relative of T.'s made the application to me because T. himself was too embarrassed."[54] Welfare officials were well aware that clothing served representational purposes beyond the merely utilitarian; in 1923, for example, the advisory board of welfare district office VII in Hamburg justified its decision to grant a young welfare client a suit to wear for his confirmation on the grounds that "it is the duty of the state to ensure that the self-respect of young people is not unnecessarily diminished." Those present at this meeting went so far as to suggest that "if young people are left to run around with worn-out clothes, then there is a danger that because their appearance is already somewhat neglected, they will [more] easily have contact with people that it would be better to keep them away from."[55]

Social workers tended to look more favorably upon the applications of welfare clients who had clearly dedicated considerable effort to the constant sewing, patching, and repairing of clothing or shoes that should long since have been replaced. In 1932, for example, a social worker in Hanover observed that "K. had previously washed, darned, and patched his own things. He has done quite a passable job with his trousers and jacket, but the underclothes are a disaster. We are granting him some undergarments so that he can have them washed regularly at the Elowa [municipal laundry]. We are also giving him the necessary shoes."[56] A male welfare client was described as being "simply but cleanly clothed. He . . . takes good care of his things, has worn the same jacket for the past five years. Now and then, he receives some clothing as gifts. His three shirts, which have been patched and darned a great deal, are so worn-out that they will not withstand the next wash. He has only one decent undershirt. I have granted him two shirts and one undershirt."[57] But when Hamburg welfare authorities considered a proposal to provide a free laundry facility for welfare clients, one commentator warned that "opening a wash house may well be desirable for many clients, but it is not the real solution because it can be doubted that most welfare clients' clothing, which is in poor condition, would in fact survive the washing process."[58]

The shoes or clothing granted by welfare agencies could become an emblem of the clients' dependent status. In 1925, Hamburg welfare authorities concluded that "wooden clogs are too old-fashioned for Hamburg."[59] But in 1932, Hamburg welfare authorities suggested that wooden shoes be given to schoolchildren on welfare because the Welfare Department's clothing budget was in danger of disappearing and also because the children were wearing out their shoes so quickly by playing soccer.[60] In 1930, a report on the activities of private welfare agencies in south Germany observed that

> in the year 1929/30, the Stuttgart welfare association gave out free, used clothing to 2,889 families and 3,858 individuals. . . . It appears that the general public approves of such clothing drives more than donations of money . . . yet . . . the people who come looking for clothes often seem to believe that these . . . depots distribute only quite good, possibly even new items (Sunday suits and coats). When their desires cannot be fulfilled, they are unhappy.[61]

That same year, the Hamburg Welfare Department reported that it had set up a "sewing room . . . where old uniforms, supplied free by the security police [*Sipo*], are taken apart, dyed, and reworked into jackets for the men who were employed in work-relief, as well as suits and coats for young boys. . . . In a number of cases, it was more appropriate to distribute used but still sturdy and well-sewn clothing instead of new, more pleasing items."[62] But the Communist newspaper complained that "when the welfare slaves who have to perform *Pflichtarbeit* have no work clothes, then SPD Neumann phones SPD Schönfelder [the police commissioner] and the *Sipo* . . . vans bring dirty, used *Sipo* uniforms to the Welfare Department warehouse, which distributes them as work clothes to the *Pflichtarbeiter*. Whoever lacks boots gets them, but they are old, worn-out slippers [*Latschen*]."[63] In 1930, one of the welfare unemployed in Hamburg claimed that when he attempted to get his worn-out boots replaced, his request was denied, even though a " 'lady' from the welfare office" made a house visit to check the condition of his boots and concluded "yes, you can't do anything with those." When the Labor Office found work for the unemployed man, it gave him a pair of boots for which, however, he was expected to pay once he had earned enough money. He claimed that he was also required to sign an agreement that "until payment of the remainder of the cost, these items remain the property of the Hamburg Labor Office and may, during this time, be neither sold nor pawned." If he did not fully respect these stipulations, the man could expect to be refused unemployment relief if he again became jobless. And if for some reason the man was unable to take up the work offered him, the boots were to be returned in brand-new condition to the Labor Office.[64]

The symbolic as well as practical significance of shoes and clothing made them the focus of important exchanges and conflicts between clients and welfare authorities. In July 1932, for example, a male social worker in St. Pauli learned from some people living in the courtyard Kohlhöfen 4/5 that an (unsuccessful) attempt had been made on the previous Monday evening (25 July) to attack him as he went about official business. The *Berufspfleger* reported that

> I had . . . official business in Hof Kohlhöfen . . . at about eight o'clock [that evening], I ran into the welfare client C. and his wife in the entranceway. Six weeks ago, C. had submitted an application to me . . . for a new suit of clothes, which had to be refused because the clothing budget was frozen but also because it was reported to me that C. still had adequate clothing in perfect condition. At that time, C. threatened me, claiming I was the one who turned down all his requests. Yesterday, when I encountered them in the entrance to the courtyard, I stopped him because I saw that he was wearing a pair

of faultless, ironed blue trousers. When I pointed this out to him he responded, "What, you call these perfect trousers?" and proceeded to show me that they had been patched many times. The wife proceeded to abuse me, saying that I should not be so "ironic," which had not even occurred to me. I responded that she should be more cautious and went my way. According to the eyewitness report of some of the residents . . . who are also welfare clients, C. [then] rounded up fifteen Communists from a bar in the Brüder-strasse and, as I was taking care of my business in the courtyard, he posted them in Hof Kohlhöfen 4/5 to lie in wait for me. That nothing worse happened was only the result of the lucky accident that I had meanwhile gone to the caretaker N. . . . where I remained for about half an hour. When I left, I saw nothing suspicious. In front of the entrance to the courtyard stood the couple C., who cast their enraged gaze at me. In the interests of public security and that of welfare personnel, I hereby petition that action be taken . . . against C. and his wife (who belong to the Communist Party and are well known in the district as malicious agitators). The state expects me to do my duty faithfully. . . . In return, I should . . . be able to expect that the state will . . . safeguard my personal secu-rity, or at least that I will get a weapon to protect myself. . . . From my small salary, I can ill afford . . . to buy new clothing if what I have gets torn while I am performing my duties—but now I must reckon with this possibility. I ask that the couple C. be dealt with severely; nowadays, a simple warning is not enough.[65]

The welfare client C. and his wife were both Communists. Yet their protest against the way they had been treated was more personal than political. C. felt he had been victimized for months by the *Berufspfleger*. Now the victim took his revenge by ridi-culing, defying, and intimidating the unprotected oppressor. It is impossible to know whether C. and his wife had intentionally positioned themselves in the entrance to the courtyard through which the *Pfleger* had to pass. But C.'s appearance there in "a pair of faultless, ironed blue trousers" was a clear provocation. The couple's verbal duel with the *Pfleger* did not promote their material interests; indeed, the social worker hinted as he left them that they would be made to pay for the momentary pleasures of verbal insubordination. But the incident did satisfy important expressive needs; the couple had challenged the competence of the *Pfleger* ("What, you call these per-fect trousers?") and symbolically rejected his authority over their lives. The social worker was not subdued by words, so he had to be attacked with blows. It was prob-ably not difficult for C. to convince a dozen or more of his friends in a nearby bar that the *Pfleger* had earned a beating, which he managed to escape purely by chance. The duel between the couple and the *Pfleger* ended in silence, with a battle of looks, rather than of fists or words.

The symbolic subversion of a welfare official's authority was also on Ernst P.'s mind when he staged a theatrical incident in a district welfare office at the end of 1932. Like the welfare client C., Ernst P. had applied for a pair of pants and was refused. Like C., Ernst P. blamed a specific official for his troubles at the welfare office. He went to this man and demanded that he give him clothing immediately. Then, according to the official, Ernst P. "pounded on the table and worked himself into such a rage that he began to foam at the mouth. He threatened to waylay me in the street and give me a sound thrashing."[66] Ernst P. was taken away by the police. He returned the following morning "with a troop of his political comrades, who had clearly come simply to disturb the office's routine." But the next time Ernst P. came to the welfare office, he was alone. The welfare officer he had been dealing with lectured him about the way he and his friends had behaved a few days earlier. Ernst P. did not respond, perhaps because he had already taken the next step in his campaign against the official:

> In the meantime, he had spread the rumor that every day I played *Skat* [a card game] in a pub. I was supposed to have lost between 10 and 15 marks a day there. As P. was behaving himself peacefully, I called him to account [for these rumors] with which I was harassed by complete strangers the whole morning long. Now he claimed that he himself had never seen me there, but his colleague had. I tried to make it clear to him that I simply did not know how to play *Skat*, never went to pubs, and, besides, I certainly had no money to do either . . . as I had five children to feed. . . . People I did not know claimed to have played cards with me, even derided me as a cheat. From these proceedings, one can see that the troublemakers pick out an employee of the welfare office at random and impugn him falsely, just to have the chance to create a disturbance.

Ernst P. needed a dramatic finale for his melodrama. After being reprimanded by the welfare officer, he went to the director's office,

> where he presented a large packet of clothing that contained, among other things, two coats, three trousers, jackets, etcetera. These items were very patched and mended. It looked as if they had been collected from somewhere for just this purpose. When P. could not get his way, he took off his trousers and sat in the outer office in his underpants and jacket for a long time, until he finally left the building in this attire.[67]

We cannot decode Ernst P.'s behavior if we dismiss his actions as no more than an irrational discharge of temper or if we search only for instrumental motives. Spreading rumors about a welfare official or taking off his pants in a welfare office was certainly not going to bring Ernst P. any closer to new clothes. But the trousers were not the main issue. An application for welfare had become a morality play. Welfare officials assessed the moral reputation of an applicant, and their judgment helped to determine whether relief would be granted. A good reputation in the neighborhood was a type of symbolic capital that could, so to speak, be cashed in for material welfare benefits in periods of distress. Welfare examiners took rumor and hearsay as evidence of an applicant's reputation. Ernst P. tried to subvert the welfare officer's authority by reversing the normal moral relationship between client and official. Could a man who allegedly gambled 10 to 15 marks at cards each day during the Depression have the moral right to deny Ernst P. or any other welfare client a pair of trousers?

Homelessness

State rent controls and measures for tenant protection had been implemented during the war and were retained and supplemented during the postwar inflation. When these state housing controls began to be relaxed in the mid-1920s, welfare offices had to deal with a new "clientele": tenants threatened with eviction.[68] Cologne welfare authorities observed in 1926, for example, that the loosening of state housing controls had combined with the effects of unemployment and the housing shortage to leave large numbers of people who did not conform to the traditional prewar image of the "homeless" vagabond without a place to live. The new homeless were old and young, male and female, sick and healthy. In Cologne, the great majority were

> native to [the city], both single people and families, whom a hard fate has thrown out onto the streets. Every month, month after month, over 1,000 . . . people pass through the office whose job it is to get a roof over their heads and also to provide them with whatever assistance in money or kind—combined with good advice—should appear necessary to sustain a simple standard of living and to preserve their health and ability to work.[69]

In September 1926, the Düsseldorf Family Care Agency cited unemployment, illness, too many children, and rents that were too high as causes of failure to keep up with rent payment.[70] By 1926, tenants who had fallen only one month behind in their rent could be threatened with fairly swift eviction. Eviction orders could now be obtained if the back rent was not paid within two weeks of the time that the landlord lodged the complaint. The courts were to notify the Welfare Department of all the eviction requests brought before them; the welfare authorities would then decide whether they wanted to prevent the evictions by offering financial assistance that would get the tenants out of debt. In Hamburg in 1926, this meant that the Welfare Department received at least forty notices each day from the courts, which created considerably more work for welfare officials and put additional pressure on the already limited funds at their disposal.[71] Between 1 July and 31 December 1926, the Hamburg Welfare Department received no fewer than 5,485 notices of impending eviction cases from the District Court, but welfare authorities approved aid in only 1,745 of these cases.[72]

In their attempts to deal with the specter of mass homelessness, Weimar welfare offices were tugged in quite different directions by their conflicting interests and priorities. Welfare authorities were certainly concerned about the effects of homelessness on German families, yet the costs of helping all families threatened with eviction were potentially enormous. In Frankfurt am Main, "a city where conditions are by no means the most unfavorable . . . the loosening of tenant protection legislation made it necessary to give the needy some 2.5 million marks as rent assistance grants [in 1926]. . . . This has meant a total shift in the focus of public assistance."[73] Welfare authorities were eager to dispel any illusion that "the welfare office was obligated to mitigate all the hardships produced by the implementation of the law."[74] Fewer than half (3,200) of the 6,900 tenants taken to court in Hamburg between the beginning of July 1926 and the end of February 1927 were able to avoid eviction with the help of the welfare office.[75] Only "worthy" and "respectable" tenants who had been unable to pay their rents through no real fault of their own could expect any consideration. Welfare authorities had no intention of coming to the aid of negligent tenants who had clearly made no sincere effort to keep up with their rent payments.[76]

Welfare offices were also careful to focus primarily upon the needs of "respectable" families with several children.[77] The Hamburg Welfare Department expressed no interest in helping single men and women or married couples with no children or just one child, even if they had made an honest effort to pay their rent.[78] Small families and single people who could have generated enough income to meet their rent by subletting space in their apartments were refused help. Indeed, welfare offices were not unhappy to see these kinds of tenants evicted so that housing could be freed up for "orderly and especially for 'child-rich' families." Welfare authorities were convinced that only "the greatest inconveniences and difficulties" could teach families threatened with eviction to assume responsibility for themselves, to become self-reliant, and to serve as good examples for other families in a similar economic position. Even if an eviction ended up costing a good deal more (for temporary shelter, for storage of the evicted family's household items, and for a new place to live) than a rent supplement, the educational benefits were thought to be well worth the price.[79]

The Hamburg welfare authorities were sometimes willing to pay the higher rents for larger dwellings for an unspecified "transitional" period of time if this was the only way to help worthy tenants keep roofs over the heads; but these tenants could not count on long-term support. People who had been unable to keep up with the rent must demonstrate that they were ready to "adjust to their changed situation" and to scale down their housing needs and expectations. If it seemed probable that, even after having been helped by the welfare authorities, the renter might get into debt once more, then requests for aid were denied, unless some exceptional circumstances indicated that it was necessary to prevent immediate homelessness—that a wife was pregnant and about to give birth, for example. If rent support was awarded, then the welfare office thought it wise to pay this money directly to the landlord to ensure that the tenant did not divert it to unintended uses.[80] Like any other form of assistance dispensed by the welfare office, money given as rent support was also supposed to be repaid. Indeed, Hamburg welfare authorities hoped that this condition "would exert a deterrent effect."

Welfare authorities in other north German cities were no more generous toward tenants threatened with eviction than were those in Hamburg. Most agreed that it was important to determine "whether, and to what extent, the tenant really tried to pay for the rent out of their own resources." Even the unemployed, especially those who were single, should be expected "to use an appropriate portion of their unemployment benefits to cover the rent." For rent support, Bremen welfare authorities generally paid only fixed sums that were already calculated into the unemployment relief, although they were prepared to consider paying more in cases where the rent was higher. Lübeck did, however, pay a special rent supplement to the unemployed, in addition to its regular public assistance rates, according to the number of children in the family. Those with one child got 50 percent of their rent, those with two children might get 66 to 75 percent, and those with three children could be given 100 percent. Like the Hamburg welfare authorities, those in Neukölln thought that money given to pay off old rent debts should be paid directly to the landlord, although they did concede that, in order to avoid degrading clients, current rent support might be given directly to the tenant "insofar as they are not unthrifty persons."[81]

Shelters for the Homeless

What happened to individuals and families whom the welfare authorities had been unable or unwilling to help avoid eviction? In the Weimar Republic, homelessness remained, as it had been under the Wilhelmine Empire, a "condition contrary to police regulations," and homeless people could be prosecuted by the police if they had not "made a real effort to find shelter." But welfare authorities began to assume greater responsibility for the homeless. Someone who became homeless might be sent to a police jail cell or one of the "work shelters" maintained by the private Association against Homelessness and Begging; in Hanover, for example, 364 homeless people were sent to the local police prison in 1928. But increasing numbers of the homeless ended up in some kind of municipal shelter or emergency housing. By 1930, Hanover was housing some 685 families with a total of 1,836 children in an assortment of emergency accommodations, including schoolhouses, poorhouses, barracks, and out-of-service railway cars, at some thirty different locations in the city. Here, families who had only recently been hit with unemployment and eviction were thrown together with problem families who had been on welfare for years.[82]

Municipal shelters for the homeless were meant to provide only short-term, emergency housing. Officials feared that families who were unable to find another place to live would take up permanent residence.[83] Reluctant to expand existing facilities, housing authorities made the conditions of entry to most shelters very unattractive. Husbands and wives were usually not allowed to continue living together, and inhabitants of municipal shelters had to accept various other restrictions. "Disorderly" families were not given places in a shelter, nor were those who did not already have a place on the Housing Office's "urgent" list (*Dringlichkeitsliste*) and who would therefore have very little motivation to keep looking for proper housing on the private market. Families who were admitted to local homeless shelters had to be made aware that they could not expect to stay there for very long and that they must continue to look for other housing.[84] New inmates of homeless shelters in Hamburg were required to sign an agreement that read, in part, "I have been . . . informed that my family and I have been granted shelter only on a temporary basis. . . . I declare myself prepared to take any other shelter offered to me, at any time, even if this involves a separation of my family."[85] In a homeless shelter set up in a former private home in the Elisenstrasse, husbands were separated from their wives and children; according to a Hamburg welfare official, this arrangement encouraged "the families to find some other place to live as soon as possible so that they can be together again. Consequently, there is a high turnover in the shelter."[86] A meeting of the welfare agencies of several north German cities confirmed this assessment.[87]

Most homeless families indeed preferred to avoid the municipal shelters. An investigation made by the Hamburg *Wohnungspflege* in 1927 revealed that "the number of families who [enter] the shelters and the emergency housing is exceptionally small. The great majority . . . take care of themselves by subletting from someone else . . . thereby increasing the burden on the old housing stock."[88] In the same year, the Hamburg office observed that of the 75 percent of the families evicted that year who had not gone into a shelter or emergency housing, "up until now apparently all of them have managed to find another place to live, even if it is only in an allotment hut or other, similarly primitive quarters. Investigations two to three months after the eviction have shown that 25 to 30 percent of the homeless families got other housing through the Housing Office, [and] 50 percent rented space as subtenants, were still in their original housing, or could no longer be traced." But the priorities of the Housing Office began to conflict with those of the Welfare Department. Housing authorities were preoccupied with strictly limiting access to homeless shelters, but welfare authorities were rapidly becoming aware of the damage done to families by this hard-line policy. Living as subtenants, as some 2,600 families in Hamburg were already estimated to be doing by 1925, subjected many, especially the "'child-rich' families . . . [to] increasingly worse housing conditions."[89] Welfare authorities sometimes had to remove children from their families and put them into orphanages until the parents could find better accommodations. When family members were forced to live apart, the costs to the welfare office (in the form of payments to foster parents or support for wives living separately from their husbands) increased considerably.[90] The housing and budget offices (*Finanzdeputation*) were content "simply to divide the homeless families, to separate the husband and the wife and refer the children to the Youth Office." But in 1925, the Welfare Department declared itself in favor of building barracks, if this allowed families to stay together "each in their own separate living spaces."[91]

Although every German city appeared to be facing similar difficulties by the mid-1920s, the responses to the problem of homelessness varied considerably. In Dortmund, where 800 evictions had taken place in the second half of 1925, "it was not possible to avoid reinstalling some of the evicted in their former housing." Barmen had built some barracks in a "pleasant wooded area" on the edge of town, but "the emergency housing is seen as only a . . . transitional stage." In Essen, evicted families were also put up in barracks that the city had rented: "Most of the barracks contain living space for individual families; only a small number have large rooms, which serve as common sleeping and living areas for several families." The university city of Göttingen had built a small number of accommodations outside the town and was negotiating with the railway authorities for the purchase of a number of railway cars. But in Karlsruhe, tenants facing eviction were left to fend largely for themselves. The police stepped in only if evicted tenants had been looking for shelter for some time without any success: "People who were evicted are put up temporarily in inns or barracks. No railway cars have been procured." Magdeburg had not yet built any barracks nor acquired any railway cars "because this form of shelter only promotes a further decline of the families in question. . . . The welfare office has granted numerous rent supplements so that tenants . . . can remain in their old housing." In Munich, municipal authorities were considering the construction of barracks for the homeless, but so far people who were evicted were housed in rental accommodations in private households. In the northern Ruhr city of Oberhausen, twenty-five railway cars had been converted into homeless shelters.[92] At the Toennisberg "settlement" in Hanover, out-of-service railway cars housed some 144 families with 263 children by 1930.[93]

Constructing more shelters was, however, no guarantee that the family lives of the homeless could be kept intact. In 1929, a Catholic women's organization in Düsseldorf warned, for example, that in one local shelter "family life is carried on in plain and open view of everyone else, day and night. Complete disruption is the inevitable outcome." The majority of these families had lived in this shelter for almost three years, where

during the day, everything is played out "on the streets," as we might say. At night, to fulfill their marital duties, the wives are forced to go over to the men's dormitory, in which the beds stand in rows, next to and above one another. In this sleeping room, there are young boys as well as older, married men. . . . It is completely understandable that the family unit is gradually destroyed in both personal and economic terms. Not only is the family deprived of every possibility of keeping itself together, it is also prevented from working its way back up again because it must give up whatever small amount of property it might still have, as the family is not allowed to have it in the shelter. . . . Whatever it can hold on to is sacrificed to premature spoilage or wear and tear because there are no cupboards in the sleeping room but just a nail to hang up clothes.[94]

The Düsseldorf Family Care Agency responded to fears that a stay in the shelters would dissolve family bonds by altering the physical layout of the institutions. In 1931, the Färberstrasse shelter was converted from separate dormitories for men and women into individual cubicles (*Einzelkajen*) "so that in future every family will have a small, enclosed space of its own."[95] While they were waiting for a place to live, women in the shelter were reeducated in disciplined household labor. A special social worker assigned to each shelter supervised the way in which the children were being cared for and arranged "sewing schools" for the mothers.[96] Voluntary workers were also active in the shelters. At the Färberstrasse shelter, a private association (Verein Paritätischer Kinderhorte) set up a kindergarten in a separate barracks: "Naturally the first task will be to get the mothers who are in the shelter to help with its work."[97] By 1929, at the Ulmenstrasse and Färberstrasse shelters, there were not only kindergarten facilities but also "at both institutions courses for instruction in the care of infants." There were also sewing rooms with machines and materials.[98] In 1930, it was reported that the inmates of the Ulmenstrasse shelter were responsible for cleaning the building themselves; no cleaning women were employed. But this attempt to put the homeless women to work and also to save the city some money did not appear to have the desired effects: "The social worker in the shelter . . . has to keep on admonishing the women to do the job properly."[99]

The intersection of mass unemployment with the progressive reduction of tenants' rights during the Depression greatly expanded the threat and the reality of homelessness.[100] One observer claimed that "in Berlin [in 1932], about 700,000 applications for rent support have been filed."[101] By 1930, between 100 and 110 evictions were taking place in Cologne each month; this meant that three or four families were made homeless each day. Although the majority were able to look after themselves, at least one family per day had to be housed by the Welfare Department.[102] The Hamburg courts handed down 5,800 eviction orders in 1930. But in the first nine months of 1931, this number rose to 8,600. At a meeting of Hamburg housing and welfare authorities in 1931, one official focused special attention upon the inordinate cost of keeping tenants "in the new housing projects with the expensive rents. . . . In north Barmbeck alone, it has been necessary to give about 700 families support that considerably exceeds the current guidelines."[103] The social-work directors warned that even if the welfare offices added as much as 50 percent to the standard rates of support, a considerable number of families would still not be in a position to hold on to their housing.[104]

President Martini urged that as many of these tenants as possible be encouraged to move from the expensive new housing (Neubauwohnungen) to cheaper accommodations in the older, prewar buildings (Altbauwohnungen), especially as the more moderately priced new housing (40 to 60 marks per month) "was much sought after by the part of the population that still had work, and landlords were not inclined to make rent concessions, as they had begun to do with much larger dwellings in new buildings." Yet although most of the unemployed "would gladly move to a cheaper dwelling, the problem is finding one."[105] Because wage cuts and unemployment were forcing more and more tenants to look for smaller, cheaper flats in the older buildings, "Germany now suffered not from a shortfall of housing per se but from a shortage of cheap dwellings and from an oversupply of costly and more spacious flats." In Berlin, 6.3 percent of the apartments with seven and more rooms were now vacant, compared to only 1.4 percent of the flats with less than three rooms.[106]

Yet even in the cheaper, smaller, and older flats, many tenants were unable to keep up with the rents. From July to the end of October 1931, 1,166 eviction notices were put into effect by the Hamburg bailiffs, most of them in the older, central parts of the city—St. Pauli, Hammerbrook, and Billwärder Ausschlag—rather than in the areas of new housing. Of the eviction notices served in October 1931, 852 were for *Altbauwohnungen*, but only 193 were for *Neubauwohnungen*.[107] Welfare authorities were well aware of the political risks involved in allowing tenants to be evicted. Evictions were increasingly resisted by the tenants, with support from sympathetic neighbors: "In Halle, even the moving companies have refused to take part in evictions."[108] Confrontations between tenants and bailiffs gave committees of the unemployed and the KPD opportunities for some particularly (melo)dramatic street theater. In 1931, a Hamburg judge observed, for example, that there had recently been a considerable increase in

> the number of instances in which the implementation of an eviction notice requires police protection. . . . Reports of the bailiffs agree that the resistance they encounter from the person to be evicted and from the crowd that quickly gathers is clearly well organized. There must be a developed system of alarms, because shortly after the bailiff shows up, a team of helpers arrives which has clearly been assigned to the location. Even though the leader of the team generally attempts to negotiate with the bailiff for a delay of the eviction, the crowd that quickly forms does not shrink back from active resistance and even violence. The tenants facing eviction repeatedly demanded that they not be separated from their families.[109]

In November 1931, the Hamburg Communist newspaper reported that an "evictions commission" organized by a local Committee of the Unemployed had recently sent twenty men to confront the bailiff when it heard that he was about to evict a neighborhood family: "The commission managed to achieve a provisional agreement with the landlord, and the family . . . gained a breathing space of fourteen days."[110] In December, the paper claimed that "a few days ago, the tenants at Kajen 41 were supposed to be evicted. Recognizing just in time that the bailiff . . . should be relieved of his nasty work, a number of the unemployed assembled at the right time and carried away all of the household items that the bailiff was supposed to impound. . . . As he arrived on the scene, all he could establish was that the items had evicted themselves."[111]

Evictions became particularly sensitive when they involved "respectable" Social Democratic workers living in the new housing estates. In 1931, for example, Neumann, the SPD senator responsible for the Hamburg Welfare Department, warned that "if there are more evictions from the new housing than have taken place up to now, even the orderly and respectable workers in, for example, north Barmbeck will find it very hard, and the existing [Communist] organizations will be able to expand their field of action here as well."[112] The Communists also tried to bring their politics into the municipal shelters for the homeless. In 1932, for example, a Cologne welfare official warned that difficulties were to be expected if a family was evicted from a municipal shelter, even though the husband had failed to make any contribution to the rent for the past nine months. The Communists threatened "not to tolerate the eviction." But the director of the welfare office insisted that the welfare authorities could not submit to this threat; "otherwise, the city will lose all its authority."[113]

Allotment Gardens and "Wild Settlements"

As the numbers of evictions rose, some of the unemployed who were now homeless took up residence in allotment huts or in "wild settlements" (wilde Siedlungen) at the edge of urban areas. In 1931, a social policy journal observed that "in the past few years . . . around every big German city, a broad belt of . . . small houses, connected with the existing allotment system, has erupted. . . . People from every class, but mainly workers and salaried employees, have bought or leased a few hundred square meters of wasteland . . . and soon begun to build small places to live out of primitive, old materials, with their own hands."[114] In Berlin, some 30,000 people were reported to be living in tent camps on the capital's outskirts or in the woods and on the banks of the lakes. Others had moved into allotment huts or toolsheds: "Although these accommodations . . . infringe the building regulations, the public agencies close an eye because the tenants' distress is so great."[115] By 1931, the Düsseldorf Family Care Agency was receiving petitions for financial and material aid from unemployed and evicted persons who wanted to build crude dwellings with their own hands. Most of these requests came from families who were not receiving sufficient rent support payments and who had been forced to move into shelters for the homeless. "Wild settlements" had already gone up in Heinefeld and behind the municipal housing *am Hellweg*, where thirty to forty families lived "in the most miserable emergency barracks." The agency suggested that it might actually be more economical to give families a lump sum equal to the amount of rent support they would normally receive over several months. At least this would allow them to buy materials they needed to put a roof over their heads.[116]

Yet mass resettlement to allotment gardens generated new conflicts between clients and welfare authorities. In October 1932, a Hamburg welfare official expressed concern about the health of infants and small children living in allotment huts, particularly during the cold and wet months of the Hamburg winter.[117] In October 1932, notices were published in the local newspapers announcing that, after the fifteenth of the month, the police and the welfare office would "remove people from the allotment huts" and the welfare office might " withdraw public assistance from those who insisted on staying." The welfare district offices were told to provide only the minimum level of support to people who remained in allotment huts.[118] By May 1933, however, families who took up residence during the summer "in their allotment gardens in Hamburg and Steilshop" might get 10 percent more than the basic standard rate "for the additional expense incurred in living on the outskirts," provided they had no dwelling in the city.[119]

Self-Help in the Depression

Critics of the Weimar welfare system saw the Depression as an opportunity to reverse social and cultural trends that they felt state welfare had promoted: the movements toward "materialism," "individualism," and "egoism."[120] The emphasis after 1929 upon returning responsibility for welfare clients to their families and relatives was more than just a cost-cutting tactic. A revival of the "family community" (*Familiengemeinschaft*) that the welfare state had, so it was argued, done a great deal to dissolve was regarded as the first step toward the reconstruction of a German "national community" (*Volksgemeinschaft*), a goal the welfare state had failed to achieve. The family was once again to become the site where Germans learned to sacrifice their individual desires for the good of the whole. Self-reliance and self-help would once again become integral virtues of German culture. Although this rhetoric originated largely from the conservative and confessional welfare interests, it was not absent from the vocabulary with which Social Democrats described the social consequences of the Depression, although the meaning of "self-help" assumed rather different forms on the socialist and trade union left. Despite their continued attachment to the belief that welfare should be primarily a responsibility of the state, Hamburg Social Democrats praised the efforts of the "unemployed manual and white-collar workers, most of whom knew each other through the trade unions of the SPD," who joined together at the beginning of 1932 to create the Verein Erwerbslosenselbsthilfe Gross-Hamburg e.V, which set up fifteen soup kitchens across the city.[121] All the work was done by the unemployed in return for meals, and the necessary food and other raw materials were supplied by private contributions and subventions from local industries and the city-state government. In addition to preparing meals for the unemployed, the Verein used unemployed cobblers to repair shoes, at the cost of the materials, as well as unemployed carpenters, tailors, and locksmiths.[122] Elsewhere, local organizations of the Arbeiterwohlfahrt ran soup kitchens as well as sewing rooms for the unemployed and collected and distributed old clothes and other household items.[123] Although these activities increasingly came to resemble nonsocialist forms of private charity, Social Democrats still represented them as genuine forms of working-class solidarity and proletarian self-help.[124] More difficult to justify was actual participation in bourgeois charitable efforts, such as the "winter help."[125]

Yet these were by no means the only forms of self-help in which welfare clients engaged during the Depression. In 1932, the Hamburg Labor Office discovered, for example, that "numbers of workers have come into the possession of several [of the] books [used to keep track of insurance contributions]. They have used one to record their shift earnings and the other to draw public assistance; welfare clients have participated in these manipulations."[126] Welfare authorities also warned the city's soup kitchens "to reject meal coupons that have not been made out properly," because some clients had altered the tickets granting them free meals so as to extend the period of their validity.[127] Some clients also turned to street trading. In July 1932, the Social Democratic paper in Cologne drew attention to the "flight into retail trade. . . . People from the poorest classes find handcarts and scales somewhere and try to make a go of it with the fruit trade on the streets. Those from higher social strata scratch their last pennies together, perhaps find a relative willing to give them a loan so they can try their luck with a cigar business. . . . Almost all of these attempts miscarry painfully."[128] Much of this street trading was unlicensed, some of it completely illegal. In 1931, for example, a Communist city council member in Düsseldorf drew attention to the case of a welfare client whose relief payments were terminated because he was discovered selling untaxed, smuggled cigarettes "in front of the building housing the unemployed benefits office." The council member insisted that this kind of illegal street trading was no longer unusual: "Today in Düsseldorf, you can find someone selling cigarettes on almost every street corner."[129] In March 1933, Hamburg welfare officials reported "that there is quite a flourishing trade in untaxed tobacco." The Hamburg police had agreed to notify the welfare authorities "when people are caught selling tobacco on which the duty has not been paid and particularly those . . . receiving support from the Welfare Department."[130] Welfare clients who had marketable skills—plumbers, carpenters, electricians, or other craftsmen—but no jobs began to sell their services at cut rates on the black market. In 1931, Hamburg authorities observed that "the difficult economic situation has produced an enormous growth of black-market labor. . . . The businesses that pay their taxes properly, especially artisans, lament the heavy damage caused by the unfair competition of illicit labor."[131] In Düsseldorf, a city council member claimed that "quite a number of welfare clients draw public assistance but also perform black-market labor and thus gain two incomes, which, however, is doubly unpleasant . . . especially for the artisans."[132]

Social experts and welfare authorities also reported an increase in child labor during the Depression. Helene Simon explained in 1931 that "unemployment and child labor create a vicious circle. When the parents are unemployed, the smallest income of the children makes a difference. At the same time, children's cheap labor competes with that of adults in the tightened labor market."[133] Ruth Weiland believed that in an increasing number of unemployed families, the only wage earners were the children younger than fourteen. Some of the work they did was permitted by the child labor laws. But teachers and social workers complained that "[while] the child labor permitted and inspected by the police has declined . . . the uncontrolled . . . work has increased almost everywhere." Children were selling flowers and begging on the streets (Düren, March 1933), "collecting coal from the tip" (Beuthen, April 1933), packing razors at home for shipment (Solingen, March 1933), and hawking and peddling on the streets and door-to-door (Kassel, March 1933). A questionnaire distributed to social workers in Magdeburg in February 1933 revealed that many children were delivering newspapers, and some were earning money by accompanying blind persons on their nightly tour of bars or by running errands for prostitutes. In Braunschweig in February 1933, children were involved in the unlicensed sale of flowers, postcards, and sundries in the streets and in the courtyards. In the Thuringian forest villages near Tannich, "child labor . . . is unquestioned. . . . For children, the word 'forest' means 'work.' They know the forest only in connection with gathering wood, picking berries, looking for fir cones, etcetera."[134]

Whether legal or illicit, most of this work "must be rejected in the interest of the child's healthy development. . . . Numerous reports from schoolteachers show that these children are in a state of permanent overexertion and fatigue. They are failing in their academic subjects. . . . In calisthenics and sport they become . . . jittery and exhausted." Observers found, however, that "it is usually quite difficult, often impossible, to convince parents embittered by distress that this child labor is in every respect damaging, especially as it is seldom possible to give them any compensation" if they kept their children from working. The directors of daycare centers reported that parents often withdrew their "educationally and socially endangered schoolchildren because they had to go out to work."[135]

CHAPTER TEN

"Welfare Is the Preservation of Labor Power"

Unemployment and Work Relief

The Unemployed in the Weimar Welfare System

After 1930, the national government progressively shifted the primary burden of unemployment relief to the local state.[1] Yet well before the onset of the Depression, local welfare offices had already become dumping grounds for those among the unemployed who were denied insurance benefits. Unemployment insurance authorities required applicants to submit to a means test designed to reject as many claims as possible or to reduce the amount of the benefits awarded. The Decree on Unemployment Relief of 13 November 1918 stipulated that only "the unemployed who were willing to work" were to receive unemployment benefits. Applicants might be denied support if they refused to take the work offered by the labor offices, even if it was far from their homes or not commensurate with their skills and training. The unemployed might also be expected to perform hard, unskilled manual labor—such as the construction of sports facilities and playgrounds—as a test of their willingness to work. After 4 January 1924, only applicants who had been employed for at least three of the previous twelve months in an occupation requiring contributions to the sickness insurance fund were eligible for unemployment benefits. Even successful applicants could count on a maximum of only twenty-six weeks of unemployment benefits. In March 1926, this was expanded to between thirty-nine and fifty-two weeks. In 1927, however, this maximum was cut back to twenty-six weeks.[2]

Women were dealt with quite differently than were adult males.[3] As early as 1918, the War Office planned to restrict any unemployment benefits for women to widows and single women. Women with several children faced additional difficulties. The Hamburg Labor Office regularly referred these women to the welfare offices, claiming that it was too difficult to find them work. Single women received benefits that were consistently lower than those of men. The support awarded women under twenty-one was lower still: By the winter of 1922/23, a single young woman received less than the amount given to a family father for one of his children, regardless of whether she was still living with her family or not. In February 1919, the unemployment relief agency (Erwerbslosenfürsorge) for greater Berlin warned that such minimal support would "deliver these women up to hunger, crime, and prostitution."

Apart from stabilizing existing wage differentials, low levels of unemployment benefits were meant to force women who had become factory workers to accept lower-paying, more traditional forms of female employment such as domestic service or agricultural labor. The Reich Finance Ministry went so far as to recommend that no payment of unemployment benefits be made to women in districts where the demand for domestic servants had not yet been filled. Thinking this too extreme, the Labor Ministry preferred instead to make the receipt of benefits dependent upon attendance at retraining courses that would prepare unemployed women for domestic service.[4] Retraining measures were used to confine unemployed women to jobs within a reconstructed "female" segment of the labor market and to encourage previously employed women to return to the family.[5] In the fiscal crisis of 1923, the Finance Ministry attempted to exclude women from Erwerbslosenfürsorge completely, but the Labor Ministry managed to defeat this motion on the grounds that it was "unsocial and unjust" and "indefensible in terms both of politics and of social policy." Thereafter, the position of women within the system of unemployment relief began to improve somewhat, although the Unemployment Insurance Law (AVAVG), which came into effect in 1927, reproduced the discrimination against women already embedded in the administration of the Erwerbslosenfürsorge since the early 1920s.[6] A series of emergency decrees during the Depression increased this discrimination, for example, denying benefits to women working less than thirty hours a week and earning under 45 marks a month (June 1930) and making the means test more severe (June 1931 and February 1932). Increasingly cut off from state unemployment benefits, women had "to find employment on the growing 'secondary' labor market" or apply for assistance from local welfare offices.[7]

The young unemployed also were excluded from many of the benefits available to adult males or were granted much lower levels of support. This discrimination reflected dominant views about the relative rights of youths and adult males, real differences in their wages and incomes before becoming unemployed, and differences in the organizational and political power of each of these groups. Even the 1927 Unemployment Insurance Law, heralded as the supreme achievement of Weimar's welfare state, specified that young people under twenty-one could be required to perform obligatory labor to qualify for unemployment benefits.[8] After the onset of the Depression, the young unemployed were successively excluded altogether from the unemployment insurance system. The emergency decree of 26 July 1930 stipulated that youths under seventeen could seek unemployment benefits only if they had absolutely no legal claim to support from their families. Young people were also allowed to work up to thirty hours per week or to earn up to 10 marks per week or 45 marks per month without being insured and hence without achieving eligibility for unemployment benefits. This provision, discriminating against the part-time and unskilled, was retained in the Notverordnung of 1 December 1930. The Emergency Decree of 5 June 1931 contained arguably the strongest assault upon the few remaining rights of young people in the unemployment insurance system. Now, it was possible to deny unemployment benefits to anyone under the age of twenty-one who had a legal claim to family support. Experts estimated that this change would get rid of about half of the unemployed youths who had previously received unemployment benefits.[9]

The restrictions and exclusions imposed by the unemployment insurance system forced many of the unemployed, especially women and young people, to turn to local welfare systems for assistance. Here, they were "certainly not received with open arms."[10] Local welfare authorities insisted on their right to judge each individual application on its own merits and according to social workers' and welfare officials' determinations of the clients' needs.[11] When the welfare office did grant relief to "young, healthy people," it insisted that every effort be made to get them work: "Anyone who refuses the job offered will be required to perform compulsory labor or will lose their public assistance."[12]

The Problem of the Welfare Unemployed

By the beginning of 1933, the national unemployment insurance system paid benefits to only 900,000 out of the total of 6.1 million officially unemployed.[13] The rest were forced to turn to local welfare systems. These welfare unemployed quickly became "the social-legal emblem of the failure of the Weimar social state."[14] By 1929, the welfare unemployed already accounted for 21.1 percent of Hamburg's welfare clients.[15] Almost two-thirds (4,108 or 64.0%) of the 6,422 able-bodied unemployed men and women receiving long-term support in 1929 were male, and 54.7 percent of these men were between eighteen and forty-five years of age. Of the unemployed males receiving welfare assistance, 59.9 percent were married but 98.5 percent of the females were either single, separated, divorced, or widowed. More than half (56.8%) of the unemployed who received welfare assistance in 1929 had been out of work for between one and six months, followed by those unemployed for six to twelve months (18.4%), one to two years (11.9%), and more than two years (10.7%). The women had been unemployed for longer than the men; 55.5 percent of the women compared to 32.8 percent of the men had been out of work for more than six months. The single largest category of the men had been receiving *Alu* (37.6%) and *Kru* (10.7%), which had now run out; 33.2 percent of the men were insured but not yet eligible for benefits, while 20.6 percent were completely uninsured. Of the women, only 20.0 percent had previously been receiving *Alu* and 3.6 percent *Kru*, whereas 31.2 percent were insured but not yet eligible, and 8.5 percent were uninsured. The three largest occupational groups represented among the male welfare unemployed were transport (16.3%), casual unskilled labor (15.1%), and sales and office personnel (15.0%); 35.3 percent of the women had previously worked as domestic servants, 12.7 percent in the garment trades, and 11.9 percent in casual labor.[16]

"Work Relief"

Weimar welfare offices wanted to get the able-bodied unemployed back into the process of production as quickly as possible. But welfare authorities had to admit that long-term unemployment had become a permanent feature of Germany's postwar economy.[17] Welfare experts felt, however, that simply giving money to the unemployed until they could once again earn a wage was an "unproductive form of help." Herta Kraus, a Social Democrat responsible for Cologne's welfare office, argued, for example, that cash support

> could encourage the feeling that [the unemployed client] has a claim to public assistance without being required to do anything in return. . . . We cannot simply eliminate this assistance, but we can improve our technique . . . [by requiring] that support be made dependent upon service. . . . This I would like to call "work relief" [*Arbeitsfürsorge*]. We should assume an unconditional obligation to support a select circle of welfare clients if they perform work in return. We clothe the support in the form of compensation for work.[18]

Welfare experts were attracted to the idea of work relief because it promised to preserve welfare clients' commitment to industrial labor discipline and their intellectual and physical abilities to resume wage labor when the opportunity arose. In 1927, at the fortieth annual meeting of the German Association for Private and Public Welfare, Frida Wunderlich told her audience that work relief would "relieve the able-bodied of the oppressive feeling that they are no longer required, prevent the deterioration of their labor power, the slacking of their spiritual energy and their desire to help themselves." Welfare offices must show their clients that work was the source of "health, happiness, strength, and trust in oneself." Because the German economy depended so heavily upon "quality work," work relief was a "necessity from the point of view of production policy. . . . We can no longer economically afford to watch valuable capacities go to waste." Wunderlich insisted, however, that the work provided by welfare authorities was more important for its psychological than for its economic effects; precisely for this reason, she urged that work relief be meaningful labor rather than the "senseless jobs that one now and then finds in prisons."[19] A welfare official in Hamburg suggested that work relief "had the ethical task of at least habituating the [unemployed] to a certain industrial discipline . . . which was the true basis of every worker's honor; without it . . . no state is thinkable."[20]

Although work relief had become an established component of welfare practices before the end of the 1920s, it assumed a new significance when the Depression created a class of long-term unemployed, dependent primarily on support from local welfare authorities. In 1930, President Martini told the Hamburg Welfare Department that 85,000 people had signed on at the local Labor Office in search of work in just the month of October 1929. It was impossible to find jobs for all of these people, and by the end of the month some 30,000 people were receiving unemployment benefits and 5,000 were on crisis relief.[21] Bremen welfare authorities agreed that "there . . . remain very many unemployed, capable of working, who cannot be placed in jobs, despite every effort, because economic conditions are so bad."[22] During the

Depression, work relief assumed two basic forms. What in Hamburg was called *Unterstützungsarbeit* and elsewhere, frequently, *Pflichtarbeit* or "obligatory labor" was used primarily to "test 'doubtful cases'" by making the receipt of welfare payments dependent upon the performance of "work useful to the common good on three days per week. . . . The client does not receive a wage but a supplement on top of the support payment." Welfare clients who refused to perform *Pflichtarbeit* were ejected from the welfare system. The unemployed welfare clients who managed to prove themselves in this first form of work relief might then be "promoted" to *Fürsorgearbeit* (welfare or relief work) "that is governed by special working conditions . . . and is paid the standard wage [*Tariflohn*] that is applicable in the relevant branch of the free economy."[23] *Fürsorgearbeit* was supposed to give welfare clients who were both able and willing to work the feeling that they had escaped the welfare system, that they were once again earning their own living through their own efforts. An unemployed welfare client admitted to the work relief program as a *Fürsorgearbeiter* was, in legal terms, no longer receiving welfare assistance but rather had entered into "a relationship that was to be regarded as a private legal employment contract, even though based upon welfare law, that was eligible for [health and unemployment] insurance and that guaranteed the worker the right to take a complaint before a labor court." By contrast, *Pfichtarbeit* was a public legal relationship between the welfare authority and the client that continued to be governed by all of the provisions of welfare law and that carried with it no right to be insured and hence no eligibility for unemployment benefits in the future. The money given to the *Pflichtarbeiter* was simply another form of assistance and not, in legal terms, a wage.[24]

Welfare authorities viewed the bodies of the unemployed as undifferentiated repositories of a relatively abstract labor power that had to be maintained and preserved during the period of unemployment by being exercised via forms of heavy manual labor. Clients on work relief were used to clean canals, to do other harbor and river work, and to construct sports facilities, new streets, and pathways for bicycles.[25] Some welfare clients, however, failed to see how these types of work relief actually helped the unemployed to preserve their ability to work. By 1930, the welfare unemployed were no longer primarily unskilled or casual laborers, as in the years before the Depression, but now included in their ranks almost all occupational groups and skill levels.[26] Representatives of the welfare clients working on the building site at the Farmsen baths insisted that "only continued exercise of a skilled trade would maintain the ability to work [in that occupation]. . . . Moreover . . . [work relief] causes an enormous wear and tear on clothing, etcetera, which our families also have to wash every day. And our health is damaged by having wet feet all day long."[27] Those with "war wounds and other physical ailments" found this heavy manual labor "nothing less than torture. . . . [People with] hand and foot complaints simply have to bite their lips if they do not want to suffer disadvantages."[28] Some clients also resented the way they were treated on the job sites. In September 1930, a mimeographed handbill offered a crudely drawn picture of a worker pushing a wheelbarrow with a fat capitalist on his shoulders. The flyer described the Stellingen sports grounds as a "thoroughly fascist workplace" where the foreman went around with a camera taking photographs of the individual workers to document their performance. When the workers objected, the foreman told them with a scornful tone that he could do whatever he wanted on this job site. The handbill also claimed that the foreman maintained a network of spies who reported on everything that was said and done on the building site and in the workers' hut.[29]

Yet these were not simply the voices of left-wing political agitators, as welfare authorities liked to insist. In December 1929, for example, a member of the conservative paramilitary organization the Stahlhelm tried to draw attention to the accidents caused by the three-class system of payment that forced relief workers to ignore safety regulations in their desperate desire to earn just a little more money. In a normal factory, the workers would not submit to this kind of exploitation, but these were "just 'welfare workers' who had to fear being flogged on their stomachs . . . if they tried to defend themselves." Those who could not stick it out lost their welfare support. What, asked the Stahlhelmer, have we done to be punished like criminals: "Yes, we have been pushed so far down that we can be told mockingly, 'If you get sick, someone else is just a telephone call away. In Hamburg, there are still lots of unemployed' . . . so we have the right to call this place 'Siberia.' The people who work here have to move eighty to ninety [tons] a day but have only dry bread, sometimes not even that, and coffee as their daily nourishment."[30]

Albert N.'s Critique

Before the Depression forced him to apply for public assistance, Albert N. had been a salesman. Required by the Hamburg welfare authorities to work as a *Pflichtarbeiter*, he became a shop steward for the welfare unemployed on work relief job sites. Although he spoke at meetings that the Communist party helped to organize, Albert N. described himself as a "social spokesmen for national workers" who believed, for example, that work relief would make sense only if the Weimar government pursued "a reasonable land policy—that is, removal of the political mistakes in the east. . . . Then, possibly, people habituated to hard physical labor could find work in agriculture."[31] Albert N. proceeded from the basic assumption, which was clearly not shared by all welfare authorities, that most of those who had been forced to turn to municipal agencies for relief could not be held personally responsible for their economic distress and therefore should not be subjected to degrading tests of their willingness to work. In a letter to the Hamburg work relief authorities that he also addressed to the Senate, the city-state Parliament, the Hamburg press, the employers associations, the trade unions, and "the producers of all estates," Albert N. posed the rhetorical question, "What have those who must draw welfare support done that is wrong?" The working conditions that the unemployed who had turned to the Hamburg welfare offices for help were forced to endure were, he claimed, "unworthy of every German employee and stamp the worker as second-class." In short, the work required by the welfare offices was nothing less than "forced labor."[32]

Albert N. insisted that the Hamburg state must pay the standard wage rates that the unions had negotiated for the building and construction trades.[33] If it refused, then relief workers had every reason to ask, "Where, then, are the guaranteed rights of those who work, that is, the Works Council Law and the constitution? Or are we engaging in social experiments with enslavement, in which case the bathing facilities at Farmsen can soon be described as 'Siberia'? Why, then, do we have collective wage agreements?"[34] It was particularly ironic that the Welfare Department for which a Social Democrat was politically responsible was engaged in the process of hollowing out these very same rights of labor: "This state is based on the idea, propagated for more than two generations, that labor power should be remunerated at the highest possible level. . . . [The fact that the state] is undermining these principles is proof either that the normal wage agreements cannot be maintained under the present economic conditions or an admission of the impracticability of Marxist demagogy."[35]

Albert N. insisted that work relief was fast becoming a form of "unfree labor" that stigmatized the welfare unemployed, making them even less attractive to employers in the free labor market: "The payment in work relief is reminiscent of the prison system." As unemployment increased, more and more people would be forced to work under these prejudicial conditions. The support provided by the unemployment insurance system would be dragged down to the levels set by the system of work relief. And "because work relief creates cheap labor power, it will not be long until public works previously paid according to the standard wage rates will now be performed as work relief."

Albert N. also failed to see how working with a pick and shovel could possibly prepare most of the welfare unemployed for a real job. Rather than preserving or restoring the ability to engage in productive labor, work relief actually caused damage to the bodies and the spirits of the welfare unemployed. The "restoration and reproduction of labor power" should, he suggested, be the responsibility not of the welfare authorities but of the doctors and the sickness insurance funds (*Krankenkasse*). But the welfare unemployed would be powerless to defend their only remaining asset, bodies capable of performing productive and remunerative labor, if they were denied any of the "rights of labor" that were an integral component of the Weimar social contract. Albert N. claimed that the welfare clients in the city's work relief program could not exercise their rights, guaranteed by Weimar labor law, because anyone who opened their mouths to complain had to fear that they would be relegated to a lower wage level. And the threat of being put back into a lower wage category was a form of tutelage over grown men who were themselves fathers of families.

Consequently, Albert N. anxiously awaited the outcome of a case taken before the Reich Labor Court in Lübeck that contested the local welfare office's refusal to pay in accordance with the relevant collective wage agreements. The federal state Labor Tribunal in Hamburg had recently declared *Fürsorgearbeiter* to be exempted from such wage agreements and had consigned them to an exceptional status, unprotected by the most basic stipulations of Weimar labor law. Albert N. hoped, however, that the outcome of the Lübeck case would halt this tendency because "everyone should have the same rights, and since 1918 every employer has had the duty to pay and every producer to earn a wage according to the *Tarif*, regardless of the branch of industry."

Albert N. did not, however, restrict his critique to the threatened status of the *Fürsorgearbeiter* who performed the more elevated form of work relief. Although "obligatory labor" (*Pflichtarbeit*) was generally used as an initial "work-test" to scare off the work-shy and the malingerers, with very little pretense of loftier motives such as the "restoration of the ability to work," Albert N. nonetheless felt that it was necessary to include *Pflichtarbeiter* in his request for better treatment: "The introduction of *Pflichtarbeit* is a further chapter in the history of social immiseration. . . . Why can't the *Pflichtarbeiter* be paid the same as the standard wage rate for part-time workers? That would . . . put an end to a degrading situation . . . and mitigate some bitter feelings and some hatred."[36] On 4 February 1930, stewards and delegates from various work relief building sites in Hamburg held a meeting at the Wucherpfennig pub in the Barmbeckerstrasse. Albert N. lamented the fact that some of the welfare unemployed "are not at all ashamed to . . . denounce their colleagues . . . who stand up for the rights of the workforce, who are then forced to leave the work site and are subjected to most disgusting reprimands and harassment in the welfare district office." But for this problem, the only remedy he could offer was to insist on the need for solidarity and "proletarian discipline," which could, for example, be demonstrated by contributing 5 pfennig per person to finance the current struggle and also by buying a copy of the "newspaper of the unemployed," *Der Arbeitslose*.[37] Moreover, all complaints and petitions for public relief should henceforth be communicated to the welfare authorities via the elected delegates of the welfare unemployed. Albert N. also proposed that the shop stewards and delegates from all Hamburg building sites should meet on a regular basis, each week, at the Wücherpfennig pub to discuss the grievances of the welfare unemployed.[38]

Yet Albert N. emphatically separated and distinguished his voice from those of the Communists with whom he shared the stage at organizational meetings and whose names appeared with his on petitions to the welfare authorities. In April 1930, for example, Albert N. petitioned welfare authorities for the reinstatement of four workers whose support had recently been cut off because they "constantly work against the current and incite the other workers." Albert N. insisted that he did not share the political opinions of the four men who had recently been disciplined. He understood that the authorities could not afford to show any weakness in the face of such insolence. Albert N. did, however, warn that the incident had afforded the Communists the opportunity to stage a walkout, using "terror tactics" to force the unwilling to join in.[39] The authorities could, of course, use physical force to end the work stoppage, but Albert N. thought this would only produce more disturbances. Respectfully suggesting that more could be achieved through reasonable discussion, Albert N. attempted to create a rhetorical space within which he could press for the four men's reinstatement without at the same time being branded as a Communist sympathizer.

Gender

Work relief programs tried to protect both women and men from "the damaging effects of unemployment . . . from the thoughtlessness and instability that comes with doing nothing for a long time."[40] Yet the forms of labor power that work relief attempted "to maintain and to strengthen" were quite gender specific. As family heads, men should not only retain the will and the ability to work but should also be seen by their wives and children to be engaged in at least some kind of productive labor.

Welfare authorities were much more interested in women's ability to perform reproductive labor in the household.[41] Indeed, unemployment seemed to afford the opportunity to redress what many welfare experts regarded as a glaring deficiency in the socialization of working-class women who had gone to work in German factories at the expense of learning the basic skills of household labor.[42] Herta Kraus described a Work Center for Women (probably the Frauenwerkstätten in Riehl, near Cologne) as "conforming to the general aim of . . . interesting women in homemaking activities." The women who came to this work center "represent all age groups and . . . many occupations." Yet only "a few special courses are held in skilled occupations not connected with homemaking, such as the manufacture of straw hats." The unemployed women at Riehl were responsible for doing all of the cleaning, washing, sewing, cooking, and child minding that was required to keep this facility going. Some of these women also provided unpaid labor for the benefit of other municipal institutions by washing and repairing their clothing and linen supplies: "Mending and laundering were also done for clients not working at the center, who were selected because of physical incapacity, old age, or pressure of work on mothers of very large families." Kraus contended that as a result of the work done in Riehl, "many a general house worker found out . . . that she really knew very little about housework, and even experienced workers enjoyed adding to their store of useful information."[43]

Kraus's positive appraisal of the Riehl Center's activities was not, however, shared by all of the women working there. In 1932, the Communist *Sozialistische Republik* published a letter from "some of the forty washerwomen who worked on two different shifts." These women labored for six hours each day and for three hours on Saturday, for which they received a wage of 50 pfennig per hour; after deduction of taxes, sick fund contributions, etcetera, they were left with only 14 to 15 marks per week. During the entire six hours of work, the women received only one fifteen-minute break: "We have scarcely eaten our bread and butter when Fräulein Meyer [overseer of the laundryroom] comes along and says, 'The break is over!'" Each Saturday, the shifts were changed; if the women had the late shift, they did not get back home until 8:00 P.M. If they then had to begin work again at 6:30 A.M. on Saturday morning, they had absolutely no time to shop for food for their families. "The regime of Fraulein Meyer" included veiled threats of physical punishment when something went wrong with the laundry machines and a prohibition against singing on the job.[44]

Women on work relief could not necessarily expect solidarity from male welfare clients. Unemployed men often appeared to have been less interested in helping to achieve the redress of women's grievances than in preserving their own male identity as the family breadwinner and as the sole rightful beneficiary of their wives' reproductive labor power. In 1930, for example, a handbill for the unemployed in Hamburg complained that "the Welfare Department has begun to require that the wives of married *Pflichtarbeiter* who receive support for their families must also work for the money. . . . The *Pflichtarbeiter* should clearly understand what it means when the wife is taken out of the household and away from the children to be condemned to *Pflichtarbeit*."[45]

The Meaning of Work in the Weimar Welfare State

The reactions of the welfare unemployed to work relief can be explained only in part by the obvious contradictions between official representations of work relief and the actual experiences of the unemployed. The ways in which the unemployed perceived work relief were structured not only by their immediate experiences but also by the meanings that since the late nineteenth century had been attached to "work" in the discourses and practices of Germany's developing welfare state. Many Weimar Germans would have found it difficult to separate their reactions to work relief from the images of work they associated with three other sites in the German welfare state: the workhouse; correctional education and youth unemployment schemes; and Weimar labor law.

The Workhouse and Compulsory Labor

In the Wilhelmine poor-law system, work was, above all, a form of discipline, indeed, of punishment for "unworthy" or irresponsible welfare clients and their relatives. Weimar welfare offices retained the right to confine in a workhouse individuals who attempted to evade their legal and moral responsibility to support themselves or their family members and other relatives.[46] Section 19 of the 1924 National Welfare Decree also allowed local welfare authorities, "in suitable cases," to make public assistance to applicants who were still physically capable of working dependent upon the "assignment of work that serves the public good . . . or . . . [upon] the performance of such work."[47] Certain groups of clients, such as "professional" tramps and beggars or prostitutes whom the welfare authorities viewed as socially marginal, deviant, and even dangerous, were routinely required to perform work in exchange for material relief and were frequently consigned to "closed" relief within the confines of a workhouse. Admittedly, work was alleged within this context not to be a punishment but rather a means of improvement or of rehabilitation. Nonetheless, the program of work prescribed, for example, in the Breitenau workhouse before World War I consisted of little more than "a relatively short, sharp shock of hard compulsory labor [that] should tear those who have sunken down out of their lethargy." The directors of the Breitenau workhouse viewed agricultural work as the ideal occupation for their inmates, even though it did not prepare them for industrial labor. The German Revolution produced no significant, immediate changes in the philosophy or practice of the workhouse, despite the political attacks to which it was subjected, particularly by the left. But during the Weimar Republic, labor in the workhouse was transformed into "work therapy," and the untrained overseers of the Wilhelmine era were replaced by qualified social workers. These changes were accompanied by demands for the decriminalization of vagabondage and prostitution. Welfare professionals argued that they could achieve better results than the judicial system, especially if they were allowed to keep inmates for much longer periods of time within the reformed workhouse, now referred to as a "custodial facility." While these more progressive formulations of the role of the workhouse prescribed better conditions for its traditional clientele, they also considerably increased the numbers and types of individuals and groups who could now potentially be consigned to a workhouse. This reshaped discourse culminated in demands voiced from quite different points in the political spectrum, for a *Bewahrungsgesetz* (preventive detention law) that would permit the long-term, even permanent, incarceration, without complicated legal procedures, of "incorrigible" beggars, vagabonds, prostitutes, and others who were thought to represent a danger to themselves and to the community.[48] One of the most prominent advocates of this kind of custodial confinement was Georg Steigertahl, former workhouse director and, from 1925 until 1950, general director of Hamburg's closed welfare institutions, with several thousand inmates. The Versorgungsheim Farmsen, under his direction, was one of the largest such institutions in Germany. By means of a highly questionable procedure for having adults declared mentally incapable (*Entmündigung*), Steigertahl managed in Hamburg to put into practice the custodial confinement that he preached so assiduously in professional welfare journals and conferences. A *Bewahrungsgesetz* would constitute the extension of practices already followed in Hamburg to the rest of Germany.[49] The division of the Hamburg welfare system headed by Ernst Jacques that was responsible for "the homeless and the wandering population" played a central role in the organization of compulsory labor. Until 1933, Jacques also supervised the treatment of chronic alcoholics in the Hansestadt, which frequently involved their incarceration at Farmsen. The threat of compulsory labor in the Farmsen workhouse was meant by Hamburg welfare authorities to discourage various categories of "difficult" welfare clients from seeking support or to compel those who had already been granted relief to repay all or part of the sum granted. Until the end of the 1920s, it was used with restraint; clients receiving only short-term support were not subjected to threats of compulsory labor, nor were those who clearly attempted to do all they could to support their families. But this limited use of compulsory labor conflicted with the labor needs of the Farmsen workhouse and with Steigertahl's notion that the most economical use of workhouse inmates' labor required relatively long periods of incarceration.[50] In July 1922, for example, Jacques complained that, despite an increase in alcoholism, the legal division of the Welfare Department had received "relatively few applications" for compulsory labor.[51] And, again, in February 1923, he observed that the district welfare offices were so busy that they were neglecting the use of compulsory labor.[52] In 1926, Jacques complained that the procedure for imposing compulsory labor (*Arbeitszwangsverfahren*) took too long and urged that the "legal department make every possible effort to speed up the process." He also encouraged the district welfare offices to simplify their applications.[53]

Reform Schools and Work Schemes for the Young Unemployed

In Wilhelmine Germany, work had also constituted the core of the therapy administered to delinquent or endangered juveniles in correctional facilities. But the rhetorical emphasis placed upon "the worth of labor" as a means of reeducation and resocialization could not hide the fact that the work assigned to reform school inmates was usually dictated by the economic needs of the institution itself, rather than by the educational needs of its inmates. In their attempts to finance their own operation, correctional facilities (the majority of which were run by private religious and charitable organizations) were quite prepared to contravene the Child Labor Law passed in 1903. It is not surprising that prewar demands for reform of correctional education focused, above all, upon the exploitation of child labor in reform schools. The German Revolution and the establishment of the Weimar Republic put fundamental reform of the system of correctional education and of the reform schools firmly on the political agenda. But reformers' pronouncements about the need to transform work from a means of exploitation to a form of training and resocialization continued to conflict with the increasingly urgent economic problems of the reform schools themselves.[54] Labor relations within reform schools constituted a significant exception to the general Weimar pattern of legally protected and guaranteed work contracts between worker and employer. This was a flagrant infringement within the welfare system of the very rights of labor to which the Weimar state was officially committed. In 1929, for example, one observer charged that in the Rickling correctional facility, "with very few exceptions . . . everyone works either in agriculture or cutting peat. . . . The workload is exceptionally heavy, and the work itself takes precedence over all educational considerations. . . . If slavery is still to be found anywhere in Germany, it is here."[55]

The administration of unemployment benefits reinforced the negative association of young welfare clients with coercive forms of labor already produced by correctional education.[56] Unemployed youths were compelled to participate in the work and educational programs that welfare authorities offered under the threat of losing all of the meager benefits they received. From February 1924 onward, the younger unemployed could qualify for support only if they "voluntarily" performed *Pflichtarbeit*, which normally took the form of "primitive physical labor."[57] Even the 1927 Unemployment Insurance Law, heralded as the crowning achievement of the Weimar welfare state, required that young people under twenty-one perform obligatory labor in order to receive unemployment benefit or crisis relief.[58]

Work had thus acquired a long association with stigmatized welfare clients that threatened to stigmatize and humiliate any client required to work in return for relief. Adult, unemployed welfare clients who were increasingly forced by welfare authorities to submit to a work test saw this maneuver as both an attack upon their constitutional rights and as a paternalistic effort to reduce them to the status of juveniles.[59] In 1930, for example, the Hamburg Communist newspaper equated work relief with the labor practices of both a Hamburg prison and a reform school: "The methods applied at the Jungiusstrasse cemetery are at a level with those in Fuhlsbüttel prison and Hahnöfersand [reformatory]. And if you explain to the colleagues that it is unheard of to do such work for 75 pfennig a day, then the foreman comes and tells you not to make mutinous speeches or he'll bust a couple of your ribs!"[60]

The Rights of Labor in the Weimar Republic

From the workhouse, the reformatory, and work schemes for the young unemployed, negative images of the role of work in welfare state practices had emerged that could all too readily color the meaning of work relief. By contrast, Weimar labor law embodied certain rights of labor that work relief threatened to assault and undermine. The Weimar constitution of 1919 was the first such document in German history to include specific reference not only to political but also to social rights.[61] Weimar Social Democrats invested great expectations in the capacity of the republic's laws, in particular its labor laws, to restructure the relationship between capital and labor.[62] Article 157 of the Weimar constitution affirmed that "labour power enjoys the special protection of the Reich. The Reich is to create a unified body of labour law." And Article 165 stated that "workers and employees are empowered to participate on equal terms in community with entrepreneurs in the regulation of wages and working conditions. . . . For the purpose of protecting their social and economic interests, workers and employees are to be legally represented in Works' Labour Councils."[63] But a radical social policy journal complained in 1928 that "'welfare workers do not have the benefit of rights deriving from the Works Council Law or the standard wages agreed on by collective bargaining. Decisions about wage payment have, until now, been totally in the hands of the welfare offices."

German labor courts responded "with considerable hesitation and vacillation to the problem of clarifying the legal position of the 'welfare worker.' "[64] A federal state labor tribunal (Landesarbeitsgericht) in Duisburg and the National Labor Court (Reichsarbeitsgericht) did decide that the employment of welfare clients in work relief programs under the provisions of paragraph 19 of the National Welfare Decree was quite distinct from the compulsory labor permitted by paragraph 20 of the same decree, and hence was subject to the wage contract (*Tarifvertrag*) governing labor relations in the relevant industrial branch.[65] In a 1929 meeting, the welfare committee of the umbrella organization of German municipal administrations (Deutscher Städtetag) conceded that *Fürsorgearbeiter* should receive payment that conformed to one of the prevailing schedule of wages, "insofar as they are fully employed and engaged in regular work that is subject to the health insurance obligation." This opinion served only to inspire municipalities to find other loopholes. When, for example, the new wage agreement for municipal and public employees went into effect on 1 March 1929, it specifically excluded "the 'welfare workers' as well as those employed . . . on the basis of [paragraph] 19 of the welfare decree of 13 February 1924. The working conditions of these workers can be regulated on a district basis without engaging in labor arbitration."[66]

Organizing the Unemployed

During the Depression, the German Communist party tried to claim the role of "tribune" of the unemployed. The KPD constructed a wide range of alternative organizations that claimed to speak for welfare clients and the unemployed: the International Workers Aid, the International League of Victims of the War and of Labor, Red Welfare, oppositional tenants' associations,[67] even a League for Healthy, Noncompulsory Motherhood."[68] The Working Group for Social Policy Organizations (ARSO), founded in 1927, which published the journal *Proletarische Sozialpolitik*, acted as an umbrella organization and coordinating instance for all of the various social policy activities carried on in the KPD orbit.[69]

But the most important organizations at the local level were the committees of the unemployed. Members of these committees did not have to be card-carrying Communists, but they did have to be "revolutionary" workers. The regional committees were supposed to organize local meetings at the unemployment offices and labor exchanges. Smaller groups would, in turn, attempt to establish direct contact with the unemployed wherever they were to be found—in the welfare offices, soup kitchens, and warming rooms. The Depression gave new life to Hamburg's regional Committee of the Unemployed, originally set up in October 1926. The chairman of the Hamburg committee, Anton Becker, a Communist deputy in the Hamburg Parliament, edited a newspaper, *Der Arbeitslose*, specifically for the unemployed.[70] *Der Arbeitslose* publicized alleged abuses in the welfare system, informed welfare clients of their rights, and encouraged them to engage in a variety of often quite original, if not markedly successful, forms of protest, resistance, or simply collective self-assertion. In its second November 1931 issue, for example, *Der Arbeitslose* advised the individual committees of the unemployed "to map out quite concretely and systematically" the neighborhoods and sections of streets in order to call tenants' meetings and to organize rent, gas, and light strikes. Other actions were to be organized to force a reduction in the frequency of the burdensome daily ritual of "signing on" at the labor exchange or welfare office.[71]

Although the KPD followed its actual and potential constituency from the factory to the labor exchange and the welfare office, the party failed to develop an adequate understanding of the differences between industrial conflicts and confrontations with state agencies. Instead, the KPD obstinately imposed "mechanical analogies with industrial struggles" on conflicts within the welfare system.[72] In October 1930, for example, some of Hamburg's welfare clients who were required to perform work in return for the public assistance they received went on strike. These *Pflichtarbeiter* complained that they received only 75 pfennig per day, an unfair wage, especially when compared to the regular municipal employees. They demanded either the abolition of obligatory labor or the payment of the standard wage.[73] But both the bourgeois and socialist press thought the strike was meaningless—indeed, silly—because the welfare office was not a normal employer. It had no particular interest in seeing that the strikers returned to work. Indeed, it had every right simply to cut off their welfare support.[74] The rapid collapse of the walkout cautioned Communists against staging another strike of Hamburg's relief workers. Welfare clients were encouraged instead to engage in passive resistance at the job sites. But this tactic proved equally ineffective. The Welfare Department simply fired these welfare clients for insufficient productivity, and the Labor Court upheld this decision.[75]

Nor was the KPD able to fashion an inclusive collective consciousness among the welfare unemployed. To begin with, the KPD was not the only party attempting to address Germans who were out of work. Donna Harsch observes that "Social Democrats in Saxony, Bavaria, the Rhineland, the Ruhr, and Hamburg began to imitate communist methods of organizing the unemployed."[76] In 1931, *Der Klassenkampf*, published by left-wing Social Democrats in Saxony, drew attention to the importance of the "street politics" created by mass unemployment:

> Everywhere, there are . . . gatherings on the streets and squares of the cities where the unemployed engage in discussions with each other. Certainly, the Communists are involved in a large number of these street discussions, but how many of the unorganized, how many of our own party comrades also have a need to go into the streets to speak

and to listen. . . . The street is organizing itself, and the SPD must direct and lead this organization in the best interests of the proletarian class struggle.

If they were successful, these attempts would "deny the Communists the material for senseless putsch attempts."[77] In Hamburg, Social Democrats were clearly at work in the local committees of the unemployed. The author of a flyer from Barmbeck-Zentrum entitled "To All the Unemployed," Karl Ulrich, was a Social Democratic member of the Hamburg Parliament. He warned that "KPD policy is senseless. . . . Germany is not Russia" and that Hitler was just waiting to be put on the throne by the German bourgeoisie as their "savior against Bolshevism." The Social Democrats, by contrast, were pressing for "demands that are not just phrases but are realistic enough to be achieved."[78] Another flyer, printed entirely in red, insisted that "the Communists are trapped in a dead-end street" and that many KPD supporters were turning to the Nazis. Because the Communists had lost heavily in the last election, they were now calling for direct action that could only hurt the unemployed. The SPD Association of the Unemployed in Hamburg-Neustadt preferred to support what it considered to be the far more constructive responses of the Social Democrats to the Depression, namely, "economic planning and immediate job creation."[79]

Even the Nazis began to target the unemployed in their search for the votes that would bring them to power.[80] Reporting in 1932 from the federal state of Hessen, the Social Democrat Anton Dey observed that the Nazis "now distinguish themselves from the most radical Communists only by the fact that their demands . . . are even more unrestrained."[81] In Hamburg, the Nazi press publicized the grievances of welfare clients in language that could scarcely be distinguished from that habitually employed by Communist newspapers.[82] And like the Communist press, the Hamburg Nazi newspaper published letters from disgruntled readers in a clear attempt to dispute the Communist claim to speak as the "tribune of the people."[83]

Neither the experience of unemployment nor the experience of work relief erased the diverse, often conflicting interests, identities, and political attachments of unemployed welfare clients. In 1928, for example, several former *Pflichtarbeiter* who described themselves as "faithful republicans and no Communists, [who] knew how to value what the Welfare Department had done," were moved to respond to Communist criticisms of the Hamburg Welfare Department. They characterized the individuals who had made these charges as "the very worst refuse" among the welfare unemployed:

> They call themselves idiots, but are in fact much worse. A dog is worth more than these mongrels. . . . Any reasonably moral person is enraged by them. . . . At the Farmsen train station there is a . . . shop . . . [where] they sit and drink until the last penny is gone. . . . Many of this gang have to go here first thing in the morning, before the work begins, to fortify themselves. Many miss work several days in the week because they are not yet sober. But if they are let go . . . then they run right away to the welfare office.[84]

The message was clear: only Communists were dissatisfied with the practices of the Hamburg welfare offices, and only degenerates were Communists.

In April 1930, a Commission of Compulsory and Welfare Workers at one of the Hamburg job sites even rejected a call for a meeting during working hours with the assertion that they were too reasonable to participate in "this kind of comedy."[85]

The two shop stewards of the *Fürsorgearbeiter* on this job site then sent a written explanation to the man who had tried to organize the meeting in which they made it very clear that

> the undersigned representatives of the Fürsorgearbeiter Ohlsdorf have nothing to do with the so-called District Committee of the Unemployed or with the Commission of Pflicht-und Fürsorgearbeiter.... Because we are neither underage children nor mentally ill ... we can speak for ourselves to the competent authorities. We will ... resist any plans for senseless ... actions at the expense of our colleagues at the Ohlsdorf building site.... Our workmates' interests can only be represented in a reasonable and objective manner.[86]

Conclusion

Toward the Nazi Racial State

Welfare State Identities

What, in summary, can we say about Weimar Germans' encounters with the welfare state? What sorts of identities and interests could be formed by these experiences? The people in the waiting room of any welfare office in the 1920s and early 1930s came from a variety of different social, economic, religious, and political milieus. These Germans had already developed a broad range of individual and collective identities well before they turned to the welfare system for help. Once inside the welfare office, however, they frequently discovered that their needs and interests were in conflict with the official identities they were now expected to assume. Some clients were even assigned several quite different and contradictory official roles. Clients who could, for example, lay claim to the relatively respectable, even privileged official status of social pensioner might, nonetheless, have to endure the humiliation of having one of their children sent to a reform school. Adolf G. certainly felt that both his official position as a social pensioner and his social honor as a father had been assailed when Stuttgart youth welfare authorities ordered correctional education for his two children:

> Certainly, I should not even have to say how much I was depressed by the way that the welfare office treated my little boy.... Why did he have to be taken into "correctional care?" ... Just to prove that I am incapable of raising my children; that I am an anti-social element and have no rights? ... [My daughter] Luise was ... also branded as a delinquent. Why?... It is written in the law that children should be helpful to their parents, but this cannot be allowed because I am antisocial and must be destroyed.[1]

Politics and the State

"In the Weimar constitution of 11 August 1919," Peukert observes, "the 'social state' received legal guarantees."[2] Weimar "republicanism" proclaimed welfare clients' rights and assured them that the "odium of the poor law" would no longer taint public assistance and stigmatize those who received it.[3] Many Weimar Germans came, however, to feel that the welfare system had failed to live up to these promises. Some were able to use the Weimar discourse of (social) democratic republicanism to draw attention to the welfare system's inadequacies and to insist upon their entitlements. Others rejected the Weimar welfare state as an unwelcome intrusion into their personal lives or even as an unfair burden on their pocketbooks. Viktor G. was dismayed, for example, that the Weimar state forced him not only to pay "high taxes . . . for the welfare system" but also to contribute to the support of a daughter from whom he had been estranged for some years. When "our ever so wonderful Social Democratic form of the state" set children against parents in this way, was it surprising, Viktor G. asked, that some people exhibited sympathy for the two doctors, "Kienle-Wolfe [*sic*]," who had recently been arrested for performing illegal abortions?[4]

Some Germans carried their political affiliations with them into the institutions of the welfare state. Others committed themselves to formal political attachments as a result of their experiences inside the welfare system. Yet welfare clients did not develop a collective political identity that could bridge the divisions among them created by the welfare state's tendency to differentiate, label, and categorize increasing numbers of subgroups, each receiving different forms of welfare treatment and benefits. Welfare clients often spoke of themselves as victims—of the war, inflation, and the Depression—who were competing with each other for scarce and shrinking welfare benefits. It was hard to reconcile this rhetoric of victimization with a Marxist language of class.[5] But Social Democrats and Communists also had trouble recognizing and responding to the needs of welfare clients, especially of women, that could not be expressed in the class categories provided by Marxist theory. Both the SPD and the KPD tried to reach out to women by engaging with "women's issues."[6] Yet in both of the left-wing parties, the actual interests of women were consistently subordinated to the ostensible interests of the working class.

The responses of welfare clients to the competing political voices that addressed them could be both volatile and inconsistent. A welfare official in Esslingen claimed that the politics of a long-term welfare client, the war victim Emil N., were motivated solely by his belief that the official's political prejudices were the source of the bad treatment Emil N. claimed to have received from the Esslingen welfare office: "Seeking revenge, he first attempted to set the International League, a left-wing organization of war victims, upon me. When that failed, he became a member of the Württemberg League of Front Soldiers, politically the exact opposite of the first organization, in an attempt to win them over against me."[7] This was an extreme example. Nevertheless, the experiences, interests, and identities of welfare clients clearly did not lead them in a single or coherent political direction. Attracted to the radical rhetoric of the Communists, welfare clients might soon abandon them for the Nazis when they found that the victories the KPD claimed were largely rhetorical.[8]

The Politics of Everyday Life

Given the extreme politicization of the Weimar welfare state and how closely public welfare was linked both positively and negatively in the popular imagination with the republic, it is surprising that explicitly political statements did not make more frequent appearances in the language of clients. This reflects, in part, the penalties attached by the authorities to the overt use of political rhetoric by clients; it simply did not pay to infringe this taboo. But it also suggests that clients' perceptions of the welfare system were often formed by their quite personal interactions with individual welfare officials and social workers. It was not an abstract state but the individual official who granted or refused a request. Ruth Fischer's "Anna," for example,

> hated the official agencies no less than anyone else who had to gain their goodwill by
> begging, wangling, and deceiving. But Anna hated them not as agencies of a world, of
> a society that she hated and that she wanted to see changed, she hated them very person-
> ally; the official she had to deal with became the object of her hatred, a raging, wild
> hatred that Anna concealed because she understood that she could get more from every
> conceivable agency through hypocritical amiability, through fake humility, through a
> whole repertoire of artful disguises for her feelings and masquerades of her sentiments
> than by gruff demands, even when the letter of the law of this state, which is now dis-
> paragingly called a "welfare state," wanted to provide her with the benefits that she
> claimed.[9]

Even welfare clients with strong political identities could often find few clues in the language of formal politics, whether left, right, or center, as to how their transactions with individual welfare officials and social workers might successfully be negotiated. The complicated nature of these negotiations derived in no small part from the fact that the welfare system was constantly engaged in the production of representations as well as in the distribution of relief.[10] To lay claim to the material and other benefits that the system had to offer (however meager these might sometimes be), clients had to construct the kind of self-representation that would bring favorable attention from the authorities or that would contest the discrimination that inevitably resulted from a negative image in official eyes. The institutions of the Weimar welfare state became arenas where official and popular representations of identities and interests confronted and challenged one another.

Gender played a central role in these confrontations. Women were normally more numerous among welfare clients than men were, at least until the Depression. Female welfare experts and social workers claimed to address women's specific needs and interests. Women could certainly benefit from the welfare system and from the relationships they formed with individual social workers, but what social workers were prepared to give female welfare clients did not always correspond to these women's own definitions of their needs and interests. Moreover, to gain access to the benefits that the welfare system could offer, women welfare clients had to submit to the female social workers' "normalizing" judgments, which were informed less by an objective, scientific knowledge than by middle-class cultural norms that many working-class women were unable or unwilling to embrace. Yet gender also exerted less obvious influences on the transactions between officials and welfare clients. All welfare clients, whether male and female, were subjected to contradictory gendered expectations "from above." Required by welfare authorities to accept what contemporaries would have considered a female subject position—subordinate and acquiescent—welfare clients were expected at the same time to embrace values and behavior considered masculine: self-reliance and a rational approach to the conduct of their daily lives—which, so the welfare authorities contended, would help clients to lift themselves out of poverty and welfare dependency.[11]

Male and female welfare clients who wanted to resist or renegotiate official representations of their identities and interests had to find ways to contest the validity of the representations themselves. This challenge could involve welfare clients in quite subtle attempts to influence and rework the official narrative of their cases. Clients might attempt to achieve legitimacy for needs and interests not originally recognized by welfare officials. Having located "some space for maneuver within the administrative framework," welfare clients could attempt to "displace and/or modify an agency's official interpretation of their needs, even without mounting an overt challenge." Welfare clients' transactions with welfare authorities might also allow them to "resist therapeutic initiatives of the social state while accepting material aid" and even to "develop practices and affiliations that are at odds with the social state's way of positioning them as clients."[12] These gains might, on occasion, be achieved through collective action, but they more commonly resulted from the successful implementation of personalized tactics and strategies.

These individual attempts to evade, contest, or subvert the power and authority of welfare officials were examples of the "everyday politics" (*Alltags-Politiken*) to which Alf Lüdtke and Thomas Lindenberger have recently drawn attention.[13] This "politics outside of politics" (*Politik ausserhalb der Politik*) can be seen, in part, as another way of directly asserting interests that might equally well have been advanced indirectly through the organizational forms and languages of conventional politics. But *Alltags-Politik* gave expression, in addition, to interests, needs, and desires that the arena of formal politics did not recognize or simply did not sanction. Frequently involving "physical or symbolic violence," the forms of self-assertion in which welfare clients engaged "offered or promised at least the possibility of a nonalienated . . . articulation of interests that took place, not at a distance, but in immediate proximity to the body and the senses."[14] This body politics allowed welfare clients to satisfy expressive and symbolic needs and to promote their material interests. As we have seen, even some material benefits—food, for example—were themselves laden with symbolic meaning derived from popular memories of recent German history. But welfare clients' various needs and interests were not necessarily compatible with each other; the satisfaction of one need could jeopardize another interest. The "pleasures of refusal" often invited painful sanctions from the authorities, which could make it more difficult to pursue longer-term, material interests.[15] The choices most clients faced were neither black nor white but rather "the varying greys of active consent, accommodation, and nonconformity."[16]

Central to the identities and interests of welfare officials and social workers was their claim to possess an expert knowledge that could produce a positive transformation of their clients' everyday lives. Yet welfare authorities could not always count on "the readiness and ability to cooperate of the person seeking the service or being subjected to it."[17] Clients wanted material assistance, not just advice, yet the economic benefits that Weimar welfare agencies were either willing or able to provide were often meager and to be had only at the cost of submitting to the investigation of intimate details of family life and of being subjected to supervision by the welfare authorities.[18] Invasive practices "of normalization and surveillance" embroiled welfare agencies in cultural conflicts with clients that damaged official claims to authority. Welfare officials' "cultural capital" was likewise depleted by the welfare system's inability to respond adequately to the "massification" of popular needs during periods of economic crisis.

During the Depression, swamped by a flood of clients that made it impossible to do much more than mechanically process cases, confronted with the threat of disturbances and even violence in the welfare office and the neighborhood, assailed in the broader public sphere by criticism from the political extremes, welfare officials and social workers experienced a fundamental crisis of their professional identities. Religion, politics, or the belief in the "mission of women" could, perhaps, give a higher meaning to work that now seemed fruitless and frustrating. Yet welfare officials and social workers sometimes found that their worldviews were in conflict with the requirements of their profession; in 1932, for example, a Protestant female social worker complained that

> as a social worker, the deaconess [*Diakonisse*] is caught in a fundamental conflict; to the needy, she is the representative of the state [and is subject to] the economic interests of the agency under which she works. The guiding principle, the motif of all her activity, is the thriftiest and most productive application of the means provided in the budget. But although the principle of economy is also present in the Innere Mission, it is not the supreme law.[19]

The Backlash against the Weimar Welfare State, 1929–1933

After 1929, the Depression tore apart the fragile, always contested political compromise that had produced the Weimar welfare state. Weimar's troubled but still functioning democratic public sphere came to play a contradictory role, both assuring continued debate yet also permitting the circulation of increasingly intemperate attacks upon the Weimar welfare state, which contributed to its ideological delegitimation and a growing readiness to embrace a completely different alternative. This growing backlash at the levels of both discourse and administrative practice created the preconditions for the subsequent construction of a Nazi "racial state."

Discourse

The assault upon the welfare state and its clients during the Depression was powered by ideological as well as financial motives. The SPD Reichstag deputy, Louise Schroeder, warned that "we now confront the greatest danger because the men who rule Germany reject the 'welfare state' not just out of economic necessity but on principle."[20] In the course of the 1920s, "Social Democracy" and the "welfare state" had become virtually synonymous terms of abuse in the vocabulary of the religious welfare interests. Karl Bopp, a spokesman for the Catholic Caritas, argued in 1932 that the socialist ideas on welfare had promoted a lamentable decline in individual self-reliance and family members' sense of responsibility for one another. Bopp worried that the "ennobled" and "generous" welfare supported by the Social Democrats threatened Germany's future, "that 'men of deeds' . . . will be reduced to people who have to be taken care of [*Versorgungsmenschen*] who believe that they may always rely upon the help of the state."[21] Bopp joined a chorus of other voices that complained that Germans had too easily become accustomed to regarding public assistance as a right that they could exercise at any time.[22] In 1926, a Stadrat in Berlin complained that "coming to rely upon welfare and refusing to change one's way of life to conform to a reduced income is, today, not uncommon."[23] In 1927, the general secretary of the German League of Free Welfare Organizations (Deutsche Liga der freien Wohlfahrtspflege) warned that

> wide circles of the sound part of our people look at the development of our current system of welfare with concern, even with skepticism. They see that an ever larger portion of the nation is going onto welfare and fear that this will lead to a moral collapse even of those circles that today still remain morally healthy. They cannot see any indication from welfare clients of an earnest desire to once again become self-reliant. Characteristic of the contemporary mood is the saying: "Behind every sick person, there are two social workers, but there is [at least] one social worker behind each healthy individual."[24]

At the 1927 Private Welfare Exhibition in the Stuttgart Stadthalle, even the director of the RAM, Dr. Brauns, complained that "with the strengthening of the public welfare system there is also the danger that feelings of mutual responsibility will be weakened. Our people all too often expect to be helped only by the state and other public bodies."[25] And a commentator in Württemberg wondered "whether the welfare and social policy that we have promoted . . . goes too far because it creates too many claims on the state and municipality and, to some extent, undermines responsibility for oneself and the inclination to take care of the family and the future."[26] A youth welfare worker with many years of experience complained in 1928 that "traditional feelings of responsibility, even toward close relatives, are in the process of disappearing. 'The city or the state must look after them,' is now heard everywhere."[27] In 1932, a conservative Hamburg newspaper charged that

> when . . . the Social Democrats came to power, they removed the state under which everyone assumed the responsibility . . . in the first instance for themselves and their families and replaced it with the "entitlement state" [*Versorgungsstaat*]. Henceforth, everyone had a claim to public money. . . . As is human, greediness grew along with these claims, and the public office that was no longer exercised in a patriarchal fashion seemed to act as an enticement. . . . The word "welfare" has created a confusion in the concepts.[28]

Bopp agreed that "there is now a danger that welfare will transform the consciousness of duty toward the state into its opposite . . . so that people will believe that they only have rights. . . . The state appears to be a cash cow that has to provide for everyone in times of need, regardless of its resources."[29] And the Social Democrats' promotion of preventive care was completely unrealistic; "The socialist belief that the extensive building up of preventive welfare will reduce the actual work of healing to a diminishing minimum remains utopian. It ignores the fact that in many cases conditions of poverty are to be traced back to causes deep within the individual . . . [that] cannot be altogether eliminated, even under the very best imaginable circumstances."[30]

Like many other critics, Bopp was also disenchanted with the spirit in which the state welfare system approached its work; state welfare, he charged, did not deal with individuals in human and personal terms but rather "abstracted the 'case' from the human being . . . and made an effective, diligent machinery, not so as to help real people but rather to satisfy [abstract] needs that arise in the population."[31] Bopp thought that "the neutrality of public welfare in matters of worldview means that its work is only ever partial. . . . A great deal of distress is ethical and inextricably bound up with the worldview of the person in need; [consequently,] public welfare can never achieve a really lasting success."[32] Bopp believed that "private welfare activity can adjust to the singularity of the individual case better . . . because it is not bound by rules and regulations . . . that restrict its ability to make decisions." Although acknowledging that state welfare would remain indispensable because "free welfare . . . cannot reach every single case,"[33] Bopp nonetheless insisted that "the hour of free welfare has sounded. Only it can provide real help because it is not bound to any schema. . . . More than ever, it is necessary to awaken and to strengthen the charitable sentiments of wide circles of the population."[34]

Writing in *Caritas* in 1931, Hans Stichler argued that a new connection, which had become lost during the Weimar years, must be forged between "the state, the *Volk*, and social welfare." For some, like Stichler, the answer was quite simply the reprivatization of welfare functions that had in the course of the Weimar Republic became more and more infused with the bureaucratic, materialistic spirit of the secular state. Stichler believed that Germany had raised "a belief in the holiness of state administration" above the "spirit of welfare." Public welfare activity always risked "the danger of becoming petrified in bureaucratic forms."[35] But the Depression seemed to offer a new chance for the "free" welfare organizations to escape the "chains of bureaucracy."[36] In August 1931, a report from south Germany observed that "the real increase of distress and the numbers of the needy set definite limits on the extent to which public welfare can make cuts and savings. . . . Consequently, the private welfare organizations . . . have been asked more than in the past to step in and help wherever the public welfare system cannot provide adequate assistance."[37] Oberregierungsrat Mailänder in Stuttgart suggested, for example, that private welfare organizations could engage in a number of activities aimed at the unemployed, such as public kitchens and the distribution of food packets to needy families. "Warming rooms" could also be set up, as could day rooms, courses for the unemployed, and workrooms where needy women from the *Mittelstand* could sew or engage in other outwork (*Heimarbeit*). Private organizations could also organize lectures, concerts, and other cultural events for the unemployed, as well as public collections of used clothing.[38] In 1931 and 1932, the district welfare association in Rottweil reported that it had provided beds, cheap food, and warming rooms, spending a total of 8,324 marks and 59 pfennig because the public welfare system was swamped.[39] In 1932, the Mergentheim district association gave out emergency relief and helped tuberculosis patients.[40] During the administrative year 1932/33, the Rottenburg district association distributed relief in cases of accident and illness, gave beds to the "child-rich," cheap shoes to the welfare unemployed, service awards to female domestic servants, and sold "welfare stamps" (*Wohlfahrtsbriefmarken*).[41] It also organized collections for the "winter help" (*Winterhilfe*), a campaign begun in 1930 by the private welfare agencies in cooperation with the social ministries of the federal states and the RAM, which elicited donations in money and kind for distribution to the needy. This program was extraordinarily successful. But it did not reinvigorate the relationship between the free welfare organizations and the republican state. In fact, the language in which these campaigns were conducted did more to legitimize the Nazi *Winterhilfe* after 1933 than to shore up the legitimacy of the Weimar Republic: "The gesture of a desire to help, which stood above political parties . . . and a diffuse model of the *Volksgemeinschaft*, could be filled at will with authoritarian, totalitarian, but only in a limited way with a democratic, content."[42]

Stichler had insisted that the public welfare system must allow "the largest possible *Lebensraum*" to the private welfare organizations "that live from and with the *Volk*."[43] Private welfare interests realized that they could not declare complete independence from the state; their own resources were too limited, the social problems generated by the Depression too great.[44] Yet the nature of the state that had made itself responsible for the welfare of the German nation could be transformed. If Germany could become a truly popular state, a *Volkstaat*, then the welfare state could perhaps begin to become a *Volksgemeinschaft*. The transition to this new state required the removal of what the enemies of Marxism regarded as its pernicious influence upon German public life. This, in part, was what Nazism promised.[45] Hamburg Nazis vowed, for instance, that as soon as they gained power they would rid the city's welfare system of "Marxist mismanagement."[46] But within a few months of Hitler's coming to power, the private welfare organizations learned just how important the democratic republic had been for the very existence of the free welfare organizations. The Innere Mission and the Caritas were not destroyed like the socialist Workers' Welfare, or absorbed into the NS-Volkswohlfahrtspflege, like some of the smaller private welfare organizations. But the Nazis' determination "to put welfare . . . under their own management" eroded the independence of the private welfare organizations, while Nazi racism assaulted their Christian values.[47]

Practices

The massification of poverty after 1929 made it virtually impossible for welfare officials to do the types of work they thought should be their primary concern. Instead of properly constructing a social diagnosis and suggesting and implementing a well-thought-out social therapy, the female social worker's job had now increasingly become a matter of the number of the cases she was able to dispose of [*abfertigen*] each day. Usually the only judgment called for was whether or not economic relief was required and justified. This in turn threatened to do considerable damage to the social worker's relationship with her clients and her image among the general public. In Frankfurt, Hanna Hellinger insisted that female social workers should be allowed to concentrate more on those cases where their training and skills could be used productively. But this meant that social workers could not be burdened with the "truly antisocial . . . the hopeless cases about which every social worker can report. . . . We can no longer afford to waste money and energy on them."[48]

Welfare officials were also disturbed that "clients are often organized and want to see their own individual case dealt with according to the guidelines of a particular organization's program. The creation of a purely human relationship of trust between the applicant and the welfare worker is frequently quite difficult."[49] Disturbances disrupted the bureaucratic routine of welfare offices. Angry welfare clients directed verbal abuse, even physical violence, against welfare officials: "Excited confrontations are often accompanied by writing tables being knocked over, by objects being thrown, and by the spitting and hysterical screaming of agitated women . . . [which] deeply disturb the normal business of the welfare office for hours at a time."[50] Local welfare authorities desperately wanted to rid themselves of the burden of the welfare unemployed. The 1924 National Welfare Decree allowed welfare authorities to require work in exchange for support, and Hamburg welfare officials were told to "ruthlessly eject anyone . . . who refuses the work they are offered without a good reason."[51] But until 1933, financial restrictions and political criticism prevented the welfare authorities from applying this work test as comprehensively as they would have liked.[52]

During the course of the Depression, the aims that the welfare authorities had hoped to achieve with work relief programs were increasingly frustrated by deflationary government policies at both the national and local levels and by the consequent budget cuts. In the city of Schleswig, for example, work relief had been in operation for a number of years; indeed, since 1925 no unemployed person received public assistance without performing some labor in a work relief scheme. But Schleswig was a provincial *Kleinstadt* with only 19,000 inhabitants and only between 12 and 163 unemployed workers.[53] Few large German cities could afford to follow this example.[54] As early as August 1931, the weekly working times for *Fürsorgearbeiter* in Hamburg were reduced to thirty-six hours for married men and thirty-two for single welfare clients. Whereas in May 1931 the Hamburg welfare system occupied about 2,300 of the city's unemployed with *Fürsorgearbeit*, by the winter of 1931/32 this number had dropped to between 600 and 700. In the early summer of 1930, about every sixth member of the welfare unemployed was engaged as a *Fürsorgearbeiter*; by the winter of 1931/32 this was only 1 percent and in December 1932 still only about 2 percent. However, the numbers engaged in "obligatory labor" (*Pflichtarbeit*) did increase almost continuously, reaching over 6,000 by the summer of 1932.[55] This clearly indicated that, in both the minds of welfare authorities and in everyday welfare practices, the educational functions of work relief were beginning to be overshadowed by the more disciplinary and deterrent functions: "With the deepening crisis . . . the authoritarian variant of *Pflichtarbeit* was strongly expanded." In Germany as a whole, the number of municipal *Fürsorgearbeiter* went, on average, from 37,000 in 1930 to 55,000 in 1931 to 47,500 in 1932. But the numbers of *Pflichtarbeiter* rose from 33,750 in 1930 to 35,600 in 1931 to 63,250 in 1932.[56]

After 1933

Demoralized by the last days of Weimar, many of the welfare officials and social workers who were not purged from the system after 1933 because they were Jews or

Social Democrats may have welcomed the Third Reich as a new beginning. Even if they had not voted for Hitler and even if they did not fully embrace the Nazis' racial program, welfare officials would have found it difficult not to be enticed by the changes the Nazis promised to make. In July 1933, for example, the new Nazi senator responsible for the Hamburg Welfare Department told welfare officials that having already put an end to the politicization that plagued the welfare system during the Weimar years, the Nazis now intended "to fill the officials once again with the feeling that loyalty, honor, and discipline are the foundation of the state and of every public agency." The Third Reich would rectify the mistakes of "the old system with its emancipation of the individual from all duties to the *Volk* and its installation of liberalism and its bolshevistic brother, Marxism, in public life." Finally, the Nazis intended to make it easier for welfare officials and social workers to do their jobs properly by reducing the numbers of "careworn, despairing, and embittered *Volksgenossen*" with which they had to deal. Since 8 March, the Welfare Department "has already registered a reduction of 10,000 welfare recipients. This success speaks for itself!" Welfare officials could expect that further reductions in their caseloads would follow.[57]

After 1933, the balance of power between welfare authorities and their clients shifted radically in favor of the former. Martini was very pleased to report in 1934 that

> in the National Socialist state, the officials can once again administer welfare with the necessary authority; they can reject the unworthy, use coercion against the "asocial," get rid of the welfare cheats. They can do all of this because standing behind them is a strong state power. The time is passed when the welfare district offices were hotbeds of the worst kinds of disturbances, when police protection was necessary, when the welfare officers had to make their decisions under pressure from the masses. The days are gone when Communist elements perpetrated their terror, officials were spat upon, bombarded with inkwells and chairs.[58]

Clients who refused to perform the obligatory labor, which was increasingly made a condition of support after 1933, played right into the hands of welfare authorities, who wanted to get rid of as many of their clients as they could. In many cities, obligatory labor became a new magic formula. Between 1933 and 1936, the national percentage of the welfare unemployed who worked as *Fürsorgearbeiter* increased from 3.0 percent to 9.4 percent, but the percentage engaged in *Pflichtarbeit* went from 3.5 percent to 20.7 percent. The larger German cities made especially active use of *Pflichtarbeit* after 1933. In Bremen, the numbers of *Pflichtarbeiter* rose from 528 in January 1933 to 2,139 in January 1934. In Düsseldorf, only 132 of the welfare unemployed were engaged in *Pflichtarbeit* in 1932, but by 1934 this number had risen to 7,162. Ayass concludes that "despite regional differences . . . the unmistakable direction taken by municipal administrations was to engage as many male welfare recipients as possible, as well as a large number of the women, in *Pflichtarbeit*."

In January 1934 in Stuttgart, for example, the municipal administration introduced a labor obligation for all of the unemployed receiving welfare assistance who were physically fit and under the age of sixty.[59] A welfare official was happy to report that of the 5,000 unemployed who had been ordered to perform obligatory labor, about one-half refused, as a result of which "they are no longer to be considered in need of assistance and are therefore removed from the welfare rolls."[60] By ordering 8,779 male welfare clients to perform *Pflichtarbeit* between late 1933 and the autumn of 1935, the Stuttgart welfare office was able drastically to decrease the numbers of welfare unemployed on its rolls from 16,631 at the end of 1932 to only 687 at the end of 1935.

The Hamburg welfare authorities created a special section of the work relief program in 1934 "whose only task was to reduce the number of single, male welfare recipients by bullying them with *Pflichtarbeit*." All of the single welfare unemployed under the age of forty-seven (with the exception of Nazi activists) were now required to perform *Pflichtarbeit* for at least six months in work camps set up some distance from Hamburg. The Welfare Department's main goal was not to intern all of the single welfare unemployed—even the largest camp, Rickling, could not accommodate more than a few hundred of the approximately 6,000 in 1934—but rather to use the threat of these external workcamps to get rid of as many clients as possible. This system worked. The great majority either failed to show up at the main Hamburg train station for transport to Rickling or one of the other camps or left the camp soon after they arrived; in either case, they were branded as malingerers and refused any further public assistance. Other local welfare authorities set up similar work camps for the welfare unemployed. At the Bremen Teufelsmoor camp, thirty-two kilometers from the city center, the inmates were required to wear institutional clothing, including striped trousers like those worn in prison, and the overseers carried pistols. Clients who submitted to these new compulsory-labor requirements "but sabotaged the work by just standing around and complaining"[61] ran the risk of being labeled "antisocial" and hence of becoming candidates for more drastic treatment.[62]

On the ruins of Weimar's contested social republic, the Nazi regime began to construct a racial state that made the "biologically unworthy," the "genetically deficient," and other "community aliens" the victims of forced sterilization, euthanasia, and extermination.[63] Ayass points out that the ideas informing this project were by no means new:

> Fundamentally new, however, was the fact that all the opponents of "race hygiene" and welfare internment practices had been reduced to silence. Only under the conditions of the dictatorship could long-standing proposals for the "weeding out" and incarceration of those who were allegedly of "lesser worth" be put into practice. The dictatorial form of Nazi domination was a decisive factor in the transition from discrimination to extermination. There was no longer a critical public sphere to hold this development in check. And, in any case, all the basic legal rights of the victims had already been destroyed.[64]

Local welfare authorities played an active role in the creation of the Nazis' murderous new racial-eugenic order. On their own initiative, without any directives from above, welfare offices had the clients they considered antisocial arrested by the police and locked up in workhouses or labor camps. Nor did welfare offices object when the Gestapo started shipping the work-shy and the antisocial to Buchenwald in 1938. The women who continued to function as social workers after 1933 were also increasingly involved in the Nazis' use of the welfare services for eugenic screening and "often ended up preparing the way for the 'selection' and elimination of so-called 'inferior life.'"[65] In Hamburg, social workers' case files played an important role in sterilization proceedings against the "genetically diseased" (*Erbkranke*) and were often included word for word in the judgments handed done by the Genetic Health Courts. Ayass concludes that "getting rid of undesirable clients simply became an unquestioned normality, with no attempt to keep it secret, with no suggestion that anything wrong or illegal was being done."[66] Many of the self-assertive practices in which clients had engaged during the Weimar Republic were now extremely dangerous, even life threatening. If they were to survive in the Nazi racial state, welfare clients could afford only the most subtle and opaque politics of everyday life.

Notes

.

Abbreviations

The following abbreviations are used throughout the notes.

BZWW	*Blätter der Zentralleitung für Wohltätigkeit in Württemberg*
DIZ	*Deutsche Invaliden Zeitung*
IM	*Die Innere Mission im evangelischen Deutschland: Organ des Centralverbandes für die Innere Mission der deutschen evangelischen Kirche*
SJDR	*Statistisches Jahrbuch für das Deutsche Reich*
SJdS	*Statistisches Jahrbuch deutscher Städte*
SJFHH	*Statistisches Jahrbuch für die Freie und Hansestadt Hamburg*
StAHH	Staatsarchiv Hamburg
StADü	Stadtarchiv Düsseldorf
StAKöln	Stadtarchiv Köln (Cologne)
StALu	Staatsarchiv Ludswigsburg
SV-Dü	*Stenographische Verhandlungs-Berichte der Stadtverordneten-Versammlung zu Düsseldorf*
ZJJ	*Zentralblatt für Jugendrecht und Jugendwohlfahrt*

Introduction

1. See Hayden White, "Historical Emplotment and the Problem of Truth," in Saul Friedlander, ed., *Probing the Limits of Representation: Nazism and the "Final Solution"* (Cambridge, Mass: Harvard University Press, 1992), pp. 42–43.

2. See especially Hans-Ulrich Wehler, *Das deutsche Kaiserreich 1871–1918* (Göttingen: Vandenhoeck and Ruprecht, 1973).

3. David Blackbourn and Geoff Eley, *The Peculiarities of German History: Bourgeois*

Society and Politics in Nineteenth-Century Germany (New York: Oxford University Press, 1984), p. 17.

4. Detlev J. K. Peukert, *Inside Nazi Germany: Conformity, Opposition, and Racism in Everyday Life*, trans. Richard Deveson (New Haven: Yale University Press, 1987), pp. 15–16.

5. Detlev J. K. Peukert, *Die Weimarer Republik: Krisenjahre der Klassischen Moderne* (Frankfurt: Suhrkamp Verlag, 1987).

6. Peukert, *Inside Nazi Germany*, p. 42.

7. Detlev J. K. Peukert, *Max Webers Diagnose der Moderne* (Göttingen: Vandenhoeck and Ruprecht, 1989), pp. 55, 60, 62–64.

8. In the past several years, there has, however, been a rapid expansion of research in this area; some of the most important works include Christoph Sachsse and Florian Tennstedt, *Geschichte der Armenfürsorge in Deutschland*, 2 Bd., *Fürsorge und Wohlfahrtspflege 1871 bis 1929* (Stuttgart: Verlag W. Kohlhammer, 1988) and 3 Bd., *Der Wohlfahrtsstaat im Nationalsozialismus* (Stuttgart: Verlag W. Kohlhammer, 1992); Detlev J. K. Peukert, *Grenzen der Sozialdisziplinierung: Aufstieg und Krise der deutschen Jugendfürsorge von 1878 bis 1932* (Cologne: Bund-Verlag, 1986); George Steinmetz, *Regulating the Social: The Welfare State and Local Politics in Imperial Germany* (Princeton: Princeton University Press, 1993); Elizabeth Harvey, *Youth and the Welfare State in Weimar Germany* (Oxford: Clarendon Press, 1993); Ewald Frie, *Wohlfahrtsstaat und Provinz: Fürsorgepolitik des Provinzialverbandes Westfalen und des Landes Sachsen, 1880–1930* (Paderborn: Ferdinand Schöningh, 1993); Marcus Gräser, *Der blockierte Wohlfahrtsstaat: Unterschichtenjugend und Jugendfürsorge in der Weimarer Republik* (Göttingen: Vandenhoeck and Ruprecht, 1995); Young-Sun Hong, "World War I and the German Welfare State: Gender, Religion, and the Paradoxes of Modernity," in Geoff Eley, ed., *Society, Culture, and the State in Germany, 1870–1930* (Ann Arbor: University of Michigan Press, 1996), pp. 345–369, and *Welfare, Modernity, and the Weimar State, 1919–1933* (Princeton: Princeton University Press, 1998); Christiane Eifert, *Frauenpolitik und Wohlfahrtspflege: Zur Geschichte der sozialdemokratischen "Arbeiterwohlfahrt"* (Frankfurt: Campus Verlag, 1993); "Der Wohlfahrtsstaat in der Stadt: Wohlfahrtspolitik und Wohlfahrtspflege in Westfalen, 1890–1945," *Westfälische Forschungen* 43 (1993); Karl Christian Führer, *Arbeitslosigkeit und die Entstehung der Arbeitslosenversicherung in Deutschland, 1902–1927* (Berlin, 1990); Greg A. Egighian, "The Politics of Victimization: Social Pensioners and the German Social State in the Inflation of 1914–1924," *Central European History* 26, no. 4 (1993): 375–404; Edward Ross Dickinson, *The Politics of German Child Welfare from the Empire to the Federal Republic* (Cambridge, Mass.: Harvard University Press, 1996).

9. George Steinmetz, "The Myth of an Autonomous State: Industrialists, *Junkers*, and Social Policy in Imperial Germany," in Eley, ed., *Society, Culture and the State*, pp. 267, 289, 295–300.

10. Sachsse and Tennstedt, *Geschichte der Armenfürsorge in Deutschland*, 2 Bd., p. 12. See also Ekkart Pankoke and Christoph Sachsse, "Armutsdiskurs und Wohlfahrtsforschung: Zum deutschen Weg in die industrielle Moderne," *Kölner Zeitschrift für Soziologie und Sozialpsychologie*, 32 Heft, 1992, p. 158. Unless otherwise noted, all translations are my own.

11. See, for example, Belinda Davis, "Home Fires Burning: Politics, Identity, and Food in World War I Berlin" (Ph.D. dissertation, University of Michigan, Ann Arbor, 1992). See also Hong, "World War I," p. 347.

12. Pankoke and Sachsse, "Armutsdiskurs und Wohlfahrtsforschung," p. 159.

13. On the economic and social consequences of the war, see Richard Bessel, *Germany after the First World War* (Oxford: Clarendon Press, 1993). On risk, see Ulrich Beck, *Risk Society: Towards a New Modernity* (London: Sage, 1992). For an extended consideration of economic historians' disagreements about the Weimar Republic, see *Geschichte und Gesellschaft* (11 Jg., 3 Heft, 1985), "Kontroversen über die Wirtschaftspolitik in der Weimarer

Republik," ed. Heinrich August Winkler, especially Jürgen von Kruedener, "Die Überforderung der Weimarer Republik als Sozialstaat," pp. 358–376.

14. Werner Abelshauser, "Die Weimarer Republik—Ein Wohlfahrtsstaat," in Werner Abelshauser, ed., *Die Weimarer Republik als Wohlfahrtsstaat: Zum Verhältnis von Wirtschafts—und Sozialpolitik in der Industriegesellschaft* (Stuttgart: Franz Steiner Verlag Wiesbaden, 1987), pp. 10–11; Pankoke and Sachsse, "Armutsdiskurs und Wolfahrtsforschung," pp. 163–164.

15. Atina Grossmann, *Reforming Sex: The German Movement for Birth Control and Abortion Reform, 1920–1950* (New York: Oxford University Press, 1995), p. viii.

16. Pankoke and Sachsse, "Armutsdiskurs und Wolfahrtsforschung," pp. 167–168. See also Hans Braun, "Das Streben nach 'Sicherheit' in den 50er Jahren: Soziale und politische Ursachen und Erscheinungsweisen," *Archiv für Sozialgeschichte*, 18 Bd., 1978, pp. 279–306. The history of the DDR seldom figures prominently, if at all, in discussions of post-1945 German social policy, although the social problems facing East Germans in the wake of unification have made the DDR tradition of social welfare, now dismantled, somewhat more visible. See Hans Günter Hockerts, "Grundlinien und soziale Folgen der Sozialpolitik in der DDR," in Hartmut Kaelble, Jürgen Kocka, and Hartmut Zwahr, eds., *Sozialgeschichte der DDR* (Stuttgart: Klett-Cotta, 1994), pp. 519–544.

17. Peukert, *Die Weimarer Republik*, pp. 137, 139.

18. Peukert, *Max Webers Diagnose der Moderne*, pp. 102–121.

19. On the rationalization of women's domestic reproductive labor, see Karen Hagemann, *Frauenalltag und Männerpolitik: Alltagsleben und gesellschaftliches Handeln von Arbeiterfrauen in der Weimarer Republik* (Bonn: Verlag J. H. W. Dietz Nachfolger, 1990), pp. 99–116, 220–305, as well as Mary Nolan, *Visions of Modernity: American Business and the Modernization of Germany* (New York: Oxford University Press, 1994), pp. 206–226. See also Tilla Siegel, "Das ist nur rational: Ein Essay zur Logik der sozialen Rationalisierung," in Dagmar Reese, Eve Rosenhaft, Carola Sachse, and Tilla Siegel, eds., *Rationale Beziehungen? Geschlechterverhältnisse im Rationalisierungsprozess* (Frankfurt: Suhrkamp Verlag, 1993), pp. 363–396.

20. Siegel, "Das ist nur rational," pp. 386–387.

21. Wolfgang Ayass, *"Asoziale" im Nationalsozialismus* (Stuttgart: Klett-Cotta, 1995), pp. 9–12, 219.

22. Seth Koven and Sonya Michel, eds., *Mothers of a New World: Maternalist Politics and the Origins of Welfare States* (New York: Routledge, 1993), pp. 29–30.

23. Kathleen Canning, "Social Policy, Body Politics: Recasting the Social Question in Germany, 1875–1900," in Laura Levine Frader and Sonya O. Rose, eds., *Gender and the Reconstruction of Working-Class History in Modern Europe* (Ithaca: Cornell University Press, 1996), pp. 212–213.

24. Eve Rosenhaft, "Women, Gender, and the Limits of Political History in the Age of 'Mass Politics,'" in Larry Eugene Jones and James Retallack, eds., *Elections, Mass Politics, and Social Change in Modern Germany: New Perspectives* (Washington, D.C.: German Historical Institute, 1992), p. 159.

25. See, for example, Ursula Nienhaus, *Vater Staat und seine Gehilfinnen: Die Politik mit der Frauenarbeit bei der deutschen Post (1864–1945)* (Frankfurt: Campus Verlag, 1995).

26. Geoff Eley, "Foreword" to Alf Lüdtke, ed., *The History of Everyday Life: Reconstructing Historical Experiences and Ways of Life* (Princeton: Princeton University Press, 1995), p. viii.

27. Alf Lüdtke, "Geschichte und Eigensinn," in Berliner Geschichtswerkstatt, ed., *Alltagskultur, Subjektivät und Geschichte: Zur Theorie und Praxis von Alltagsgeschichte* (Münster: Westfälisches Dampfboot, 1994), p. 147.

28. Charles Tilly, *Big Structures, Large Processes, Huge Comparisons* (New York: Russell Sage Foundation, 1984).

29. William H. Sewell, Jr., "How Classes Are Made: Critical Reflections on E. P. Thompson's Theory of Working-Class Formation," in Harvey J. Kaye and Keith McClelland, eds., *E. P. Thompson: Critical Perspectives* (Philadelphia: Temple University Press, 1990), p. 66; this is Sewell's rendering of Anthony Giddens's arguments.

30. Sachsse and Tennstedt, *Geschichte der Armenfürsorge in Deutschland*, 2 Bd., p. 12.

31. Ralph Jessen argues that this need for the client's cooperation was one of the reasons why before World War I in Prussia "welfare" functions (such as housing inspection) were taken from the police, who were associated with repressive practices, and assigned to specialized, new welfare agencies; see Ralph Jessen, "Polizei, Wohlfahrt und die Anfänge des modernen Sozialstaats in Preussen während des Kaiserreichs," *Geschichte und Gesellschaft*, 20 Jg., 2 Heft, 1994, p. 178.

32. Eley, "Foreword," p. x.

33. Lüdtke, "Geschichte und Eigensinn," pp. 147, 151.

34. Thomas Lindenberger, *Strassenpolitik: Zur Sozialgeschichte der öffentlichen Ordnung in Berlin 1900 bis 1914* (Bonn: Verlag J. H. W. Dietz Nachfolger, 1995), p. 284.

35. Michel de Certeau, *The Practice of Everyday Life* (Berkeley: University of California Press, 1984), p. 96.

36. Gräser, *Der blockierte Wohlfahrsstaat*, pp. 218, 222.

37. See Jochen-Christoph Kaiser, "Freie Wohlfahrtsverbände im Kaiserreich und in der Weimarer Republik: Ein Überblick," *Westfälische Forschungen* 43 (1993): 28.

38. Detlev J. K. Peukert, "Wohlfahrtsstaat und Lebenswelt," in Lutz Niethammer et al., *Bürgerliche Gesellschaft in Deutschland: Historische Einblicke, Fragen, Perspektiven* (Frankfurt: Fischer Taschenbuch Verlag, 1990), p. 348; Egighian, "The Politics of Victimization," pp. 400–401.

39. See, for example, Braun, "Das Streben nach 'Sicherheit,'" pp. 279–306, and also Werner Abelshauser, "Arbeit, Für- und Vorsorge," and Hans Günter Hockerts, "Vorsorge und Fürsorge: Kontinuität und Wandel der sozialen Sicherung," both in Axel Schildt and Arnold Sywottek, eds., *Modernisierung im Wiederaufbau: Die westdeutsche Gesellschaft der 50er Jahre* (Bonn: Verlag J. H. W. Dietz Nachfolger, 1993), pp. 203–206, 224–241.

40. Peukert, "Wohlfahrtsstaat und Lebenswelt," p. 348.

41. Bessel, *Germany after the First World War*, p. 102.

42. Kaiser, "Freie Wohlfahrtsverbände im Kaiserreich," p. 28. Kaiser points out that the term "welfare state," with positive connotations, is an Anglo-Saxon import that first became popular in Germany in the 1950s.

43. See, for example, Dirk Kurbjuweit, "Der Sozialstaat ist sein Geld wert," *Die Zeit*, Nr. 33, 9 Aug., 1996.

44. See, in particular, Abelshauser, *Die Weimarer Republik*, and W. J. Mommsen and Wolfgang Mock, eds., *The Emergence of the Welfare State in Britain and Germany, 1850–1950* (London: Croom Helm, 1981).

45. Kaiser, "Freie Wohlfahrtsverbände im Kaiserreich," p. 27.

46. Wilfried Rudloff, "Unwillkommene Fürsorge: Inflation und Inflationsfolgen in der Fürsorge am Beispiel Münchens," *Westfälische Forschungen* 43 (1993): 180.

47. *SJDR*, 51 Jg., 1932, p. 411, 52 Jg., 1933, p. 507. In 1925, the total population of Germany was 62,410,619. *SJDR*, 48 Jg., 1929, p. 15.

48. *SJdS*, 23 Jg., 1928, 25 Jg., 1930, 26 Jg., 1931.

49. *SJFHH*, 1932/33, p.161.

50. Thomas Lindenberger and Michael Wildt, "Radical Plurality: History Workshops as a Practical Critique of Knowledge," *History Workshop Journal*, no. 33 (1992): 85.

51. Eley, "Foreword," pp. viii–ix.
52. Grossmann, *Reforming Sex*, p. vii.
53. In 1925, Hamburg had 985,083 Protestants and 60,017 Catholics. "Die Bevölkerung des Deutschen Reichs nach der Ergebnissen der Volksählung 1925," *Statistik des Deutschen Reichs*, 401 Bd., 1 (Berlin: Reimar Hobbing, 1930), pp. 356-357. In the Hamburg Bürgerschaft elections, the distribution of votes between Social Democrats, Communists, and Nazis was as follows:

Year	Social Democrats	Communists	Nazis
1919	50.5%		
1921	40.6%	11.0%	
1924	32.4%	14.7%	
1927	38.2%	17.0%	1.5%
1928	35.9%	16.7%	2.2%
1931	27.8%	21.9%	26.3%
1932	30.2%	16.0%	31.2%

Ursula Büttner, *Politische Gerechtigkeit und sozialer Geist: Hamburg zur Zeit der Weimarer Republik* (Hamburg: Christians Verlag, 1985), p. 288.
54. *SJFHH*, 1928/29, Table 7, "Die Wohnbevölkerung des hamburgischen Staates nach dem Hauptberuf (Haupterwerb) der Erwerbstätigen nach Wirtschaftszweigen, Wirtschafts-gruppen und Wirtschaftsabteilungen am 16. Juni 1925," pp. 15–19.
55. In 1925, Düsseldorf had 128,820 Protestants and 273,198 Catholics; Cologne had 130,457 Protestants and 538,154 Catholics. *Statistik des Deutschen Reichs*, 401 Bd., 1, pp. 356–357. In the municipal elections held between 1923 and 1927, the relative strengths of the major parties in Düsseldorf, Cologne, and Stuttgart were as follows:

Party	Düsseldorf	Cologne	Stuttgart
Communists	24.3%	16.7%	15.4%
Social Democrats	8.8%	12.2%	24.8%
Center	27.5%	31.8%	9.8%
DVP	8.9%	9.2%	8.7%
DDP	4.1%	3.8%	17.3%
DNVP	16.0%	5.7%	17.0%
Wirtschaftspartei		6.4%	
Others	8.4%	12.6%	7.0%

Dr. August Busch, Direktor des Statistischen Amtes der Stadt Frankfurt a.M., "Städtische Kollegien und die letzten städtischen Wahlen," *SJdS*, 23 Jg., 1928, pp. 282–283.
56. Stuttgart had 259,003 Protestants and 64,825 Catholics in 1925. *Stastik des Deutschen Reichs*, 401 Bd., 1, pp. 356–357. Source for employment figures: "Volks-, Berufs- und Betriebszählung vom 16. Juni 1925: Die berufliche und soziale Gliederung der Bevölkerung in den deutschen Grossstädten," *Statistik des Deutschen Reichs*, 406 Bd. (Berlin: Reimar Hobbing, 1929), pp. 434–448, 450–464, 706–720.
57. *Württemberg in Wort und Zahl*, ed. Württ. Statistischen Landesamt (Stuttgart: Verlag von W. Kohlhammer, 1930), pp.18, 21, 23.
58. Ibid., p. 36. One hectare is 2.471 acres.
59. Alf Lüdtke, "Einleitung: Was ist und wer treibt Alltagsgeschichte?" in Alf Lüdtke, ed., *Alltagsgeschichte: Zur rekonstruktion historischer Erfahrungen und Lebensweisen* (Frankfurt: Campus, 1989), p. 12.
60. David Warren Sabean, *Property, Production, and Family in Neckarhausen, 1700–1870* (Cambridge: Cambridge University Press, 1990), p. 11.

61. Ibid., pp. 71, 76, 79, 99.

62. On the importance of the definitional powers of central European police, see, for example, Alf Lüdtke, ed., *"Sicherheit" und "Wohlfahrt": Polizei, Gesellschaft und Herrschaft im 19. und 20. Jahrhundert* (Frankfurt: Suhrkamp Verlag, 1992), pp. 97–160.

63. Adelheid von Saldern, with Karen Heinze and Sybille Küster, " 'Eine Sensation stösst ins Leere': Gertrude Polley im Mittelpunkt eines Diskurses," in Adelheid von Saldern, *Neues Wohnen: Wohnungspolitik und Wohnkultur in Hannover der Zwanziger Jahre*, Hannoversche Studien, Bd. 1 (Hanover, 1993), p. 92.

Chapter One

1. Detlev Peukert, "Zur Erforschung der Sozialpolitik im Dritten Reich," in Hans-Uwe Otto and Heinz Sünker, eds., *Soziale Arbeit und Faschismus: Volkspflege und Pädagogik im Nationalsozialismus* (Bielefeld: K-T Verlag, 1986), p. 129.

2. See especially Detlev J. K. Peukert, "Die Genesis der 'Endlösung' aus dem Geist der Wissenschaft," in *Max Webers Diagnose der Moderne*, pp. 102–121.

3. Kaiser, "Freie Wolfahrtsverbände im Kaiserreich," pp. 39–41.

4. Karl Seidel, "Die kommunale Wohlfahrtspflege, ihr Begriff und ihre Bedeutung, unter Berücksichtigung der kommunalen Wohlfahrtspflege der Stadt Cassel" (Dissertation, Universität Marburg, 1922), p. 235.

5. *Wohlfahrtsamt: Jahresbericht 1925* (Hamburg, 1926), p. 26.

6. *Tätigkeitsbericht der Fraktion der Deutschen Demokratischen Partei in der Hamburger Bürgerschaft, 1921–1924*, ed. von der Fraktion (Hamburg: Verlag der DDP, 1924), p. 40.

7. Rudloff, "Unwillkommene Fürsorge," p. 189.

8. Kaiser, "Freie Wolfahrtsverbände im Kaiserreich," pp. 30, 42–43.

9. D. Reinhold Seeberg, Berlin, "Innere Mission und Staat," *IM*, 18 Jg., 8 Heft, Berlin, Aug. 1983, pp. 143–144.

10. Ludwig Preller, *Sozialpolitik in der Weimarer Republik* (Düsseldorf: Droste, 1978), p. 221.

11. Kaiser, "Freie Wolfahrtsverbände im Kaiserreich," p. 44.

12. Dr. Ruland, Frankfürt, "Die 'Kommunalisierung' der privaten Fürsorge vom Standpunkte des Steuerzahlers," *BZWW*, 73 Jg., Nr. 1, 10 Jan. 1920, p. 135.

13. Preller, *Sozialpolitik in der Weimarer Republik*, p. 246.

14. Staatsminister A. Stegerwald, M.d.R., Berlin, "Vom Arbeitsgeist des Wohlfahrtsamtes," in Prof. Dr. Chr. Klumker and Prof. Dr. B. Schmittmann, eds., *Wohlfahrtsämter* (Stuttgart: Verlag von Ferdinand Enke, 1920), pp. 1–3, 7–8.

15. "Die Stellung der privaten Fürsorge im neuen Staat," *BZWW*, 73 Jg., Nr. 3, 24 Jan. 1920, pp. 10–11.

16. Dr. Alexander Göbel, *Das Wohlfahrtsamt: Zweck, Einrichtung und Richtlinien für den weiteren Ausbau*, Soziale Tagesfragen, 47 Heft, ed. Volksverein für das Kath. Deutschland (M. Gladbach: Volksvereins-Verlag, 1923), pp. 23–24.

17. Universitätsprofessor Dr. Joseph Löhr, Breslau, "Geist und Wesen der Caritas II: Die Wirksamkeit der Caritas," *Caritas*, 1 Jg., Neue Folge, 1922, pp. 57–58.

18. Kaiser, "Freie Wolfahrtsverbände im Kaiserreich," p. 47.

19. Frie, *Wohlfahrtsstaat und Provinz*, pp. 196–197, 199.

20. Kaiser, "Freie Wolfahrtsverbände im Kaiserreich," pp. 45, 48, 49.

21. See Lucio Coletti, "Bernstein and the Marxism of the Second International," in Lucio Coletti, *From Rousseau to Lenin: Studies in Ideology and Society* (London: New Left Books, 1972), pp. 45–108.

22. See R. Rürup, "Problems of the German Revolution," *Journal of Contemporary History* Vol. 3, No. 4, Oct. (1968): 109–126.

23. See, for example, Adelheid von Saldern, "'Nur ein Wetterleuchten': Zu den historischen Komponenten des 'Novembergeistes' von 1918/19," in Jürgen Kocka, Hans-Jürgen Puhle, and Klaus Tenfelde, eds., *Von der Arbeiterbewegung zum modernen Sozialstaat: Festschrift für Gerhard A. Ritter zum 65. Geburtstag* (Munich: K. G. Saur, 1994), pp. 93–113.

24. Comments of Louis Korell, the head of the Arbeiterwohlfahrt in Hamburg and a member of that city-state's welfare administration, at a conference of Social Democratic women from the Hamburg/North-West district in Nov. 1921, *Hamburger Echo*, 28 Nov. 1921, Abend-Ausgabe.

25. Christoph Sachsse, *Mütterlichkeit als Beruf: Sozialarbeit, Sozialreform und Frauenbewegung, 1871–1929* (Frankfurt: Suhrkamp Verlag, 1986), pp. 173–182.

26. Hedwig Wachenheim, *Republik und Wohlfahrtspflege: Eine Rededisposition von Hedwig Wachenheim* (Berlin: Hauptausschuss für Arbeiterwohlfahrt, 1927), p. 8.

27. Peukert, "Wohlfahrtsstaat und Lebenswelt," p. 348.

28. Hedwig Wachenheim, "Der Vorrang der öffentlichen Wohlfahrtspflege: Grundsatzliches zur Krise in der rheinischen Jugendwohlfahrtspflege," *Arbeiterwohlfahrt*, 1 Jg., 3 Heft, 1 Nov. 1926, pp. 67–69.

29. Stadtrat Dr. Heimerich, "Die Zusammenarbeit der öffentlichen Fürsorge mit der privaten Fürsorge und den Trägern der Sozialversicherung," *Die Gemeinde*, 1 Jg., 1924, p. 467.

30. Wachenheim, "Der Vorrang," p. 70.

31. Paula Kurgass, "Die sozialistische Fürsorgerin: Gegen die Isolierung der Wohlfahrtspflege," *Arbeiterwohlfahrt*, 1 Jg., 5 Heft, 1 Dec. 1926, pp. 133–136.

32. "Bezirkskonferenz der Ortsausschüsse der Arbeiterwohlfahrt," *Beilage der Volkszeitung*, 36 Jg., Nr. 7, Düsseldorf, Freitag, 9 Jan. 1925, and Wachenheim, "Der Vorrang," p. 69.

33. Eifert, *Frauenpolitik und Wohlfahrtspflege*, pp. 54, 56, 63.

34. See Annemarie Hermberg, "Die soziologische Bedeutung der öffentlichen und freien Wohlfahrtspflege," *Arbeiterwohlfahrt*, 4 Jg., 16 Heft, 15 Aug. 1929, p. 491.

35. Eve Rosenhaft, "Communisms and Communities: Britain and Germany between the Wars," *Historical Journal* 26, no. 1 (1983): 229.

36. See Beatrix Herlemann, *Kommunalpolitik der KPD im Ruhrgebiet, 1924–1933* (Wuppertal: Peter Hammer Verlag, 1977), pp. 90–112.

37. See, for example, *SV-Dü*, Nr. 4, Sitzung, 16 Mar. 1929, p. 116.

38. *SV-Dü*, Nr. 1, Sitzung, 29 Jan. 1926, p. 16.

39. "Der Segen der 'sozialen Einrichtungen,'" *Hamburger Volkszeitung*, 17 July 1923. In the 1927 elections for the Hamburg Bürgerschaft, the SPD and the KPD actually commanded a majority between them (SPD, 38.2%; KPD, 17%); however, talks between the two parties, along with the trade-union federation, quickly fell apart amid mutual recriminations; see Axel Schildt, "Als Arbeiterpartei im Senat: Vorsichtige Reformen, sozialistische Propaganda, und Verteidigung der Republik: Die Hamburger SPD, 1924–1933," in Ulrich Bauche et al., eds., *"Wir sind die Kraft": Arbeiterbewegung in Hamburg von den Anfängen bis 1945: Katalogbuch zu Ausstellungen des Museums für Hamburgische Geschichte* (Hamburg: VSA-Verlag, 1988), pp. 184–192.

40. Sen. Paul Neumann, *Russland ein Vorbild? Eine vergleichende Darstellung russischer und hamburgischer Sozialpolitik* (Hamburg, n.d.), p. 4.

41. "Was leistet die Hamburger Bürgerschaft für die proletarischen Frauen," *Hamburger Volkszeitung*, 13 June 1923.

42. "Die Frauenkonferenz glänzend verlaufen," *Sozialistische Republik*, 10 July 1928.

43. StALu, E191 2588, *Schwäbische Tagewacht*, Stuttgart, 43 Jg., Nr. 31, 7 Feb. 1923, p. 3.

44. Hedwig Wachenheim, "Ausbildung zur Wohlfahrtspflege," *Die Neue Zeit*, 39 Jg., 2 Bd., 1921, p. 303.

45. Jeremy Leaman, "The Gemeinden as Agents of Fiscal and Social Policy in the Twentieth Century," in W. R. Lee and Eve Rosenhaft, eds., *The State and Social Change in Germany, 1880–1980* (Oxford: Berg Publishers, 1990), p. 260.

46. Neumann, *Russland ein Vorbild?*; Reichstagsabgeordnete Otto Thiel, "Sozialpolitik und kommunale Wohlfahrtspflege," in Gustav Wittig, ed., *Kommunalpolitik und Deutsche Volkspartei* (Berlin, 1929), p. 92. Welfare was often the largest single item in municipal budgets. Critics of the SPD charged that under its influence local government welfare expenditure accounted for at least one-third of the total budget of most municipalities. See Dr. F. D. von Hansemann, "Wir und die Sozialdemokraten," in Wittig, *Kommunalpolitik und Deutsche Volkspartei*, p. 102.

47. "Schul- und Fürsorgewesen," *Schwäbische Tagewacht*, 17 Oct. 1929.

48. Emma Woytinsky, *Sozialdemokratie und Kommunalpolitik (Gemeindearbeit in Berlin)* (Berlin: E. Lausche Verlagsbuchhandlung, 1929), p. 67.

49. *SV-Dü*, Nr. 12, Sitzung, 1 July 1919, p. 241; *SV-Dü*, Nr. 9, Sitzung, 11 May 1921, p. 115; *SV-Dü*, Nr. 16, Sitzung, 30 Oct. 1923, p. 162.

50. "Bezirkskonferenz der Ortsausschüsse der Arbeiterwohlfahrt," *Beilage der Volkszeitung*, Düsseldorf, 36 Jg., Nr. 7, 9 Jan. 1925.

51. Dr. med. Kurt Erichson, *Die Fürsorge in Hamburg: Ein Überblick über ihre Entwicklung, ihren gegenwärtigen Stand und dessen gesetzliche Grundlagen* (Hamburg: Friederichsen, de Gruyter, 1930), p. 77.

52. Büttner, *Politische Gerechtigkeit und sozialer Geist*, p. 289. Typically, an elected political official assumed overall responsibility for each of these departments, but a professional bureaucrat acted as the administrative director.

53. Hanna Stolten, "Die Fachgruppe der sozialistischen Fürsorgerinnen, Hamburg," *Arbeiterwohlfahrt*, 6 Jg., 1931, p. 27.

54. Sen. Paul Neumann, "Aufbau und Leistungen der staatlichen Wohlfahrtspflege in Hamburg," *Arbeiterwohlfahrt*, 3 Jg., 15 Heft, 1 Aug., 1928, p. 455.

55. StAHH, SB I EF 12.14, "Zusammenarbeit zwischen öffentlicher und privater Wohlfahrtspflege," 1 Bd., 1921–1930, Sitzung des Beirats der Wohlfahrtsstelle IV, 15 May 1922.

56. StAHH, SB I VG 24.23, Niederschriften über die Leitersitzungen (hereafter Leitersitzungen), 7 May 1923.

57. StAHH, SB I EF 12.14, Auszug aus der Niederschrift über die Sitzung des Beirats der Wohlfahrtsstelle I, 28 June 1923.

58. StAHH, SB I EF 12.14, letter to Martini, 4 Apr. 1924.

59. *Wohlfahrtsamt: Jahresbericht, 1925*, p. 26.

60. StAHH, SB I EF 12.14, Auszug aus der Niederschrift über die Sitzung des Beirats der Wohlfahrtsstelle II, 26 Apr. 1927.

61. K. Joerger, Generalsekretär des Deutschen Caritasverbands, "Der 27. deutsche Caritastag vom 25. bis 29. Mai 1926 zu Trier," *Caritas*, 31 Jg., 3 Heft, 5 Neue Folge, Mar. 1926, p. 213.

62. "Sitzung der Stadtverordneten," *Beilage der "Volkszeitung,"* Düsseldorf, 35 Jg., Nr. 256, Donnerstag, 30 Oct. 1924.

63. Hedwig Wachenheim, "Kulturkampf gegen den Sozialismus," *Die Gemeinde*, 1926, p. 548.

64. Caritasdirektor Dr. Braekling, Paderborn, "Die Arbeiterwohlfahrt und die Caritas," *Caritas*, 31 Jg., 5 Heft, Neue Folge, May 1926, pp. 130–131, 133–134.

65. Löhr, "Geist und Wesen der Caritas II," p. 64.

66. Dr. Kurt Lücken, Darmstadt, "Grundsätzliches und Kritisches zur Caritasarbeit der Gegenwart. III (Schluss)," *Caritas*, 12 Jg., Neue Folge, 1932, pp. 58–59.

67. Generalsekretär F. X. Rappenecker, Freiburg, "25 Deutscher Caritastag vom 10. bis 14. Juni 1924 zu Breslau," *Caritas*, 3 Jg., Neue Folge, Nr. 7, 1924, p. 128.

68. K. Joerger, "Der 27. deutsche Caritastag," p. 213.

69. "Vom Caritasverband für Württemberg," *BZWW*, 79 Jg., Nr. 10, Stuttgart, Oct. 1926, p. 186.

70. Regierungsrat Mailänder, "Geist und Formen der neuzeitlichen Wohlfahrtspflege," *BZWW*, 78 Jg., Nr. 10/11, Stuttgart, May 1925, p. 76.

71. Erichson, *Die Fürsorge in Hamburg*, p. 127.

72. Dr. Franz Kloidt, Berlin, "Die Berufsethik des katholischen Wohlfahrtspflegers," *Caritas*, 8 Jg., Neue Folge, 1929, p. 393.

73. Oskar Martini, Präsident der Wohlfahrtsbehörde Hamburg, "Herz und Verstand in der öffentlichen Fürsorge," *Wohlfahrtsblatt der freien Hansestadt Bremen*, 2 Jg., Nr. 2, Bremen, June 1929, p. 9.

74. Lic. Steinweg, Dahlem, "Zur gegenwärtigen Lage in der Wohlfahrtspflege," *IM*, 22 Jg., 1927, pp. 69–70.

75. Generalsekretär Wilh. Wiesen, O.S.C., Freiburg, "Christliche Liebestätigkeit und behördliche Wohlfahrtspflege," *Caritas*, 32 Jg., 6 Neue Folge, 4 Heft, Apr. 1927, p. 100.

76. Lic. Steinweg, Dahlem, "Seelsorge und Fürsorge," *IM*, 22 Jg., 1 Heft, Berlin, Jan. 1927, p. 3–5.

77. D. Erfurth, Elberfeld-Barmen, "Die evangelisch orientierte Wohlfahrtspflege," *IM*, 24 Jg., 1929, pp. 437–438.

78. Martini, "Herz und Verstand in der öffentlichen Fürsorge," pp. 9, 11.

Chapter Two

1. Neumann, "Aufbau und Leistungen," p. 454; see also Erichson, *Die Fürsorge in Hamburg*.

2. Neumann, "Aufbau und Leistungen," pp. 454–455; see also Erichson, *Die Fürsorge in Hamburg*, pp. 158–169.

3. Lohalm, "Wohlfahrtspolitik und Modernisierung Bürokratisierung, Professionalisierung und Funktionsausweitung der Hamburger Fürsorgebehörde im Nationalsozialismus," in Frank Bajor, ed., *Norddeutschland im Nationalsozialismus* (Hamburg: Ergebnisse Verlag, 1993), p. 389.

4. Neuman, "Aufbau und Leistungen," p. 455. The number of volunteers rose to 2,528 by January 1930 and to 2,867 by December 1932; the ratio of professional to unpaid welfare workers was 1:3 in 1929 but 1:1.3 at the end of 1932; Lohalm, "Wohlfahrtspolitik und Modernisierung," p. 390. In 1925, Cologne had 347 professional staff and 2,181 volunteers, Dusseldorf had 292 professionals and 1,133 volunteers, and Stuttgart had 213 professionals and 735 volunteers; *SJdS*, 22 Jg., 1927, pp. 436–437.

5. Dr. Clara Friedheim, *Führer durch die Wohlfahrtseinrichtungen Hamburgs*. Umgearbeitete Neuauflage des Handbuchs für den Hamburger Wohlfahrtspfleger, ed. Maria Hinrichs, Institut für Soziale Arbeit, Hamburg, 17 Heft (Hamburg: Verlag Ackermann and Wulff Nachfolger, 1926), p. 8.

6. Neumann, "Aufbau und Leistungen," pp. 454–461.

7. Friedheim, *Führer*, p. 8. When quoting directly, I have not attempted to change the gendered form of the language employed in these official regulations, which consistently referred to clients as if they were always male, when in fact, they were more often female.

8. Neumann, "Aufbau und Leistungen," pp. 454–461.

9. Klaus Weinhauer, *Alltag und Arbeitskampf im Hamburger Hafen, 1914–1933* (Paderborn: Ferdinand Schöningh, 1994), p. 153.

10. Neumann, "Aufbau und Leistungen," pp. 454–461.

11. See Egighian, "The Politics of Victimization."

12. Neumann, "Aufbau und Leistungen," pp. 454–461.

13. See "Die öffentliche Fürsorge in Hamburg," *Hamburger Echo*, 25 July 1929; Neumann, *Russland ein Vorbild?*; Harvey, *Youth and the Welfare State in Weimar Germany*, p. 23.

14. Neumann, "Aufbau und Leistungen," p. 459; *Wohlfahrtsamt. Jahresbericht 1925*, p. 24.

15. StAHH, SB I VG 43.00, "Organisation der männlichen Aussenfürsorge, 1923–1930"; Wohlfahrtsamt, Wohlfahrtsstelle XI, An das Präsidialbüro, Hier, Hamburg, 16 Apr. 1927.

16. "Die grösseren politischen Parteien in Hamburg," *Hamburger Statististicher Monatsberichte*, 1924, *Sonderbeitrag*, p. 137.

17. Ibid.

18. "Sonderbeitrag: Amtliches Ergebnis der Bürgerschaftswahl am 27. Sept. 1931," *Aus Hamburgs Verwaltung und Wirtschaft: Monatsschrift des Statistischen Landesamts*, 8 Jg., Nr. 8, 15 Oct. 1931, p. 242.

19. Paul Neumann was born in Chemnitz in 1869. A typesetter by trade, he joined the SPD in 1898. In 1912, he became editor of the *Hamburger Echo*. He served as a member of the Hamburg city parliament from 1921 to 1933. See Schildt, "Als Arbeiterpartei im Senat," p. 176. Oskar Martini "entered the Hamburg state service in 1910 and gained experience in the finance administration." See Lohalm, "Wohlfahrtspolitik und Modernisierung," p. 389.

20. StAHH, SB I VG 24.22, Leitersitzungen, 31 July 1922; Lohalm, "Wohlfahrtspolitik und Modernisierung," p. 389.

21. Christiane Rothmaler, "'. . . aus dem tiefsten und heiligsten Instinkt ihres Geschlechtes heraus.' Probleme der Sozialen Frauenschule und des Sozialpädagogischen Instituts in Hamburg, 1919–1945," in Evelyn Glensk and Christiane Rothmaler, eds., *Kehrseiten der Wohlfahrt: Die Hamburger Fürsorge auf ihrem Weg von der Weimarer Republik in den Nationalsozialismus* (Hamburg: Ergebnisse, 1992), p. 82.

22. StAHH, Pressestelle I–IV, 3183, 1 Bd., 1923–1939, "The Economic Crisis and the Hamburg Poor: An Interview with President Martini of the Hamburg Wohlfahrtsamt," *American News*, 13 Feb. 1926.

23. Sen. Paul Neumann, "Von Armenpflege zur sozialen Fürsorge," *Hamburger Echo*, Nr. 32, 1 Feb. 1928.

24. Dr. med. et phil. E. G. Dresel, Privatdozent für Hygiene in Heidelberg, "Ausbildung der Wohlfahrtsbeamten," in Klumker and Schmittmann, *Wohlfahrtsämter*, p. 109.

25. Carl Mennicke, Direktor des Sozialpädagogischen Seminars der Deutschen Hochschule für Politik, "Die Ausbildung männlicher Sozialbeamten," *Jugend und Volkswohl*, 1 Jg., Nr. 11, Feb. 1926, p. 3.

26. Dresel, "Ausbildung der Wohlfahrtsbeamten," p. 109.

27. Ibid.

28. Mennicke, "Die Ausbildung männlicher Sozialbeamten," p. 3.

29. Magistratssyndikus Dr. Kantorowicz, Kiel, "Die Wohlfahrtsarbeit auf Grund der Fürsorge-Pflicht-Verordnung," in *Bezirksausschuss für Arbeiterwohlfahrt für den Bezirk Schleswig-Holstein, Protokoll der Bezirkskonferenz vom 5. bis 7. September 1925 im Landesjugendheim zu Cismar* (n.p.: n.d.), p. 18.

30. Dr. Marie Baum, *Familienfürsorge: Eine Studie*, Neue Folge der Schriften des Deutschen Vereins für öffentliche und private Fürsorge, 12 Heft (Karlsruhe: Verlag E. Braun, 1927), p. 93.

31. StAHH, SB I VG 24.22, Leitersitzungen, 31 July 1922.

32. "Die Wohlfahrtspflege in Hamburg," *Hamburger Volkszeitung*, 19 July 1923.

33. StAHH, SB I VG 24.22, Leitersitzungen, 17 July 1922; StAHH, SB I VG 24.24, Leitersitzungen, 3 Jan. 1924.

34. StAHH, SB I VG 24.22, Leitersitzungen, 31 July 1922, 16 Oct. 1922.

35. StAHH, SB I VG 24.26, Leitersitzungen, 26 Apr. 1926.

36. "Wie das Wohlfahrtsamt hilft," *Hamburger Volkszeitung*, 29 Sept. 1926.

37. SV-Dü, Nr. 2, Sitzung, 2 Mar. 1926, p. 27.

38. StAHH, SB I VG 43.00, "Organisation der männlichen Aussenfürsorge, 1923–1930"; "Dienstanweisung für die Ermittler," 2 May 1923, der Präsident des Wohlfahrtsamtes.

39. StAHH, SB I VG 43.00, Hamburg, 12 May 1926.

40. StAHH, SB I VG 43.00, Leitersitzungen, 16 May 1927.

41. StAHH, SB I VG 43.00, "Dienstanweisung für die Berufspfleger," 2 May 1923; see also StAHH, SB I PA 40.14, "Berufsamtliche Pfleger . . ." , 2 Bd., 1922–1930.

42. StAHH, SB I VG 43.00, Statistik über die Tätigkeit der Aussendienstbeamten vom 13.III–9.IV 1927 in der Wohlfahrtsstelle VI.

43. StAHH, SB I VG 43.00, "Dienstanweisung für die Berufspfleger," 2 May 1923.

44. StAHH, SB I VG 43.00, Rundschreiben, Nr. 17, betreffend den Aussendienst in den Wohlfahrtsstellen, 15 Feb. 1926, Der Präsident des Wohlfahrtsamtes, Martini.

45. StAHH, SB I VG 43.00, Wohlfahrtsamt, Wohlfahrtsstelle X, An die Verwaltungsabteilung, Hamburg, 21 Apr. 1927.

46. StAHH, SB I VG 43.00, Hamburg, 12 May 1926.

47. StAHH, SB I VG 43.00, Leitersitzungen, 24 Jan. 1927.

48. "Ehrenamtliche Mitarbeiter in der Wohlfahrtspflege," Von Oskar Kienast, Vorsteher der 42. Wohlf.-Kommission, *Berliner Wohlfahrtsblatt*, 5 Jg., Nr. 3, 3 Feb. 1929, p. 11.

49. Min. Rat. Dorothea Hirschfeld, "Die Verordnung über die Fürsorgepflicht vom 13. Februar 1924," *Kommunale Praxis: Allgemeine Fürsorge* (Berlin: Dietz, 1924), p. 9.

50. S. Wronsky, "Die Idee der ehrenamtlichen Arbeit in der Wohlfahrtspflege bei Führern des Deutschen Vereins," *Berliner Wohlfahrtsblatt*, 6 Jg., Nr. 16, 28 Sept. 1930, p. 139.

51. StAHH, Allgemeine Armenanstalt II/64, "Mitwirkung von Arbeitern als Pfleger in der öffentlichen Armenpflege," p. 6, Herr Direktor Dr. Lohse tragt folgendes vor.

52. StAHH, Allgemeine Armenanstalt II/64, Hamburg, 5 Aug. 1919, Hamburgisches Arbeitsamt An die Allgemeine Armenanstalt Direktor-Dr. Löhse.

53. SV-Dü, Nr. 12, Sitzung, 1 July 1919, p. 243.

54. Neumann, "Aufbau und Leistungen," p. 455.

55. "Allgemeine Armenanstalt oder neuzeitliche Wohlfahrtspflege," *Hamburger Echo*, 16 Oct. 1924.

56. Stadtrat G. Binder, Bielefeld, "Ehrenamtliche Mitarbeit der Arbeiterschaft in der Wohlfahrtspflege," *Arbeiterwohlfahrt*, 1 Jg., 4 Heft, 15 Nov. 1926, pp. 103, 110. Binder was director of a welfare office in Westphalia.

57. "Allgemeine Armenanstalt oder neuzeitliche Wohlfahrtspflege," *Hamburger Echo*, 16 Oct. 1924.

58. Binder, "Ehrenamtliche Mitarbeit," p. 111.

59. StAHH, Allgemeine Armenanstalt II/66, 1 Bd., 1922–1928, "Ausschuss zur Prüfung der Eignung ehrenamtlicher Organe."

60. StAHH, Allgemeine Armenanstalt II/66, 1 Bd., 1922–1928, Hamburg, 10 Feb. 1925.

61. Stadtrat Zachow, Berlin-Kreuzberg, "Wohlfahrtspfleger und Wohlfahrtsamt," *Berliner Wohlfahrtsblatt*, 5 Jg., Nr. 3, 3 Feb. 1929, p. 18.

62. Binder, "Ehrenamtliche Mitarbeit," p. 112.

63. StAHH, SB I VG 24.26, Leitersitzungen, 6 Sept. 1926, 27 Sept. 1926.

64. Hans Vogel, Calau, N.-L., "Die organisation der Nachbarschaftshilfe in einem Landkreis," *Die Gemeinde*, 2 Jg., 22 Heft, 2 Nov. 1925, p. 912.

65. *Jahresbericht der Verwaltungsbehörden der freien und Hansestadt Hamburg, 1925*, p. 638.

66. StAKöln, 902, Nr. 198, Fasc. 3, pp. 1–500 (1927–1930).

67. Vogel, "Die organisation der Nachbarschaftshilfe," p. 911.

68. Doris Schlüter, "Sozialpolitik und Sozialfürsorge der Stadt Hannover in der Weimarer Republik" (Ph.D. dissertation, Universität Hannover, 1990), p. 87.

69. StAKöln, 902, Nr. 198, Fasc. 3, pp. 1–500 (1927–1930).

70. Zachow, "Wolfahrtspfleger und Wohlfahrtsamt," pp. 17–19.

71. "Ehrenamtliche und berufsamtliche Arbeit in der Wohlfahrtspflege," *Hamburger Echo*, 19 Feb. 1927.

72. Wronsky, "Die Idee der ehrenamtlichen Arbeit," p. 138.

73. Baum, *Familienfürsorge*, p. 90.

74. StADü, III 4069, Zusammenarbeit mit der freien Wohlfahrtspflege, 1932–1933, "Zusammenstellung der ehrenamtlichen Fürsorger- und Fürsorgerinnen der Familienfürsorge der Stadt-Düsseldorf."

75. D. Otto Ohl-Langenberg, "Ehrenamtlicher und beruflicher Dienst in ihrer Arbeitsverbundenheit," *IM*, 1933, p. 11.

76. "Ehrenamtliche Mitarbeiter in der Wohlfahrtspflege," *Berliner Wohlfahrtsblatt*, 4 Jg., Nr. 26, 23 Dec. 1928, pp. 397–398.

77. Dr. G. Vöhringer, "Sparmassnahmen für das Gebiet der freien Wohlfahrtspflege," *BZWW*, 80 Jg., Nr. 1, Stuttgart, Jan. 1927, p. 1.

78. "Aus der ehrenamtlichen Arbeit: Vorträge und Arbeitsgemeinschaften aus dem Bereich der Wohlfahrtspflege," *Wohlfahrtsblätter der Stadt Köln*, Nr. 6/7, Sept./Oct. 1926, pp. 29, 40.

79. StAHH, SB I VG 24.28, Leitersitzungen, 5 Mar. 1928.

80. Vogel, "Die organisation der Nachbarschaftshilfe," p. 915.

81. *Hamburger Fremdenblatt*, 22 Dec. 1926.

82. "Die Ausgestaltung einer Bezirksversammlung," von Bezirksvorsteher Lingens, *Wohlfahrtsblätter der Stadt Köln*, Nr. 6/7, Sept./Oct. 1926, p. 31.

83. "Fürsorgeberichte," *Wohlfahrtsblätter der Stadt Köln*, Nr. 12, Mar. 1927, p. 53.

84. StAHH, SB VG I 24.27, Leitersitzungen, 2 May 1927.

85. StAHH, SB I VG 43.00, Leitersitzungen, 2 May 1927.

86. StAHH, SB I VG 42.11, "Allgemeine Erörterungen über die Familienfürsorge und ihre Durchführung in Hamburg, 1928–32," Leitersitzungen, 19 Nov. 1928, pp. 4–6.

87. StAHH, SB I VG 24.26, Leitersitzungen, 20 Apr. 1925, 1 July 1926.

88. StAHH, SB I VG 42.11, Leitersitzungen, 19 Nov. 1928, pp. 4–6, 10.

89. StAHH, SB I VG 24.21, Leitersitzungen, 24 Oct. 1921.

90. StAHH, SB I VG 24.23, Leitersitzungen, 19 Mar. 1923.

91. StAHH, SB I VG 24.27, Leitersitzungen, 1 July 1927.

92. StAHH, SB I AF 42.10, Mieteunterstützungen, 4 Bd., 1928–1930.

93. Ibid., 1 July 1927.

94. StAHH, SB I VG 24.28, 8 Oct. 1928, pp. 8–9.

95. StAHH, SB I VG 24.24, Leitersitzungen, 20 Oct. 1924, p.14.

96. StAHH, SB I VG 24.23, Leitersitzungen, 7 May 1923, pp. 10, 13; "Und nochmals der SPD—Bauch von der Veddel," *Hamburger Tageblatt*, 4 Apr. 1932.

97. StAHH, SB I VG 24.27, Leitersitzungen, 7 Mar. 1927.

98. StAHH, SB I VG 24.31, Leitersitzungen, 7 Oct. 1931, p. 20.

Chapter Three

1. Quoted in Gräser, *Der blockierte Wohlfahrtsstaat*, p. 223.

2. Ibid., p. 224.

3. Susanne Zeller, *Volksmütter—mit staatlicher Anerkennung—Frauen im Wohlfahrtswesen der zwanziger Jahre* (Düsseldorf: Schwann, 1987), p. 101.

4. Dr. Else Wex, *Die Entwicklung der Sozialen Fürsorge in Deutschland (1914 bis 1927)* (Berlin: Carl Heymanns Verlag, 1929), p. 77.

5. Alice Salomon, *Leitfaden der Wohlfahrtspflege*, with the assistance of S. Wronsky (Leipzig: Verlag und Druck von B. J. Teubner, 1921), pp. iv, 72.

6. Ibid., p. 4.

7. StAHH, Staatl. Pressestelle I–IV, 3125, "Gutachten, Auskünfte, Berichte der öffentl. Jugendfürsorge, 1922–1929," n.d. (18 Jan. 1927 in margin), press release; see Dr. Hertz, Direktor des Jugendamtes, "Aus der amtlichen Jugendschutzarbeit," *Hamburger Echo*, 19 Jan. 1927.

8. Wohlfahrtsamtsdirektor Wodtke, Plön, "Aus der Jugendpflegearbeit im Kreise Plön," *Schleswig-Holsteinische Wohlfahrtsblätter*, Erster Jg., Nr. 4, 1925, p. 38.

9. Salomon, *Leitfaden der Wohlfahrtspflege*, p. 2.

10. Seidel, "Die kommunale Wohlfahrtspflege," p. 240.

11. Richard Münchmeier, *Zugänge zur Geschichte der Sozialarbeit* (Munich: Juventa Verlag, 1981), p. 100.

12. Dr. Hanna Hellinger, *Das kleine Lehrbuch: Ratgeber für unsere Helfer in der öffent-lichen Wohlfahrtspflege*, ed. Hauptausschuss für Arbeiterwohlfahrt, 2 Bd. (n.p., n.d.), p. 17.

13. Elizabeth Neumann, Kreisfürsorgerin, Senftenberg, "Die Kreisfürsorgerin," *Die Nachbarschaft: Zeitschrift für praktische Wohlfahrtspflege: Amtsblatt des Kreiswohlfahrt-samtes, Calau N-L.*, 2 Jg., Nr. 4, 30 Jan. 1922, p. 40.

14. Jürgen Reyer, *Alte Eugenik und Wohlfahrtspflege: Entwertung und Funktionalisierung der Fürsorge vom Ende des 19. Jahrhunderts bis zur Gegenwart* (Freiburg: Lambertus Verlag, 1991), p. 73.

15. Young-Sun Hong, "The Contradictions of Modernization in the German Welfare State: Gender and the Politics of Welfare Reform in First World War Germany," *Social History* 17, no. 2 (1992): 266.

16. Christine Thomas, "Caritas und Wohlfahrtspflegerin," *Caritas*, 1 Jg., Neue Folge, 1922, pp. 141, 143.

17. Sachsse, *Mütterlichkeit als Beruf*, p. 181.

18. Kurgass, "Die sozialistische Fürsorgerin," p. 134.

19. Hanna Stolten, "Etwas vom Fürsorgedienst im Selbstgespräch," *Jugend und Volkswohl*, 4 Jg., 1928, pp. 9–11.

20. Kurgass, "Die sozialistische Fürsorgerin," pp. 133–136.

21. Clara Henriques, "Psychologische Schwierigkeiten und Möglichkeiten sozialistischer Wohlfahrtsarbeit," *Arbeiterwohlfahrt*, 2 Jg., 15 Heft, 1 Aug. 1927, pp. 454–456.

22. Stolten, "Etwas vom Fürsorgedienst im Selbstgespräch," pp. 9–11.

23. Henriques, "Psychologische Schwierigkeiten und Möglichkeiten sozialistischer Wohlfahrtsarbeit," p. 457; see also Stolten, "Etwas vom Fürsorgedienst im Selbstgespräch," pp. 9–11.

24. See, for example, "Wie sollen gute Berichte aussehen," in Hellinger, *Das kleine Lehrbuch*, pp. 38–40.

25. See Michel Foucault, *Power/Knowledge: Selected Interviews and Other Writings, 1972–1977*, ed. Colin Gordon (New York: Pantheon, 1980).

230 Notes to Pages 50–54

26. Nancy Fraser, "Foucault on Modern Power: Empirical Insights and Normative Confusions," in Nancy Fraser, *Unruly Practices: Power, Discourse, and Gender in Contemporary Social Theory* (Minneapolis: University of Minnesota Press, 1989), p. 23.

27. Sonya Michel and Seth Koven, "Womanly Duties: Maternalist Politics and the Origins of Welfare States in France, Germany, Great Britain, and the United States, 1880–1920," *American Historical Review* 95, no. 4 (1990): 1076–1108.

28. Hong, "The Contradictions of Modernization," p. 263.

29. Norbert Preusser, "Fürsorge zwischen Massennot und Opfergang," in Hedwig Stieve, *Tagebuch einer Fürsorgerin* (Weinheim: Beltz Verlag, 1983), p. 107.

30. See, for example, Rothmaler, "Probleme der Sozialen Frauenschule," pp. 77–78; Schlüter, "Sozialpolitik und Sozialfürsorge," pp. 60, 65; Ministerialrat Schmidt in württemb, Ministerium des Innern, Stuttgart, "Die beruflichen Verhältnisse der Fürsorgerinnen in Württemberg," *BZWW*, Sept. 1925, Nr. 18, p. 175.

31. Baum, *Familienfürsorge*, pp. 129–133.

32. Dresel, "Ausbildung der Wohlfahrtsbeamten," pp. 103–106.

33. Ibid., p. 106, quoting Alice Salomon.

34. Ibid., pp. 109, 112, 113–114.

35. Preusser, "Fürsorge zwischen Massennot und Opfergang," p. 107.

36. Rothmaler, "Probleme der Sozialen Frauenschule," p. 82; see also Baum, *Familienfürsorge*, p. 122.

37. Schmidt, "Die beruflichen Verhältnisse der Fürsorgerinnen," pp. 176–177.

38. Schlüter, "Sozialpolitik und Sozialfürsorge," pp. 65–66, 70.

39. *Wohlfahrtsamt. Jahresbericht 1925* (Hamburg, 1926), p. 7.

40. StADü, V, 58, 10 May 1919, 7 Aug. 1919.

41. Stefan Bajohr, *Die Hälfte der Fabrik: Geschichte der Frauenarbeit in Deutschland, 1914–1945* (Marburg, 1979), p. 63.

42. Gertrud Bäumer, "Die Stellung der Sozialbeamtin und der Sinn der Wohfahrtspflege," *Die Frau*, 31 Jg., 9 Heft, 1924, pp. 262–265, quoted in Schlüter, "Sozialpolitik und Sozialfürsorge," p. 67.

43. Quoted in Baum, *Familienfürsorge*, p. 122.

44. Ibid.

45. Stolten, "Etwas vom Fürsorgedienst im Selbstgespräch," pp. 9–11.

46. Schmidt, "Die beruflichen Verhältnisse der Fürsorgerinnen," p. 176.

47. Baum, *Familienfürsorge*, pp. 120–121.

48. Dr. Phil. Margarete Cordemann, Bielefeld, "Familienfürsorge," *Soziale Berufsarbeit*, 6 Jg., 11/12 Heft, Nov./Dec. 1927, p. 7.

49. Rosenhaft, "Women, Gender, and the Limits of Political History," p. 159.

50. Emilie Zadow, *Kinder des Staates* (Hamburg: Agentur des Rauhen Hauses, 1929), pp. 15–17.

51. "Jugendamt und Jugendfürsorge," *Rheinische Zeitung*, Nr. 252–253, Donnerstag, 26 Oct. 1922.

52. Stieve, *Tagebuch einer Fürsorgerin*, p. 80.

53. Preusser, "Probleme der Sozialen Frauenschule," p. 131.

54. Schlüter, "Sozialpolitik und Sozialfürsorge," p. 73.

55. Ida Solltman, "Die Frau in der Verwaltung," *Soziale Arbeit*, 7 Bd., 1–2 Heft, Ausg. A, 1930, p. 3, quoted in Susanne Zeller, "Zum Geschlechtsverhältnis zwischen Fürsorgerinnen und Sozialbeamten in Wohlfahrtsämtern der Zwanziger Jahre," in Verena Fesel, Barbara Rose, and Monika Simmel, eds., *Sozialarbeit—ein deutscher Frauenberuf: Kontinuitäten und Brüche im 20. Jahrhundert* (Pfaffenweiler: Centaurus-Verlagsgesellschaft, 1992), pp. 45–46.

56. Eifert, *Frauenpolitik und Wohlfahrtspflege*, pp. 62–63.

57. Schwester Martha Mehl, Backnang, "Beamtenabbau und Fürsorgerinnen," *BZWW*, Nr. 4, Apr. 1924, pp. 37–38.

58. Quoted in Eifert, *Frauenpolitik und Wohlfahrtspflege*, p. 63.

59. See, for example, Dr. rer. pol. Karl Bopp, *Die Wohlfahrtspflege des modernen deutschen Sozialismus: Eine soziale und wirtschaftliche Studie* (Freiburg: Caritasverlag, 1930), p. 85.

60. Kloidt, "Die Berufsethik des katholischen Wohlfahrtspflegers," p. 397.

61. Jane Lewis, "Gender, the Family, and Women's Agency in the Building of 'Welfare States': The British Case," *Social History* 19, no. 1 (January 1994): 48.

62. StAHH, SB I VG 42.11, "Allgemeine Erörterungen über die Familienfürsorge und ihre Durchführung in Hamburg, 1928–32," Leitersitzung, 5, Nov. 1928, pp. 3–4.

63. Lewis, "Gender, the Family, and Women's Agency," p. 48.

64. Baum, *Familienfürsorge*, p. 89.

65. Ibid., pp. 19, 18; see also Ute Daniel, *Arbeiterfrauen in der Kriegsgesellschaft: Beruf, Familie, und Politik im Ersten Weltkrieg* (Göttingen: Vandenhoeck and Ruprecht, 1989), pp. 35–124.

66. StAHH, SB I VG 42.11, p. 40.

67. Baum, *Familienfürsorge*, pp. 5, 27, 31, 51, 57–66, 69.

68. Lutz Niethammer, "Ein langer Marsch durch die Institutionen: Zur Vorgeschichte des preussischen Wohnungsgestezes von 1918," in Lutz Niethammer, ed., *Wohnen im Wandel: Beiträge zur Geschichte des Alltags in der bürgerlichen Gesellschaft* (Wuppertal: Peter Hammer Verlag, 1919), pp. 363–384.

69. Dr. Jur. Adalbert Oehler, *Düsseldorf im Weltkrieg: Schicksal und Arbeit einer deutschen Grossstadt* (Düsseldorf:Lintz, 1927).

70. StADü, III, 4059, 19 July 1921, 18 Apr. 1923, 22 Dec. 1925.

71. StADü, III, 4060, 1 May 1930, 26 June 1930.

72. StADü, III, 4060, Aug. 1919; see also Prof. Chr. J. Klumker, Wilhelmsbad, "Familienfürsorge und Kinderfürsorge," *ZJJ*, 19 Jg., Nr. 11, Berlin, Feb. 1928, p. 288.

73. StADü, III, 4059, 18 Apr. 1923.

74. StADü, III, 4059, n.d.

75. StADü, III 4060, 15 Oct. 1931.

76. Baum, *Familienfürsorge*, pp. 64–65.

77. StAHH, SB I VG 42.11, "Die Organization der Bezirksfürsorge in Berlin," p. 5, Hamburg, 1 Nov. 1928, Herrn Präsidenten ergebenst vorzulegen.

78. Hanna Hellinger, "Familienfürsorge-Einheitsfürsorge," *Arbeiterwohlfahrt* 4 Jg., 1927, pp. 104–105.

79. StAHH, SB I VG 42.11, Städtisches Fürsorgeamt Fürsorge-Direktion, Frankfurt am Main, 20 Nov. 1928, An die Wohlfahrtsbehörde Hamburg, Entwurf einer vorläufigen Geschäftsanweisung für die Fürsorgerinnen des städtischen Jugend und Wohlfahrtsamtes.

80. Schlüter, "Sozialpolitik und Sozialfürsorge," p. 70.

81. Schmidt, "Die beruflichen Verhältnisse der Fürsorgerinnen," p. 176.

82. Preusser, "Probleme der Sozialen Frauenschule," p. 106.

83. Baum, *Familienfürsorge*, p. 86.

84. StAHH, SB I VG 42.11, Leitersitzung, 5 Nov. 1928, Frau Regierungsrat Dr. Albers, p. 4.

85. StAHH, SB I VG 42.11, Hedwig Bickhoff, Oberfürsorgerin, *"Zur Einführung der Familienfürsorge in Dortmund,"* p. 40.

86. For example, Frankfurt; see StAHH, SB I VG 42.11, Städtisches Fürsorgeamt, Fürsorge-Direktion, An die Wohlfahrtsbehörde Hamburg, Frankfurt am Main, 20 Nov. 1928; "Entwurf einer vorläufigen Geschäftsanweisung für die Fürsorgerinnen des städtischen Jugend-und Wohlfahrtsamts; B. Aufgaben der Fürsorgerinnen; II. Aus dem Gebiete der Wirtschafts-fürsorge, 3) Prüfung von Darlehensanträgen."

87. "Sinn und Aufgaben der Familienfürsorge (Aus einer Vortragsreihe des Wohlfahrtsamtes)," *Wohlfahrtsblätter der Stadt Köln*, Nr. 12, Mar. 1927, p. 49.

88. Siddy Wronsky, *Methoden der Fürsorge* (Berlin: Carl Heymanns Verlag, 1930), p. 11.

89. Siddy Wronsky and Prof. Dr. Kronfeld, *Sozialtherapie und Psychotherapie in den Methoden der Fürsorge* (Berlin: Carl Heymanns Verlag, 1932), p. 32.

90. Siddy Wronsky, "Behandlungsmethoden in der Fürsorge," *Jugend und Volkswohl* (Hamburg), 6 Jg., Nr. 10/11, Jan./Feb. 1931, pp. 202–203.

91. Wronsky, *Methoden der Fürsorge*, p. 16.

92. Hauptausschuss für Arbeiterwohlfahrt, ed., *Das kleine Lehrbuch*, 2 Bd. (Berlin, 1928), p. 17.

93. Wronsky, "Behandlungsmethoden in der Fürsorge," pp. 202–203.

94. StAHH, SB I VG 24.28, Leitersitzungen, 5 Nov. 1928, pp. 3–4.

95. Wronsky, *Methoden der Fürsorge*, p. 25.

96. Neumann, "Die Kreisfürsorgerin," p. 39.

97. StAHH, SB I VG 24.27, Leitersitzungen, 13 June 1927, p. 10.

98. Lotte Lemke, "Zeitschriften für die Fürsorgerin (Zeitschriftenschau)," *Arbeiterwohlfahrt*, 2 Jg., 23 Heft, 1 Dec. 1927, p. 761.

99. Baum, *Familienfürsorge*, p. 65.

100. "Wie leben unsere Wohlfahrtserwerbslosen? 73 Fürsorgerinnen-Berichte aus der Stadt Hannover," *Schriftenreihe des Wohlfahrtsamtes der Stadt Hannover*, 4 Heft (Hannover, 1932), pp. 27, 29, 39, 42–43.

101. *Das kleine Lehrbuch*, 2 Bd., pp. 38–39.

102. StAHH, SB AF 70.03, Herausnahme von Familien mit Kinder aus Strassen in denen Prostitution betrieben wird, 1 Bd., 1923–1932, p. 5.

103. StAHH, SB I VG 26.31, Berichte und Beschwerde der Kreisdienststelle 3a, 1938–1943, Li. 5681./333. I would like to thank Dr. Uwe Lohalm, Hamburg, for bringing this document to my attention.

104. "Dienstanweisungen für die Fürsorgerinnen der Stadt Hannover: Hannover 1923," quoted in Schlüter, "Sozialpolitik und Sozialfürsorge," pp. 73–74.

105. Sachsse, *Mütterlichkeit als Beruf*, p. 283.

106. See, for example, StAHH, SB I VG 42.11, Leitersitzung, 5 Nov. 1928, pp. 3–4.

107. StAHH, SB I VG 25.11, 1 Bd., 1926–1935, Niederschrift über die Oberfürsorgerinnensitzung (hereafter, Oberfürsorgerinnensitzungen), 10 Mar. 1926.

108. Oberinspektor Hanna Dünkel, "Familienfürsorge," review of Baum', *Familienfürsorge, Jugend und Volkswohl*, 3 Jg., Nr. 10, 1927, p. 189.

109. Baum, *Familienfürsorge*, pp. 116, 117, 96, 102.

110. StADü, III, 4059, 18 Apr. 1923, Nov./Dec. 1923.

111. Preusser, "Probleme der Sozialen Frauenschule," p. 127.

112. "Sinn und Aufgaben der Familienfürsorge" (Aus einer Vortragsreihe des Wohlfahrtsamtes), *Wohlfahrtsblätter der Stadt Köln*, Nr. 12, Mar. 1927, pp. 50–51.

113. Baum, *Familienfürsorge*, pp. 94, 118, 119–120.

114. Ibid., pp. 119–120. See also Solltman, "Die Frau in der Verwaltung," pp. 45–46.

115. See, for example, StAKöln 903, Nr. 194 (Billstein), "Gang mit der Wohlfahrtspflegerin," *Stadt-Anzeiger zu Köln*, 18 Apr. 1926, Nr. 195, and Zadow, *Kinder des Staates*, pp. 14–15.

116. Stolten, "Etwas vom Fürsorgedienst im Selbstgespräch," pp. 9–11.

117. Neumann, "Die Kreisfürsorgerin," p. 39.

118. Baum, *Familienfürsorge,* pp. 39, 37, 40.

119. Neumann, "Die Kreisfürsorgerin," p. 37.

120. Dr. Hoffmann, Steinau a. Oder, "Die Tätigkeit der Kreisfürsorgerinnen und ihre Bedeutung für den Haushaltsplan eines Landeskreises," *Schleswig-Holsteinische Wohlfahrtsblätter*, 6 Jg., Nr. 10, Oct. 1930, p. 117.

121. Dr. Gertrud Bäumer, "Die Fürsorgerin in der öffentlichen Meinung," *Soziale Berufsarbeit; Organ der Arbeitsgemeinschaft der Berufsverbände der Wohlfahrtspflegerinnen Deutschlands*, 10 Jg., 3 Heft, Mar. 1930, p. 27.

122. Schwester Martha Mehl, Backnang, "Beamtenabbau und Fürsorgerinnen," *BZWW*, Nr. 4, Apr. 1924, pp. 37–38.

123. Baum, *Familienfürsorge*, pp. 109–110.

124. Stieve, *Tagebuch einer Fürsorgerin*, p. 41.

125. Baum, *Familienfürsorge*, pp. 207, 211.

126. Zadow, *Kinder des Staates*, pp. 107, 99, 27.

127. Bäumer, "Die Fürsorgerin in der öffentlichen Meinung," p. 27.

128. Helene Weber, "Der katholische Gedanke in der beruflichen Wohlfahrtspflege," *Die Christliche Frau*, Jan. 1928, quoted in Kloidt, "Die Berufsethik des katholischen Wohlfahrtspflegers," p. 394.

129. Kloidt, "Die Berufsethik des katholischen Wohlfahrtspflegers," pp. 395, 397.

Chapter Four

1. "Ein Vormittag in der Wohlfahrtskreisstelle," *Wohlfahrtsblätter der Stadt Köln*, Nr. 2/3, May/June 1926, pp. 9–10.

2. Rudloff, "Unwillkommene Fürsorge, p. 165.

3. Dr. Wilh. Niemeyer, "Frankfurt," in *Die örtliche und soziale Herkunft der öffentlich unterstützten Personen, insbesondere der verwahrlosten Familien* (Leipzig: Kommissionsverlag bei B. G. Teubner, 1927), pp. 31, 41.

4. Wilhelm Steinhilber, "Esslingen a.N.," in *Die örtliche und soziale Herkunft*, pp. 65, 66–67.

5. "Die wirtschaftliche Fürsorge der Stadt Nürnberg in den letzten zehn Jahren," *Wohlfahrtsblätter der Stadt Nürnberg*, 8 Jg., Nr. 4, Nüremberg, Oct. 1929, p. 8.

6. *Wohlfahrtsamt. Jahresbericht 1925* (Hamburg, 1926), p. 8.

7. *Jahresbericht der Verwaltungsbehörden der freien und hansestadt Hamburg 1925*, p. 641.

8. Büttner, *Politische Gerechtigkeit und sozialer Geist*, pp. 181, 182.

9. Anthony McElligott, "Mobilising the Unemployed: The KPD and the Unemployed Workers' Movement in Hamburg-Altona during the Weimar Republic," in Richard J. Evans and Dick Geary, eds., *The German Unemployed: Experiences and Consequences of Mass Unemployment from the Weimar Republic to the Third Reich* (New York: St. Martin's Press, 1987), p. 235; see also Weinhauer, *Alltag und Arbeitskampf*, p. 147. In 1925, trade employed 23.7 percent of the workforce, transport, 11.9 percent. "1. Endgültige Ergebnisse der Personenstandsaufnahme im hamburgischen Staat am 10. Oktober 1926," *Aus Hamburgs Verwaltung und Wirtschaft*, 4 Jg., 1927, p. 107.

10. Peukert, *The Weimar Republic*, pp. 87–88.

11. "Sonderbeiträge: Die Altersgliederung der Wohnbevölkerung Hamburgs zu Beginn des Jahres 1932," *Aus Hamburgs Verwaltung und Wirtschaft*, 9 Jg., Nr. 10, 1932, p. 206.

12. Niemeyer, "Frankfurt," pp. 25–26.

13. "Vom Wohlfahrtsamt Hamburg laufend unterstützte Parteien (nach dem Stande vom 10. July 1927)," *Jugend und Volkswohl*, 3 Jg., Nr. 8/9, Oct./Nov., 1927, p. 169.

14. Dr. Heinz Kaufmann, *Die soziale Gliederung der Bevölkerung und ihre Auswirkungen*

auf das Wohlfahrtsamt, Veröffentlichungen der Schleswig-Holsteinischen Universitäts-Gesellschaft, Ortsgruppe Altona, 2 Heft (Altona: In Kommission bei Hammerich und Lesser, 1928), pp. 81–82.

15. Hagemann, *Frauenalltag und Männerpolitik*, p. 356.

16. Sonderbeiträge, 1 "Die berufliche und soziale Gliederung der Bevölkerung Hamburgs nach den Zählungen von 1925 und 1907," *Hamburger Statistische Monatsberichte*, 1926, pp. 145, 150.

17. Karen Hagemann, "'Wir werden alt vom Arbeiten': Die soziale Situation alternder Arbeiterfrauen in der Weimarer Republik am Beispiel Hamburgs," *Archiv für Sozialgeschichte*, 30 Bd., 1990, p. 252.

18. Steinhilber, "Esslingen," p. 62.

19. Kaufmann, *Die soziale Gliederung der Bevölkerung*, p. 87.

20. Niemeyer, "Frankfurt," p. 17.

21. Büttner, *Politische Gerechtigkeit und sozialer Geist*, p. 240.

22. Heinrich August Winkler, *Der Weg in die Katastrophe: Arbeiter und Arbeiterbewegung in der Weimarer Republik, 1930 bis 1933* (Berlin: Verlag J. H. W. Dietz Nachfolger, 1987), pp. 23, 26, 30.

23. Ayass, *"Asoziale" im Nationalsozialismus*, p. 20.

24. StAHH, SB I VG 24.23, Leitersitzungen, 24 Oct. 1923, 3 Dec. 1923; I VG 24.24, 10 Jan. 1924, 19 May 1924; I VG 25.11, 1 Bd., 1926–1935, Oberfürsorgerinnensitzungen, 28 Nov. 1928, "Verschiedenes: Mitarbeit im Werftarbeiterstreik"; "Wohlfahrt in Front gegen Werftarbeiter," Arbeiterkorrespondenz Nr. 5758, *Hamburger Volkszeitung*, 21 Dec. 1928.

25. *Soziale Nachrichten: Aus den Ämtern und der Freien Wohlfahrtspflege der Stadt Köln*, No. 5, 1929, pp. 42, 43, 44.

26. *Berliner Wohlfahrtsblatt*, 7 Jg., Nr. 4, 15 Feb. 1931, p. 29.

27. Rudloff, "Unwillkommene Fürsorge," pp. 181, 182.

28. SV-Dü, Nr. 1, Sitzung, 29 Jan. 1926, p. 16,

29. *Wohlfahrtsamt. Jahresbericht 1925*, p. 11.

30. *Das kleine Lehrbuch*, pp. 15–16.

31. StAHH, SB I VG 24.21, Leitersitzungen, 9 Sept. 1921.

32. StAHH, SB I VG 24.22, Leitersitzungen, 17 July 1922.

33. StAHH, SB I VG 24.22, Leitersitzungen, 31 July 1922.

34. *Wohlfahrtsamt. Jahresbericht 1925*, p. 11.

35. Regierungsrat Mailänder, "Geist und Formen der neuzeitlichen Wohlfahrtspflege," *BZWW*, Nr. 10/11, May 1925, p. 76.

36. StAHH, SB I VG 24.26, Leitersitzungen, 4 Jan. 1926.

37. StAHH, SB I VG 24.26, Leitersitzungen, 12 Apr. 1926.

38. Bürgermeister Friedrich Kleeis, Aschersleben, "Die 'Individualisierung' der öffentlichen Fürsorge," *Arbeiterwohlfahrt*, 6 Jg., 8 Heft, 15 Apr. 1931, pp. 227–228.

39. StADü, III, 4060, 19 Feb. 1932.

40. Hermine Bäcker, "Im Gängeviertel Hamburgs," *Die Rundschau: Mitteilungsblatt der Inneren Mission*, 3 Jg., Nr. 1, 1932, p. 1.

41. "Aus der Praxis des Wohlfahrtsamtes," *Hamburger Volkszeitung*, Nr. 170, July 1927.

42. StADü, III, 4059, 20 July 1929.

43. "Aus dem Dunkel der Altstadt," *Wohlfahrts-Woche*, 4 Jg., Nr. 18, Hanover, 5 May 1929, p. 139.

44. StALu, F202 II-796, 12 Mar. 1930, Schultheissenamt An das Amtsoberamt Stuttgart.

45. StALu, E180 II-V-77, Württ. Oberamt Waiblingen, 28 Nov. 1932, An die Ministerialabteilung für Bezirks und Körperschaftsverwaltung.

46. StALu, F164 II-725, Oberamt Esslingen, Esslingen, 24 Feb. 1926, An das verehrl.

Oberamt Esslingen, Beschwerdesache des Kriegsbeschädigten Emil N. gegen Geschäftsführer S. bei BFB-E.

47. StALu, E180 II-V-75, Ministerialabteilung für Bezirks und Körperschaftsverwaltung, Bezirksfürsorgebehörde Biesigheim, 23 Oct. 1930, An das Wirtschaftsministerium Stuttgart durch das Oberamt Biesigheim.

48. StALu, F164 II-725, Oberamt Esslingen, Esslingen, 2 Mar. 1927, Bezirksfürsorgebehörde, Rechnungsrat.

49. Rudloff, "Unwillkommene Fürsorge," p. 179.

50. "Aussprache," (Link)-Frau Stadtdirektor Dr. Kraus, Cologne, *Arbeitsfürsorge: Bericht über den 40. Deutschen Fürsorgetag in Hamburg 23. bis 25. Mai 1927* (Karlsruhe: Verlag G. Braun, 1927), p. 55.

51. StALu, F202 II-794, Stuttgart Amtsoberamt, Bürgermeisteramt Stuttgart, 10 Oct. 1931.

52. StALu, F202 II-794, Bürgermeisteramt Vaihingen a. F., 20 Oct. 1931. In this particular instance, the rent support was being paid directly to the landlord.

53. *Jahresbericht der Verwaltungsbehörden der freien und Hansestadt Hamburg, 1925*, pp. 643–644.

54. StAHH, SB I VG 24.22, Leitersitzungen, 8 May 1922.

55. StALu, F164 II-725, Die Bezirksleitung, An Württ. Oberamt Esslingen, 16 Nov. 1927.

56. StAHH, SB I VG 24.24, Leitersitzungen, 8 Sept. 1924.

57. StALu, F164 II-725, Bezirksfürsorgebehörde Esslingen, Niederschrift über die Verhandlungen des Bezirksfürsorgeausschusses, 16 Mar. 1927.

58. StALu, F164 II-725, Esslingen, An das verehrl. Oberamt Esslingen, Beschwerdesache des Kriegsbeschädigten Emil N. gegen Geschäftsführer S. bei Bezirksfürsorgebehörde Esslingen, 24 Feb. 1926.

59. StALu, F164 II-725, Esslingen, Württembergischer Kriegerbund Stuttgart, Landesverband des Deutschen Reichskriegerbunds Kyffhäuser, An das Oberamt Esslingen, 3 June 1927.

60. "Bezirkskonferenz der Ortsausschüsse der Arbeiterwohlfahrt," *Beilage der Volkszeitung*, 36 Jg., Nr. 7, Düsseldorf, Freitag, 9 Jan. 1925.

61. StAHH, SB I AK 31.22, "Erhebung über die Lage der Kleinrentner, 1927–1929," Dr. Marie Elisabeth Lüders, Mitglied des Reichstages, "Zur Kleinrentnerfrage," *Berliner Tageblatt*, Nr. 19, 11 Jan. 1929.

62. StAHH, SB I VG 24.21, Leitersitzungen, 9 Sept. 1921.

63. StAHH, SB I VG 24.22, Leitersitzungen, 6 Feb. 1922.

64. StAHH, SB I VG 24.25, Leitersitzungen, 2 Mar. 1925.

65. StAHH, SB I VG 24.26, Leitersitzungen, 4 Jan. 1926.

66. StAHH, SB I VG 24.26, Leitersitzungen, 19 July 1926, pp. 8, 9. For Württemberg, see StALu, F210 II-967, Oberamt Waiblingen, Ministerialabteilung für Bezirks und Körperschaftsverwaltung, An die Oberämter, Stuttgart, 15 Feb. 1932.

67. StAHH, SB I VG 24. 26, Leitersitzungen, 19 July 1926.

68. StAHH, SB I VG 24. 26, Leitersitzungen, 2 Aug. 1926.

69. StAHH, SB I VG 24. 26, Leitersitzungen, 12 Apr. 1926.

70. *Berliner Wohlfahrtsblatt*, 7 Jg., Nr. 4, 15 Feb. 1931.

71. See, for example, StALu, F177 II-315, Oberamt Künzelsau, Fürsorge-Protokoll, Begonnen, 1 Oct. 1926.

72. Eghigian, "The Politics of Victimization," pp. 400–401.

73. Ibid., p. 383.

74. Rudloff, "Unwillkommene Fürsorge," p. 169.

75. StALu, E180 II-V-68, Pauline Heller in Oberteuringen An das Württ. Innenministerium, Ministerialabteilung für Bezirks und Körperschaftsverwaltung, Stuttgart, Oberteuringen, 10 Mar. 1929, Beschwerde gegen Bescheid der Bezirksfürsorgebehörde Tettnang, 21 Jan. 1929.

76. StALu, E180 II-V-68, Bezirks-Fürsorge-Auschuss Tettnang, 10 July 1929.

77. StALu, E 180 II-V-68, Ministerialabteilung für Bezirks und Körperschaftsverwaltung, 13 Aug. 1929.

78. StALu, F164 II, Sozialrentnerfürsorge, 1927–1938, 723 (Esslingen), Betreff Friedrich K. (Hilfsarbeiter), Abschrift, Esslingen, Mit vorzüglicher Hochachtung, Friedrich K. Weberstr. 17 (included a copy of the bread bill), 27 Apr. 1926.

79. StALu, F164 II, Sozialrentnerfürsorge, 1927–1938, 723 (Esslingen), Betreff Friedrich K. (Hilfsarbeiter), Esslingen am Neckar, Eingaben und Beschwerden (4 May 1922–May 1941), Städt. Fürsorgeamt Esslingen a.N., 17 May 1926.

80. StALu, F164 II, Sozialrentnerfürsorge, 1927–1938, 723 (Esslingen), BFB Esslingen, Auszug aus der Niederschrift über die Verhandlungen des Bezirksfürsorgeauschusses, 26 Apr. 1927.

81. StALu, F164 II, Sozialrentnerfürsorge, 1927–1938, 723 (Esslingen), RAM to K. Berlin, 21 Sept. 1927.

82. StALu, F164 II, Sozialrentnerfürsorge, 1927–1938, 723 (Esslingen), Stadt Fürsorgeamt An das Oberamt Esslingen, 11 June 1930.

83. StALu, F164 II, Sozialrentnerfürsorge, 1927–1938, 723 (Esslingen), BFB Esslingen An OA Esslingen, 21 Nov. 1933.

84. StALu, F164 II, Sozialrentnerfürsorge, 1927–1938, 723 (Esslingen), Regierungsrat An den Herrn Württ. Wirtschaftsminister Landeswirtschaftsamt für den Wehrwirtschaftsbezirk Va in Stuttgart, 10 May 1941.

85. StAKöln, 902, Nr. 198, Fasc. 3, pp. 501–1052, 24 Sept. 1930.

86. See Christa Hempel-Küter, *Die kommunistische Presse und die Arbeiterkorrespondentenbewegung in der Weimarer Republik* (Frankfurt, 1989), pp. 240–244.

87. The veracity of the reports carried in the *Hamburger Volkszeitung* were, indeed, frequently challenged, resulting in numerous court cases and fines. As a result, the editors increasingly demanded that worker correspondents supply supporting evidence or name witnesses who could confirm their claims; see ibid.

88. Patrice Petro, *Joyless Streets: Women and Melodramatic Representation in Weimar Germany* (Princeton: Princeton University Press, 1989), p. 26.

89. Ibid., pp. 29–31, quoting Peter Brooks, *The Melodramatic Imagination: Balzac, Henry James, Melodrama, and the Mode of Excess* (New Haven, 1976), p. 53.

90. See Rosenhaft, "Women, Gender, and the Limits of Political History," pp. 164–165.

91. "Misstände bei der Abfertigung am Wohlfahrtsamt," *Hamburger Volkszeitung*, 18 Sept. 1923.

92. "Bummelei auf dem Wohlfahrtsamt," *Hamburger Volkszeitung*, 15 Aug. 1927.

93. *Hamburger Volkszeitung*, 4 Sept. 1923.

94. *Hamburger Volkszeitung*, 25 Jan. 1929.

95. Ibid.; "Ein netter Wohlfahrtspfleger!" *Hamburger Volkszeitung*, 14 Sept. 1923.

96. "Wie das Wohlfahrtsamt hilft," *Hamburger Volkszeitung*, 29 Sept. 1926.

97. "Mehr Rücksicht gegenüber den Wohlfahrtsempfängern," *Hamburger Volkszeitung*, 12 Apr. 1927.

98. Judith R. Walkowitz, *City of Dreadful Delight: Narratives of Sexual Danger in Late-Victorian London* (Chicago: University of Chicago Press, 1992), p. 93.

99. See Pierre Bourdieu, *Language and Symbolic Power* (Cambridge, Mass: Harvard University Press, 1991).

100. See David Crew, "Gewalt 'auf dem Amt,' Beispiele aus der Wohlfahrtsverwaltung der Weimarer Republik," *WerkstattGeschichte*, 4 Heft (1993): pp. 33–42.

101. *Hamburger Volkszeitung*, 23 Jan. 1929.

102. StAHH, SB I VG 24.28, Leitersitzungen, 5 Nov. 1928.

103. StAHH, SB I VG 24.24, Leitersitzungen, 3 Mar. 1924.

104. StAHH, SB I VG 24.26, Leitersitzungen, 15 Feb. 1926.

105. StAHH, SB I VG 24.28, Leitersitzungen, 16 July 1928.

106. StAHH, SB I VG 24.26, Leitersitzungen, 1 Nov. 1926.

107. StAHH, SB I VG 24.28, Leitersitzungen, 16 Jan. 1928.

108. StAHH, SB I VG 24.28, Leitersitzungen, 19 Nov. 1928.

109. StAHH, SB I VG 24.29, Leitersitzungen, 29 July 1929.

110. SV-Dü, Nr. 1, Sitzung, 29 Jan. 1926.

111. "Spitzel in der ganzen Stadt," *Sozialistische Republik*, Nr. 197, 2 Blatt, 23 Aug. 1929.

112. StAKöln, 902, Nr. 198, Fasc. 3, pp. 1–500 (1927–1930), Abschrift, 9 Aug. 1929.

113. StALu, 164 II-725, Oberamt Esslingen, Beschwerde Kriegsbeschädigten Karl L. in Esslingen, jetzt in Heilbronn gegen die Bezirksfürsorgebehörde Esslingen, Bezirksfürsorgebehörde Esslingen An das Oberamt hier, 2 Mar. 1927.

114. StADü, III, 4052,Verschiedenes (1930/31–1933), 14 July 1931.

115. "Die weibliche Kriminalpolizei berichtet," *Hamburger Anzeiger*, 9 May 1930.

116. StAHH, I VG 24.26, Leitersitzungen, 15 Feb. 1926.

117. *Stenographische Berichte über die Sitzungen der Bürgerschaft zu Hamburg im Jahre 1927*, J. Henningsen (DNP), 11 Sitzung, p. 282.

118. Wohlfahrtspflegerin Gertrud Maas, "Der Vierte Fürsorgebezirk," *Blätter für Wohlfahrtspflege der Stadt Altona*, 1 Jg., Nr. 8, 28 Aug. 1920, p. 84.

119. StAHH, SB I VG 24.25, Leitersitzungen, 29 July 1925.

120. StAHH, SB I VG 24.29, Leitersitzungen, 29 July 1929.

121. StAHH, SB I AF 81.30, "Unterstützung von selbständigen Gewerbetreibenden und Geschäftsleuten: Allgemeines (ausser Gewerbeschein)," 1 Bd., 1900–1935, An die Polizeibehörde Hamburg, 7 Nov. 1929 (8 Dec. 1929).

Chapter Five

1. See Gerhard A. Ritter, *Social Welfare in Germany and Britain: Origins and Development* (New York: Berg Publishers, 1986), pp. 33–58.

2. Karl Christian Führer, "Für das Wirtschaftsleben 'mehr oder weniger wertlose Personen': Zur Lage von Invaliden- und Kleinrentner in den Inflationsjahren, 1918–1924," *Archiv für Sozialgeschichte*, 30 Bd., 1990, p. 158.

3. Eghigian, "The Politics of Victimization," p. 378.

4. Führer, "Für das Wirtschaftsleben," pp. 158, 168–169.

5. "Forderungen des Deutschen Rentnerbundes e.V. an den Hohen Reichstag," *Der Rentner*, Nr. 7, 1924.

6. Eghighian, "The Politics of Victimization," p. 386.

7. Rudloff, "Unwillkommene Fürsorge," p. 170.

8. See especially Michael L. Hughes, *Paying for the German Inflation* (Chapel Hill, N.C.: University of North Carolina Press, 1988).

9. These figures are for social pensioners in 1924 and small capital pensioners in 1925; see Eghigian, "The Politics of Victimization," p. 378, and Führer, "Für das Wirtschaftsleben," pp. 168–169.

10. See Klaus Saul, "Der Kampf um die Jugend zwischen Volksschule und Kaserne: Ein Beitrag zur 'Jugendpflege' im Wilhelminischen Reich, 1890–1914," *Militärgeschichtliche Mitteilungen*, Nr. 1, 1971, pp. 97–142.

11. See Harvey, *Youth and the Welfare State*; Dickinson, *The Politics of German Child Welfare*, pp. 113–203.

12. Sen. Neumann, "Wohlfahrtsamt und Wirtschaftlage," *Jugend und Volkswohl*, 2 Jg., Nr. 6, Sept. 1926, p. 41.

13. StAHH, SB I VG 25.11, 1 Bd., 1926–1935, Oberfürsorgerinnensitzungen, 15 Dec. 1931.

14. StAHH, SB EF 70.13, "Fürsorge für sittlich Gefährdete: Allgemeines," 1 Bd. (1924–1932), Vereinigung Nordwestdeutscher Wohlfahrtsämter, July 1931.

15. StAHH, SB I VG 25.11, 1 Bd., 1926–1935, Oberfürsorgerinnensitzungen,4 Mar. 1931.

16. Führer, "Für das Wirtschaftsleben," p. 145.

17. Egighian, "The Politics of Victimization," p. 389.

18. *DIZ*, 7 Jg., Nr. 6, Berlin, June 1925, p. 41.

19. StAHH, SB I VG 24.21, Leitersitzungen, 20 Sept. 1921.

20. Rudloff, "Unwillkommene Fürsorge," pp. 174, 175, 176, 178–179.

21. StALu, E191, Zentralleitung Wohltätigkeitsverein, 25779-2582-2591/2590, *Deutsche Tageszeitung*, Nr. 329, 17 July 1921, 1. Beiblatt, Hilfsmassnahmen für die Kleinrentner.

22. StAHH, SB I AK 33.10, "Angelegenheiten der Organisation der Klein- und Sozialrentner," 7 June 1926.

23. Egighian, "The Politics of Victimization," p. 396.

24. StAHH, SB I AK 33.10, 29 Jan. 1923, An die Ortsgruppe Eilbeck des Deutschen Rentnerbundes, z Hd. von Frau Josephine Kreplin, 8 Aug. 1923.

25. Führer, "Für das Wirtschaftsleben," p. 173.

26. Rudloff, "Unwillkommene Fürsorge," pp. 178–179.

27. StALu E191, Zentralleitung Wohltätigkeitsverein, 25779-2582-2591/2589, 15 Sept. 1922, Schultheissenamt Wasseralfingen, gez Straub.

28. StADü, III, 4064, "Neuordnung der Düsseldorfer Armenpflege: Begründung," n.d. [1922].

29. StAKöln, 902, Nr. 198, Fasc. 1, pp. 1–400 (1915–1927), to Herrn Oberbürgermeister Adenauer, Cöln-Lindenthal, 10 Nov. 1923, Klosterstrasse N.110.

30. StAHH, SB I VG 24.22, Leitersitzungen, 16 Oct. 1922.

31. StAHH, SB I VG 24.24, Leitersitzungen, 17 Mar. 1924.

32. StAHH, SB I VG 24.23, Leitersitzungen, 5 Feb. 1923.

33. SV-Dü, Nr. 5, Sitzung, 22. Mar. 1921, p. 58, Stadtverordnete Frau Schweigel (D.N.V.).

34. Rudloff, "Unwillkommene Fürsorge," p. 169.

35. "3. Die Arbeitsfürsorge für Frauen des Mittelstandes,"*BZWW*, 84 Jg., 1931, "Tätigkeitsbericht für die Jahre 1928/29 und 1929/30; II: Überblick über die Tätigkeit der Zentralleitung in den Kriegs und Nachkriegsjahren bis zum Jahre 1928," p. 4.

36. "3 Jahre Verkaufsstelle der Mittelstandsnothilfe in Stuttgart," *BZWW*, 78 Jg., Nr. 16, Aug. 1925, p. 125.

37. StAHH, SB I AK 33.10, "Angelegenheiten der Organisation der Klein und Sozialrentner," 14 Apr. 1925, letter to Frau Regierungsrat Dr. Westphal, Deutscher Rentnerbund Ortsgruppe Barmen.

38. Führer, "Für das Wirtschaftsleben," p. 178.

39. StALu, F164 II-725, Esslingen, Entschliessung, 10 Apr. 1924.

40. StALu, F202 II-790, K. Amtsoberamt Stuttgart, 17 June 1924.

41. See *Reichsgrundsätze über Voraussetzung, Art und Mass der öffentlichen Fürsorge vom 4. Dezember 1924*, B. Besondere Bestimmungen.

42. *DIZ*, 7 Jg., Nr. 6, June 1925, p. 41.

43. *DIZ*, 11 Jg., Nr. 8, Aug. 1929, p. 62.

44. *DIZ*, 11 Jg., Nr. 9, Sept. 1929, p. 71.

45. *DIZ*, 11 Jg., Nr. 12, Dec. 1929, p. 91.

46. StALu, F202 II-789, Württ. Arbeits und Ernährungsministerium an sämtliche Oberämter

und das Stadtschultheissenamt Stuttgart, Stuttgart, 9 June 1925, RAM Schreiben to Sozial-ministerien der Länder 3 Juni ds. Js.

47. StAHH, SB I VG 24.21, Leitersitzungen, 5 Dec. 1921.

48. StALu, F202 II-790, Bezirksfürsorgebehörde Stuttgart-Amt an das Wü. Innenmini-sterium, Auf den Erlass, 11 Feb. 1929.

49. StALu, F202 II-795, Amtsoberamt Stuttgart, "Verweigerung der Unterstützungspflicht," Stuttgart, 5 Feb. 1925; sent to various local newspapers.

50. StAHH, SB I VG 24.31, Leitersitzungen, 28 Jan. 1931.

51. Oberfürsorgerin Kathe Ehlers, "Altersfürsorge in dem Staatlichen Versorgungsheim in Hamburg," *Jugend und Volkswohl*, 5 Jg., Nr. 1/2, Apr–May 1929, p. 8.

52. StAHH, SB I VG 24.22, Leitersitzungen, 31 July 1922.

53. StAHH, SB I VG 24.23, Leitersitzungen, 19 Mar. 1923; StAHH, SB I VG 24.31, Leitersitzungen, 25 Feb. 1931.

54. StAHH, SB I VG 24.24, Leitersitzungen, 23 June 1924.

55. StAHH, SB I VG 24.24, Leitersitzungen, 18 Feb. 1924.

56. *Wohlfahrtsnachrichten der Stadt Altona*, 6 Jg., Nr. 9/10, June/July 1930, p. 104.

57. StALu, E180 II-V-75, Bezirksfürsorgebehörde Besigheim An das Wirtschaftsministerium Stuttgart durch das Oberamt Besigheim, 23 Oct. 1930.

58. StALu, F164 II-732, Bezirksfürsorgebehörde Esslingen a.N, Auszug aus der Nieder-schrift über die Verhandlungen des Bezirksfürsorgeausschusses, 13 Apr. 1931, Beschwerde der Frau Sofie H., Sozialrentnerin in Plochingen-Reichenbach wegen Ablehnung ihres Antrags auf Soz-Rentner Unterstützung.

59. StALu, E180 II-V-75, Bezirkswohlfahrtsamt Rottweil An die Ministerialabteilung für Bezirks und Körperschaftsverwaltung, Bezirkswohlfahrtsamt Rottweil-Beschwerde des Wilhelm B, 2 Jan. 1933.

60. StALu, E180 II-V-71, 4 Oct. 1929.

61. StALu, E180 II-V-71, Bezirkswohlfahrtsamt Ulm a.D. an das Oberamt Ulm a.D, 4 Oct. 1929.

62. See, for example, the repeated directives against this practice issued to the federal state (*Länder*) social and welfare ministries by RAM in Berlin in StALu, F202 II-791. Such com-plaints were, however, already quite frequent by the mid-1920s.

63. See, for example, StAHH, SB I VG 24.31, Leitersitzungen, 28 Jan. 1931.

64. StALu, F164 II-711–713, Oberamt Esslingen, Stadt. Fürsorgeamt Esslingen, 10 Jan. 1930.

65. *DIZ*, 10 Jg., Nr. 2, Berlin, Feb. 1928, p. 15, "Gau Bayern."

66. Edmund Scharein, "Falsche Ansichten, Unterhaltspflicht und Familie: Rentnerjugend, Sterbende Kulturträger: Was sagt die Kirche?" *Der Rentner*, Nr. 1, Feb. 1927, p. 15.

67. StALu, F 164 II, Oberamt Esslingen, Esslinger Volkszeitung, Nr. 278, 26 Nov. 1929.

68. *DIZ*, 8 Jg., Nr. 11, Berlin, Nov. 1926.

69. *DIZ*, 7 Jg., Nr. 6, June 1925, p. 42.

70. *DIZ*, 8 Jg., Nr. 6, June 1926, and 10 Jg., Nr. 2, Feb. 1928, p. 15.

71. *DIZ*, 11 Jg., Nr. 9, Sept. 1929, p. 66.

72. *DIZ*, 7 Jg., Nr. 4, Apr. 1925, pp. 1, 29.

73. *DIZ*, 12 Jg., Nr. 7, July 1930, pp. 80–81.

74. StALu, F164 II-723, Oberamt Esslingen, Ausschnitt aus Volkszeitung, Nr. 110, 13 May 31.

75. StALu, F164 II-723, Oberamt Esslingen, Bezirksfürsorgebehörde Esslingen a.N. Auszug aus der Niederschrift über die Verhandlungen des Bezirksfürsorgeausschusses, 12 May 1931.

76. StALu, E 180 II-V-71, Volksrechtspartei (Reichspartei für Volksrecht und Aufwertung)

Notes to Pages 100–104

Stuttgart, 8 Dec. 1931, Der Reichsparteivorstand an das Württ, Innenministerium Stuttgart, Adolf B., Oberschulrat, Stuttgart, Holderlinstr. 57.

77. StALu, E180 II-V-71, Wohlfahrtsamt Stuttgart, 30 June 1931.

78. Stephan Leibfried, "Existenzminimum und Fürsorge-Richtsätze in der Weimarer Republik," in Stephan Leibfried et al., *Armutspolitik und die Entstehung des Sozialstaats: Entwicklungslinien sozialpolitischer Existenzicherung im historischen und internationalen Vergleich*, Grundrisse sozialpolitischer Forschung, Nr. 3 (Bremen, 1985), pp. 186–240.

79. *DIZ*, 15 Jg., Nr. 2, Feb. 1933, p. 17.

80. *DIZ*, 12 Jg., Nr. 4, 1930, p. 44.

81. See, for example, StAHH, SB I StA 23.71, "Ständige Ausschüsse in den Wohlfahrts-stellen gemäss Geschäftsordnung von 1930 #39 Allgemeines, 1930–1935."

82. *DIZ*, 12 Jg., Nr. 2, Berlin, Feb. 1930, "Um den Ausbau der Fürsorge."

83. *Der Rentner*, Nr. 7, 1924, p. 1.

84. *Der Rentner*, Nr. 6, June 1925.

85. *DIZ*, 7 Jg., Nr. 8, Berlin, Aug. 1925, p. 60; *DIZ*, 7 Jg., Nr. 9, Berlin, Sept. 1925, p. 66; StALu, F202 II-789, Auszug aus dem Protokoll . . . im Rathaus in Vaihingen a. Fildern, 22 July 1927.

86. *DIZ*, 12 Jg., Nr. 2, Berlin, Feb. 1930.

87. See Robert Scholz, "'Heraus aus der unwürdigen Fürsorge': Zur sozialen Lage und politischen Orientierung der Kleinrentner in der Weimarer Republik," in Christoph Conrad and Hans-Joachim Kondratowitz, eds., *Gerontologie und Sozialgeschichte: Wege zu einer historischen Betrachtung des Alters: Beiträge einer internationalen Arbeitstagung am Deutschen Zentrum für Altersfragen, Berlin, 5.–7. July 1982* (Berlin, 1983), pp. 319–350.

88. See, for example, *DIZ*, 12 Jg., Nr. 2, Berlin, Feb. 1930, "Kiel 4: Verbandstag," in which two functionaries of the Zentralverband who were also Communist party members spoke out against "the divisive activities of the Communist counterorganization."

89. *DIZ*, 11 Jg., Nr. 3, Mar. 1929, p. 19.

90. *DIZ*, 10 Jg., Nr. 9, Sept. 1928, p. 70.

91. *DIZ*, 10 Jg., Nr. 10, Oct. 1928, p. 76.

92. "Ein halbes Jahre Arso-Arbeit in Ostsachsen," *Proletarische Sozialpolitik*, 2 Jg., 1929, p. 222.

93. See, for example, the *Vollmacht* given to Hans W., a representative of the IB, Gau Württemberg, in StALu, F164 II-732, "Renten- und Fürsorgeverfahren," 25 May 1932.

94. *DIZ*, 11 Jg., Nr. 6, Berlin, June 1929, p. 44.

95. See, for example, StAHH, Pressestelle I–IV, 3222, Bau und Einweihung des Alter-sheimes Gross-Borstel, 1928–1929.

96. StAHH, Pressestelle I–IV, 3189, "Versorgungsheim Barmbeck ist modernisiert," *Hamburger Echo* (SPD), Nr. 89, 30 Mar. 1930.

97. "Gnadenbringende Weihnachtszeit . . . ," *Hamburger Volkszeitung*, Nr. 280, 12 Dec. 1932.

98. *DIZ*, 12 Jg., Nr. 6, Berlin, June 1930, p. 66, "Nationalsozialistische Wohlfahrtspflege."

99. *DIZ*, 13 Jg., Nr. 3, Berlin, Mar. 1931, p. 31, "Nazimoral."

100. *DIZ*, 12 Jg., Nr. 8, Berlin, Aug. 1930, p. 88.

101. *DIZ*, 11 Jg., Nr. 5, Berlin, May 1929, p. 37.

102. StALu, E191 2590, 20 Dec. 1922.

103. *DIZ*, 8 Jg., Nr. 9, Berlin, Sept. 1926.

104. *DIZ*, 7 Jg., Nr. 6, Berlin, June 1925, p. 42.

105. A 1925 survey came to the conclusion that about two-thirds of small capital pen-sioners were women; the percentage of female social pensioners was probably lower. Small capital pensioners over the age of sixty accounted for between 60 and 85 percent of the total.

See Führer, "Für das Wirtschaftsleben," pp. 168–169; see also Ruth Köppen, *Die Armut is weiblich* (Berlin: Elefanten Press, 1985), pp. 87–88.

106. StALu, E191 2587, *Süddeutsche Zeitung*, Nr. 53, 6 Feb. 1923, Kleinrentnernot und Kleinrentnerfürsorge,von Ober-Reg. Rat Roster.

107. Niemeyer, "Frankfurt," p. 32.

108. Calculations based on figures presented in *Schriften des Deutschen Vereins für öffentliche und private Fürsorge*, 14 Heft (Neue Folge), *Sozialversicherung und öffentliche Fürsorge als Grundlagen der Alters- und Invalidenversorgung* (Karslruhe: Verlag G. Braun, 1930), p. 89.

109. Köppen, *Die Armut is weiblich*, p. 88.

110. Oberfürsorgerin A. Dohrmann, Hamburg, "Die Lebensverhältnisse der Sozialrentner in Zahlen," *Jugend und Volkswohl*, 5 Jg., Nr. 1–2, Apr./May 1929, pp.15–18.

111. *DIZ*, 7 Jg., Nr. 4, Apr. 1925, p. 29.

112. Dohrmann, "Die Lebensverhältnisse der Sozialrenter," pp. 15–17.

113. Elisabeth Ludy, *Erwerbstätige Mutter in vaterlosen Familien* (Berlin, 1930), p. 18.

114. StALu, F202 II-796, Schultheissenamt Plattenhardt to Oberamt Stuttgart, 9 Oct. 1925.

115. *DIZ*, 7 Jg., Nr. 4, Apr. 1925, p. 29.

116. Robert Weldon Whalen, *Bitter Wounds: German Victims of the Great War, 1914–1939* (Ithaca: Cornell University Press, 1984), pp. 110–111, 160–162.

117. See, for example, Emmy Schräder, *Die Kleinrentnerfürsorge: Ein Leitfaden für die Praxis* (Berlin, 1928).

118. See, for example, "Vertagung," *Der Rentner*, Nr. 2, Feb. 1928.

119. Paula Mueller-Otfried, M.d.R., *Kleinrentnernot: Aus Deutschlands Not und Ringen*, 1 Heft (Berlin: Deutschnationale Schriftenvertreibsstelle, 1927).

120. *Der Rentner*, Nr. 2, Feb. 1925.

121. See, for example, the photographs accompanying the *DIZ* report of the 1925 demonstrations in Berlin in *DIZ*, 7 Jg., Nr. 4, Berlin, Apr. 1925, pp. 1, 29.

122. See, for example, "'Soziale Fürsorge' in Biedenkopf," *DIZ*, 12 Jg., Nr. 7, Berlin, June 1930, p. 79.

123. On the central importance of gender, see Chris Phillipson, *Capitalism and the Construction of Old Age* (London: Macmillan, 1982), pp. 61–75.

124. The phrase quoted in the subhead is taken from a complaint lodged by Adolf G., StALu E180 II-V-76, Ministerialabteilung für Bezirks- und Körperschaftsverwaltung Sozialrentnerfürsorge, G-J, 1924–1943 (hereafter StALu, E180 II-V-76), to Kriminalabteilung z.H. der behandelten Krimm. Komis, 21 Oct. 1931.

125. StALu, E180 II-V-76, "Strafsache gegen den am 18.4.1892 zu Schlatt Bez. Amts Engen, geb., in Bad Canstatt, Sulzbachgasse 2. wohn. verh. Sattler, Adolf G. wegen übler Nachrede . . . Sitzung vom 23. July 1937."

126. StALu, E180 II-V-76, Einschreiben An das Arbeitsministerium Stuttgart sowie An das Ministerium des Innern ferner An das Reichsarbeitsministerium, Canstatt, 14 Mar. 1927.

127. StALu, E180 II-V-76, "Württ. Verwaltungsgerichtshof. Urteil. . . . 9 November 1938."

128. StALu, E180 II-V-76, Adolf G. to Arbeits- und Ernährungsministerium Stuttgart, Stuttgart, 27 Dec. 1925.

129. StALu, E180 II-V-76, Adolf G. to Arbeitsministerium, Abtlg. Wohlfahrt, Stuttgart, 16 Feb. 1926.

130. StALu, E180 II-V-76, letter of 12 Jan. 1926, Stuttgart.

131. StALu, El80 II-V-76, letter included with a decision of the Württ. Amtsgericht/ Stuttgart II in the matter of Stadtgemeinde Stuttgart vs. Adolf G. and Ehefrau, n.d. (probably 1926).

132. StALu, E180 II-V-76, Einschreiben An das Arbeitsministerium Stuttgart, sowie An das Ministerium des Innern, ferner. An das Reichsarbeitsministerium, Canstatt, 14 Mar. 1927.

133. Peukert, *Grenzen der Sozialdisziplinierung*, pp. 263–304.

134. StALu, E180 II-V-76, An die Kriminalabteilung z.H. der behandelten Krimm Komisar [*sic*] Herrn Schelling, Canstatt, 21 Oct. 1931.

135. StALu, E180 II-V-76, An das württ. Wirtschaftsministerium, Stuttgart, Canstatt, 16 May 1930. It is interesting that Adolf G. sent copies of this letter to all the political parties in the city council. By this time, he also had his own address stamp to affix to his letters of complaints.

136. StALu, E180 II-V-76, Canstatt, 16 Mar. 1930.

137. StALu, E180 II-V-76, Stadtschultheissenamt Stuttgart to Herr Adolf G., Canstatt, Sülzbachgasse 2, 5 May 1930, signed by Bürgermeister.

138. StALu, E180 II-V-76, Stuttgart-Canstatt, 11 May 1930, Dem RAM Unterabtlg. 5B Ständiger Auschuss für städt. Wohnungswesen, Abschriftlich Herrn Bürgermeister Sigloch Stuttgart (Einschreiben).

139. StALu, E180 II-V-76, RAM to Adolf G., Berlin, 15 May 1930.

140. StALu, E180 II-V-76, WA Stuttgart an das Württ. Wirtschaftsministerium, 4 June 1930.

141. StALu, E180 II-V-76, An die Kriminalabteilung, Canstatt, 21 Oct. 1931.

142. StALu, E180 II-V-76, Wohlfahrtsamt Stuttgart to Ministerialabteilung für Bezirks- und Körperschaftsverwaltung, 7 Dec. 1931.

143. StALu, E180 II-V-76, Beschwerde . . . dem RAM, Abschriftlich der Ministerial-abteilung für Bezirks- und Körperschaftsverwaltung, Stuttgart, Canstatt, 20 Dec. 1931.

144. StALu, E180 II-V-76, Canstatt, 30 May 1927.

145. StALu, E191 4119, "Schwäb. Bund zum Schutze der kinderreichen Familien."

146. StALu, E180 II-V-76, Stuttgart–Bad Canstatt, 1 Jan. 1937, Dem Chef der Kanzlei des Führers der NSDAP, Berlin W8.

147. StALu, E180 II-V-76, Schöffengericht Stuttgart II in Bad Canstatt, 23 July 1927, Strafsache gegen den am 18 Apr. 1892 . . . geb . . . Sattler, Adolf G. wegen übler Nachrede.

148. StALu, E180 II-V-76, Stuttgart, Württ. Verwaltungsgerichtshof . . . Urteil, 9 Nov. 1938.

149. Ibid.; for a fascinating discussion of the way that criticism of the "little Fuehrers" contributed to Hitler's own charisma, see Ian Kershaw, *The Hitler Myth* (Oxford: Clarendon Press, 1987), pp. 83–104.

150. StALu, E180 II-V-76, Stadt Stuttgart, Geschäftsstelle Bad Canstatt, Abt. Wohl-fahrtswesen, An das Städt. Wohlfahrtsamt Stuttgart, 15 Feb. 1937.

151. StALu, E180 II-V-76, Adolf G. An die Kriminalpolizei, z.H. des Herrn Kriminal-komis, Schelling Stuttgart, 17 Oct. 1931.

152. See, for example, "Reinfall eines Denunzianten," *DIZ*, 12 Jg., Nr. 7, July 1930, p. 78.

Chapter Six

1. See, for example, Helgard Kramer, "Frankfurt's Working Women: Scapegoats or Win-ners of the Great Depression?" in Evans and Geary, *The German Unemployed*, pp. 108–14.

2. SV-Dü, Nr. 11, Sitzung, 12 May 1920, p. 150.

3. Lewis, "Gender, the Family, and Women's Agency," pp. 52, 54.

4. Henny Schumacher, *Die proletarische Frau und ihre Erziehungs-Aufgabe: Mit einem Vorwort von Marie Juhacz* (Berlin: J. H. W. Dietz Nachfolger, 1929).

5. Wronsky, "Behandlungsmethoden in der Fürsorge," pp. 202–203.

6. StAHH, SB I VG 42.11, "Zur Einführung der Familienfürsorge in Dortmund" (Hedwig Bickhoff, Oberfürsorgerin), p. 40.

7. Hagemann, *Frauenalltag und Männerpolitik*, p. 211; see also Melitta Lorenzen, "Einiges aus meiner Arbeit als Lauenburgische Landesfürsorgerin," *Schleswig-Holsteinisches Wohlfahrtsblätter*, Nr. 12, 1925, p. 163.

8. Hagemann, *Frauenalltag und Männerpolitik*, pp. 209–210.

9. Sachsse and Tennstedt, *Geschichte der Armenfursorge in Deutschland*, 2 Bd., p. 124.

10. Hagemann, *Frauenalltag und Männerpolitik*, p. 211.

11. Hauptstaatsarchiv Stuttgart, E 151 i II, Jugendamt-Göppingen 1919–1939, Zeitungsausschnitt aus Der Hohenstaufen, Göppingen, Nr. 181, 5 Aug. 1922, "Die Aufgaben des Jugendamts von E. Krauss beim JA. Göppingen."

12. Dr. Ellen Simon, "Mutter- und Säuglingsschutz," *Jugend und Volkswohl*, 5/6 Heft, 1929.

13. Hagemann, *Frauenalltag und Männerpolitik*, p. 213.

14. StAHH, Medizinalkollegium I K27a, 4 Bd. (1929–1931), annual report of Dr. Plate for 1928–1929, Schularztbezirk 22.

15. Lene Overlach, "Licht, Luft, und Sonne: Frauen und Reichsgesundheitswoche," *Hamburger Volkszeitung*, 7 Apr. 1926.

16. Lorenzen, "Einiges aus meiner Arbeit," p. 163.

17. "Wohlfahrtspflege auf dem Lande," *Die Gemeinde*, 3 Jg., 1926, p. 34.

18. "Zu wenig besucht: Die Beratungsstelle für werdende Mütter," *Hamburger Anzeiger*, 23 Apr. 1930.

19. StAHH, Jugendbehörde I/293, "Fürsorge für unverheiratete Schwangere, 1918–1933"; StAHH, Medizinalkollegium II C 3c, "Säuglingsfürsorge in Hamburg" (9 May 1916–1938), Hamburg, Sept. 1923, Arbeitsweise in der Säuglings- und Kleinkinderfürsorge.

20. Sachsse and Tennstedt, *Geschichte der Armenfursorge in Deutschland*, 2 Bd., p. 123.

21. See, for example, *Proletarische Sozialpolitik*, 1 Jg., Nr. 6, 1928, p. 187.

22. StAHH, SB I AF 85.11, "Wochenhilfe und Wochenfürsorge," 2 Bd. 1925–1932, "Aus der Praxis der Wochenfürsorge," *Nachrichtendienst*, Nr. 67, Nov. 1925.

23. StAHH, SB I AF 85.11, "Wochenhilfe und Wochenfürsorge," 2 Bd., 1925–1932, "Ausbau der Mutterschaftshilfe," *Hamburger Echo*, Nr. 189, 11 July 1926.

24. StAHH, SB I VG 24.28, Leitersitzungen, 2 Jan. 1928.

25. Med.-Rat Dr. Brockerhoff, (Hagen, "Schwangerenfürsorge in der Stadt Hagen i.W.," *Zeitschrift fur Schulgesundheitspflege und soziale Hygiene*, 40 Jg., Nr. 4, 1927, pp. 189, 191.

26. StADü, III, 4082, Beamte und Angestellte des Gesundheitsamtes, Fürsorgerinnen, Abschrift, der Minister für Handel und Gewerbe, Berlin, 27 Oct. 1924, Betrifft Zusammenarbeit mit den Kreis und Stadtfürsorgerinnen zur besseren Durchführung des Schwangeren und Wöchnerinnenschutzes.

27. StAHH, SB I AF 85.11, "Wochenhilfe und Wochenfürsorge," 2 Bd., 1925–1932.

28. StAHH, Medizinalkollegium II C 3c, "Säuglingsfürsorge in Hamburg" (9 May 1916–1938).

29. Stadt- und Medizinalrat Dr. med. Friedrich Wolf, Freital, "Wie ist die Kommunalisierung des Hebammenstandes, wenn auch zunächst nur in einzelnen Gemeinden, vom Standpunkt der öffentlichen Gesundheitspflege zu beurteilen? Welche Vorteile und welche Nachteile hat sie für die Bevölkerung und den Hebammenstand gegenüber dem bisher üblichen System?" *Das Wohlfahrtswesen der Industriestadt Freital*, 3 Jg., Nr. 2, 1 Feb. 1920, pp. 2–3.

30. StAHH, Medizinalkollegium II C 3c, "Säuglingsfursorge in Hamburg" (9 May 1916–1938), Hamburg, Sept. 1918, Arbeitsweise in der Säuglings- und Kleinkinderfürsorge.

31. StADü, III, 4052, 1932.

32. StADü, III, 4052, 19 Feb. 1932.

33. See Paul Th. Hoffmann, *Neues Altona, 1919–1929: Zehn Jahre Aufbau einer deutschen Grossstadt, Dargestellt im Auftrage des Magistrats der Stadt Altona* (Jena: Eugen Diederichs Verlag, 1929), p. 259.

34. Nikolas Rose, *Governing the Soul: The Shaping of Private Life* (London: Routledge, 1990), pp. 130–131.

35. Plaschke, "Die Niedergang des Krippenwesens," *Mutter und Kind*, 1 Jg., Nr. 9/10, Ausgabe A und B, Sept–Oct. 1923, p. 35.

36. Schuhmacher, *Die proletarische Frau*, p. 20.

37. Stadtarchiv Frankfurt am Main, Akten der Stadtverordnetenversammlung Kinderhorte und Volkskindergärten 1888, Magistrats-Vorlage, Errichtung eines Kinderhortes in der Siedlung Praunheim, 28 Aug. 1928.

38. StAHH, SB I VG 25.11, 1 Bd., 1926–1935, Oberfürsorgerinnensitzungen, 21 Nov. 1930, p. 5.

39. For example; the depiction of Gertrude Polley as a woman who had led a sexually "irregular" life helped to undermine the legitimacy of her claims and grievances against local housing and welfare authorities. See von Saldern et al., "Eine Sensation stösst ins Leere," pp. 87–88.

40. Regina Schulte, *Sperrbezirke, Tugendhaftigkeit und Prostitution in der bürgerlichen Welt* (Frankfurt am Main: Syndikat, 1979), pp. 174–175.

41. See, for example, "Sysyphusarbeit," *Das Blatt der Frau:Frauenbeilage der Volkszeitung*, Düsseldorf, 29 Nov. 1924.

42. See, for example, Dora Brede, Kiel, "Fürsorge für gefährdete Mädchen," *Schleswig-Holsteinische Wohlfahrtsblätter*, Kiel, 3 Jg., Nr. 10, Oct. 1927.

43. *Enzyklopädisches Handbuch des Kinderschutzes und der Jugendfürsorge*, ed. Mitwirkung Hervorragender Fachleute von Ludwig Clostermann, Dr. Theodor Heller, Medizinalrat Dr. P. Stephani (Leipzig: Akademische Verlagsgesellschaft, 1930), pp. 829–830. See also StALu, F152 III-27, FE.

44. StAHH, Jugendbehörde I/293, Zur Schwangerenfürsorge, Bemerkungen des Referendar Adler nebst Anlagen, 2 Oct. 1919.

45. See, for example, W. Kützner, Siegen, "Die Fahndung nach Unterhaltspflichtigen und deren Heranziehung in der Ausübung der Vormundschaft," *Die Nachbarschaft*, Calau, Nr. 4, July 1929, pp. 64–68, and also StAHH, I FR 42.2, "Statistik über Arbeitszwangsverfahren, 1924–1939." In 1931, illegitimate births constituted 12.8 percent of live births in Hamburg, 15.2 percent in Hanover, 11.2 percent in Cologne, 8.4 percent in Düsseldorf, and 15.0 percent in Stuttgart. See *SJdS*, 27 Jg., 1932, p. 312.

46. See, for example, Dr. Annemarie Wulff, *Das Schicksal der unehelichen in Berlin* (Frankfurt, 1928), pp. 13–14, and also StALu, F177 II-315, Oberamt Künzelsau.

47. StALu, F181 III-677, Oberamt Ludwigsburg, Erteilung einer Unterhalts-bezw. Ersatzleistungsauflage gemäss, 23RFV.

48. StALu, F181 III-677, Bezirkfürsorgebehörde Besigheim, 23 Nov. 1930, to Jugendamt Abt. 2, 14 Nov. 1930.

49. StALu, F181 III-677, Städtisches Jugendamt Heilbronn, 11 Aug. 1931.

50. StALu, F154 II-3969–3974, Oberamt Besigheim, Stadtschultheissenamt Lauffen am Neckar, 15 May 1931, Vernommen wird Christian F.

51. StALu, F154 II-3969–3974, Oberamt Besigheim, Beschluss, 5 Aug. 1931, Städtisches Jugendamt Heilbronn, 28 July, 1931, An das Oberamt Besigheim.

52. StALu, F154 II-4051, Oberamt Besigheim, Einzelne Fälle, Vormundschaftswesen 1930–1937; Oberamt Besigheim, 18 Sept. 1930, to Jugendamt.

53. StALu, F154 II-4051, Dr. H. Pfaehler, Rechtsanwalt, Stuttgart, 19 Apr. 1933, letter of complaint on behalf of Alfred S. to Oberamt Besigheim.

54. StALu, F154 II-4051, Jugendamt Besigheim, 18 Jan. 1930, An das Oberamt Besigheim.

55. StALu, F154 II-4051, Jugendamt Besigheim, 1 Mar. 1930.

56. Erna Maraun, Bezirksjugendamt Prenzlauer Berg, "Was tun wir? Bericht über die Jahresarbeit einer Familienfürsorgerin," *Berliner Wohlfahrtsblatt*, 5 Jg., Nr. 7, 31 Mar. 1929, p. 59.

57. Margarete Cohn-Radt, "Berliner Pflegekinder: Untersuchung über die Grunde des Pflegestellenwechsels in 4 Berliner Bezirken," *Waisenhilfe: Zeitschrift des Reichsverbandes für Waisenfursorge*, 51 Jg., Berlin, Nov. 1931, pp. 5, 7.

58. Direktor Eberhard Giese, Görlitz, "Ein Notjahr im Jugendamt," *ZJJ*, 23 Jg., Apr. 1931–Mar. 1932, p. 168.

59. Cohn-Radt, "Berliner Pflegekinder," p. 61. See also "Bericht aus der Praxis," *Schleswig-Holsteinische Wohlfahrtsblätter*, 6 Jg., Nr. 7, Kiel, July 1930, pp. 90–91.

60. Direktor Dr. Hertz, Hamburg, "Pflegestellenpolitik," *ZJJ*, 23 Jg., Nr. 3, Berlin, June 1931, p. 87.

61. StAHH, Jugendbehörde I/298, An Einen Hohen Senat, "Abhaltung von Mütterabenden, 1926–1931," 16 Sept. 1926.

62. StAHH, Jugendbehörde I/298, Magistrat der Hauptstadt Breslau, Städt. Jugendamt, 17 Mar. 1931.

63. "Die Möglichkeit von Strafmassnahmen im Rahmen der Pflegekinderaufsicht," *Nachrichtendienst des Deutschen Vereins für öffentliche und private Fürsorge*, 9 Bd., 4 Apr. 1928, pp. 132–133.

64. Stieve, *Tagebuch einer Fürsorgerin*, pp. 50, 27, 49.

65. In 1927, for example, no less than a quarter of all households in Hamburg contained subtenants. The three highest concentrations of subtenants in Hamburg could be found in the older, poorer, inner city districts of St. Pauli-Nord (44.1%), St. Pauli-Sud (38.4%), and St. Georg-Nord (38.3%). See "Die Untermieter in der Stadt Hamburg nach der Wohnungszählung vom 16. Mai 1927," *Aus Hamburgs Verwaltung und Wirtschaft: Monatschrift des Statistischen Landesamts*, Jan. 1928, Hamburg, 5 Jg., Nr. 1, 1 Mar. 1928, p. 1. Of the 37,848 people living as subtenants in Hamburg, 24,600 were renting from people to whom they were not in any way related, while 13,248 rented from relatives who, for the most part, were either their parents, their in-laws, or their grandparents. See StAHH, Pressestelle IV, 2003, 1928–1929, "Verwandtschaftsbeziehungen der Hauptmieter und Untermieter in Hamburg," *Hamburger Nachrichten*, 13 Nov. 1928.

66. See Hagemann, "'Wir werden alt vom Arbeiten,'" pp. 252–266.

67. StAHH, SB I VG 24.24, 18 Feb. 1924.

68. Ludy, *Erwerbstätige Mütter in vaterlosen Familien*, pp.18, 20.

69. See, for example, StAHH, SB I VG 24.31, Leitersitzungen, 28 Jan. 1931, 4 Nov. 1931.

70. Rosi Wolfstein, "Das Wohnungselend und die Frauen," *Sozialistische Republik*, Cologne, Nr. 16, 20 Jan. 1921.

71. StAHH, SB I EF 50.16, *Jahresberichte der Behörde für Wohnungspflege 1926*, pp. 8–9.

72. Adelheid von Saldern, "Sozialdemokratie und kommunale Wohnungsbaupolitik in den 20er Jahren am Beispiel von Hamburg und Wien," *Archiv für Sozialgeschichte* 25 Bd., 1985, pp. 202–203.

73. Karen Hagemann, "'Wir hatten mehr Notjahre als reichliche Jahre . . .': Lebenshaltung und Hausarbeit Hamburger Arbeiterfamilien in der Weimarer Republik," in Klaus Tenfelde, ed., *Arbeiter im 20. Jahrhundert* (Stuttgart: Klett-Cotta, 1991), p. 218.

74. Dr. Kuno Bergerhoff, *Wohnungspflege* (Stuttgart: Verlag von Ferdinand Enke, 1922), pp. 72–79.

75. StADü, III, 4060, 1 May 1930, Betr. Vortragsreihe über Fragen der Wohnungsaufsicht und Wohnungspflege.

76. StADü, III, 4060, 1 May 1930.

77. Quoted in Hagemann, *Frauenalltag und Männerpolitik*, p. 115.

78. StAHH, SB I EF 50.16, *Jahresbericht der Behörde für Wohnungspflege 1925*.

79. Hagemann, *Frauenalltag und Männerpolitik*, pp. 115–116.

80. Bergerhoff, *Wohnuingspflege*, pp. 64, 83.

81. StAHH, SB I EF 50.16, *Jahresbericht der Behörde für Wohnungspflege 1925*.

82. Oberbaurat Dr. Brandt, Hamburg, "Die Bedeutung der Altwohnung," *Jugend und Volkswohl*, 3 Jg., Nr. 10, Dec. 1927, pp. 181–182.

83. "Reform der Altwohnungen," *Hamburger Echo*, 13 Jan. 1928.

84. Brandt, "Die Bedeutung der Altwohnung," p. 181.

85. "Vorträge über 'Reform der Altwohnungen,'" *Hamburger Echo*, 15 Dec. 1927.

86. "Wohnungspflege als Schulfach," *Die Gemeinde*, 8 Jg., 1931, p. 565.

87. Hagemann, *Frauenalltag und Männerpolitik*, p. 117.

88. "Hausbesuche," *Wohlfahrtsblätter der Stadt Köln*, Nr. 1, Apr. 1926, pp. 4–5.

89. Hauptstaatsarchiv Stuttgart, E 151 i II, Jugendamt-Göppingen, 1919–1939, Ausschnitt aus der *Süddeutschen-Arbeiter-Zeitung*, Nr. 42, 20 Feb. 1931, "Das Ideale Jugendamt Feuerbach" (Arbeiter-Korrespondenz).

90. Frieda Rosenthal, Berlin, "Die anerkannten Spitzenverbände der privaten Wohlfahrt—Die Arbeiterwohlfahrt," *Proletarische Sozialpolitik*, 5 Heft, 1928, p. 139.

91. StAHH, I VG 24.28, Leitersitzungen, 19 Nov. 1928.

92. *Hamburger Volkszeitung*, Nr. 19, 23 Jan. 1929, "Das Wohlfahrtsamt kann Sie nicht bis zu Ihrem 80. Lebensjahre ernähren! . . ."

93. *Sozialistische Republik*, Cologne, 5 July 1932.

94. StAKöln, 902, Nr. 198, Fasc. 3, pp. 501–1052, Cologne, 24 Sept. 1930.

95. StAHH, SB I VG 24.32, Leitersitzungen, 14 Dec. 1932.

96. Quoted in Führer, "Für das Wirtschaftsleben," p. 178.

97. Wronsky and Kronfeld, *Sozialtherapie und Psychotherapie*, p. 39.

98. Linda Gordon, *Heroes of Their Own Lives—The Politics and History of Family Violence: Boston, 1880–1960* (New York: Viking, 1988).

99. Ruth Fischer and Franz Heimann, *Deutsche Kindheiten 1932: Wohlfahrt, Krankheit, Hunger, Krise* (Düsseldorf: W. Schroeder Verlag, 1986), pp. 203–204.

100. Zadow, *Kinder des Staates*, pp. 47–48.

101. Münchmeier, *Zugänge zur Geschichte der Sozialarbeit*, pp. 101–106.

102. Stieve, *Tagebuch einer Fürsorgerin*, p. 53.

Chapter Seven

1. In her article "Die Schutzaufsicht und ihre Durchführung als Aufgabe der Arbeiterwohlfahrt," Lotte Möller used the phrase "Eine Elternschaft zu Dritt," which can be translated as "parenting in threes," to signal the involvement of the social worker, along with the mother and father, in the task of raising children properly. See *Arbeiterwohlfahrt*, 2 Jg., 1927, p. 727.

2. For more detailed discussion of the origins of this law and its provisions, see Peukert, *Grenzen der Sozialdisziplinierung*, pp. 37–142 ; Harvey, *Youth and the Welfare State*, pp. 176–183.

3. "Prussian Enforcement Law of the National Youth Welfare Act of July 9, 1922," in John W. Taylor, *Youth Welfare in Germany: A Study of Governmental Action Relative to Care of the Normal German Youth* (Nashville, Tenn., 1936), pp. 214–215.

4. Landesrat Wingender, "'Modernisierung' der Fürsorgeerziehung," *Die Gemeinde*, 1 Jg., 1924, pp. 187–190.

5. See, for example, "Kinderfürsorge und Arbeiterwohlfahrt," *Rheinische Volkswacht*, 14 July 1925.

6. Irma Fechenbach, Berlin, "Schulfürsorge: Wie sie ist und wie sie sein soll," *Arbeiterwohlfahrt*, 2 Jg., 23 Heft, 1 Dec. 1927, p. 724.

7. Direktor K. Joerger, Freiburg, "Der 29. Deutsche Caritastag vom 28. August bis 4. September 1929 zu Freiburg i. Br.," *Caritas*, 1929, p. 455.

8. Hans Windelkinde Jannasch, *Alarm des Herzens: Aus den Papieren eines Helfers* (Stuttgart: Verlag Gerhard Merian, 1928).

9. *Enzyklopädisches Handbuch des Kinderschutzes und der Jugendfürsorge*, pp. 829–830.

10. StALu, F190 II-1184, Oberamt Nürtingen, case of W., Otto, Friedrich, geb. 20 May 1910, Tübingen; Abschrift, An das Amtsgericht Nürtingen (Jugendamt stamp July 1929).

11. See especially Peukert, *Grenzen der Sozialdisziplinierung*, pp. 240–245. On the work therapy that remained the core of rehabilitation in most reformatories, see Joachim Fenner, *Durch Arbeit zur Arbeit erzogen: Berufsausbildung in der preussischen Zwangs- und Fürsorgeerziehung, 1878–1932* (Kassel: Eigenverlag des LWV Hessen, 1991).

12. See Peukert, *Grenzen der Sozialdisziplinierung*; StAHH, Jugendbehörde, "Die Anträge auf Fürsorgeerziehung im Rechnungsjahre 1929 in Hannover," *Wohlfahrts-Woche*, Nr. 28, 1930, p. 332.

13. Margarete Kahle, *Beziehungen weiblicher Fürsorgezöglinge zur Familie* (Leipzig: Verlag von Johann Ambrosius Barth, 1931), p. 75.

14. Gräser, *Der blockierte Wohlfahrtsstaat*, pp. 229–230.

15. StALu, F164 UU-Oberamt Esslingen 739, Ministerialabteilung für Bezirks und Körperschaftsverwaltung to Oberamt Esslingen, 7 Oct. 1922.

16. StALu, F190 II-1184, Oberamt Nürtingen, An das Städt. Jugendamt Worms and Jugendamt Ludwigshafen a Rh, 22 Mar. 1928.

17. StALu, F190 II-1184, Oberamt Nürtingen, An das Amtsgericht Nürtingen, 30 Apr. 1928, petition for *FE*; An das Städt. Jugendamt Worms and Jugendamt Ludwigshafen a Rh, 22 Mar. 1928.

18. StALu, F190 II-1184, Oberamt Nürtingen, An das Amtsgericht Nürtingen, 30 Apr. 1928, petition for *FE*.

19. StALu, F190 II-1184, Oberamt Nürtingen, Jugendamt Nürtingen to Jugendamt Mannheim, 16 Mar. 1928; An die WLFB Stuttgart, Nürtingen, 25 June 1928, Jugendamt.

20. StALu, F190 II-1184, Oberamt Nürtingen, An das Amtsgericht Nürtingen, 30 Apr. 1928, petition for *FE*; An das Städt. Jugendamt Worms and Jugendamt Ludwigshafen a Rh, 22 Mar. 1928.

21. StALu, F190 II-1184, Oberamt Nürtingen, Abschrift Amtsgericht Nürtingen als Vormundschaftsgericht, 3 May 1928.

22. Ibid., testimony of Marie W. herself.

23. Ibid.

24. StALu, F190 II-1184, Oberamt Nürtingen, 14 Nov. 1928; Abschrift Amtsgericht Nürtingen als Vormundschaftsgericht, 3 May 1928.

25. StALu, F190 II-1184, Oberamt Nürtingen, Amtsgericht Nürtingen als Vormundschaftsgericht, 6 May 1926, Beschluss.

26. StALu, F190 II-1184, Oberamt Nürtingen, Kriminalpolizei Augsburg, 3 Sept. 1925.

27. StALu, F190 II-1184, Oberamt Nürtingen, Amtsgericht Nürtingen als Vormund-schaftsgericht, 6 May 1926, Beschluss.

28. StALu, F190 II-1184, Oberamt Nürtingen, Direktor des St. Konradihaus, Schelklingen, 4 Aug. 1928; Der Anstaltsvorstand, Direktor an das St. Konradihaus, 19 July 1928.

29. StALu, F190 II-1184, Oberamt Nürtingen, Jugendamt-Nürtingen An das Konradihaus Schelklingen, 13 July 1928.

30. StALu, F190 II-1184, Oberamt Nürtingen.

31. StALu, F190 II-1184, Oberamt Nürtingen, Amtsgericht Nürtingen als Vormund-schaftsgericht, 6 May 1926, Beschluss.

32. StALu, F190 II-1184, Oberamt Nürtingen, Polizeipräsident Stuttgart, Fürsorgestelle; Bericht der Pol/Fürsorgerin, Stuttgart, 11 Jan. 1926, sent to Jugendamt Nürtingen, 14 Jan. 1926.

33. StALu, F190 II-1184, Oberamt Nürtingen, 2 Feb. 1926, Bericht der Polizeifürsorgerin, gez. Dora Reis, sent to Jugendamt Nürtingen, 6 Feb. 1926.

34. StALu, F190 II-1184, Oberamt Nürtingen, 8 Apr. 1926, Bericht der Polizeifürsorgerin, gez. Dora Reis.

35. StALu, F190 II-1184, Oberamt Nürtingen, 8 Apr. 1926, Jugendamt Nürtingen, Antrag auf Erhebung der FE, 21 Apr. 1926.

36. StALu, F190 II-1184, Oberamt Nürtingen, WLFB-Jugendamt-Nürtingen, Stuttgart, 11 May 1926; WLFB-An Jugendamt-Nürtingen, 8 Apr. 1929.

37. StALu, F190 II-1184, Oberamt Nürtingen, WLFB to Jugendamt-Nürtingen, 10 Aug. 1928.

38. StALu, F190 II-1184, Oberamt Nürtingen, Direktion des St. Konradihauses an WLFB Stuttgart, 22 Aug. 1928.

39. StALu, F190 II-1184, Oberamt Nürtingen, die WLFB, 13 Aug. 1928.

40. StALu, F190 II-1184, Oberamt Nürtingen, Direktor des St. Konradihaus, Schelklingen, to Jugendamt-Nürtingen, 27 Mar. 1929, der Anstaltsvorstand.

41. StALu, F190 II-1184, Oberamt Nürtingen.

42. StALu, F190 II-1184, Oberamt Nürtingen, WLFB-JA-Nürtingen, Stuttgart, 11 May 1926; WLFB-An Jugendamt-Nürtingen, 8 Apr. 1929.

43. Gräser, *Der blockierte Wohlfahrtsstaat*, pp. 229–230.

44. Lene Mann, Frankfurt, "Zur Krisis der Jugendämter," *ZJJ*, 20 Jg., Nr. 9, Dec. 1929, p. 242.

45. StAKöln, 903, Nr. 171, *Jugendamt der Stadt Köln Jahres-Bericht*, 1 Apr. 1925–31 Mar. 1926.

46. Möller, "Die Schutzaufsicht," pp. 727, 728.

47. Fürsorger Gustav Buchhierl, Berlin-Friedrichshain, "Grossstädtische Schutzaufsicht," *ZJJ*, Nr. 6, Sept. 1926, pp. 154–156.

48. *Oberfürsorgerin* Gertrud Embden,"Die Schutzaufsicht in der Praxis," *Jugend und Volkswohl*, Hamburg, Nr. 3, June 1926, pp. 16–17.

49. Stadtpfarrer Wuterich, "Uber Schutzaufsicht," *BZWW*, 79 Jg., Sept. 1926, pp. 139, 137.

50. StALu, F190 II-1184, Oberamt Nürtingen.

51. StALu, F190 II-1184, Oberamt Nürtingen, Jugendamt to Amtsgericht.

52. StALu, F190 II-1184, Oberamt Nürtingen, Staatsanwaltschaft Stuttgart, Kirchheim-Teck, 29 July 1926, gez. Stadtpfarrer Blum.

53. StALu, F190 II-1184, Oberamt Nürtingen, Jugendamt to Amtsgericht.

54. StALu, F190 II-1184, Oberamt Nürtingen, Amtsgericht Kirchheim-Beschluss, 24 July 1930, ordering *FE*.

55. StALu, F190 II-1184, Oberamt Nürtingen, Kirchheim-Teck, 27 June 1930, In der Strafsache gegen Erwin F. Bericht der Sekretäre, Helfer- und Helferinnen, gez. Kurcher.

56. StALu, F190 II-1184, Oberamt Nürtingen, An die WLFB Stuttgart, Direktion des Konradihauses, Schelklingen, 23 Sept. 1932.

57. StAKöln, 903, Nr. 14, Die Neuorganisation der Schülfursorge, proposal from Amalie Lauer, Cologne, 1 Apr. 1924, to Bürgermeister.

58. Dr. Herford, "Vorbeugende Fürsorge als Sparmassnahme," quoted in *Soziale Nachrichten aus den Ämtern und der freien Wohlfahrtspflege der Stadt Köln*, No. 2, 1929, StAKöln, 902, Nr. 198, Fasc. 3, pp. 501–1052.

59. StALu, F152 III-24, Backnang, Oberamtsärztlicher Jahresbericht für 1929, Oberamtsbezirk Backnang-Marbach.

60. See, for example, Stadtoberschularzt Dr. Georg Wolff, Berlin, "Schulkinderfürsorge und soziale Hygiene," *Arbeiterwohlfahrt*, 5 Jg., 3 Heft, 1 Feb. 1930, p. 83.

61. George Benjamin, "Ausbau der Schulhygiene!" *Der Sozialistische Arzt*, 3 Jg., Nr. 1, Apr. 1926, p. 15.

62. StAHH, Medizinalkollegium II 57a, Protokolle über die Sitzungen der Schulärzte, 1907–1932; Niederschrift über eine am 17 Nov. 1932, 11 Uhr vorm., im grossen Sitzungssal der Gesundheitsbehörde stattgefundene Schularztsitzung, p. 10.

63. StAHH, Medizinalkollegium I K27a, 3 Bd., Jahresberichte der Schulärzte, 1925–1928, Abt. Schulärztlicher Jahresbericht, 1 May 1927–31 Mar. 1928, p. 11.

64. StAHH, Medizinalkollegium I K27a, 4 Bd., 1929–1931, Jahresbericht Schularztbezirk 22.

65. StAHH, Medizinalkollegium I K27a, 5 Bd., 1932–1933, annual report of Dr. Ferdinand Plate, May 1932.

66. StAHH, Medizinalkollegium I K27a, 3 Bd., Jahresberichte der Schulärzte, 1925–1928, 1 May 1927–31 Mar. 1928, pp. 9–11.

67. See Paul Levy, "Die ärztliche Versorgung der Wohlfahrtskranken," *Die Gemeinde*, 9 Jg., 8 Heft, 2 Apr. 1932, pp. 343–344.

68. Benjamin, "Ausbau der Schulhygiene!" pp. 13–14; StAHH, SB I VG 25.11, 1 Bd., 1926–1935, Oberfürsorgerinnensitzungen, 17 Oct. 1927.

69. StAHH, Medizinalkollegium I K 27a, 5 Bd., 1932–1933, Dr. med. Helmuth Simon, Hamburg, Schäferkampsallee 18, 10 May 1932, Bericht über die schulärztliche Tätigkeit während des Berichtsjahres 1931/32.

70. StAHH, Medizinalkollegium I K 27a, 5 Bd., 1932–1933, Hamburg, May 1933, Schularztbericht für das Jahr 1932/33.

71. StAHH, Medizinalkollegium I K27a, 3 Bd., Jahresberichte der Schulärzte, 1925–1928, Volksschulen, 4 June 1925.

72. StAHH, SB I VG 25.II, 1 Bd., 1926–1935, Oberfürsorgerinnensitzungen, 22 Mar. 1929.

73. StAHH, Medizinalkollegium I K27a, 5 Bd., 1932–1933, annual report of Dr. Schall, Sievekingsalleee 50, 1 Apr. 1932.

74. StAHH, Medizinalkollegium I K 27a, 5 Bd., 1932–1933, Dr. H. Strauss, An die Gesundheitsbehörde, Hamburg, 7 May 1932.

75. Benjamin, "Ausbau der Schulhygiene!" p. 15.

76. Irma Fechenbach, Berlin, "Schulfürsorge: Wie sie ist und wie sie sein soll," *Arbeiterwohlfahrt*, 2 Jg., 23 Heft, 1 Dec. 1927, p. 723.

77. StAHH, Medizinalkollegium II, S7a, Protokolle über die Sitzungen der Schulärzte, 1907–1932, 25 Feb. 1929.

78. "Kinderfürsorge und Arbeiterwohlfahrt," *Rheinische Volkswacht*, 14 July 1925.

79. August Brandt, Berlin, "Überweisung öffentlicher Fürsorgeaufgaben an die private Wohlfahrt (Fortsetzung)," *Proletarische Sozialpolitik*, 2 Jg., 9 Heft, 1929, pp. 272–273.

80. Otto Wehn, *Die Bekämpfung schädlicher Erwerbsarbeit von Kindern,* 4 Heft (Langensalza: Fr. Manns Pädagogisches Magazin, 1925), pp. 62, 65–67.

81. Helen Simon, "Arbeitslosigkeit, Doppelverdiener, Kinderwerbsarbeit (Fortsetzung)," in *Soziale Praxis,* 40 Jg., 30 Heft, 1931, p. 997.

82. Wehn, *Die Bekämpfung,* pp. 57, 59–61.

83. Wohlrabe, Chemnitz, "Zur Ueberwachung der Kinderarbeit: Aus der Praxis eines grosstädtischen Jugendamtes," *Arbeiterwohlfahrt,* 5 Jg., 1930, pp. 679–684.

84. StADü, III, 5425, Städt. Polizeiverwaltung, Düsseldorf, 14 Nov. 1928; S. W. u G. Abt. Gesundheitsamt, Düsseldorf, 6 Jan. 1929.

85. StADü, III, 5425, Städt. Polizeiverwaltung, Düsseldorf, 3 Aug. 1929; S. W. und G-J-Düsseldorf, 14 Aug. 1929, to Polizeiverwaltung; Städt. Polizeiverwaltung, Düsseldorf, 16 Dec. 1929; Städt. Polizeiverwaltung, Düsseldorf, 19 May 1930.

86. StADü, III, 5425, betr. die Arbeitskarten für schulpflichtige Kinder, 1904/7–1932, Der Oberbürgermeister W. und G/Jugendamt, Düsseldorf, 13 June 1925, urschriftlich dem Gewerbeaufsichtsamt, hier.

87. Wehn, *Die Bekämpfung,* p. 89.

88. Ruth Weiland, "Kinderarbeit," *Arbeiterwohlfahrt,* 8 Jg., 10 Heft, 15 May 1933, pp. 289–291.

89. Christopher Lasch, *Haven in a Heartless World* (New York, 1977); Jacques Donzelot, *The Policing of Families* (New York: Pantheon, 1979); Philippe Meyer, *The Child and the State* (Cambridge, 1983).

90. Michel and Koven, "Womanly Duties," pp. 1076–1108.

91. Gordon, *Heroes of Their Own Lives.*

92. See especially Elizabeth Wilson, *Women and the Welfare State* (London: Tavistock Publications, 1977).

93. Jürgen Habermas, *The Theory of Communicative Action,* vol. 2, *Lifeworld and System: A Critique of Functionalist Reason,* trans. Thomas McCarthy (Boston: Beacon Press, 1987), p. 362.

94. Meyer, *The Child and the State,* p. 42.

95. Donzelot, *The Policing of Families,* pp. 96–168.

96. Clara Henriques, "Psychologische Schwierigkeiten und Möglichkeiten sozialistischer Wohlfahrtsarbeit," *Arbeiterwohlfahrt,* 2 Jg., 15 Heft, 1 Aug. 1927, p. 456.

97. Erika S. Fairchild, "Women Police in Weimar: Professionalism, Politics, and Innovation in Police Organizations," *Law and Society Review* 21, no. 3 (1987): 387.

98. Eckart Pankoke, "Von 'guter Policey' zu 'socialer Politik': 'Wohlfahrt,' 'Glückseligkeit,' und 'Freiheit' als Wertbindung aktiver Sozialstaatlichkeit," in Christoph Sachsse and Florian Tennstedt, eds., *Soziale Sicherheit und soziale Disziplinierung: Beiträge zu einer historischen Theorie der Sozialpolitik* (Frankfurt, 1986), p. 171; see also Jessen, "Polizei, Wohlfahrt und die Anfänge."

99. StAHH, Staatl. Pressestelle I–IV, 3125, "Gutachten, Auskünfte, Berichte der öffentl. Jugendfürsorge, 1922–1929," n.d. (18 Jan. 1927 in margin).

100. Seidel, "Die kommunale Wohlfahrtspflege," p. 181.

101. Stieve, *Tagebuch einer Fürsorgerin,* p. 50.

102. Siddy Wronsky and Alice Salomon with the assistance of Eberhard Giese, *Soziale Therapie: Ausgewählte Akten aus der Fürsorge-Arbeit: Für Unterrichtszwecke* (Berlin: Carl Heymanns Verlag, 1926), pp. 78, 80, 83, 84, 86.

103. StALu, F190 II-1184, Amtsgericht Nürtingen als Vormundschaftsgericht, 30 Dec. 1926.

104. StALu, F190 II-1184, probably from Jugendamt an das Schultheissenamt Linsenhofen, Oberamt Nürtingen, 14 July 1930.

105. StALu, F190 II-1184, Schultheissenamt.

106. StALu, F190 II-1184, news clipping, Nürtingen, *Nürtinger Tagblatt,* 9 Jg., Nr. 197,

25 Aug. 1930, Amtsblatt der Staats-Stadt- und Gemeindebehörden des Bezirks Nürtingen Heilbronn, 24 Aug. 1930, Kindsraub.

107. StALu, F190 II-1184, Jugendamt Nürtingen-Urach to Herrn Pfarrer Held, Linsenhofen, 13 Aug. 1930.

108. StALu, F190 II-1184, Jugendamt Nürtingen to WLFB Stuttgart, 23 May 1934.

109. StALu, F190 II-1184, an das Gesundheitsamt hier, 14 Nov. 1935.

110. StALu, F190 II-1184, Erbgesundheitsgericht beim Amtsgericht Stuttgart I an das Jugendamt Nürtingen, 4 Feb. 1937.

111. Gisela Bock, "Racism and Sexism in Nazi Germany: Motherhood, Compulsory Sterilization, and the State," in Renate Bridenthal, Atina Grossmann, and Marion Kaplan, eds., *When Biology Became Destiny: Women in Weimar and Nazi Germany* (New York: Monthly Review Press, 1984), p. 279.

Chapter Eight

1. In 1932, 144,845 people were receiving long-term cash support, and 98,934 were given one-time assistance. *Statistisches Jahrbuch für die Freie und Hansestadt Hamburg, 1932/ 33*, ed. Statistisches Landesamt (Hamburg, 1933), p. 161.

2. "Die gegenwärtige Lage in der Fürsorge," *Jugend und Volkswohl*, 10/11Heft, Jan./Feb. 1931, p. 205.

3. "Die Wohlfahrtserwerbslosen im hamburgichen Staat nach Bezirksfürsorgeverbänden und Gemeinden" (Sonderbeitrag), *Aus Hamburgs Verwaltung und Wirtschaft: Monatsschrift des Statistischen Landesamts*, 9 Jg., Nr. 6, Hamburg, 15 Aug. 1932, p. 1, and *Aus Hamburgs Verwaltung und Wirtschaft*, 9 Jg., Nr. 1, 1932, p. 13.

4. "Die gegenwärtige Lage in der Fürsorge," *Jugend und Volkswohl*, 10/11 Heft, Jan./Feb. 1931, pp. 208, 207.

5. Stadtrat Dr. Michel, Frankfurt, "Probleme der kommunalen Wohlfahrtspflege um die Wende 1932/33," *Arbeiterwohlfahrt*, 8 Jg., 1933, pp. 4, 5, 8.

6. Stadtrat Dr. Michel, Frankfurt, "Die Notmassnahmen in der Wohlfahrtspflege," *Arbeiterwohlfahrt*, 6 Jg., 20 Heft, 15 Oct. 1931, p. 614.

7. Oliver Schmeer, "Sozialpolitik in Duisburg, 1930–1933: Staatliche Sozialpolitik und kommunale Selbstverwaltung in der Krise der Weimarer Republik," in *Duisburger Forschungen: Schriftenreihe für Geschichte und Heimatkunde Duisburgs*, ed. Stadtarchiv Duisburg in Verbindung mit der Mercator-Gesellschaft, 37 Bd., 1990, p. 210.

8. Ibid., p. 76; see also Heidrun Homburg, "Vom Arbeitslosen zum Zwangsarbeiter: Arbeitslosenpolitik und Franktionierung [sic] der Arbeiterschaft in Deutschland, 1930–1933, am Beispiel der Wohlfahrtserwerbslosen und der kommunalen Wohlfahrtshilfe," *Archiv für Sozialgeschichte*, 30 Bd., 1985, pp. 251–298.

9. Schmeer, "Sozialpolitik in Duisburg," pp. 209–212.

10. Michel, "Die Notmassnahmen," p. 613.

11. Leibfried, "Existenzminimum und Fürsorge-Richtsätze, p. 221.

12. Quoted in ibid.

13. Ibid., p. 222.

14. "Die Handhabung der öffentlichen Fürsorge im rheinisch-westfälischen Industriegebiet," *Arbeiterwohlfahrt*, 7 Jg., 1932, pp. 50, 51, 52.

15. StAHH, SB I VG 38.52, Bericht über Prüfung der ehrenamtlichen betreuten Fälle des Bezirk 167, 28 May 1932.

16. StAHH, SB I VG 38.52, 22 Nov. 1932, Wohlfahrtsstelle 6, An die Verwaltungsabteilung.

17. StAHH, SB I VG 38.52, 13 Feb. 1933, Wohlfahrtsstelle 6, An die Verwaltungs-abteilung, regarding Bezirk 176.

18. Annemarie Hermberg, "Die Lebenshaltung der Lohnempfänger und der Unterstützen," *Arbeiterwohlfahrt*, 6 Jg., 24 Heft, 15 Dec. 1931, pp. 741–742, 743, 744.

19. D. Adolf Stahl, Berlin, "Sorge um die deutsche Familie: Eine nachdenkliche Wanderung durch die neue Fachliteratur," *IM*, 1932, p. 76.

20. "Vom Verein der württ. Bezirksfürsorgerinnen," *BZWW*, 84 Jg., Nr. 5, May 1931, p. 111.

21. "Familienfeindlichkeit in Gesetzen und Verordnungen," *Die Rundschau: Mitteilungs-blatt der Inneren Mission*, 3 Jg., Nr. 7, 1932, p. 110.

22. Stahl, "Sorge um die deutsche Familie," pp. 76–80.

23. "Die Berücksichtigung des Arbeitseinkommens in der Familiengemeinschaft bei Bemessung der Fürsorgeleistungen," *Nachrichtendienst des Deutschen Vereins für öffentliche und private Fürsorge*, 1931, pp. 354–358.

24. "Die Handhabung der öffentlichen Fürsorge im rheinisch-westfälischen Industriegebiet," *Arbeiterwohlfahrt*, 7 Jg., 1932, p. 53.

25. "Die Berücksichtigung des Arbeitseinkommens in der Familiengemeinschaft bei Bemessung der Fürsorgeleistungen," *Nachtichtendenst des Deutschen Vereins für öffentliche und private Fürsorge*, 1931, p. 354.

26. StAHH, SB I VG 24.32, Leitersitzungen, 15 June 1932.

27. StAHH, SB I VG 24.31, Leitersitzungen, 1 Bd., 28 Jan. 1931.

28. Dr. Marie Baum, Heidelberg, "Die Familie in Sozial- und Fürsorge-Politik der Gegenwart," *Soziale Politik*, 41 Jg., 27 Heft, 1932, pp. 833–834.

29. S. Packert, Zwickau, "Ein Dolchstoss auf die 'Familiengemeinschaft,'" *Die Gemeinde*, 10 Jg., 1933, p. 126.

30. Bertha Finck, "Familie und Fürsorge im Zeichen der Volksnot," *Die Rundschau: Mitteilungsblatt der Inneren Mission*, 3 Jg., Nr. 7, 1932, p. 105.

31. Dr. H. Bolzau, Cologne, "Der Schutz der Familie in der Sozialversicherung unter besonderer Berücksichtigung der Notverordnungen des Reichspräsidenten," *Caritas*, 12 Jg., Neue Folge, 1932, pp. 116–117.

32. See, for example, Christine Teusch-Köln, M.d.R., "Sozialpolitik und Familie," *Caritas*, 11 Jg., Neue Folge, 7 Heft, July 1932, p. 307.

33. StADü, III, 4060, 10 Dec. 1931.

34. StAHH, SB I VG 25.11, 1 Bd., 1926–1935, Oberfürsorgerinnensitzungen, 26 Nov. 1931.

35. Stadtrat Zachow, "Die Zusammensetzung der Wohlfahrtserwerbslosen im Verwaltungs-bezirk Kreuzberg," *Berliner Wohlfahrtsblatt*, 6 Jg., Nr. 14, 31 Aug. 1930, p. 93.

36. "Not und Armut schaffen Konflikte: Wohlfahrtsbeamte mussen darunter leiden," *Hamburger Echo*, Nr. 134, 16 May 1930.

37. StAHH, SB I VG 24.31, Leitersitzungen, 25 Feb. 1931.

38. StAHH, SB I VG 24.32, Leitersitzungen, Revierkommissar Fischer, 12 Dec. 1932.

39. "Wohlfahrtsbeamte: Eine Zuschrift aus unserem Leserkreise und ein Kommentar dazu," *Hamburger Anzeiger*, 17 Sept. 1931.

40. "Die Bureaus der Kölner Armenverwaltung," *Rheinische Zeitung*, Cologne, 20 Oct. 1922.

41. "Unhaltbare Zustände in den Wohlfahrtsstellen," *Hamburger Volkszeitung*, 1 Oct. 1926.

42. StAHH, SB I VG 24.28, Leitersitzungen, 19 Nov. 1928.

43. *Berliner Wohlfahrtsblatt*, 7 Jg., Nr. 4, 15 Feb. 1931, p. 29.

44. StAHH, I VG 24.32, Leitersitzungen, 21 Sept. 1932.

45. StAHH, I VG 24.31, Leitersitzungen, 25 Feb. 1931.

46. StAHH, I VG 24.32, Leitersitzungen, 21 Sept. 1932.

47. *Berliner Wohlfahrtsblatt*, 7 Jg., Nr. 4, 15 Feb. 1931.

48. "Verprügelte Wohlfahrtsbeamte," *Hamburger Anzeiger*, Nr. 112, 15 May 1930.

49. StAHH, SB I VG 24.23, Leitersitzungen, 6 Oct. 1923.

50. StAHH, SB I VG 74.12, "Sicherungsmassnahmen gegen Ausschreitungen" (hereafter "Sicherungsmassnahmen"), 1 Bd., 1923–1932, Leitersitzungen, 1 Nov. 1926, Auszug.

51. StAHH, SB I VG 74.12, "Sicherungsmassnahmen," 13 Oct. 1927, Wohlfahrtsamt, Herr Präsident Martini.

52. StAHH, SB I VG 74.12, "Sicherungsmassnahmen," 19 Nov. 1927, Wohlfahrtsstelle 6.

53. StAHH, SB I VG 74.12, "Sicherungsmassnahmen," 5 Nov. 1927, Wohlfahrtsstelle 8 an Martini.

54. StAHH, SB I VG 74.12, "Sicherungsmassnahmen," Leitersitzungen, 17 Oct. 1927, Auszug.

55. StAHH, SB I VG 74.12, "Sicherungsmassnahmen," 28 Nov. 1927, Wohlfahrtsstelle 2 an den Herrn Präsidenten des Wohlfahrtsamtes, Hamburg.

56. StAHH, SB I VG 74.12, 18, "Sicherungsmassnahmen," Dec. 1929, Wohlfahrtsstelle 2 an die Verwaltungsabt, Rentzelstrasse 68.

57. StAHH, SB I VG 74.12, "Sicherungsmassnahmen," 7 Aug. 1930, Wohlfahrtsstelle 10 an Abt I.

58. StAHH, SB I VG 74.12, "Sicherungsmassnahmen," 16 Aug. 1930, Wohlfahrtsstelle 1.

59. StAHH, SB I VG 74.12, "Sicherungsmassnahmen," 8 Oct. 1930, Der Präsident des Wohlfahrtsamtes, Schreiben an Amtsgerichtspräsidenten Dr. Blunk.

60. StAHH, SB I VG 74.12, "Sicherungsmassnahmen," 12 Dec. 1932, Wohlfahrtsstelle 6 an die Verwaltungsabt.

61. StAHH, SB I VG 74.12, "Sicherungsmassnahmen," Hamburg, 24 June 1931, An die Wohlfahrtsbehörde zu Hamburg, Vorgelegen im Bezirk II zur Sitzung, 24 June 1931.

62. "Unhaltbare Zustände in den Wohlfahrtsstellen," *Hamburger Volkszeitung*, 1 Oct. 1926.

63. See especially Klaus Theweleit, *Männerphantasien*, 1 Bd., *Frauen, Flüten, Körper* (Frankfurt: Verlag Roter Stern, 1977).

64. *Hamburger Nachrichten*, 11 Oct. 1923.

65. Zadow, *Kinder des Staates*, pp. 13–14.

66. StAHH, SB I VG 25.11, 1 Bd., 1925–1936, Oberfürsorgerinnensitzungen, 22 Oct. 1932.

67. StAHH, SB I VG 24.23, Leitersitzungen, 24 Oct. 1923.

68. StAHH, SB I VG 74.12, 12 Dec. 1932, Wohlfahrtsstelle 6 an die Verwaltungsabt.

69. StAHH, SB I VG 24.32, Leitersitzungen, 14 Dec. 1932, Sonderniederschrift über die Besprechung betreffend Unruhen in den Wohlfahrtsstellen.

70. StAHH, SB I AW 00.93, "Bewegungen gegen die Unterstützungsarbeit (Sammelakte mit 5 Einzelakten), 1930–1931," 21 Oct. 1930, Wohlfahrtsstelle 6, report by Walter Gross, Glashüttenstr 110 Hs. II.

71. StAHH, SB I VG 24.32, Leitersitzungen, 14 Dec. 1932.

72. StAHH, SB I VG 74.12, Polizeibehörde Hamburg—Abschrift Abtlg. IV Ordnungspolizei Hamburg, 27 Jan. 1930.

73. StAHH, SB I VG 74.12, 5 Nov. 1927, Wohlfahrtsstelle 7.

74. On this connection see, in general, Bourdieu, *Language and Symbolic Power*.

75. StAHH, Staatl. Pressestelle I–IV, 3186, "Rüpeleien in Wohlfahrtsstellen, 'Organisiert den Hungermarsch,'" *Hamburger Echo*, 25 Jan. 1930, On the *Hamburger Volkszeitung*, see Hempel-Küter, *Die Kommunistische Presse*, pp. 240–244.

76. "Senator Neumann, wo sind die Beweise?" *Hamburger Volkszeitung*, Nr. 268, 17 Nov. 1930.

77. "Eine Stunde im Kampf um Unterstützung," *Hamburger Volkszeitung*, 13 Oct. 1930.

78. "Senator Neumann, wo sind die Beweise?" *Hamburger Volkszeitung*, Nr. 268, 17 Nov. 1930.

79. Pierre Bourdieu, *Outline of a Theory of Practice* (Cambridge: Cambridge University Press, 1987).

80. See, for example, Alf Lüdtke, "Gewalt im Alltag: Herrschaft, Leiden, 'Körpersprache'? Formen direkter und 'sanfter' Gewalt in der bürgerlichen Gesellschaft," in Jorg Calliess, ed., *Gewalt in der Geschichte: Beiträge zur Gewaltaufklärung im Dienste des Friedens* (Düsseldorf: Schwann Verlag, 1983), pp. 271–296.

81. StAHH, SB I VG 24.31, Leitersitzungen, 13 June 1931, Wohlfahrtsstelle 13.

82. StAHH, SB I VG 74.12, 25 July 1931, 30 July 1931, 4 Aug. 1931, 17 Aug. 1931.

83. StAHH, SB I VG 24.32, Leitersitzungen, 14 Dec. 1932.

Chapter Nine

1. Alf Lüdtke, "Hunger in der Grossen Depression: Hungererfahrungen und Hungerpolitik am Ende der Weimarer Republik," *Archiv für Sozialgeschichte*, 27 Bd., 1987, pp. 145–176.

2. Bernhard Michael Menapace, *"Klein-Moskau" wird braun: Geesthacht in der Endphase der Weimarer Republik (1928–1933)* (Kiel: Neuer Malik Verlag, 1991), p. 97.

3. Michael Wildt, *Am Beginn der "Konsumgesellschaft": Mangelerfahrung, Lebenshaltung, Wohlstandshoffnung in Westdeutschland in den fünfziger Jahren* (Hamburg: Ergebnisse Verlag, 1994), p. 21.

4. Alf Lüdtke, " 'Ihr könnt nun wissen, wie die Glocken eigentlich leuten sollen': Brotration und Arbeiter (Über) Leben im Sommer 1919–ein Beispiel aus Bochum," in Alf Lüdtke, *Eigen-Sinn: Fabrikalltag, Arbeitererfahrungen, und Politik vom Kaiserreich bis in den Faschismus* (Hamburg: Ergebnisse Verlag, 1993), p. 219.

5. Wildt, *Am Beginn der "Konsumgesellschaft,"* p. 21.

6. "Lebenshaltung minderbemittelten Familien in Hamburg in den Jahren 1907, 1925 und 1926 nach Haushaltsrechnungen," *Aus Hamburgs Verwaltung und Wirtschaft: Monatsschrift des Statistischen Landesamts*, 4 Jg., Nr. 11, Nov. 1927, pp. 198–199.

7. Wildt, *Am Beginn der "Konsumgesellschaft,"* p. 26.

8. See Daniel, *Arbeiterfrauen in der Kriegsgesellschaft*, pp. 215–232, and Karin Hartewig, *Das unberechenbare Jahrzehnt: Bergarbeiter und ihre Familien im Ruhrgebiet, 1914–1924* (Munich: Verlag C. H. Beck, 1993), pp. 153–190.

9. StAHH, SB I EF 50.16, Jahresbericht der Behörde für Wohnungspflege 1925.

10. Davis, "Home Fires Burning," pp. 328–370.

11. StAHH, SB I VG 25.11, 1 Bd., 1926–1935, Oberfürsorgerinnensitzungen, 12 Oct. 1930.

12. *SV-Dü*, Nr. 18, Sitzung, 30 Nov. 1921, p. 248.

13. *Das Kommunalprogramm der kommunistischen Partei Deutschlands* (Berlin, 1923), pp. 42–43.

14. StADü, III, 4066, 1 Mar. 1924.

15. StADü, III, 4066, 5 Oct. 1928.

16. StADü, III, 4066, "Richtlinien für die Volksspeisung," 1925/26.

17. StAHH, SB I VG 25.11, 1 Bd., 1926–1935, Oberfürsorgerinnensitzungen, 12 Oct. 1930.

18. StADü, III, 4066, 5 Feb. 1927.

19. StAHH, SB, I VG 25.11, 1 Bd., 1926–1935, Oberfürsorgerinnensitzungen, 12 Oct. 1930, pp. 5–6.

20. StAHH, SB I VG 25.11, 1 Bd., 1926–1935, Oberfürsorgerinnensitzungen, 15 Sept. 1932.

21. StAHH, I VG 73.11, "Erwerbslosen-Ausschuss und ähnl. 1929–1933."

22. StAHH, SB I VG 25.11, 1 Bd., 1926–1935, Oberfürsorgerinnensitzungen, 4 Dec. 1929.

23. "Vorwort," in "Wie leben unsere Wohlfahrtserwerbslosen?" p. 4.

24. StADü, III, 4069, "Entschliessung," n.d., no signatures, but following document dated 20 June 1932.

25. StADü, III, 4069, 1932, Im Rahmen der Winterhilfe hauswirtschaftliche Beratung" (Haushaltsstunden).

26. StADü, III, 4069, Bericht über die Haushaltsstunde, 20 June 1932.

27. "Wie Leben unsere Wohlfahrtserwerbslosen?" p. 47.

28. See especially Lüdtke, "Hunger in der Grossen Depression," pp. 145–176.

29. "Dr. Baumanns Kalorienberechnung. . . ," *Hamburger Volkszeitung*, 2 Sept. 1930.

30. Ibid.

31. "Wie Leben unsere Wohlfahrtserwerbslosen?" p. 13.

32. Lüdtke, "Hunger in der Grossen Depression," p. 151.

33. "Neue Richtsätze für Wohlfahrtserwerbslose. . . ," *Hamburger Volkszeitung*, Nr. 150, 1 July 1932.

34. "Der Selbstverpfleger schreibt: Mein Diner im GW. Arbeiterkorrespondenz 2725," *Hamburger Volkszeitung*, 16 Dec. 1932.

35. "Aus 'Wohlfahrts'-Neumanns Praxis. . . ," *Hamburger Volkszeitung*, Nr. 176, 1 Aug. 1930.

36. StAHH, SB I VG 25.11, 1 Bd., 1926–1935, Oberfürsorgerinnensitzungen, 17 Oct. 1927.

37. StAHH, SB I VG 25.11, 1 Bd., 1926–1935, Oberfürsorgerinnensitzungen, 4 Dec. 1929.

38. StAHH, Staatliche Pressestelle I–IV, 3202, 1 Bd., "Winterhilfswerk, 1929–1933"; "Niederschrift über die Besprechung des Arbeitsausschusses für das Winterhilfswerk am 25 September 1931," p. 5.

39. StAHH, Medizinalkollegium I K 27a, 5 Bd., 1932–1933, Dr. H. Strauss, An die Gesundheitsbehörde, Hamburg, 7 May 1932.

40. StAHH, Medizinalkollegium I K 27a, 5 Bd., 1932–1933, Dr. Strauss, Hamburg, 5 May 1933, An die Gesundheitsbehörde, Abteil. III, Schulärztlicher Jahresbericht.

41. "Die Schande der SPD- und naziführer. . . ," *Hamburger Volkszeitung*, Nr. 94, 22 Apr. 1932.

42. *Der Arbeitslose*, Nr. 46, 1 Beilage, Zweite Nov., Ausgabe.

43. "Frauen demonstrieren vor den Wohlfahrtsämtern. . . ," *Hamburger Volkszeitung*, Nr. 167, 21 July 1932.

44. StAHH, SB I VG 25.11, 1 Bd., Oberfürsorgerinnensitzungen, 26 Nov. 1931.

45. StAHH, SB I VG 25.11, 1 Bd., Oberfürsorgerinnensitzungen, 15 Sept. 1932.

46. StALu, F202 II-794, Bürgermeisteramt Echterdingen an das Amtsoberamt Stuttgart, 10 Oct. 1931.

47. StAHH, SB I VG 25.11, 1 Bd., 1926–1935, Oberfürsorgerinnensitzungen, 4 Dec. 1929.

48. Schmeer, "Sozialpolitik in Duisburg," p. 275.

49. Wildt, *Am Beginn der "Konsumgesellschaft,"* p. 23.

50. Schmeer, "Sozialpolitik in Duisburg," pp. 275–276, 277.

51. "Felddiebstähle nehmen zu im Zeichen der Not und der moralischen Verwahrlosung," *Rheinische Zeitung*, Cologne, Nr. 182, 4 Aug. 1932.

52. "Erwerbslos dem Elend preisgegeben: Arbeiterkorrespondenz 3785," *Hamburger Volkszeitung*, 5 Nov. 1927.

53. Karl Christian Führer, "Unterstützung und Lebensstandard der Arbeitslosen, 1918–1927," in Tenfelde, *Arbeiter im 20. Jahrhundert*, p. 284. This instruction was clearly often ignored, especially during the Depression.

54. "Wie Leben unsere Wohlfahrtserwerbslosen?" p. 32.

55. StAHH, SB I VG 24.23, Leitersitzungen, 5 Feb. 1923.

56. "Wie Leben unsere Wohlfahrtserwerbslosen?" p. 9. The Elowa, or Erwerbslosenwäsche, was "a facility of the welfare office's work-relief program. One pound [*Pfund*] of laundry could be washed, ironed, . . . and repaired here for 10 pfennig. The work was done by female welfare clients who were required to perform obligatory or welfare work."

57. Ibid., p. 26.

58. StAHH, SB I VG 25.11, 1 Bd., 1926–1935, Oberfürsorgerinnensitzungen, 19 May 1932.

59. StAHH, SB I VG 24.25, Leitersitzungen, 2 Feb. 1925.

60. StAHH, SB I VG 25.11, 1 Bd., 1926–1935, Oberfürsorgerinnensitzungen, 10 May 1932.

61. Oberregierungsrat Mailänder, Stuttgart, "Die Not der Arbeitslosen: Wie kann die freie Wohlfahrtspflege zu ihrer Linderung beitragen?" *BZWW*, Stuttgart 83 Jg., Nr. 11, Nov. 1930, pp. 223–224.

62. StAHH, SB I VG 25.11, 1 Bd., 1926–1935, Oberfürsorgerinnensitzungen, 28 Feb. 1930.

63. "Unterstützt den Streik der Pflichtarbeiter. . . ," *Hamburger Volkszeitung*, Nr. 247, 23 Oct. 1930.

64. "Wohlfahrtserwerblose sind schlimmer als die Sklaven dran," *Hamburger Volkszeitung*, 13 Oct. 1930.

65. StAHH, SB I VG 74.12, "Sicherungsmassnahmen," 1 Bd., 1923–1932. Ergebenst gez. Ad. Bussau Berufspfleger Bezirk 24, 26 July 1932, Wohlfahrtsstelle 1.

66. StAHH, SB I VG 74.12, "Sicherungsmassnahmen," Pl. 5722, Bez. 160, Ernst P. Abschrift aus der Akte der Wohlfahrtsbehorde, Blatt 12, 13, 14.

67. Ibid., 12 Dec. 1933. gez. Lüders.

68. StAHH, SB I AF 42.10, "Mieteunterstützungen," 2 Bd., 1926, Auszug aus der Niederschrift über die Referentenbesprechung, 13 July 1926, Herrn Dr. Hollburg referiert über die Aenderung des Mieterschutzgesetzes. For a detailed discussion of these measures, see Karl Christian Führer, *Mieter, Hausbesitzer, Staat und Wohnungsmarkt, 1914–1960* (Stuttgart: Franz Steiner Verlag, 1995), esp. pp. 47–116.

69. "Einrichtungen der Kölner Obdachlosenfürsorge," *Wohlfahrtsblätter der Stadt Köln*, Nr. 2/3, May/June 1926, p. 11.

70. StADü, III, 4060, Städtisches Wohlfahrts- und Gesundheitsamt-Familienfürsorgeamt II D, 7 Sept. 1929.

71. StAHH, SB I AF 42.10, "Mieteunterstützungen," 2 Bd., 1926, Auszug aus der Niederschrift uber die Referentenbesprechung, 13 July 1926.

72. StAHH, SB I AF 42.10, "Mieteunterstützungen," 3 Bd., 1927–1928, An den Herrn Senatsreferenten Dr. Lippman, 31 Mar. 1927, from Wohlfahrtsamt.

73. Dr. Max F. Michel, Frankfurt, "Der Abbau der Wohnungszwangswirtschaft und die Aufgaben der Wohlfahrtspflege," *Arbeiterwohlfahrt*, 2 Jg., 23 Heft, 1 Dec. 1927, p. 708.

74. StAHH, SB I AF 42.10, "Mieteunterstützungen," 2 Bd., 1926, Auszug aus der Niederschrift über die Leitersitzung, 19 July 1926.

75. Hagemann, *Frauenalltag und Männerpolitik*, p. 55.

76. See, for example, StAHH, SB I AF 42.10, "Mieteunterstützungen," 2 Bd., 1926, Auszug aus dem Protokoll der Beiratssitzung, 20 Aug. 1926, Wohlfahrtsstelle 7.

77. StAHH, SB I AF 42.10, "Mieteunterstützungen," 2 Bd., 1926, Bericht über die Anzahl der an die Wohlfahrts-Stellen abgegebene Mitteilungen des Amts-Gerichts.

78. StAHH, SB I AF 42.10, "Mieteunterstützungen," 2 Bd., 1926, 29 Apr. 1926, An die Finanzdeputation, Domänenverwaltung . . . Verwaltern der Staatsgrundstücke in der Alt- und Neustadt, den Herrn Groth and Gottschalk, etc.

79. StAHH, Wohnungsamt I/104, 18 Dec. 1924.

80. StAHH, SB AF 44.12, "Mieterschutz u. Mieteeinigungsämter," 1 Bd., Rundschreiben an die Herren Bezirksvorsteher und Pfleger, from Der Präses des Wohlfahrtsamtes, Paul Neumann, Hamburg, 19 Aug. 1926.

81. StAHH, SB I AF 42.10, "Mieteunterstützungen," 2 Bd., 1926, Niederschrift über die 26. Sitzung des Hauptfürsorgeauschusses 16. Aug. 1926.

82. Adelheid von Saldern, *Häuserleben: Zur Geschichte städtischen Arbeiterwohnens von Kaiserreich bis heute* (Bonn, 1975), pp. 146, 147.

83. StAHH, Allgemeine Armenanstalt II/369, 1924–1925, Bericht über die Unterbringung obdachloser Familien in Dienstgebäude der Wohlfahrtsstelle 5, Dorotheenstr. 137, Hamburg, 19 Feb. 1925, pp. 7–8.

84. StAHH, Allgemeine Armenanstalt II/369, 1924–1925), Hamburg, 21 May 1924.

85. StAHH, Wohnungsamt I/104, Hamburg, 18 Dec. 1924.

86. StAHH, SB I EF 61.51, "Beschaffung von Asylwohnungen für Obdachlose Familien," 1 Bd., 1925–1929, "Niederschrift einer Besprechung über Beschaffung von Asylwohnungen für obdachlose Familien am 31. Juli 1926 im Sitzungssaal der Baudeputation," *Wohlfahrtsamt. Jahresbericht 1925*, p. 21.

87. StAHH, SB I AF 42.10, "Mieteunterstützungen," 2 Bd., 1926, "Die Ergebnisse der Besprechung der Kommission der Vereinigung nordwestdeutscher Wohlfahrtsämter über ergänzende Unterstützung Erwerbsloser, insbesondere durch Mietegewährung am 4 August 1926 im Rathaus zu Lüneburg."

88. StAHH, SB I AF 42.10, "Mieteunterstützungen," 3 Bd., 1927–1928, Brandt, Behörde für Wohnungspflege Hamburg, 13 May 1927, An das Wohlfahrtsamt.

89. StAHH, Wohnungsamt I/104, "Niederschrift einer Besprechung vom 28. Sept. 1927 über die Beschaffung von Asylwohnungen für obdachlosen Familien."

90. Ibid., Abt. II to Martini.

91. StAHH, Sozialbehörde I EF 61.51, "Beschaffung von Asylwohnungen für Obdachlose Familien," 1 Bd., 1925–1929, Besprechung unter Vorsitz von Herrn Staatsrat Rautenberg, 25 Nov. 1925, meetings of various agencies: Welfare Office, Housing Office, Youth Office, police.

92. StAHH, Wohnungsamt I/104, Der Bürgermeister, Stadt. Wohnungsamt, Wesel, 16 Dec. 1925, An das Wohnungsamt Hamburg.

93. Adelheid von Saldern, "Arme und Obdachlose im Hannover der Weimarer Republik," in Hans-Dieter Schmid, eds., *Hannover Am Rande der Stadt*, Hannoversche Schriften zur Regional und Lokalgeschichte, 5 Bd. (Bielefeld: Verlag für Regionalgeschichte, 1992), p. 244.

94. StADü, III, 4059, Stadtverband für Frauenbestrebungen, Kath. Deutscher Frauenbund, Abschrift, Denkschrift für die Obdachlosenfürsorge, 15 July 1929.

95. StADü, III, 4060, 20 Jan. 1931.

96. StADü, III, 4059, *Verwaltungsbericht*, 1925–1927.

97. StADü, III, 4059, 27 Dec. 1926.

98. StADü, III, 4059, 25 July 1929.

99. StADü, III, 4060, 26 June 1930.

100. Von Saldern, *Häuserleben*, pp. 142–145.

101. Georg Schumann, M.d.R., Thüringen, "Die Mieterschaft muss kämpfen!" *Proletarische Sozialpolitik*, 5 Jg., 9 Heft, Sept. 1932, p. 275.

102. Dr. Hanna Meuter, *Heimlosigkeit und Familienleben* (Eberswalde bei Berlin: Verlagsgesellschaft R. Müller, 1932), pp. 26–27.

103. StAHH, Wohnungsamt I/109, "Niederschrift über die Besprechung am Montag, dem 2 November 1931 11 Uhr, im Sitzungssaal der Finanzdeputation." In 1931, Hamburg welfare authorities were able to provide some amount of rent support in 20,719 cases; however, this figure dropped to 12,976 in 1932. *SJFHH*, 1932/33, p. 163.

104. StAHH, SB I VG 25. 11, 1 Bd., 1926–1935, Oberfürsorgerinnensitzungen, 13 Oct. 1930.

105. StAHH, Wohnungsamt I/109, "Niederschrift über die Besprechung am Montag, dem 2 November 1931 11 Uhr, im Sitzungssaal der Finanzdeputation."

106. Karl Christian Führer, "Managing Scarcity: The German Housing Shortgage and the Controlled Economy, 1914–1990," *German History, The Journal of the German History Society* 13, no. 3 (1995): 335.

107. StAHH, Wohnungsamt I/109, "Niederschrift über die Besprechung am Montag, dem 2 November 1931 11 Uhr, im Sitzungssaal der Finanzdeputation."

108. Schumann, "Die Mieterschaft muss kämpfen!" p. 275.

109. StAHH, Wohnungsamt I/109, "Niederschrift über die Besprechung am Montag, dem 2 November 1931 11 Uhr, im Sitzungssaal der Finanzdeputation," pp. 3–4.

110. "Exmittierungskommission erzwingt Aufschub," *Hamburger Volkszeitung*, Nr. 195, 16 Nov. 1931.

111. "Dem Gerichtsvollzieher die Arbeit abgenommen," *Hamburger Volkszeitung*, Nr. 213, 8 Dec. 1931.

112. StAHH, Wohnungsamt I/109, "Niederschrift über die Besprechung am Montag, dem 2 November 1931 11 Uhr, im Sitzungssaal der Finanzdeputation."

113. StAKöln, 902, Nr. 198, Fasc. 4, pp. 501–596, 28 June 1932.

114. *Soziale Praxis*, 36 Heft, 3 Sept. 1931, p. 1214, Abschrift in StAHH, Arbeitsbehörde I/161, "Planung vorstädtischer Kleinsiedlungen u. Überlassung von Gartenland an Erwerbslose 1931–1933."

115. Schumann, "Die Mieterschaft muss kämpfen!" p. 275.

116. StADü, III, 4052, 29 Sept. 1931.

117. StAHH, SB I VG 25.11, 1 Bd., 1925–1936, Oberfürsorgerinnensitzungen, 22 Oct. 1932.

118. StAHH, SB I VG 24.32, Leitersitzungen, 19 Oct. 1932.

119. StAHH, SB I VG 25.11, 1 Bd., 1925–1936, Oberfürsorgerinnensitzungen, 4 May 1933.

120. See Adelheid von Saldern, "Kommunale Verarmung und Armut in den Kommunen während der grossen Krise (1929 bis 1933): Am Beispiel der Finanz- und Wohnungs(bau)-politik," *Soziale Bewegungen: Geschichte und Theorie, Jahrbuch 3, Armut und Ausgrenzung* (Frankfurt: Campus Verlag, 1987), p. 69.

121. See "Neues Leben blüht aus den Ruinen . . . ," in Projektgruppe Arbeiterkultur Hamburg, eds., *Vorwärts—und nicht vergessen: Arbeiterkultur in Hamburg um 1930* (Berlin, 1980), p. 54; see also StAHH, Pressestelle I–IV, 3251, Erwerbslosenselbsthilfe Gross-Hamburg e.V., 1932–1933.

122. "Selbsthilfe der Erwerbslosen: 'Arbeiten aus Hilfswillen und dem Geist der Zeit,'" in Projektgruppe Arbeiterkultur Hamburg, eds., *Vorwärts—und nicht vergessen*, p. 56.

123. See Eifert, *Frauenpolitik und Wohlfahrtspflege*, pp. 79–83, 95–97.

124. See, for example, "Ein Aufruf der Erwerbslosenselbsthilfe: Notruf an alle Schaffenden," *Hamburger Echo*, Nr. 198, 18 Aug. 1932.

125. See StAHH, Staatliche Pressestelle I–IV, 3201, 1 Bd., "Winterhilfswerk, 1929–1933," p. 42.

126. StAHH, SB I VG 24.32, 1 Bd., 1932, Leitersitzungen, 23 Mar. 1932.

127. StAHH, SB I VG 24.31, Leitersitzungen, 2 Dec. 1931.

128. "Leben und doch nicht verzweifeln! . . . ," *Rheinische Zeitung*, Cologne, Nr. 160, 9–10 July 1932.

129. Stadtverordneter Geisler (KP), SV-Dü, Nr. 6, Sitzung, 26 June 1931, p. 178.

130. StAHH, SB I VG 24.33, Leitersitzungen, 9 Mar. 1933.

131. StAHH, Pressestelle I–IV, 3334, "Massnahmen gegen Schwarzarbeit, 1931–1933," press release, printed in Hamburg newspapers, 7 Jan. 1931.

132. Stadtverordneter Schöpwinkel, Wirtschaftsbund, SV-Dü, Nr. 3, Sitzung, 15 Mar. 1929, p. 62.

133. Helene Simon, "Arbeitslosigkeit, Doppelverdiener, Kindererwerbsarbeit (Fortsetzung)," *Soziale Praxis*, 40 Jg., 30 Heft, 1931, p. 997.

134. Ruth Weiland, "Kinderarbeit," *Arbeiterwohlfahrt*, 8 Jg., 10 Heft, 15 May 1933, pp. 289–292; see also Hubert R. Knickerbocker, *German Crises* (New York, 1932).

135. Weiland, "Kinderarbeit," pp. 289–292.

Chapter Ten

1. The title of this chapter is from the German headline, "Wohlfahrtspflege ist Erhaltung der Arbeitskraft!" attributed to the Cologne newspaper *Stadt-Anzeiger* by the Communist *Sozialistische Republik* in an article "Stadt-Anzeiger lobt Arbeitsfürsorge in Köln: Wie sie in Wirklichkeit aussieht," *Sozialistische Republik*, 22 July 1929.

2. Führer, "Unterstützung und Lebensstandard der Arbeitslosen, 1918–1927," pp. 281, 283, 286, 277–280.

3. Susanne Rouette, *Sozialpolitik als Geschlechterpolitik: Die Regulierung der Frauenarbeit nach dem Ersten Weltkrieg* (Frankfurt: Campus Verlag, 1993), p. 232.

4. Karl Christian Führer, *Arbeitslosigkeit und die Entstehung der Arbeitslosenversicherung in Deutschland, 1902–1927* (Berlin, 1990), pp. 489–492; Rouette, *Sozialpolitik als Geschlechterpolitik*, pp. 249–250.

5. Rouette, *Sozialpolitik als Geschlechterpolitik*, pp. 249–250.

6. Führer, *Arbeitslosigkeit*, p. 492.

7. Kramer, "Frankfurt's Working Women," p. 133.

8. Harvey, *Youth and the Welfare State*, p. 117.

9. Gräser, *Der blockierte Wohlfahrtsstaat*, pp. 181–182.

10. Führer, "Unterstützung und Lebensstandard der Arbeitslosen, 1918–1927," p. 287.

11. StAHH, SB I VG 24.22, Leitersitzungen, 2 Jan. 1922; SB I VG 24.23, Leitersitzungen, 17 Dec. 1923, 6 Oct. 1923; SB I VG 24.24, Leitersitzungen, 4 Feb. 1924, 18 Feb. 1924.

12. StAHH, SB I VG 24.24, Leitersitzungen, 17 Mar. 1924; see also 23 June 1924 and SB I VG 24.25, Leitersitzungen, 7 Dec. 1925.

13. Von Saldern, "Kommunale Verarmung," p. 76.

14. Ayass, *"Asoziale" im Nationalsozialismus*, p. 19.

15. "Tab. 1. Die im Jahr 1929 Unterstützten und Höhe des Aufwandes," in *Statistisches Jahrbuch für die Freie und Hansestadt Hamburg 1929/30*, ed. Statistisches Landesamt (Hamburg: Kommissionsverlag von Lutcke and Wulff, 1930), pp. 298–299. By 1932, this had risen to 61.2 percent. See *Statistisches Jahrbuch für die Freie und Hansestadt Hamburg*, 1932/33, ed. Statistisches Landesamt (Hamburg: Kommissionsverlag von Lütcke and Wulff, 1933), p. 161.

16. "Tab. 3. Die von der Wohlfahrtsbehörde laufend unterstützten erwerbslosen Arbeitsfähigen am 16. Februar 1929, c) Die Unterstützten nach der Berufszugehörigkeit," *Statistisches Jahrbuch für die Freie und Hansestadt Hamburg, 1928/29*, ed. Statistisches Landesamt (Hamburg: Kommissionsverlag von Lütcke and Wulff, 1929), pp. 296, 297.

17. StAHH, SB I AF 42.10, "Mieteunterstützungen," 2 Bd., 1926, Rundschreiben an die Herren Bezirksvorsteher u Pfleger, 19 Aug. 1926.

18. Frau Stadtdirektorin Dr. Kraus, Cologne, "Aussprache," in *Arbeitsfürsorge: Bericht über den 40. Deutschen Fürsorgetag in Hamburg 23. bis 25 Mai 1927*, Neue Folgen der

Schriften des Deutschen Vereins für öffentliche und private Fürsorge, 11 Heft (Karlsruhe: Verlag G. Braun, 1927), p. 55.

19. Dr. Frida Wunderlich, Berlin, "Die Arbeitsfürsorge für hilfsbedürftige Personen vom Standpunkt der Wirtschaft und der Wohlfahrtspflege," in ibid., pp. 3–4, 19–20, 18.

20. StAHH, SB I AW 00.54, Betrifft Pflichtarbeiter, Hamburg, 15 May 1930, An die Wohlfahrtsbehörde, Abtlg. Unterstützungsarbeit zu Hd. Herrn Regierungsrat Dr. Marx.

21. "Arbeitsfürsorge für Wohlfahrtserwerbslose," Nach einem von Präsident Martini vor Beamten und Angestellten der Wohlfahrtsbehörde gehaltenen Vortrag, *Jugend und Volkswohl*, 5 Jg., Nr. 9/10, Dec. 1929/Jan. 1930, p. 153.

22. "Fürsorgeamt und Wirtschaftskrise," *Wohlfahrtsblatt der Freien Hansestadt Bremen*, 2 Jg., Nr. 6, Bremen, Mar. 1930, p. 44.

23. StAHH, Pressestelle I–IV, 3204, *Hamburger Anzeiger*, Nr. 41, 18 Feb. 1930; see also *Hamburger Fremdenblatt*, Nr. 49, 18 Feb. 1930.

24. Martini, "Arbeitsfürsorge für Wohlfahrtserwerbslose," p. 160.

25. StAHH, SB I AW 00.65, Zusammenfassende Berichte und Übersichten über Arbeitsgelegenheiten für Wohlfahrtserwerbslose, 3 Bd., 1931–1932.

26. StAHH, SB I VG 24.30, Leitersitzungen, 17 Mar. 1930, p. 70, 5 May 1930, p. 89. By August 1930, about 20 percent of the unemployed in Hamburg who were welfare clients received work relief.

27. StAHH, SB I AW 00.54, Arbeitsfürsorge, Angriffe, und Beschwerden, 1928–1931, Hamburg, 5 Jan. 1930, Baustelle, Badeanstalt Farmsen-Arbeitsfürsorge, Ergebenst für die Belegschaft I. A.

28. StAHH, SB I AW 00.54, 11 Nov. 1929, An die Wohlfahrtsbehörde, Abt. Arbeitsfürsorge.

29. StAHH, SB I AW 00.54, Flugblatt, "Der Pranger der Baustelle" or "Der Wohlfahrtssklave" (probably Sept. 1930).

30. StAHH, SB I AW 00.54, Hamburg, 2 Dec. 1929, Betrifft Baustelle Badeanstalt Farmsen An die Wohlfahrtsbehörde, Abtlg. Arbeitsfürsorge, Ergebenst für die Belegschaft, Die Vertrauensleute.

31. StAHH, SB I AW 00.54.

32. StAHH, SB I AW 00.54, Hamburg, 20 Jan. 1930, Ergebenst I. A., Albert N., Hbgr. 21, Winterhudeweg 49, Hs 4, Obmann (his reports and letters are typed or mimeographed). Albert N. was listed as a Kaufmann in the *Hamburger Adressbuch* 936-IV, 1930.

33. StAHH, SB I AW 00.54, Albert N. speaking at meeting of Obleute and delegates from several public building sites in Hamburg, 2 Feb. 1930.

34. StAHH, SB I AW 00.54, petition signed by 34 workers, 11 Nov. 1929, An die Wohlfahrtsbehörde, Abteilung Arbeitsfürsorge. The Works Councils Law (Betriebsrätegesetz) of 4 February 1920 provided for the election of councils by the employees (manual and white collar) of enterprises employing at least twenty people. The councils were meant to represent the interests of employees within the firm, but their powers to influence hiring, firing, and social measures and to exercise oversight were quite limited. See Preller, *Sozialpolitik in der Weimarer Republik*, pp. 249–252.

35. StAHH, SB I AW 00.54, petition signed by 34 workers, 11 Nov. 1929, An die Wohlfahrtsbehörde, Abteilung Arbeitsfürsorge.

36. StAHH, SB I AW 00.54, Hamburg, 20 Jan. 1930, to "Wohlfahrtsbehörde, Arbeitsfürsorge, hohen Senat, Bürgerschaft, Hamburger Presse," employers' associations, trade unions, and "the producers of all estates."

37. StAHH, SB I AW 00.54, Hamburg, 2 Feb. 1930.

38. StAHH, SB I AW 00.54, Hamburg, 2 Feb. 1930, Der Kommission für Pflicht und Facharbeiter I. A. Nitzschke, Niebuhr.

39. StAHH, SB I AW 00.54, n.d., follows newspaper article.

40. "Arbeitsfürsorge für Frauen in Riehl," *Wohlfahrtsblätter der Stadt Köln*, Nr. 8/9, Nov./ Dec. 1926, ed. Wohlfahrtsamt der Stadt Köln in monatlicher Folge, pp. 33–34.

41. Rouette, *Sozialpolitik als Geschlechterpolitik*, p. 259.

42. Silke Schütter, "Arbeitlosigkeit, Arbeitsmarkt, und Arbeitsmarktpolitik in den Altkreisen Beckum und Warendorf, 1918 bis 1927," *Westfälische Forschungen*, 43, no. (1993): 226.

43. Herta Kraus, *Work Relief in Germany* (New York: Russell Sage Foundation, 1934), pp. 63, 55, 57.

44. "Wäschereiarbeiterinnen unter der Knute: Die Notstandsarbeiterinnen in der Riehler Heimstätte (Notstandsarbeiterinnen-Korrespondenz)," *Sozialistische Republik*, Cologne, 29 July 1932.

45. "Die Frau als Pflichtarbeiterin," StAHH, SB I VG 25.11, 1 Bd., 1926–1935, Ober-fürsorgerinnensitzungen, 28 Feb. 1930.

46. Schlüter, "Sozialpolitik und Sozialfürsorge," p. 274.

47. Ayass, *"Asoziale" im Nationalsozialismus*, p. 58.

48. Wolfgang Ayass, *Das Arbeitshaus Breitenau: Bettler, Landstreicher, Prostituierte, Zuhälter, und Fürsorgeempfänger in der Korrektions- und Landesarmenanstalt Breitenau (1874–1949)* (Kassel: Verein für hessische Geschichte und Landeskunde, 1992), pp. 179, 189, 243, 245, 246, 247; see also Ayass, *"Asoziale" im Nationalsozialismus*, pp. 13–18.

49. Ayass, *Breitenau*, p. 249.

50. Christiane Rothmaler, "'. . . um sie nachher in der offenen Fürsorge gefügig und arbeitswillig zu machen: Der Fürsorgerechtliche Arbeitszwang in der Weimarer Republik und im Nationalsozialismus," in Christiane Rothmaler and Evelyn Glensk, eds., *Kehrseiten der Wohlfahrt: Die Hamburger Fürsorge auf ihrem Wege von der Weimarer Republik in den Nationalsozialismus* (Hamburg: Ergebnisse Verlag, 1992), pp. 243–245.

51. StAHH, SB I VG 24.22, Leitersitzungen, 31 July 1922.

52. StAHH, SB I VG 24.23, Leitersitzungen, 19 Feb. 1923.

53. StAHH, SB I VG 24.26, Leitersitzungen, 15 Feb. 1926.

54. Fenner, *Durch Arbeit zur Arbeit erzogen*, pp. 93–94, 138.

55. August Brandt, *Gefesselte Jugend in der Zwangsfürsorgeerziehung* (Berlin, [1929]), p. 6, quoted in Fenner, *Durch Arbeit zur Arbeit erzogen*, p. 138.

56. See Harvey, *Youth and the Welfare State*, pp. 113–151, and Führer, *Arbeitslosigkeit*, pp. 487–505.

57. Führer, *Arbeitslosigkeit*, p. 503.

58. Harvey, *Youth and the Welfare State*, p. 117. The so-called Voluntary Labor Service (Freiwilliger Arbeitsdienst; FAD), the Brüning government's "main initiative to deal with mass youth unemployment," assumed increasing importance as local authorities ran out of funds to support their own work schemes. Right-wing nationalists "wanted to see the scheme paving the way for the introduction of general labor conscription for all young men." See Harvey, *Youth and the Welfare State*, p. 137. See also StAHH, Pressestelle I–IV, 334a, "Freiwilliger Arbeitsdienst: Arbeitsdienstpflicht, 1933–1934."

59. See, for example, "Die 'Arbeitsfürsorge' der Wohlfahrtsämter," *Proletarische Sozial-politik*, 1 Jg., 2 Heft, July 1928, p. 41.

60. "Neumanns Wohlfahrt in der Welt voran!: Arbeiterkorrespondenz 1854," *Hamburger Volkszeitung*, Nr. 125, 2 June 1930. This reference is particularly ironic as Hahnöfersand, Hamburg's youth prison on an island in the Elbe, had gained considerable publicity as a pro-gressive educational experiment conducted in the early 1920s by Walter Herrmann and Curt Bondy, who were in turn inspired by Karl Wilker's work in the Berlin reformatory, Lindenhof. These reforms "sought to build up a more intensive pedagogical relationship between staff

and inmates, to involve inmates actively in discussions and decisions concerning prison routine, and to create a progressive regime stressing incentives and rewards for good behaviour as well as punishments for misbehaviour." Harvey, *Youth and the Welfare State*, p. 212.

61. See Eckart Pankoke, *Die Arbeitsfrage: Arbeitsmoral, Beschäftigungskrisen und Wohlfahrtspolitik im Industriezeitalter* (Frankfurt: Suhrkamp Verlag, 1990), pp. 138–168.

62. See especially Keith Tribe, ed., *Social Democracy and the Rule of Law: Otto Kirchheimer and Franz Neumann* (London: Allen and Unwin, 1987).

63. Reproduced in ibid., pp. 199, 200–201.

64. "Die rechtliche Lage der 'Wohlfahrts-Arbeiter,'" *Proletarische Sozialpolitik*, 2 Jg., 1 Heft, Jan. 1929, pp. 200–201.

65. "Eine wichtige Entscheidung des Landesarbeitsgerichts Düsseldorf über tarifliche Entlohnung von Wohlfahrtserwerbslosen," *Proletarische Sozialpolitik*, 1 Jg., 7 Heft, Berlin, Dec. 1928, p. 209.

66. "Die rechtliche Lage der 'Wohlfahrts-Arbeiter,'" *Proletarische Sozialpolitik*, 2 Jg., 1 Heft, Jan. 1929, pp. 200–202.

67. Johanna Piiper, *Die Frauenpolitik der KPD in Hamburg, 1928 bis 1933* (Cologne: Pahl-Rugenstein Verlag, 1988), pp. 70–71.

68. StALu, E191 3928, W. Landeskriminalpolizeiamt, 26 June 1925, Württ. Polizeipräsidium Stuttgart.

69. Piiper, *Die Frauenpolitik der KFD*, p. 70.

70. McElligott, "Mobilising the Unemployed," pp. 241–242, 233, 236.

71. *Der Arbeitslose*, Nr. 46, 1 Beilage, Zweite Nov. Ausgabe, "Organisatorische Richtlinien zum Ausbau der Erwerbslosenbewegung," Apr. 1931.

72. Rosenhaft, "Communisms and Communities," p. 229.

73. StAHH, SB I AW 00.93, "Bewegungen gegen die Unterstützungsarbeit (Sammelakte mit 5 Einzelakten) 1930–31," 9 Aug. 1930, *Hamburger Volkszeitung*, Nr. 239, 14 Oct. 1930.

74. StAHH, SB I AW 00.93, *Hamburger Anzeiger*, 15 Apr. 1930, *Hamburger Echo*, 16 Oct. 1930.

75. "Einstellung der Notstandsarbeiten-Entlassung der Notstandsarbeiter," *Hamburger Anzeiger*, Nr. 197, 25 Aug. 1931.

76. Donna Harsch, *German Social Democracy and the Rise of Nazism* (Chapel Hill, N.C.: University of North Carolina Press, 1993), pp. 214–215, referring here to the fall of 1932.

77. Siegfried Wagner, Dresden, "In den Betrieben—An den Stempelstellen: Eine notwendige Aufgabe der Partei in der Gegenwart," *Der Klassenkampf*, 5 Jg., Nr. 4, 1931, pp. 116–117.

78. StAHH, SB I VG 73.11, "Erwerbslosen-Ausschüsse und ähnl, 1929–1933," n.d.; Flugblatt from Barmbeck-Zentrum, 19, 13 Feb. 1933; see also StAHH, Handschrift 1754.

79. StAHH, SB I VG 73.11, "Erwerbslosen-Ausschüsse und ähnl, 1929–1933," n.d.

80. Walter Auerbach, Berlin, "Was wollen die Nationalsozialisten in den Gemeinden," *Die Gemeinde*, 8 Jg., 1931, pp. 493–494.

81. Anton Dey, Offenbach, "Nationalsozialismus und Wohlfahrtspflege," *Die Gemeinde*, 9 Jg., 1932, p. 410.

82. See, for example, "Und nochmals die Wohlfahrt . . . ," *Hamburger Tageblatt*, Nr. 116, 19 May 1932.

83. "Ein Wohlfahrtserwerbsloser schreibt an Senator Neumann," *Hamburger Tageblatt*, Nr. 194, 26 Aug. 1932.

84. StAHH, SB I AW 00.54.

85. StAHH, SB I AW 00.54, Hamburg, 6 Apr. 1930, to Marx.

86. Ibid., signed Der Obleute der Fürsorge-arbeiter Ohlsdorf, Franz Schlomsky, Karl Schulz.

Conclusion

1. StALu, E180 II-V-76, Ministerialabteilung für Bezirks- und Körperschaftsverwaltung, Sozialrentnerfürsorge G-J, 1924–1943, "An die Kriminalabteilung z.h. der behandelten Krimm. Kommissar" from Adolf G., Canstatt, 21 Oct. 1931.

2. Peukert, "Wohlfahrtsstaat und Lebenswelt," p. 348.

3. Sen. Paul Neumann, Wohlfahrtsamt, "Von Armenpflege zur sozialen Fürsorge," *Hamburger Echo*, Nr. 32, 1 Feb. 1928.

4. StALu, F181 III-676, Victor Gretsch, Feuerbach to OA Ludwigsburg, 27 Oct. 1932, on being required to contribute to the support of an estranged daughter. On Else Kienle and her colleague Friedrich Wolf, see Grossmann, *Reforming Sex*, pp. 87–88.

5. Egighian, "The Politics of Victimization," pp. 400–401.

6. Rosenhaft observes, however, that the KPD's efforts always "stopped short at the mechanical functions of 'reaching out' and 'mobilizing' [women] as one of a series of 'allied strata.'" See Rosenhaft, "Communisms and Communities," p. 228.

7. StALu, F164 II-725, Oberamt Esslingen, Esslingen, 24 Feb. 1926, An das verehrl. OA Esslingen; Beschwerdesache des Kriegsbeschädigten Emil N. gegen Geschäftsführer S. bei BFB-E.

8. Rosenhaft, "Communisms and Communities," p. 229.

9. Fischer and Heimann, *Deutsche Kindheiten 1932*, pp. 202–203.

10. On the power of representations, see Walkowitz, *City of Dreadful Delight*, pp. 7–10.

11. Habermas recognizes that the "form of the administratively prescribed treatment by an expert is for the most part in contradiction with the aim of the therapy, namely, that of promoting the client's independence and self-reliance," but he does not explore the gendered aspects of this contradiction. Habermas, *Lifeworld and System*, p. 363.

12. Nancy Fraser, "Struggle over Needs: Outline of a Socialist-Feminist Critical Theory of Late-Capitalist Political Culture," in Linda Gordon, ed., *Women, the State, and Welfare* (Madison: University of Wisconsin Press, 1990), pp. 215–216.

13. Lüdtke, *Eigen-Sinn*; Lindenberger, *Strassenpolitik*, p. 16.

14. Lindenberger, *Strassenpolitik*, pp. 17–18.

15. Dick Hebdige, "Hiding in the Light: Youth Surveillance and Display," in Dick Hebdige, *Hiding in the Light: On Images and Things* (London: Routledge, 1989), pp. 17–36.

16. Peukert, *Inside Nazi Germany*, p. 243.

17. Habermas, *Lifeworld and System*, p. 363, quoting E. Reidegeld, "Vollzugsdefizite sozialer Leistungen," in R. Voigt, ed., *Verrechtlichung* (Frankfurt, 1980), p. 281.

18. Stadtrat Dr. Hans Muthesius, Berlin-Schöneberg, "Fürsorge und fürsorgerische Haltung," *Jugend und Volkswohl*, Feb. 1933, 8 Jg., Nr. 5, p. 133.

19. "Mensch und Amt in der Fürsorge: Von einer in der kommunalen Fürsorge tätigen Diakonisse," *IM*, 1932, p. 112.

20. Louise Schroeder, M.d.R., Altona, "Gemeinden und Fürsorge," *Die Gemeinde*, 10 Jg., 5/6 Heft, 1–2 Mar. 1933, p. 221.

21. Bopp, *Die Wohlfahrtspflege des modernen deutschen Sozialsmus*, pp. 79, 83.

22. See, for example, Lic. Steinweg, Dahlem, "Zur gegenwärtigen Lage in der Wohlfahrtspflege," *IM*, 22 Jg., 1927, pp. 67–68.

23. Stadtrat Plath, Berlin-Steglitz, "Alte und neue Wohlfahrtspflege," *Berliner Wohlfahrtsblatt*, 2 Jg., Nr. 10, Oct. 1926, p. 147.

24. Vöhringer, "Sparmassnahmen für das Gebiet der freien Wohlfahrtspflege," *BZWW*, 80 Jg., Nr. 1, Stuttgart, Jan. 1927, p. 1.

25. StAHH, SB I EF 12.14, "Zusammenarbeit zwischen öffentlicher und privater Wohlfahrtspflege," 1 Bd., 1921–1930, *Hamburger Correspondent*, 7 May 1927, "Staatliche und freie Wohlfahrtspflege, Stuttgart 6 Mai."

26. Regierungsrat Mailänder, "Geist und Formen der neuzeitlichen Wohlfahrtspflege," *BZWW*, Nr. 10/11, May 1925, p. 76.

27. Jannasch, *Alarm des Herzens*, p. 6.

28. "Hamburgs neue Wohlfahrt und alte Armenpflege," *Hamburger Nachrichten*, 6 Nov. 1932.

29. Josef Beeking, "Behördliche und private Jugendfürsorge," *Jugendwohl*, Jg. 11, 1922, pp. 1–2, quoted in Bopp, *Die Wohlfahrtspflege des modernen deutschen Sozialismus*, p. 79.

30. Bopp, *Die Wohlfahrtspflege des modernen deutschen Sozialismus*, p. 77.

31. Friedrich Dessauer, *Philosophie der Technik*, 107, cited in Franz Keller, *Caritas*, 33 Jg., 1928, p. 9, quoted in ibid., p. 68.

32. Quoted in Bopp, *Die Wohlfahrtspflege des modernen deutschen Sozialismus*, p. 85.

33. Ibid., p. 87.

34. Dr. Karl Bopp, review of Helene Wessel, *Lebenshaltung aus Fürsorge und aus Erwerbstätigkeit* (Eberswalde-Berlin: R. Muller, 1931), *Caritas*, 1932, p. 107.

35. Hans Stichler, Rothenburg o.T., "Staat, Volk, Soziale Fürsorge," *Caritas*, 1931, pp. 454–457.

36. Kaiser, "Freie Wohlfahrtsverbände in Kaiserreich," p. 50.

37. "Die freie Fürsorge und die Not der Gegenwart," *BZWW*, 84 Jg., Nr. 8, Stuttgart, Aug. 1931, p. 137.

38. Oberregierungsrat Mailänder, Stuttgart, "Die Not der Arbeitslosen," *BZWW*, 83 Jg., Nr. 11, Nov. 1930, pp. 222, 223–224.

39. StALu, E191 4667, Bezirkswohltätigkeitsverein Rottweil, Geschäftsübersicht über die Kalenderjahre 1931 u 1932, Rottweil, 29 May 1933.

40. StALu, E191 4667, Rechenschaftsbericht des Bezirkswohltätigkeitsverein Mergentheim für das Jahr 1932.

41. StALu, E191 4607, Rechenschaftsbericht des Bezirkswohltätigkeitsverein Rottenburg für das Jahr 1932/33, Rottenburg, 16 Nov. 1933.

42. Kaiser, "Freie Wohlfahrtsverbände in Kaiserreich," p. 50.

43. Stichler, "Staat, Volk, Soziale Fürsorge," p. 457.

44. Dr. rer. pol. Alfred Depuhl, Hanover, "Winterhilfe eines evangelischen Landeswohlfahrtsdienstes," *Innere Mission*, 27 Jg., 2 Heft, Feb. 1932, p. 33.

45. See D. Adolf Stahl-Wiesbaden, "Oeffentliche und freie Jugendwohlfahrtspflege im neuen Staat," *IM*, 1933, p. 130; "Der Neue Geist in der Wohlfahrtspflege," *Schleswig-Holsteinische Wohlfahrtsblätter*, 8 Jg., Nr. 3, Kiel, May 1933, p. 34.

46. "Gegen die rote Herrschaft in der Wohlfahrtsbehörde: Schafft mit den Nationalsozialisten reinen Tisch! Wählt Liste 2! Wählt Hitler," *Hamburger Tageblatt*, Nr. 93, 20 Apr. 1932.

47. Kaiser, "Freie Wohlfahrtsverbände in Kaiserreich," p. 50.

48. Dr. Hanna Hellinger, "Möglichkeiten und Schwierigkeiten grossstädtischer familienfürsorgerischer Arbeit der Gegenwart," *Arbeiterwohlfahrt*, 8 Jg., 6 Heft, 15 Mar. 1933, pp. 162, 165.

49. Martini, "Herz und Verstand in der öffentlichen Fürsorge," *Wohlfahrtsblatt der freien Hansestadt Bremen*, p. 17.

50. StAHH, SB I VG 74.12, 1 Bd., Schreiben an Amtsgerichtspräsidenten Dr. Blunk, Der Präsident des Wohlfahrtsamts, 8 Oct. 1930.

51. "Die gegenwärtige Lage in der Fürsorge," *Jugend und Volkswohl*, 10/11 Heft, Jan./Feb. 1931, p. 209.

52. Ayass, *"Asoziale" im Nationalsozialismus*, p. 61.

53. Richard Claussen, "Die Arbeitsfürsorge für ausgesteuerte Erwerbslose," *Schleswig-Holsteinische Wohlfahrtsblätter*, 5 Jg., Nr. 7, Kiel, July 1929, p. 165.

54. "Arbeitsfürsorge für Wohlfahrtserwerbslose," *Jugend und Volkswohl*, 5 Jg., Nr. 9/10, Dec. 1929/Jan. 1930, p. 157.

55. Uwe Lohalm, "Die Wohlfahrtskrise, 1930–1933: Vom ökonomischen Notprogramm zur rassenhygienischen Neubestimmung," in Frank Bajohr, Werne Johe, and Uwe Lohalm, eds., *Zivilisation und Barbarei: Die widersprüchlichen Potentiale der Moderne: Detlev Peukert zum Gedenken* (Hamburg: Christians Verlag, 1991), p. 204.

56. Sachsse and Tennstedt, *Geschichte der Armenfürsorge in Deutschland*, 3 Bd., p. 72.

57. "Die Wohlfahrtsbehörde im neuen Staat. Senator v. Allwörden vor den Beamten seiner Behörde," *Hamburger Fremdenblatt*, 28 July 1933.

58. Ayass, *"Asoziale" im Nationalsozialismus*, p. 120.

59. Ibid., pp. 59, 74, 60; figures for Bremen and Düsseldorf are on pp. 59–60; see also p. 85.

60. Roland Müller, *Stuttgart zur Zeit des Nationalsozialismus* (Stuttgart: Konrad Theiss Verlag, 1988), p. 85.

61. Ayass, *"Asoziale" im Nationalsozialismus*, pp. 76, 61–63, 69, 77.

62. See also Lisa Pine, "Hashude: The Imprisonment of 'Asocial' Families in the Third Reich," *German History: The Journal of the German History Society* 13, no. 2 (1995): 182–197.

63. Michael Burleigh and Wolfgang Wippermann, *The Racial State: Germany, 1933–1945* (Cambridge: Cambridge University Press, 1991).

64. Ayass, *"Asoziale" im Nationalsozialismus*, p. 222.

65. Adelheid von Saldern, "Victims or Perpetrators? Controversies about the Role of Women in the Nazi State," in David F. Crew, ed., *Nazism and German Society, 1933–1945* (London: Routledge, 1994), p. 149.

66. Ayass, *"Asoziale" im Nationalsozialismus*, pp. 113, 222–223.

Bibliography

Archival Materials

The following list gives the *Bestände* used in each archive; individual files used within each *Bestand* are not listed separately.

Hauptstaatsarchiv Düsseldorf (Kalkum), Regierung Düsseldorf, 254, 264, 268, 572, 33507, 33512, 33513, 34269.

Hauptstaatsarchiv Stuttgart, E 151 i I, E 151 i II, E 151 i III, E 151 f II.

Staatsarchiv Hamburg, Allgemeine Armenanstalt II, Jugendbehörde I, Medizinal-Kollegium, Sozialbehörde I–II, Staatliche Pressestelle I–IV, Wohnungsamt.

Staatsarchiv Ludwigsburg, E180 II-V-68, 69, 71, 73, 74, 75, 76, 79, 80, 1426; E191 4106, 4108, 4115, 4312–4339, 5504, 5753, 5807, 5808, 5809; E258 II; F154 II; F164-II-715, 722, 723, 725, 727, 732, 736, 737, 738, 739; F177 II-312–316; F181 III-676, 677; F202 II-791, 792, 794, 795, 796; F210 II-967.

Stadtarchiv Bochum, Sozialamt, Bo 50, Bo 500/39, Bo 500/297(2), Bo 500/298.

Stadtarchiv Dortmund, Stadtverwaltung 1815–1929, Bestand 3–971–984; Polizeiverwaltung, Bestand 536, 537, 538.

Stadtarchiv Düsseldorf, III 4048, 4049, 4050, 4051, 4052, 4054, 4056, 4059, 4060, 4061, 4065, 4071,4072, 5149,5425, 7858, 7860, 7878, 11636, 11643.

Stadtarchiv Essen, Rep. 102, Abt 1, Nr. 575, Nr. 1099; Abt 22, Nr. 168, Nr. 179.

Stadtarchiv Frankfurt, Stadtverordneten-Versammlung 1.736, 1.685, 1.857, 1.869, 1.880, 1.865, 1.8691, 1.737, 1.868, 1.694, 1.738, 1.706, 1.909, 1.777, 1.784, 1.734, 1.803, 1.878, 1.841, 1.751.

Stadtarchiv Köln, 535; 610; 902, Nr. 198, Fasc. 3, pp. 501–1052; 903, Nr. 171, 176, 194, 258, 317, 334; 904; 905; 1138.

Contemporary Printed Sources

Articles from the contemporary periodicals consulted most extensively for this study are not listed individually.

Periodical Volumes: Series

Arbeiterwohlfahrt. Ed. Hauptausschuss der Arbeiterwohlfahrt. 1 (1926) to 8 (1933).
Berliner Wohlfahrtsblatt. Ed. Zentralarbeitsgemeinschaft der öffentlichen und freien Wohlfahrtspflege in Berlin. 1 (1925) to 9 (1933).
Blätter der Zentralleitung für Wohltätigkeit in Württemberg, Neue Folge, 71 (1918) to 86 (1933).
Blätter für die Wohlfahrtspflege (Sachsen). Ed. Sächsisches Landesamt für Wohlfahrtspflege. 1 (1921) to 5 (1925).
Caritas: Zeitschrift für Caritaswissenschaft und Caritasarbeit. Ed. Deutscher Caritasverband, Neue Folge, 1 Jg. (1922) to 12 (1933).
Der Rentner. 1924 to 1932.
Der sozialistische Arzt. Zeitschrift des Vereins sozialistischer Aerzte. 2 (1927) to 7 (1932).
Deutsche Invaliden Zeitung. 6 (1924) to 14 (1932).
Die Gemeinde: Halbmonatsschrift für sozialistische Arbeit in Stadt und Land. 1 Jg. (1924) to 10 (1933).
Die Innere Mission im evangelischen Deutschland. Organ des Centralverbandes für die Innere Mission der deutschen evangelischen Kirche. 15 (1920) to 28 (1933).
Die Kommune: Zeitschrift für kommunistische Kommunalpolitik. 10 (1930) to 11 (1931).
Die Nachbarschaft: Zeitschrift für praktische Wohlfahrtspflege: Amtsblatt des Kreiswohlfahrtsamtes Calau N-L. 1 (1921) to 12 (1932).
Die Wohlfahrtspflege in der Rheinprovinz: Zeitschrift für alle Zweige der Wohlfahrtspflege. 1 (1925) to 9 (1933).
Dortmund: Wohlfahrtsblätter. Ed. städt. Wohlfahrtsamt. 1 (1925) to 3 (1927).
Jugend und Volkswohl: Hamburgische Blätter für Wohlfahrtspflege und Jugendhilfe. 1 (1925) to 8 (1932).
Kommunale Praxis: Wochenschrift für Kommunalpolitik und Gemeindesozialismus. 1 (1914) to 5 (1918).
Proletarische Sozialpolitik: Organ der Arbeitsgemeinschaft sozialpolitischer Organisationen. 1 (1928) to 6 (1933).
Schleswig-Holsteinische Wohlfahrtsblätter. 1 (1925) to 6 (1930).
Soziale Berufsarbeit: Organ der Arbeitsgemeinschaft der Berufsverbande der Wohlfahrtspflegerinnen Deutschlands. 6 (1927) to 10 (1930).
Soziale Praxis und Archiv für Volkswohlfahrt. 28 (1918/19) to 42 (1933).
Stenographische Verhandlungs-Bericht der Stadtverordneten-Versammlung, Düsseldorf. 1921–1932.
Wohlfahrtswoche, Zeitschrift für Wohlfahrtskunde, Wohlfahrtspflege und Wohlfahrtspolitik. Organ des Wohlfahrtsamtes und des Kriegsfürsorgeamtes der Hauptstadt Hannover. 1 (1926) to 8 (1933).
Zentralblatt für Jugendrecht und Jugendwohlfahrt. 16 (1924/5) to 27 (1935).

Periodicals: Single Volumes or Parts of Volumes

Berliner Wohlfahrtsblatt, 7 Jg., Nr. 4, 15 Feb. 1931.
Das Wohlfahrtswesen der Industriestadt Freital, 3 Jg., Nr. 2, 1 Feb. 1920.

Der Klassenkampf, 5 Jg., Nr. 4, 1931.
Jahresbericht der Verwaltungsbehörden der freien und Hansestadt Hamburg, 1925.
Jahresberichte der Behörde für Wohnungspflege (Hamburg, 1926).
Soziale Nachrichten aus den Ämtern und der freien Wohlfahrtspflege der Stadt Köln,
    No. 5., 1929.
Wohlfahrtsblatt der freien Hansestadt Bremen, 2 Jg., 1929.
Wohlfahrtsamt. Jahresbericht 1925 (Hamburg, 1926).
Wohlfahrtsblätter der Stadt Nürnberg, 8 Jg., 1929.
Wohlfahrtsnachrichten der Stadt Altona, 1 Jg., 1924.25, and 6 Jg., 1929/30).

Statistics

Aus Hamburgs Verwaltung und Wirtschaft. 4 (1927) to 15 (1938).
Hamburger Statistische Monatsberichte. 1 (1924) to 3 (1926).
Statistik des Deutschen Reichs. 401/1 (1929) and 406 (1930).
Statistik des Hamburgischen Staates. 27 (1918) to 34 (1928).
Statistisches Handbuch für den Hamburgischen Staat. 1920.
Statistisches Jahrbuch deutscher Städte. 22 (1927) to 28 (1933).
Statistisches Jahrbuch für das Deutsche Reich. 46 (1927) to 51 (1932).
Statistisches Jahrbuch für die freie und Hansestadt Hamburg. 1925, 1926/27, 1927/28,
    1929/30, 1930/31, 1932/33.

Newspapers

Cologne
    Sozialistische Republik (KPD) 1929–1932.

Düsseldorf
    Volkszeitung. Organ für das werktätige Volk am Niederrhein (SPD), 1919–1927.

Hamburg
    Hamburger Echo (SPD), 1919–1933.
    Hamburger Volkszeitung (KPD) (press clippings in StAHH, Staatliche Pressestelle
    I–IV, 1923–1932).
    Press clippings from *Anzeiger* (DDP), *Correspondent, Fremdenblatt, Nachrichten*
    (DNVP), *Tageblatt* (NSDAP) in StAHH, Staatlicher Pressesstelle I–IV.

Stuttgart
    Schwäbische Tagewacht (SPD), 1929.
    Süddeutsche Arbeiter-Zeitung (KPD), 1922, 1924–1925.

Books and Articles

Allgemeine Fürsorge: Referate auf der Reichstagung der Arbeiterwohlfahrt am 12.–13.
    September 1924 in Hannover (Berlin: J. H. W. Dietz Nachfolger, 1924).
Baum, Dr. Marie. *Familienfürsorge: Eine Studie.* Neue Folge der Schriften des Deutschen
    Vereins für öffentliche und private Fürsorge, 12 Heft (Karlsruhe: Verlag E. Braun,
    1927).
Bergerhoff, Dr. Kuno. *Wohnungspflege* (Stuttgart: Verlag von Ferdinand Enke, 1922).
Bopp, Dr. rer. pol. Karl. *Die Wohlfahrtspflege des modernen deutschen Sozialismus: Eine*
    soziale und wirtschaftliche Studie (Freiburg: Caritasverlag, 1930).

Erichson, Dr. med. Kurt , *Die Fürsorge in Hamburg: Ein Überblick über ihre Entwicklung, ihren gegenwärtigen Stand und dessen gesetzliche Grundlagen* (Hamburg: Friederichsen, de Gruyter, 1930).

Friedheim, Dr. Clara. *Führer durch die Wohlfahrtseinrichtungen Hamburgs.* Umgearbeitete Neuaflage des Handbuchs für den Hamburger Wohlfahrtspfleger, bearb. von Maria Hinrichs. 17 Heft, Institut für Soziale Arbeit, Hamburg. (Hamburg: Verlag Ackermann and Wulff Nachfolger, 1926).

Göbel, Dr. Alexander. *Das Wohlfahrtsamt: Zweck, Einrichtung und Richtlinien fur den weiteren Ausbau.* Soziale Tagesfragen, 47 Heft, ed. Volksverein für das Kath. Deutschland (M. Gladbach: Volksvereins-Verlag, 1923).

Hauptauschuss für Arbeiterwohlfahrt, ed., *Das kleine Lehrbuch*: 1–9 Bde. (Berlin, 1928–1931).

Jannasch, Hans Windelkinde. *Alarm des Herzens: Aus den Papieren eines Helfers* (Stuttgart: Verlag Gerhard Merian, 1928).

Kaufmann, Dr. Heinz. *Die soziale Gliederung der Bevölkerung und ihre Auswirkungen auf das Wohlfahrtsamt.* Veröffentlichungen der Schleswig-Holsteinischen Universitäts-Gesellschaft, Ortsgruppe Altona, 2 Heft (Altona: In Kommission bei Hammerich und Lesser, 1928).

Klumker, Prof. Dr. Chr., and Prof. Dr. B. Schmittmann, eds. *Wohlfahrtsämter* (Stuttgart: Verlag von Ferdinand Emke, 1920).

Kraus, Herta. *Work Relief in Germany* (New York: Russell Sage Foundation, 1934).

Neumann, Sen. Paul. *Russland ein Vorbild? Eine vergleichende Darstellung russischer und hamburgischer Sozialpolitik* (Hamburg, n.d.).

Salomon, Alice, with the assistance of S. Wronsky. *Leitfaden der Wohlfahrtspflege* (Leipzig: Verlag und Druck von B. J. Teubner, 1921).

Schriften des Deutschen Vereins für öffentliche und private Fürsorge, Neue Folge, 14 Heft, *Sozialversicherung und öffentliche Fürsorge als Grundlagen der Alters- und Invalidenversorgung* (Karslruhe: Verlag G. Braun, 1930).

Schwarzbuch der Kleinrentnerfürsorge. Ed. Pressestelle des Deutschen Rentnerbundes (Kassel, 1929).

Seidel, Karl. "Die kommunale Wohlfahrtspflege, ihr Begriff und ihre Bedeutung, unter Berucksichtigung der kommunalen Wohlfahrtspflege der Stadt Cassel." Dissertation, Universität Marburg, 1922.

Stieve, Hedwig. *Tagebuch einer Fürsorgerin* (Weinheim; Beltz Verlag, 1983).

Wachenheim, Hedwig. "Ausbildung zur Wohlfahrtspflege." *Die Neue Zeit*, 39 Jg., 2 Bd., 1921.

———. *Republik und Wohlfahrtspflege: Eine Rededisposition von Hedwig Wachenheim* (Berlin: Hauptausschuss für Arbeiterwohlfahrt, 1927).

———. "Der Vorrang der öffentlichen Wohlfahrtspflege: Grundsätzliches zur Krise in der rheinischen Jugendwohlfahrtspflege." *Arbeiterwohlfahrt*, 1 Jg., 3 Heft, 1 Nov. 1926, pp. 67–69.

Wex, Dr. Else. *Die Entwicklung der Sozialen Fürsorge in Deutschland (1914 bis 1927)* (Berlin: Carl Heymanns Verlag, 1929).

Wilden, Dr. Josef. *Auf dem Wege zur Wohlfahrtspflege: Dargestellt an den Düsseldorfer Einrichtungen* (Düsseldorf, 1921).

Wildenhayn, F. with a foreword by Carl Mennicke. *Die Auflösung der Familie* (Potsdam: Alfred Protte Verlag, 1931).

Wronsky, Siddy. "Behandlungsmethoden in der Fürsorge." *Jugend und Volkswohl* (Hamburg), 6 Jg., Nr. 10/11, Jan./Feb. 1931.

———. *Methoden der Fürsorge* (Berlin: Carl Heymanns Verlag, 1930).

Wronsky, Siddy, and Prof. Dr. Kronfeld. *Sozialtherapie und Psychotherapie in den Methoden der Fürsorge* (Berlin: Carl Hegnanns Verlag, 1932).
Wronsky, Siddy, and Alice Salomon with the assistance of Eberhard Giese. *Soziale Therapie: Ausgewählte Akten aus der Fürsorge-Arbeit: Für Unterrichtszwecke* (Berlin: Carl Heymanns Verlag, 1926).

Selected Secondary Sources

Abelshauser, Werner, ed. *Die Weimarer Republik als Wohlfahrtsstaat: Zum Verhältnis von Wirtschafts-und Sozialpolitik in der Industriegesellschaft* (Stuttgart: Franz Steiner Verlag Wiesbaden, 1987).
Ayass, Wolfgang. *Das Arbeitshaus Breitenau: Bettler, Landstreicher, Prostituierte, Zuhälter, und Fürsorgeempfänger in der Korrektions- und Landesarmenanstalt Breitenau (1874–1949)* (Kassel: Verein für hessische Geschichte und Landeskunde, 1992).
―――. *"Asoziale" im Nationalsozialismus* (Stuttgart: Klett-Cotta, 1995).
Bajohr, Frank, Werner Johe, and Uwe Lohalm, eds., *Zivilisation und Barbarei: Die widersprüchlichen Potentiale der Moderne: Detlev Peukert zum Gedenken* (Hamburg: Christians Verlag, 1991).
Bauche, Ulrich, Ludwig Eiber, Ursula Wamser, and Wilfried Weinke, eds. *"Wir sind die Kraft": Arbeiterbewegung in Hamburg von den Anfängen bis 1945: Katalogbuch zu Ausstellungen des Museums für hamburgische Geschichte* (Hamburg: VSA-Verlag, 1988).
Bessel, Richard. *Germany after the First World War* (Oxford: Clarendon Press, 1993).
Bourdieu, Pierre. *Outline of a Theory of Practice* (Cambridge: Cambridge University Press, 1987).
Burleigh, Michael, and Wolfgang Wippermann. *The Racial State: Germany, 1933–1945* (Cambridge: Cambridge University Press, 1991).
Büttner, Ursula. *Politische Gerechtigkeit und sozialer Geist: Hamburg zur Zeit der Weimarer Republik* (Hamburg: Christians Verlag, 1985).
Crew, David. "'Eine Elternschaft zu Dritt'—staatliche Eltern?: Jugendwohlfahrt und Kontrolle der Familie in der Weimarer Republik, 1919–1933." In Alf Lüdtke, ed., *"Sicherheit" und "Wohlfahrt": Polizei, Gesellschaft und Herrschaft im 19. und 20. Jahrhundert* (Frankfurt: Suhrkamp Verlag, 1992), pp. 267–294.
―――. "German Socialism and Democracy, 1890–1933." In Ursula Hoffmann-Lange, ed., *Social and Political Structures in West Germany: From Authoritarianism to Postindustrial Democracy* (Boulder: Westview Press, 1991), pp. 105–123.
―――. "Gewalt 'auf dem Amt': Beispiele aus der Wohlfahrtsverwaltung der Weimarer Republik." *WerkstattGeschichte*, 4 (1993): 33–42.
―――. "'Wohlfahrtsbrot ist bitteres Brot': The Elderly, the Disabled, and the Local Welfare Authorities in the Weimar Republic, 1924–1933." *Archiv für Sozialgeschichte*, 30 Bd., 1990, pp. 217–245.
Crew, David, ed. *Nazism and German Society, 1933–1945* (London: Routledge, 1994).
De Certeau, Michel. *The Practice of Everyday Life* (Berkeley: University of California Press, 1984).
Dickinson, Edward Ross. *The Politics of German Child Welfare from the Empire to the Federal Republic* (Cambridge, Mass.: Harvard University Press, 1996).
Ebbinghaus, Angelika, Heidrun Kaupen-Haas, and Karl Heinz Roth, eds., *Heilen und Vernichten im Mustergau Hamburg: Bevölkerungs- und Gesundheitspolitik im Dritten Reich* (Hamburg: Konkret Literatur-Verlag, 1984).

Egighian, Greg A. "The Politics of Victimization: Social Pensioners and the German
    Social State in the Inflation of 1914–1924." *Central European History* 26, no. 4
    (1993): 375–404.
Eifert, Christiane. *Frauenpolitik und Wohlfahrtspflege: Zur Geschichte der
    sozialdemokratischen "Arbeiterwohlfahrt"* (Frankfurt: Campus Verlag, 1993).
Evans, Richard J., and Dick Geary, eds. *The German Unemployed: Experiences and
    Consequences of Mass Unemployment from the Weimar Republic to the Third Reich*
    (New York: St. Martin's Press, 1987).
Fischer, Ruth, and Franz Heimann. *Deutsche Kindheiten 1932: Wohlfahrt, Krankheit,
    Hunger, Krise* (Düsseldorf: W. Schroeder Verlag,1986).
Foucault, Michel. *Discipline and Punish: The Birth of the Prison.* Trans. Alan Sheridan
    (London: Allen Lane, 1977).
———. *Power/Knowledge: Selected Interviews and Other Writings, 1972–1977.* Ed.
    Colin Gordon (New York: Pantheon, 1980).
Fraser, Nancy. "Struggle over Needs: Outline of a Socialist-Feminist Critical Theory of
    Late-Capitalist Political Culture." In Linda Gordon, ed., *Women, the State, and
    Welfare* (Madison: University of Wisconsin Press, 1990).
Frie, Ewald. *Wohlfahrtsstaat und Provinz: Fürsorgepolitik des Provinzialverbandes
    Westfalen und des Landes Sachsen, 1880–1930* (Paderborn: Ferdinand Schöningh,
    1993).
Führer, Karl Christian. *Arbeitslosigkeit und die Entstehung der Arbeitslosenversicherung
    in Deutschland, 1902–1927* (Berlin: Colloquium Verlag, 1990).
———. "Für das Wirtschaftsleben 'mehr oder weniger wertlose Personen': Zur Lage von
    Invaliden- und Kleinrentner in den Inflationsjahren, 1918–1924." *Archiv für
    Sozialgeschichte*, 30 Bd., 1990, pp. 145–180.
———. "Unterstützung und Lebensstandard der Arbeitslosen 1918–1927." In Klaus
    Tenfelde, ed., *Arbeiter im 20. Jahrhundert* (Stuttgart: Klett-Cotta, 1991), pp. 275–
    298.
Glensk, Evelyn, and Christiane Rothmaler, eds. *Kehrseiten der Wohlfahrt: Die Hamburger
    Fürsorge auf ihrem Weg von der Weimarer Republik in den Nationalsozialismus*
    (Hamburg: Ergebnisse Verlag, 1992).
Gräser, Marcus. *Der blockierte Wohlfahrtsstaat: Unterschichtenjugend und
    Jugendfürsorge in der Weimarer Republik* (Göttingen: Vandenhoeck and Ruprecht,
    1995).
Grossmann, Atina. *Reforming Sex: The German Movement for Birth Control and Abortion
    Reform, 1920–1950* (New York: Oxford University Press, 1995).
Habermas, Jürgen. *The Theory of Communicative Action.* Vol. 2, *Lifeworld and System: A
    Critique of Functionalist Reason.* Trans. Thomas McCarthy (Boston: Beacon Press,
    1987).
Hagemann, Karen. *Frauenalltag und Männerpolitik: Alltagsleben und gesellschaftliches
    Handeln von Arbeiterfrauen in der Weimarer Republik* (Bonn: Verlag J. H. W. Dietz
    Nachfolger, 1990).
———. "'Wir hatten mehr Notjahre als reichliche Jahre . . .': Lebenshaltung und Hausarbeit
    Hamburger Arbeiterfamilien in der Weimarer Republik." In Klaus Tenfelde, ed.,
    Arbeiter im 20. Jahrhundert (Stuttgart: Klett-Cotta, 1991), pp. 200–240.
Harvey, Elizabeth. *Youth and the Welfare State in Weimar Germany* (Oxford: Clarendon
    Press, 1993).
Hempel-Küter, Christa. *Die kommunistische Presse und die
    Arbeiterkorrespondentenbewegung in der Weimarer Republik* (Frankfurt: Peter Lang,
    1989).

Homburg, Heidrun. "Vom Arbeitslosen zum Zwangsarbeiter: Arbeitslosenpolitik und Franktionierung [*sic*] der Arbeiterschaft in Deutschland 1930–1933 am Beispiel der Wohlfahrtserwerbslosen und der kommunalen Wohlfahrtshilfe." *Archiv fur Sozialgeschichte*, 35 Bd., 1985, pp. 251–298.

Hong, Young- Sun. "Femininity as a Vocation: Gender and Class Conflict in the Professionalization of German Social Work." In Geoffrey Cocks and Konrad H. Jarausch, eds., *German Professions, 1800–1950* (New York: Oxford University Press, 1990), pp. 232–251.

———. "World War I and the German Welfare State: Gender, Religion, and the Paradoxes of Modernity." In Geoff Eley, ed., *Society, Culture, and the State in Germany, 1870–1930* (Ann Arbor: University of Michigan Press, 1996), pp. 345–369.

Kaiser, Jochen-Christoph, and Martin Greschat, eds., *Sozialer Protestantismus und Sozialstaat: Diakonie und Wohlfahrtspflege in Deutschland 1890 bis 1938* (Stuttgart: Kohlhammer, 1996).

Köppen, Ruth. *Die Armut is weiblich* (Berlin: Elefanten Press, 1985).

Lee, W. R., and Eve Rosenhaft, eds. *The State and Social Change in Germany, 1880–1980* (Oxford: Berg Publishers, 1990).

Leibfried, Stephan. "Existenzminimum und Fürsorge-Richtsätze in der Weimarer Republik." In Stephan Leibfried et al., *Armutspolitik und die Entstehung des Sozialstaats: Entwicklungslinien sozialpolitischer Existsicherung im historischen und internationalen Vergleich*. Grundrisse sozialpolitischer Forschung, Nr. 3 (Bremen,1985), pp. 186–240.

Lindenberger, Thomas. *Strassenpolitik: Zur Sozialgeschichte der öffentlichen Ordnung in Berlin, 1900 bis 1914* (Bonn: Verlag J. H. W. Dietz Nachfolger, 1995).

Linton, Derek. *"Who Has the Youth Has the Future": The Campaign to Save Young Workers in Imperial Germany* (New York: Cambridge University Press, 1991).

Lohalm, Uwe. "Die Wohlfahrtskrise, 1930–1933: Vom ökonomischen Notprogramm zur rassenhygienischen Neubestimmung." In Frank Bajohr, Werner Johe, and Uwe Lohalm, eds., *Zivilisation und Barbarei: Die widersprüchlichen Potentiale der Moderne: Detlev Peukert zum Gedenken* (Hamburg: Christians Verlag, 1991), pp. 193–225.

———. "Wohlfahrtspolitik und Modernisierung: Bürokratisierung, Professionalisierung und Funktionsausweitung der Hamburger Fürsorgebehörde im Nationalsozialismus." In Frank Bajohr, ed., *Norddeutschland im Nationalsozialismus* (Hamburg: Ergebnisse Verlag, 1993), pp. 387–413.

Lüdtke, Alf. *Eigen-Sinn: Fabrikalltag, Arbeitererfahrungen, und Politik vom Kaiserreich bis in den Faschismus* (Hamburg: Ergebnisse Verlag, 1993).

———. "Gewalt im Alltag: Herrschaft, Leiden, 'Körpersprache'? Formen direkter und 'sanfter' Gewalt in der bürgerlichen Gesellschaft." In Jorg Calliess, ed., *Gewalt in der Geschichte: Beiträge zur Gewaltaufklärung im Dienste des Friedens* (Düsseldorf: Schwann Verlag,1983), pp. 271–296.

———. "Hunger in der Grossen Depression: Hungererfahrungen und Hungerpolitik am Ende der Weimarer Republik." *Archiv fur Sozialgeschichte*, 27 Bd., 1987, pp. 145–176.

Lüdtke, Alf, ed. *Alltagsgeschichte: Zur rekonstruktion historischer Erfahrungen und Lebensweisen* (Frankfurt: Campus Verlag, 1989).

Mallmann, Klaus-Michael. *Kommunisten in der Weimarer Republik: Sozialgeschichte einer revolutionären Bewegung* (Darmstadt: Wissenschaftliche Buchgesellschaft,1996).

Michel, Sonya, and Seth Koven. "Womanly Duties: Maternalist Politics and the Origins of

Welfare States in France, Germany, Great Britain, and the United States, 1880–1920." *American Historical Review* 95, no. 4, (1990): 1076–1108.

Otto, Hans-Uwe, and Heinz Sünker, eds. *Politische Formierung und soziale Erziehung im Nationalsozialismus* (Frankfurt: Suhrkamp, 1991).

———. *Soziale Arbeit und Faschismus: Volkspflege und Pädagogik im Nationalsozialismus* (Bielefeld: K-T Verlag, 1986).

Peukert, Detlev J. K. *Grenzen der Sozialdisziplinierung: Aufstieg und Krise der deutschen Jugendfürsorge von 1878 bis 1932* (Cologne: Bund-Verlag, 1986).

———. *Inside Nazi Germany: Conformity, Opposition, and Racism in Everyday Life.* Trans. Richard Deveson (New Haven: Yale University Press, 1987).

———. *Max Webers Diagnose der Moderne* (Göttingen: Vandenhoeck and Ruprecht, 1989).

———. *The Weimar Republic: The Crisis of Classical Modernity*, trans. Richard Deveson (New York: Hill and Wang, 1989).

Pine, Lisa. "Hashude: The Imprisonment of 'Asocial' Families in the Third Reich." *German History: The Journal of the German History Society* 13, no. 2 (1995): 182–197.

Preller, Ludwig. *Sozialpolitik in der Weimarer Republik* (Düsseldorf: Droste, 1978).

Projektgruppe Arbeiterkultur Hamburg, eds. *Vorwärts- und nicht vergessen: Arbeiterkultur in Hamburg um 1930*; Materialien zur Geschichte der Weimarer Republik (Berlin: Fröhlich and Kaufmann, 1982).

Reagin, Nancy. *A German Women's Movement: Class and Gender in Hanover, 1880– 1933* (Chapel Hill, N.C.: University of North Carolina Press, 1995).

Reyer, Jürgen. *Alte Eugenik und Wohlfahrtspflege: Entwertung und Funktionalisierung der Fürsorge vom Ende des 19. Jahrhunderts bis zur Gegenwart* (Freiburg: Lambertus Verlag, 1991).

Ritter, Gerhard A. *Social Welfare in Germany and Britain: Origins and Development* (New York: Berg Publishers, 1986).

Rosenhaft, Eve. "Communisms and Communities: Britain and Germany between the Wars." *Historical Journal* 26, no. 1 (1983): 221–236.

———. "Women, Gender, and the Limits of Political History in the Age of 'Mass Politics.'" In Larry Eugene Jones and James Retallack, eds., *Elections, Mass Politics, and Social Change in Modern Germany: New Perspectives* (Washington, D.C.: German Historical Institute, 1992), pp. 149–173.

Rouette, Susanne. *Sozialpolitik als Geschlechterpolitik: Die Regulierung der Frauenarbeit nach dem Ersten Weltkrieg* (Frankfurt: Campus Verlag,1993).

Sachsse, Christoph. *Mütterlichkeit als Beruf: Sozialarbeit, Sozialreform, und Frauenbewegung, 1871–1929* (Frankfurt: Suhrkamp Verlag, 1986).

Sachsse, Christoph, and Florian Tennstedt. *Geschichte der Armenfürsorge in Deutschland.* 2 Bd., *Fürsorge und Wohlfahrtspflege, 1871 bis 1929* (Stuttgart: Verlag W. Kohlhammer, 1988).

———. *Geschichte der Armenfürsorge in Deutschland*, 3 Bd., *Der Wohlfahrtsstaat im Nationalsozialismus* (Stuttgart: Verlag W. Kohlhammer, 1992).

Schlüter, Doris. "Sozialpolitik und Sozialfürsorge der Stadt Hannover in der Weimarer Republik" (Ph.D. dissertation, Universität Hannover, 1990).

Siegel, Tilla. "Das ist nur rational: Ein Essay zur Logik der sozialen Rationalisierung." In Dagmar Reese, Eve Rosenhaft, Carola Sachse, and Tilla Siegel, eds., *Rationale Beziehungen? Geschlechterverhältnisse im Rationalisierungsprozess* (Frankfurt: Suhrkamp Verlag, 1993), pp. 363–396.

Steinmetz, George. *Regulating the Social: The Welfare State and Local Politics in Imperial Germany* (Princeton: Princeton University Press, 1993).

Stieve, Hedwig. *Tagebuch einer Fürsorgerin* (Weinheim: Beltz Verlag, 1983).

Von Saldern, Adelheid. "Arme und Obdachlose im Hannover der Weimarer Republik." In Hans-Dieter Schmid, ed., *Hannover Am Rande der Stadt.* Hannoversche Schriften zur Regional und Lokalgeschichte, 5 Bd. (Bielefeld: Verlag für Regionalgeschichte, 1992), pp. 221–254.

———. *Häuserleben: Zur Geschichte städtischen Arbeiterwohnens vom Kaiserreich bis heute* (Bonn: Verlag J. H. W. Dietz Nachfolger, 1995).

———. "Kommunale Verarmung und Armut in den Kommunen während der grossen Krise (1929 bis 1933): Am Beispiel der Finanz- und Wohnungs(bau)politik." In *Soziale Bewegungen: Geschichte und Theorie.* Jahrbuch 3, *Armut und Ausgrenzung* (Frankfurt: Campus Verlag, 1987), pp. 69–109.

———. *Neues Wohnen: Wohnungspolitik und Wohnkultur im Hannover der Zwanziger Jahre.* Hannoversche Studien, 1 Bd. (Hanover: Hahnsche Buchhandlung, 1993).

———. "'Nur ein Wetterleuchten': Zu den historischen Komponenten des 'Novembergeistes' von 1918/19." In Jürgen Kocka, Hans-Jürgen Puhle, and Klaus Tenfelde, eds., *Von der Arbeiterbewegung zum modernen Sozialstaat: Festschrift für Gerhard A. Ritter zum 65. Geburtstag* (Munich: K. G. Saur, 1994), pp. 93–113.

———. "Victims or Perpetrators? Controversies about the Role of Women in the Nazi State." In David F. Crew, ed., *Nazism and German Society, 1933–1945* (London: Routledge,1994), pp. 141–165.

———. "The Workers' Movement and Cultural Patterns on Urban Housing Estates and in Rural Settlements in Germany and Austria During the 1920s." *Social History* 15, no. 3 (1990): 333–354.

Von Saldern, Adelheid, ed. *Stadt und Moderne: Hannover in der Weimarer Republik* (Hamburg: Ergebnisse Verlag, 1989).

Weindling, Paul. *Health, Race, and German Politics Between National Unification and Nazism, 1870–1945* (Cambridge: Cambridge University Press, 1989).

"Der Wohlfahrtsstaat in der Stadt: Wohlfahrtspolitik und Wohlfahrtspflege in Westfalen, 1890–1945." *Westfälische Forschungen* 43 (1993).

Zeller, Susanne. *Volksmutter—mit staatlicher Anerkennung—Frauen im Wohlfahrtswesen der zwanziger Jahre* (Düsseldorf: Schwann, 1987).

———. "Zum Geschlechtsverhältnis zwischen Fürsorgerinnen und Sozialbeamten in Wohlfahrtsämtern der Zwanziger Jahre." In Verena Fesel, Barbara Rose, and Monika Simmel, eds., *Sozialarbeit—ein deutscher Frauenberuf: Kontinuitäten und Brüche im 20. Jahrhundert* (Pfaffenweiler: Cantaurus-Verlagsgesellschaft,1992), pp. 41–54.

Index